SOTHIS PRESS

Sothis Press aims to completely reimagine the public domain book with an emphasis on universal access to captivatingly designed print editions. We believe that technology will enable every single book ever published to be perpetually accessible in beautiful print form. Sothis is beauty in ubiquity.

www.sothis.press
1 Waterhouse Square, London, EC1N 2ST

A Book of Forms

Containing 600 of the Most Approved Precedents for Conveyancing, and for Practice in the Courts of the Commonwealth; Also, for Use in Public Offices and for Men of Business Generally; Adapted to the Present Acts of Assembly; With Explanatory Notes and Ref

James D. Dunlap

SOTHIS PRESS

ISBN 978-1-0368-0452-7

This edition is published by
Sothis Press © 2023. The company
is registered in England and Wales.
The Company Number is 14900389.

OPINIONS

From the Hon. Archibald Randall, Judge of the District Court of the United States, for the Eastern District of Pennsylvania.

Philadelphia, April 16, 1845.

GENTLEMEN: I have examined the sheets of "Dunlap's Conveyancing and Forms" submitted to me, and have no hesitation in recommending it as superior to any work of the kind now in use here. The number of useful forms not heretofore in print, and their admirable arrangement, will render it invaluable to the profession, and very useful to the citizen engaged in other pursuits. Very respectfully, yours, &c.

Messrs. E. C. & J. BIDDLE. ARCHD. RANDALL.

From the Hon. Edward King, President Judge of the First Judicial District of Pennsylvania, composed of the city and county of Philadelphia.

Philadelphia, March 27, 1845.

DEAR SIRS: The examination I have given to "Dunlap's Conveyancing and Forms," enables me to say with entire conviction, that it is one of the best books of its kind. It will be found equally advantageous to the citizen as well as the professional man; being replete with useful practical forms, calculated to aid all in transacting business, with legal accuracy and precision. Very respectfully, &c.

Messrs. E. C. & J. BIDDLE. EDWARD KING.

From the Hon. Ellis Lewis, President Judge of the Second Judicial District of Pennsylvania, composed of the county of Lancaster.

Lancaster, January 8, 1845.

DEAR SIRS: I have examined the manuscript copy of "Dunlap's Conveyancing and Forms," and am truly rejoiced to perceive that the legal profession, and the business community are about to be presented with a work of so much value. The many changes made in the legislation of the State, and our increasing business in the Orphans' Court, have rendered such a work highly necessary. From the examination I have made, and from the high character for ability, of Mr. Dunlap, I can cordially recommend the work to the profession and to the public. Yours truly,

Messrs. E. C. & J. BIDDLE. ELLIS LEWIS.

From the Hon. John Banks, President Judge of the Third Judicial District of Pennsylvania, composed of the counties of Berks, Northampton and Lehigh.

Reading, March 31, 1845.

GENTLEMEN: I have examined a large portion of the Forms prepared for publication by James D. Dunlap, Esq., and approve of the same. They have been prepared with care, and accommodated, with accuracy, to the various changes which have been recently made in our acts of Assembly. When published, they will be of great value to the legal profession, the Clerks of our various Courts, Justices of the Peace and Scriveners. JOHN BANKS.

Messrs. E. C. & J. BIDDLE.

From the Hon. Gaylord Church, President Judge of the Sixth Judicial District of Pennsylvania, composed of the counties of Erie, Crawford, Venango and Warren.

Meadville, Pa., Dec. 27, 1844.

GENTLEMEN: Having perused the manuscript of "Dunlap's Conveyancing and Forms," I feel confident the work will fully answer the character claimed for it by the author. The many recent changes in our Statute Laws seem to render it necessary to vary somewhat many of the forms of practice heretofore used, and I think this work will in a degree meet the exigency.

I most cheerfully recommend it to the Profession and the business community generally. Very respectfully, yours, &c.

Messrs. E. C. & J. BIDDLE. GAYLORD CHURCH.

From the Hon. Samuel Hepburn, President Judge of the Ninth Judicial District of Pennsylvania, composed of the counties of Cumberland, Perry and Juniata.

Carlisle, March 30, 1845.

GENTLEMEN: From the examination which I have been enabled to make of the number of sheets, which you have already published, of "Dunlap's Conveyancing and Forms," I should consider the work one of great practical utility; and coming from the hand of its able and accomplished author, I feel no hesitation in recommending it to the business community generally, as a book calculated to facilitate their labours in all the branches within the scope of the author's design.

Very respectfully, yours, &c., SAMUEL HEPBURN.

Messrs. E. C. & J. BIDDLE.

From the Hon. Nathaniel B. Eldred, President Judge of the Twelfth Judicial District of Pennsylvania, composed of the counties of Dauphin and Lebanon.

Harrisburg, Dec. 21, 1844.

I have examined the manuscript of "Dunlap's Conveyancing and Forms." I believe it to be a useful and convenient work, and as such recommend it to the favourable notice of the Profession and the public generally.

Messrs. E. C. & J. Biddle. NATHANIEL B. ELDRED.

From the Hon. John N. Conyngham, President Judge of the Thirteenth Judicial District of Pennsylvania, composed of the counties of Susquehanna, Bradford and Tioga.

Harrisburg, March 12, 1845.

Gentlemen: I have had an opportunity of examining some of the manuscript intended for the Book of Legal Forms and Precedents now being prepared by James D. Dunlap, Esq., of Erie county, and from what I have seen of the proposed contents, and understood of the plan, I am satisfied, that the work will be valuable as well to the profession as other business members of society.

Mr. Dunlap has the reputation of being an accurate and careful lawyer, knowing the wants, in this respect, of the profession and also the community at large, and knowing too, that much litigation and trouble are occasioned by the careless following of ill prepared forms; and it is believed his book will be an important assistant in endeavouring to remove these difficulties. Respectfully, yours, &c.

Messrs. E. C. & J. Biddle. JOHN N. CONYNGHAM.

From the Hon. James Thompson, President Judge of the District Court, composed of the counties of Erie, Crawford and Mercer, Pa.

Erie, Dec. 30, 1844.

Dear Sirs: I have examined the manuscripts of Forms collated by James D. Dunlap, Esq., of Erie, for his Form Book, and think the plan of the work, the number and variety of the precedents designed to be contained in it, and the arrangement generally will make the work a desirable book for the business community, as well as useful and convenient to gentlemen of the legal profession. Yours truly,

Messrs. E. C. & J. Biddle. JAMES THOMPSON.

From the Hon. Alexander L. Hayes, President Judge of the District Court for the city and county of Lancaster, Pa.

Lancaster, April 5, 1845.

Gentlemen: Having examined the proof sheets of the greater portion of "Dunlap's Conveyancing and Forms," I believe this work will furnish the public with a very desirable guide in the transaction of business. Its importance must be obvious to all who are conversant with courts of justice, and know how much of the litigation with which they are occupied, arises from ill-prepared writings. Many persons unaware of the difference between formalities and forms, treat both with equal neglect, without reflecting that the latter afford in general the best preservative of the life and substance of business; the bark being hardly more essential to the existence of the tree, than are forms of contracts and proceedings to the full and faithful expression of the meaning of parties. Hence the disastrous mistakes so often observed in last wills, deeds, written agreements and other instruments, drawn by unskilful hands, without the aid of precedents. Such evils the work of Mr. Dunlap is well adapted to prevent, being judiciously planned, and, so far as I have examined it, executed with judgment and ability. It will doubtless prove most useful to the community at large, and be of no little assistance to the legal profession. A wide circulation is therefore much to be wished; and this I am glad to learn you have provided for by a large edition and a moderate price. Respectfully your obt. servt.,

Messrs. E. C. & J. Biddle. A. L. HAYES.

From the Hon. John Reed, LL.D., Professor of Law in Dickinson College, and author of "The Pennsylvania Blackstone."

Carlisle, March 29, 1845.

Gentlemen: I have had an opportunity of examining the proof-sheets of "Dunlap's Conveyancing and Forms," which you are about to publish. I commend the book cordially to practising Lawyers, Scriveners, and every one who may have occasion to prepare for himself, or for others, writings in any way affecting property. The collection is copious, and well arranged. If properly consulted, it may avoid thousands of law-suits which grow out of instruments of writing, unskilfully and inartificially drawn. The book should be widely diffused through the community.

Very respectfully your obt. servt.,

Messrs. E. C. & J. Biddle. JOHN REED.

A BOOK OF FORMS:

CONTAINING

600 OF THE MOST APPROVED

PRECEDENTS FOR CONVEYANCING,

AND

FOR PRACTICE IN THE COURTS

OF THE COMMONWEALTH:

ALSO,

FOR USE IN PUBLIC OFFICES AND FOR MEN OF BUSINESS GENERALLY.

ADAPTED

TO THE PRESENT ACTS OF ASSEMBLY.

WITH

EXPLANATORY NOTES AND REFERENCES,

AND

A GLOSSARY OF TECHNICAL LAW TERMS.

BY JAMES D. DUNLAP,
COUNSELLOR AT LAW, ETC. ETC.

PHILADELPHIA:
E. C. & J. BIDDLE, NO. 6 SOUTH FIFTH STREET.

PHILADELPHIA:
T. K. & P. G. COLLINS,
PRINTERS.

PREFACE.

The facility afforded for the despatch of business, to those engaged in the practice of the law, or in conveyancing, by the possession of a hand-book of forms, and the importance to all business men, of an acquaintance with the forms by which the various transactions connected with their several pursuits may be safely and correctly conducted, prompted the compiler of this book to its preparation, in the belief that it would meet the wants of the classes referred to.

Several valuable works on Forms, to which the compiler of this volume is considerably indebted, have issued from the press; but these are generally too expensive and not sufficiently plain for business men not of the legal profession. Other works on the same subject, and of a very useful character, but containing too small a number of precedents, and these too limited in variety, fully to supply the wants of the community, have been published. This collection of forms, it is believed, will be found to combine copiousness and variety with perspicuity, and its cost to be within the means of most persons desiring its aid.

The position of the compiler as a member of the legal profession, and for several years past, of the legislature of this commonwealth, has made him familiar with the changes in the statute laws to which the forms in this work are accommodated, as also with the practice in the various public offices, and it is presumed, will be considered a sufficient guarantee for its correctness.

In preparing it for the press, it has been the especial design and aim of the compiler to make it plain and practical.

The precedents are such as lawyers and the various other classes of business men usually need. Forms for writs have not been inserted, as officers generally have printed blanks for them. Some of the forms contained in this work are to be met with in none other. Those for practice in Admiralty Courts, contained in an

Appendix, are to be found elsewhere only in works devoted exclusively to that subject.

Most of the precedents are drawn *in full*, this being more convenient for the lawyer, and more easily understood by others, than the plan of referring to several parts of forms to complete one.

Remarks generally accompany each class of forms, explanatory of their use and manner of application, and notes are frequently added, to make plain that which may be intricate. In addition to these remarks and notes, references to the various Acts of Assembly are made, and the decisions of the Supreme Court and other authorities given. A glossary of Technical Law Terms is appended, and reference to any particular form made easy by means of a copious index.

Trusting that this volume may be found well adapted to the purposes for which designed, and that it may promote care in the transaction of business, and tend to the prevention of litigation and losses, which so frequently arise from incorrectness in the form of instruments of writing, or from the want of written contracts,—the compiler submits it to the examination of the public.

ERIE, January 1st, 1845.

INDEX.

PAGE

ACCOUNT.
——— of Administrators - - - - - - - - 25
——— of Executors - - - - - - - - 26
——— of Guardians - - - - - - - - 27
ACKNOWLEDGMENTS.
Remarks on - - - - - - - - - 28
——— of a Deed, &c., by one person - - - - - - 29
——— by Husband and Wife - - - - - - - 29
——— by virtue of a Letter of Attorney - - - - - 31
——— of Sheriff's Deed - - - - - - - - 31
——— by a Corporation - - - - - - - - 32
——— by Special Partners - - - - - - - 32
——— of a writing in English, with a copy in another language - - 33
——— for Affidavits, where a deed has not been acknowledged, &c. See Affidavits.
——— of a Trustee selling a trust estate, and also the acknowledgment of the one for whose use the same was sold - - 162
ACQUITTANCE.
Remarks on Acquittances - - - - - - - 33
——— for money received on a sale - - - - - - 33
——— for money received in part of a bond - - - - - 34
——— for interest due on a bond - - - - - - - 34
AFFIDAVITS AND OATHS.
Remarks on - - - - - - - - - 34
AFIDAVIT where the debt or damages exceed 100 dollars - - - 34
——— to an Account - - - - - - - - 35
——— to a Petition, &c. - - - - - - - - 35
——— on an Appeal from an award of Arbitrators - - - 35
——— of Defence - - - - - - - - - 36
——— of the service of Notices, &c. - - - - - - 36
——— of Administrators, Executors or Guardian to a final account - 36
——— of an Alien on Petition to become a citizen - - - 37
——— of a Citizen on the application of an alien - - - 37
——— where a witness to a deed is deceased or absent - - - 37
——— where a deed has not been acknowledged, but proved by a subscribing witness - - - - - - - - 30
——— of another form, where a deed has not been acknowledged, &c. - - - - - - - - - - 30
——— of a Partner under limited partnership law - - - 38
——— to sustain a Writ of Certiorari - - - - - 38
——— on an appeal from the Orphans' Court to the Supreme Court - 38
——— of the publication of notice - - - - - 38
——— by wife, in action by husband and wife for work by her before marriage - - - - - - - - 39
——— to support a Writ of domestic attachment - - - - 39
——— on an appeal - - - - - - - - 39

PAGE

AFFIDAVIT by executor or administrator of his cause of action - - 40
——— and certificate for land settled on - - - - - 70
——— and certificate for land improved but not settled - - - 70
——— and certificate for unimproved lands - - - - - 71
——— of applicant for lands prior to the last purchase of 1784, (under the Act of 13th April, 1807) - - - - 71
——— of witness to an agreement to arbitrate - - - - 78
——— of appraisers of a decedent's estate - - - - 182
——— by administratrix to petition, inventory, and debts on application to court to sell Real Estate - - - - - 255
——— to petition for divorce - - - - - - 276
OATH by kissing the book - - - - - - - - 40
——— of a witness on a trial - - - - - - - 40
——— of *voir dire* - - - - - - - - 40
——— by lifting up the right hand - - - - - - 40
——— by affirmation - - - - - - - - 40
——— of foreman of a grand jury - - - - - - 41
——— of the other grand jurors - - - - - - 41
——— of traverse jury in the civil courts - - - - - 41
——— of traverse jury in the criminal courts - - - - 41
——— of referees under the Act of 1810 - - - - - 41
——— of referees in trespass - - - - - - - 41
——— of referees in trover and conversion - - - - 42
——— of jurors in proceedings to recover possession after sale by sheriff - - - - - - - - - 42
——— of claimant of land sold by sheriff, in proceedings to deliver possession under the Act of 16th June, 1836 - - - 42
——— of jurors under landlord and tenant Act of 1825 - - - 42
——— of inquest in Partition in the Common Pleas - - - 42
——— of inquest on real estate under execution - - - - 43
——— of inquest on Writ of Inquiry - - - - - 43
——— of inquest on Writ of Liberari Facias - - - - 43
——— of Arbitrators - - - - - - - - 43
——— of Executors or Administrators - - - - - 43
——— of Constable attending upon a jury - - - - 44
——— of a witness to a grand jury - - - - - 44
——— of an Attorney at Law on his admission to the bar - - 44
——— of Clerk of Markets - - - - - - - 44
——— of Constable - - - - - - - - 44
——— of Overseers of the Poor - - - - - - 45
——— of appraising of goods distrained for rent - - - - 45
——— of Deputy Surveyor - - - - - - - 45
——— of Notary Public - - - - - - - - 45
——— of Sheriff and County Commissioners before the selection of jurors - - - - - - - - - 45
AGREEMENTS AND CONTRACTS.
Remarks upon - - - - - - - - 46
——— for the sale of land - - - - - - - 46
——— in another form for sale of land - - - - - 47
——— also in another form for sale of land . - - - - 48
——— for purchase of cordwood - - - - - - 49
——— for building a house - - - - - - - 50
——— for performing bricklayer's and plasterer's work in building a house - - - - - - - - - 51
——— with a Millwright - - - - - - - - 52
——— on a sale of wheat - - - - - - - - 53
——— for the sale and delivery of coal - - - - - 54
——— between a housekeeper and his lodger - - - - 55
——— for sale of a parcel of trees growing, and liberty to cut down and carry them away - - - - - - 56

	PAGE
AGREEMENT with a manager - - - - - - -	57
——— or articles of co-partnership between partners - - -	58
——— or articles of co-partnership between an active and silent partner - - - - - - - - -	60
——— or articles of co-partnership between two tradesmen - -	61
——— or articles for special or limited partnership - - -	64
——— of dissolution of partnership - - - - - -	64
——— and covenant to be inserted in partnership contracts, if desired, not to trust any one whom the co-partner shall forbid -	65
——— do. not to be bound, or endorse bills - - - -	65
——— where neither party is to assign his interest - - -	65
——— where parties are to draw quarterly - - - -	66
——— to continue a partnership by endorsement on the old articles -	66
——— in relation to party walls - - - - - - -	66
——— for renewing a Policy of Insurance by endorsement - -	67
AMICABLE ACTION.	
Remarks on - - - - - - - - -	68
——— agreement to institute a suit - - - - - -	68
——— to revive a lien - - - - - - -	68
——— for judgment, after rule of reference entered - - -	69
——— to waive inquisition and condemnation of land taken in execution - - - - - - - -	69
APPLICATION FOR WARRANTS.	
——— for taking out a warrant by a settler for lands settled on -	70
——— form of affidavit and certificate on application for warrants. See AFFIDAVIT.	
APPRENTICE.	
Remarks concerning - - - - - - -	71
Indenture of Apprenticeship - - - - - -	73
Another form of indenture of apprenticeship - - -	74
Indenture of apprenticeship by Overseers of the Poor - -	75
Approbation of the apprenticeship of paupers - - -	76
ARBITRATION AND AWARD.	
Remarks on - - - - - - - -	76
——— under the Act of 1836. Agreement to refer - - -	77
——— for affidavit of witness to an agreement to arbitrate. See AFFIDAVIT.	
Awards of arbitrators in debt or case - - - - -	78
Award in replevin for rent - - - - - -	79
——— in replevin, when property is to be returned - - -	79
ASSIGNMENT.	
Remarks on - - - - - - - - -	79
——— of Dower by the heir - - - - - - -	79
——— of a Deed - - - - - - - - -	80
——— of a Lease - - - - - - - -	81
——— in another form - - - - - - - -	81
——— of a Debt - - - - - - - - -	82
——— of a Judgment - - - - - - - -	82
——— of Moneys due upon account - - - - -	83
——— of a Mortgage - - - - - - - -	83
——— of a Bond where the assignor is liable - - - -	84
——— of a Bond where the assignor is not liable - - -	84
——— where the assignor is liable in another form - - -	85
——— where the assignor is not liable in another form - - -	85
——— of a Note, where the assignor is liable - - - -	86
——— of a Note, where the assignor is not liable - - -	86
——— of an Apprentice - - - - - - - -	86
——— of a Servant - - - - - - - -	86
——— of shares in a company - - - - - -	87
——— of a Policy of Insurance - - - - - - -	87

PAGE

ATTESTATION.
Remarks on - - - - - - - 87
——— where there are interlineations or erasures in instruments of writing - - - - - - - - 88
——— by a Blind person - - - - - - - 88
——— where there are erasures - - - - - - 88
BILLS, NOTES, &c.
Remarks on - - - - - - - 88
BILL of Sale of Goods and Chattels - - - - - - 89
——— of Sale of Goods and Stock, in consideration of maintenance, &c. 90
——— of Sale of a Vessel - - - - - - - 91
——— of Exchange, 1st - - - - - - - 91
——— of Exchange, 2d and 3d - - - - - - - 92
——— of Exchange (Domestic) - - - - - - - 92
Draft - - - - - - - - 93
Note to Bank - - - - - - - 93
Check - - - - - - - - 93
Due Bill - - - - - - - - 94
Promissory Note - - - - - - - 94
Judgment Note - - - - - - - 94
Note with security, or for two or more persons - - - 94
Note on Demand - - - - - - - 95
BONDS.
Remarks on - - - - - - - 95
——— Common form - - - - - - - 96
——— Judgment Bond - - - - - - - 97
——— from one to two - - - - - - - 98
——— from two to one - - - - - - - 98
——— of Indemnity to Bail - - - - - - 99
——— to refund to Executors on payment of a Legacy - - 100
——— to refund, given by distributee under approval of court, (sec. 41 and 57 of Act of 24th of Feb.,
- - 101
——— of - 102
——— to
- 103
——— er
- 104
——— an to
- - - 104
——— - - - - 104
——— to - - - - 104
——— to - - - - 105
——— to - - - - 105
——— to - - - - 106
——— to maintain Parents in another form - - - - 106
——— to keep a person during life - - - - - 107
——— to execute a Conveyance at a time to come, and that the obligee receive the profits - - - - - - 107
——— for services of an Apprentice - - - - - 108
——— of an Attorney to account to his Constituent - - - 108
——— of a Treasurer of a Company - - - - - 108
——— to a Mother of a bastard child - - - - - 109
——— of Indemnity to Surety in a Bond - - - - 109
——— of Indemnity to Bail in Bail Bond - - - - 110
——— of Indemnity to Special Bail - - - - - 110
——— of Indemnity to Bail in Recognizance - - - - 111
——— of Indemnity to Surety in an Administration Bond - - 111
——— of Indemnity to Executor on Payment of a Legacy - - 112
——— of Indemnity to save harmless on paying Rent - - - 112
——— of Indemnity against Claim for Dower - - - - 113

PAGE

Bond of Indemnity for a Bond mislaid or lost - - - - - 113
——— to the County for a bastard child - - - - - 114
——— to refund Money on failure of Contract - - - - - 115
——— in Replevin to Sheriff by Plaintiff - - - - - 115
——— in Replevin to Sheriff by Defendant - - - - - 116
——— of Indemnity in case of Foreign Attachment - - - - 117
——— of Indemnity upon Levy and Sale - - - - - 117
——— of Indemnity for the Payment of an Annuity during life - - 118
——— of Indemnity to discharge Incumbrances - - - - 119
——— to Indemnify Indorsers - - - - - - - 119
——— for Payment of Money after a person's death - - - - 120
——— of Indemnity by an Executor who retains Money in his hands directed by the Will to be put out at Interest - - - 120
——— of a Constable for faithful performance, &c. - - - 121
——— to leave Money to a Wife - - - - - - 121
——— to Indemnify Lessee on payment of Rent - - - - 122
——— for payment of an Annuity during the Life of a Feme Covert - 122
——— of Indemnity on paying Money to a person who had not taken out Letters of Administration - - - - - 123
——— to suffer a Wife to live apart from her Husband - - 123
——— to suffer a Wife to live apart, to have all her effects, and to behave quietly to her - - - - - - - 124

Case Stated.
Remarks on - - - - - - - - 125
——— Form for, - - - - - - - - 126

Caveat.
Remarks on - - - - - - - - 126
——— against the Probate of a Will - - - - - - 126
——— against granting Letters of Administration - - - 126

Certiorari.
Remarks on a - - - - - - - - 127
——— to a Justice of the Peace - - - - - - 127
——— return of Magistrate to be indorsed on the Writ - - - 127

Cognovit Actionem.
Remarks on a - - - - - - - - 127
Cognovit in Action of Debt - - - - - - - 128
——— in Assumpsit - - - - - - - - 128

Commission.
Remarks on - - - - - - - - 129
Caption to Interrogatories on a Commission - - - - 129
Caption to Cross Interrogatories to the same - - - - 129
Rule for a Commission - - - - - - - 130

Commission to examine Witnesses, - - - - - - 130
Letter of Instruction to Commissioners - - - - - 131
Interrogatories to Garnishee in Foreign Attachment - - - 133
Interrogatories to Witness in proceedings for a Divorce - - 134

Composition.
Remarks on Composition in Contracts - - - - - 135
General Form of Composition with Creditors - - - - 135
A Deed of Composition of Debts by Partners - - - - 136

Conditions of Sale.
Remarks on - - - - - - - - 137
——— of Lands - - - - - - - - - 137
Agreement following Conditions - - - - - - 138
Receipt at the foot of Conditions - - - - - - 139
Form of Vendue Article - - - - - - - 139
Another form of Vendue Article - - - - - - 139

Deeds.
Remarks on - - - - - - - - 140
Common form of Deed - - - - - - - 141
Deed with full Covenants - - - - - - - 143
——— by Attorney - - - - - - - - 144

	PAGE
DEED without Covenants	145
——— Quit Claim	145
——— by Executors	145
——— by Executors under a special authority in a Will	147
——— Poll	147
——— Poll on Disfranchising a Member of a Company	148
——— Poll for Unpatented Lands, with Clause of Special Warranty	149
——— for Lands sold by Administrators, by order of Orphans' Court, in Partition	149
——— by Administrators, by order of Court, to satisfy debts, &c.	152
——— by an Administrator of Land which his Intestate had bound himself to Convey	154
——— by Sheriff on a Venditioni	154
——— by Sheriff on a Levari Facias	156
——— of Trust or Assignment for the benefit of Creditors	158
——— to a Wife by Intervention of Trustees	159
——— from same Trustee by direction of the Wife to Sell her Trust estate	161
——— of Marriage Settlement of a Wife's fortune (consisting of lands, goods, &c.) to her use as a separate and distinct estate	162
——— of a Water Course	165
——— of an Alley or Passage	166
——— by gift of Lands	166
——— Partition	167
——— of Rent Charge	169
——— of Release	170
——— of Exchange of Lands	171
mation	172
Covenant of Warranty to Deed	173
Covenant for Quiet Enjoyment	173
Covenant for further Assurance	173
Covenant against Incumbrances	174
Joint-Covenant, of two or more, to one person	174
Joint and several Covenant, of two or more, to one person	174
A several Covenant of two or more	174
DEPOSITION.	
Remarks on	175
Caption of a Deposition under a Rule of Court	175
A Deposition in the hand-writing of the Witness	175
DEPUTATION.	
Deputation to a Deputy Register	176
DISCHARGE.	
Remarks on.	
——— of an Insolvent Debtor from Arrest,	176
——— of a Prisoner charged with a Criminal Offence	177
EXECUTION.	
Property exempt from Execution, &c.	183
INTEREST.	
Remarks on	177
An Interest Table	180
A Table showing the number of days from any day in the month to the same day in any other month throughout the year	181
INVENTORY.	
Inventory of Appraisers of a Decedent's Estate	181
Remarks on the duties, &c., of Executors and Administrators	182
LANDLORD AND TENANT.	
Remarks on	184
Warrant of Landlord to distrain for Rent	185
Notice of Distress	185
Schedule	186
Notice to remove in 15 (or 30) days under the act of 3d April, 1830	186

LANDLORD AND TENANT. PAGE
(Note on the Act of 3d April, 1830) - - - - - 186
Landlord's Affidavit or Complaint - - - - - - 187
Form of Appraisement - - - - - - - 187
Notice of Sale - - - - - - - - 187
Notice to quit after expiration of the Term - - - 188
Notice to quit at the expiration of the Term - - - 188
Complaint to two Justices - - - - - - - 188
LEASE,
Remarks on - - - - - - - - 189
——— for years of a House and Lands, with Exceptions and Special Covenants, &c. - - - - - - - - 190
——— of a House - - - - - - - - 192
——— of a Farm - - - - - - - - 193
Special Covenants in a Lease not to pursue certain occupations 193
Clause to be inserted in a Lease to inhabit part of the premises 194
Clause not to assign or underlease - - - - - 194
Clause to be inserted in a Lease, if required, that lessor shall pay the Taxes - - - - - - - - 194
Clause to insure the premises from Fire, and to rebuild in case of Damage - - - - - - - - 194
LETTER OF ATTORNEY,
Remarks on - - - - - - - - 195
General form of Letter of Attorney to receive Debts - - - 195
General Letter of Substitution - - - - - - - 196
Letter of Attorney to receive money on a Bond - - - - - 196
——— of Revocation, &c. - - - - - - - 197
——— of Attorney to receive dividends of Stock - - - 197
——— to receive the back pay of a deceased Soldier - - - 198
——— to receive a Legacy - - - - - - - 198
——— of Attorney to convey Lands - - - - - - 199
——— to acknowledge a Deed - - - - - - - 199
——— of Attorney in short form to transfer Stock - - - - 199
——— from the President and Directors of a Corporation to collect Debts 199
——— of Attorney to deliver possession of Lands - - - 200
——— of Attorney to receive Debts - - - - - - 201
——— from one to his Wife, to receive Wages, &c. - - - 201
——— to receive principal and interest of the Public Debt - - 201
——— of Attorney to make Partition - - - - - - 202
——— to Attorney at Law to appear to suit for Defendant - - 202
——— by Plaintiff to institute a Suit - - - - - 203
——— by Plaintiff to conduct Suit already brought - - - 203
LETTERS OF LICENSE,
Remarks on - - - - - - - - 204
Letter of License from Creditors - - - - - - - 204
LETTERS OF CREDIT.
Letter of Credit for Goods - - - - - - - 204
——— for a limited sum of money - - - - - - 205
MARRIAGES,
Remarks on - - - - - - - - - 205
Form for a Marriage Ceremony - - - - - - 207
Form of Certificate of Marriage - - - - - - 207
MECHANIC'S LIEN,
Remarks on - - - - - - - - - 208
Form of Claim by a House Carpenter, against one who is owner and contractor, for work and materials for a building - 209
Plaintiff's Bill of Particulars - - - - - - - 210
Form of Claim filed by a House Carpenter against William Burns, owner, and Samuel Dean, contractor, for work and materials for a building - - - - - - - - - 210
Form of Claim filed by a Brickmaker against one who is owner and contractor, for materials furnished for one building - 211

MECHANIC'S LIEN. PAGE

Form of Claim filed by a Brickmaker against William Burns, owner, and Samuel Dean, contractor, for materials furnished for one building - - - - - - - 211

Form of Claim filed against William Burns, owner, and Samuel Dean, contractor, by a Bricklayer, for work - - - 212

Form of Claim filed against one who is owner and contractor, by a Bricklayer, for work - - - - - - - 212

Form of Claim filed by a Lumberman against one who is owner and contractor, for lumber furnished for one building - - 213

Form of Claim filed by a Lumberman against William Burns, owner, and Samuel Dean contractor, for lumber furnished for one building - - - - - - - - 214

Form of Claim filed by a Painter and Glazier, against one who is owner and contractor, for work and materials for one building 214

Form of Claim by a Painter and Glazier, against William Burns, owner, and Samuel Dean, contractor, for work and materials for one building - - - - - - - - 215

Form of Claim filed by a Brickmaker against one who is owner and contractor, for materials furnished for two or more buildings where the amount claimed is equally divided - - 215

Form of Claim filed by a Brickmaker against one who is owner and contractor, for materials furnished for two or more buildings, where the amount claimed is unequally divided - - 216

Form of Claim filed by a Brickmaker against William Burns, owner, and Samuel Dean, contractor, for materials furnished for two or more buildings, where the amount claimed is unequally divided - - - - - - - - 217

Form of Claim filed by Lumber-merchants (partners) against one who is owner and contractor, for lumber furnished for two or more buildings, where the amount claimed is unequally divided 218

MORTGAGES,

Remarks on - - - - - - - - - 219

A Mortgage of Indemnity to Bail - - - - - 221

A common form of Mortgage for securing the payment of money due on a Bond - - - - - - - - 222

For continuing a Mortgage by Indorsement - - - - 223

Mortgage to secure indorsers in Bank - - - - - 224

A short Mortgage of Goods - - - - - - 225

Form of acknowledgment where Deeds and Evidences are delivered to Mortgagee upon the execution of the Mortgage - - 225

NOTICES,

Remarks on - - - - - - - - - 225

Notice to Respondent of the taking of Depositions in application for Divorce - - - - - - - - 226

——— of the execution of a Writ of Inquiry - - - - - 226

——— of the filing of accounts in Courts - - - - - 226

——— to Constable of a desire to vote for an increase of the number of Justices in a District - - - - - - - 226

——— of an Election to change the place of holding Township Elections 227

——— by Constable, of the time and place of holding such Election - 227

——— of an Appeal by Overseers of the Poor, from an order of Removal 227

——— of Captain of Militia to non-commissioned officers and privates on a requisition from the Governor or President - - 228

——— to Officers of their election - - - - - - 228

——— of a Rule to take Depositions - - - - - - 228

——— of proceedings to remove Pauper - - - - - 228

——— of a Motion upon a Justice's Judgment - - - - - 229

——— of Lumber taken up in Rivers - - - - - - 229

——— of Sale in Attachment - - - - - - - 229

——— of Landlord to Sheriff or Constable to pay Rent out of the proceeds of Sale - - - - - - - - 229

PAGE

Notice to Justice of intention to bring suit unless he tender amends - 230
——— by Commissioners of the time and place of taking Depositions 230
——— of time and place of taking Depositions on Rule of Court - 230
——— of Special Matter - - - - - - - 231
——— of Justification - - - - - - - - 231
——— to produce Papers - - - - - - - 231
——— to Constable before bringing suit against him for acts done under the authority of a Warrant - - - - - - 231
——— by Purchaser at Sheriff's Sale, to tenant in possession - - 232
——— to Overseers of the Poor who neglect or refuse to comply with the orders of relief - - - - - - 232
——— of Bail - - - - - - - - - 232
——— of exception to Bail - - - - - - 232
——— of justification of Bail - - - - - - 233

Paper Book,
Remarks with regard to a - - - - - 233
Form of - - - - - - - - - 233

Patents.
Information to persons having business at the Patent Office at Washington, under the act of Congress, August 29th, 1842 - 234
Fees payable at the Patent Office - - - - 235
Form of Petition - - - - - - - - 236
Form of Specification - - - - - - - 237
Form of Oath - - - - - - - - 238
Form of withdrawal - - - - - - - 238
Form of surrender of a patent for re-issue - - - 239
Form of assignment of a right in a patent - - - 239
Form of Disclaimer - - - - - - - 240
Form of Caveat - - - - - - - - 240
Form for addition of new improvements - - - - 241
Form of assignment before obtaining Letters Patent, and to be recorded preparatory thereto - - - - 241
Form of application for Patents or designs under the Act of August 29th, 1842 - - - - - - - 242
Form of Specification - - - - - - - 242
Form of Oath - - - - - - - - 242
Letters Patent for a new invention - - - - 243

Petitions.
Remarks on - - - - - - - - - 243
Petition to the Governor of a State - - - - - - 244
——— to the Congress of the United States - - - - 244
——— to the Legislature of Pennsylvania - - - - 244
——— for laying out a Road - - - - - - 244
——— for appointment of Viewers - - - - - 244
Return of Viewers in favour of the Road - - - 245
Return of Viewers against the Road - - - - 245
Order of Confirmation - - - - - - 246
——— for Review - - - - - - - - 246
Appointment of Reviewers - - - - - - 246
Report of reviewers in favour of the Road - - - 247
Report of reviewers against the Road - - - - 247
——— to vacate a Road - - - - - - - - 247
Appointment of Viewers - - - - - - - 247
Report of viewers in favour of vacation - - - - 248
Report of viewers against the vacation - - - - 248
Confirmation by the Court - - - - - - 248
——— to value lands in case of a Public Road - - - - 248
——— to value lands in case of a Private Road - - - 249
Appointment of viewers - - - - - - - 249
Oath of viewers - - - - - - - - - 249
Report of viewers - - - - - - - - 249
Another form of report - - - - - - - 250

	PAGE
Petition for a Gate	250
Appointment of viewers	250
Report of viewers	251
Confirmation by the Court	251
—— for a Bridge	251
Appointment of viewers	251
Report of viewers	252
—— of Commissioners	252
Order	252
Report of viewers	253
Confirmation by Court	253
—— where a deed is lost, or has become defaced	253
—— for guardian by minor under the age of fourteen years	253
—— for guardian for minor over the age of fourteen years	254
—— for sale of land by administratrix	254
Inventory of Property and debts	254
—— of administratrix for further time for sale of premises	256
Return upon order of sale	256
Affidavit upon return of sale	257
—— by guardian for sale of land	257
—— where master compels apprentice to work at another business, beats him, &c.	258
—— where apprentice has been disobedient, idle, &c.	258
—— where apprentice has committed larceny, &c.	259
—— for inquest to make partition	259
—— for review of account under the act of 13th October, 1840	260
—— for the appointment of seven men to make partition	261
—— for citation to widow to accept or refuse a devise or bequest	261
—— for a rule on the heirs to come in and accept or refuse to take the real estate of decedent at the valuation	262
—— for citation to executors to give security for the execution of their trust	262
—— for Habeas Corpus, where petitioner is under arrest on civil process	263
—— for Habeas Corpus, where the petitioner is in the criminal department	264
—— for Habeas Corpus, where petitioner is deprived of liberty by master or any other person	264
—— for Habeas Corpus by a parent for a child	265
—— for Habeas Corpus ad testificandum	265
—— to enter an appeal from an order of removal of pauper	265
—— for Mandamus	266
—— for the appointment of persons to appraise assigned property	266
—— for a Pedlar's license	266
—— for the appointment of auditors on the accounts of guardian	267
—— where trustees of a fund is insolvent, mismanaging, &c.	267
—— where trustee under marriage settlement is insolvent, &c.	268
—— after trustee is dismissed, for appointment of a new one	268
—— for leave to prove contract of decedent to convey	269
—— for commission *de inebritate inquirendo*	270
—— of defendant, alleging reformation, and praying the court to revoke the original order	271
—— for a tavern license	271
—— to the Legislature for a Turnpike Road	272
—— to the Legislature for a State Road	273
—— for erecting a bridge on county line	273
—— to authorize the Recorder to enter satisfaction upon a mortgage	274
—— to compel a deed for property sold by former sheriff	275
—— where former sheriff has gone out of office	275
—— for subpœna in divorce for desertion	275
—— for subpœna in divorce for intolerable treatment	276

PAGE

Petition for subpœna in divorce for adultery - - - - 277
——— for divorce from bed and board, and for alimony, for abandonment of family - - - - - - - 277
——— for divorce from bed and board, and for alimony, on the ground of intolerable treatment - - - - 277
——— of a Husband, respondent, that the Decree of Divorce, *a mensa et thoro*, be annulled - - - - - - - 278
——— to the Legislature of Pennsylvania for Divorce, - - - 279
Note on Legislative Divorces - - - - - 279
——— to Incorporate a Religious Society - - - - 279
Note relative to Courts incorporating religious and other societies 281

Precipes.

Remarks on - - - - - - - - 281

Precipe for an Original Writ in the Common Pleas - - - 281
——— in Foreign Attachment - - - - - - 281
——— for Writ of Inquiry of Damages - - - - - - 282
——— for *Scire Facias* to Garnishee - - - - - - 282
——— in Domestic Attachment - - - - - - - 282
——— in Attachment against Vessels - - - - - - 282
——— for *fi. fa.* for Residue of Judgment - - - - - 282
——— for Certiorari to Justice of the Peace - - - - - 283
——— for Summons in Covenant . - - - - - 283
——— for execution on Judgment affirmed on Certiorari - - 283
——— for Writ of Replevin - - - - - - - 283
——— for *sci. fa.* on Writ of Inquiry - - - - - 283
——— for *fi. fa.* against Plaintiff for Costs - - - - - 283
——— for *sci. fa.* to revive Judgment - - - - - 283
——— for *sci. fa.* on - - - - - - - 284
——— for Certiorari on Proceedings, to deliver Possession to Sheriff's Vendee - - - - - - - - 284
——— for a Writ in Trespass - - - - - - - 284

Proclamation.

Remarks on - - - - - - - - 284
——— of a Court Crier on opening Court - - - - - 284
——— for Grand Jurors - - - - - - - - 285
——— for Returns of Constables - - - - - - 285
——— for Discharge of Insolvent Debtors - - - - - 285
——— for forfeiting Recognizances - - - - - - 285
——— for acknowledgment of Sheriff's Deeds - - - - 285
——— of Sheriff for holding Court . - - - - - - 285

Public Schools.

Form of Bond of District Treasurer - - - - - 286
Form of Bond of District Collector - - - - - 287
Form of Warrant to Collector of School Tax - - - 287
Form of Certificate of Assessment of School Tax - - 288
Form of Order on District Treasurer - . - - - 289
Form of Certificate of Non-payment of Tax on unseated land - 289
Form of Deed of Land to School Directors - - - 289
Form of Lease of School-house and Lot to School Directors - - 290
Form of Agreement between School Directors and Teacher - 291
Form of Certificate to a Teacher - - - - - 291

Receipts.

Remarks on - - - - - - - - 292
General Form of a Receipt - - - - - - 292

Receipt for Rent - - - - - - - - - 292
——— in another form - - - - - - - - 292
——— paid by a Third Person - - - - - - - 293
——— for Money received from a Third Person - - - 293
——— for Money received for the use of another - - - 293
——— for money received in part of a Bond - - - - 293
——— for interest due on a Bond - - - - - 293

PAGE
Receipt to an Administrator - - - - - - 294
——— for a Promissory Note - - - - - - 294
——— for an Order drawn upon a third person - - - - 294
——— for writings left in a person's hands - - - - 294
——— for Grain from a Miller - - - - - - 294
——— for Cattle or Horses put out to Winter - - - - 295
——— for Lading - - - - - - - - 295
——— for money in part payment, for Lading receipted - - 295
——— for a Legacy - - - - - - - 296
——— for Boarding - - - - - - - 296
——— for money at coming of Age - - - - - 296
——— in another form for a Legacy - - - - - 296

Recitals.
Remarks on - - - - - - - - 296
Recital of title by Patent - - - - - - - 297
——— of title by Grant - - - - - - - 297
——— of title by Devise - - - - - - - 297
——— of title by Descent - - - - - - 298
——— of title by Sheriff - - - - - - - 298
——— of title by Attorney - - - - - - 298
——— of title by Executors - - - - - - 299
——— of title by Administratrix - - - - - - 299
——— of title by partition by Writ - - - - - 299
——— of title partition by Deed - - - - - - 300
——— of Sale by order of Orphans' Court - - - - 300
——— of title by Deed - - - - - - - 300
——— of title by Will - - - - - - - 301
——— of title by Deed and Will - - - - - 301
——— of estate of an Intestate, conveyed by the heirs - - - 301
——— of same, valued by order of Court and accepted by one of the heirs - - - - - - - - 302
——— of title by Sheriff - - - - - - 302

Release.
Remarks on - - - - - - - - 302
Release to an Executor - - - - - - - 303
——— to an Administrator - - - - - - 303
——— to Guardian - - - - - - - 304
——— to the father of a bastard - - - - - - 304
——— of all demands - - - - - - - 305
——— upon a Mortgage - - - - - - - 305
——— between co-partners or traders, on settling accounts - - 306
——— of Dower by Indorsement - - - - - 307

Report.
Remarks on - - - - - - - - 308
Report of Examiners of Attorney at Law - - - - 308
——— of an Alien - - - - - - - - 308
——— of Auditors to Orphans' Court on application of Executor, Administrator or Guardian, to sell or mortgage Real Estate - 309
——— of Auditors on settlement of an Account - - - - 309
——— of Commissioners appointed to lay out State Road - - 309
For Report of Viewers, &c., see Petitions.

Returns by Sheriff.
Remarks on - - - - - - - - - 310
A great variety of Returns by Sheriff from page 310 to page 318.

Return by Constable.
Constable's Return to Court of Constable's election - - 318
Notice to Constables elected - - - - - - 319
Constable's Return to Court - - - - - - 319
Return of Constable on Domestic Attachment - - - 319
Return of Constable on Warrant - - - - - - 320
Another Return of Constable on a Warrant - - - 320
Return of Constable on Warrant for Affray - - - 320

PAGE

SUBPŒNA.
Remarks on - - - - - - - - 320
—— with Clause of Duces Tecum - - - - - - 320
Common form of Subpœna before Arbitrators - - - 321
WILL.
Remarks on - - - - - - - - 321
Form for a Will - - - - - - - - 322
Another form of a Will - - - - - - - 323
Another form of a Will - - - - - - - 324
Another form of a Will - - - - - - - 326
Codicil, or Supplement to a Will - - - - - 327
Another form of Codicil or Supplement to a Will - - 327
Clause forgiving Debts due from Relations - - - 328
Proviso, in case a Wife should sue for Dower and Thirds - 328
To make void Limitations where persons dispute the Validity of a Will - - - - - - - - 328
Clause concerning Disputes - - - - - - 329
Clause of Guardianship of Children - - - - - 329
Conclusion and Attestation of a Will written on several sheets 329
Renunciation of Executorship - - - - - - 330
Release of Right to Administration by Widow - - - 330
Appointment of a Guardian by a Father for his Son - - 330
Note on the subject of appointing Guardians, &c. - - 331
Nuncupative Wills - - - - - - - 331
Proviso for a Will - - - - - - - - 331
WRIT OF ERROR.
Precipe for Writ of Error to Supreme Court - - - 332
Affidavit - - - - - - - - - 332
Recognizance - - - - - - - - 332
A Glossary of Technical Law Terms - - - - - - 333

APPENDIX.

PRECEDENTS FOR PROCEEDINGS IN ADMIRALTY COURTS.
Remarks on - - - - - - - - 345
Libel for Mariners' Wages, with a Claim and Answer - - - 345
—— in a Cause of Personal Damage, with an Answer - - - 347
—— do. do. do. - - - - - - 350
—— for Collision, with a Claim and Answer - - - - - 351
—— by a dissentient Part-Owner (having a majority or a moiety of interest) of a Ship, in order to procure possession; with an Answer 355
—— by dissentient Part-Owners (owning less than a moiety) of a Ship, in order to obtain security; with a Stipulation thereupon - 356
—— by a Painter, for Painting and Furnishing a Ship; with an Answer 357
—— in a Cause of Salvage, with a Claim and Answer - - 359

ERRATA.

Page 28—18th line from bottom, for *county* read *country.*

" 80—9th line of "Assignment of a Deed," insert, after the word *less,* the following [*here insert the chain of title*].

" 114—13th line from top, for *County* (in the title to the precedent on that page) read *Township.*

" 114—17th line from top, for *county* read *township.*

" 233—4th line from bottom, for *sustained* read *overruled.*

ADMINISTRATORS' ACCOUNT.

The Account of John Duncan and James Jones, Administrators of all and singular the goods and chattels, rights and credits, which were of William Dickinson, late of the township of Springfield, in the county of Erie, yeoman, deceased.

1844.	DR.	Dolls.	cts.
	* The said accountants charge themselves with all and singular the goods and chattels, rights and credits, which were of the said deceased, agreeably to an inventory thereof, filed in the Register's Office in Erie, amounting to - - - - - - - - - - - -	8325	50
1845. May 1.	To dividend received on bank stock, - - - - -	65	00
	To rent received of Charles Ames, - - - - -	50	00
		8440	50
	May 2d, 1845.		

1844.	CR.	Dolls.	cts.
	The said accountants crave allowance for the following disbursements, made out of the estate aforesaid, to wit:		
May 1.	By cash paid Register for letters of administration, -	2	62
" 7.	Funeral expenses, as per receipt, - - - - -	72	50
	Medicine, as per ditto, - - - - - - - -	8	25
	Servant's wages, as per receipt, - - - - - -	32	12
" 14.	Note in the Erie Bank, - - - - - - - - -	100	00
1845.	Sundry book debts charged in the inventory, not recoverable, - - - - - - - - - - - -	50	00
May 1.	Loss in the sale of the goods of the deceased, -	70	00
	Paid Register for examining and passing this account, &c., - - - - - - - - - - - -	6	00
	Paid Clerk of Orphans' Court, - - - - - - -	1	00
	Administrators' charge for settling the estate, - -	200	00
	Balance in favour of the estate, - - - - - -	7898	01
		8440	50
	JOHN DUNCAN, JAMES JONES.		

* The following is an extract from the opinion of the Supreme Court of Pennsylvania, in the case of "John Heister's Estate." "All executors or administrators should charge themselves with the whole inventory, noting desperate or doubtful debts. In stating their accounts they should take a credit from the amount of their inventory for all expenses incurred and debts paid within the year," stating the same on the credit side as above.

Five per cent. has been the usual commission charged on all moneys received and paid, but it is now a well-established rule that executors and administrators have a right to charge a reasonable allowance without regard to any fixed per centum. This account should be accompanied with an affidavit by the administrators for which, see Affidavit of Administrators, Executors or Guardians to a Final Account.

EXECUTORS' ACCOUNT.*

The Account of John Selden and James Spencer, Executors of the last Will and Testament of William Snowden, of the city of Philadelphia, merchant, deceased.

1844.	DR.	Dolls.	cts.
	The said accountants charge themselves with all and singular the goods and chattels, rights and credits, which were of the said deceased, agreeably to an inventory thereof, filed in the Register's Office at Philadelphia,		
1845.	amounting to - - - - - - - - - -	7040	48
April 1.	To an increase on the sale of goods, - - - - -	100	50
	To one-half year's dividend on stock of the Bank of North America, - - - - - - - - - -	100	00
	To interest on bonds and notes, received since the inventory was filed, - - - - - - - -	100	50
		7341	48
	April 3d, 1845.		

1844.	CR.	Dolls.	cts.
	The accountants crave allowance for the following disbursements, made out of the estate aforesaid, to wit:		
	By cash paid Register for probate of Will, &c., - -	3	85
	" " John Spencer, as per receipt, - -	300	00
	" " James [illegible], " " - -	250	00
	" " John [illegible], " " - - -	42	00
	By amount of goods bequeathed to the widow, and charged in the inventory, amounting to - - - - - -	1000	00
	By cash paid Counsel for the estate, - - - -	20	00
	" " for stating this account, - - - -	5	00
	" " Register for examining and passing this account, - - - - - - - - - - - - -	6	00
	By cash paid Clerk of Orphans' Court, - - -	1	00
	Accountants' charge for settling the estate, - - -	300	00
	Balance in favour of the estate, - - - - -	5413	63
		7341	48

JOHN SELDEN,
JAMES SPENCER.

* This account should be accompanied by an affidavit by the executors, for which, see Affidavit of Administrators, Executors or Guardian to a Final Account.

GUARDIAN'S ACCOUNT.*

John Bush, Guardian of John Allen, one of the children and heirs of James Allen, late of Harrisburg, yeoman, deceased, in account with the said John Allen.

1845.	DR.	Dolls.	cts.	1845.		CR.	Dolls.	cts.
January	The guardian charges himself as follows:					The guardian asks an allowance for the following		
4.	Amount received of James Hughes, Executor of the			January		sums, paid on account of his said Ward:		
	said James Allen, being the proportion due the said			4.	No. 1.	Paid Robert F. Black, clerk's fees, - - $2 50		
	John Allen as one of the heirs of said James Allen,	1000	50	7.	2.	" James Norton, attorney's fee, - - 8 00 =	10	50
"	Amount received of Ira Glazier, in full of the said			11.	3.	Paid James Sanders for six months' boarding, -	36	00
"	John Allen's proportion of one year's rent of the farm			"	4.	" John Shelby for one year's schooling, - -	10	00
	of the said James Allen, - - - - - - -	100	00	"	5.	" Thos Jones for clothes furnished the said Ward,	20	25
	Ditto ditto, - - - - - - -	100	00	15.	6.	" John Wythe for school books, - - -	6	00
						Balance in hands of guardian, - - - -	1117	75
		1200	50				1200	50
	May 1st, 1845.					JOHN BUSH.		

* This account should be accompanied by an affidavit, for which, see Affidavit of Administrators, Executors or Guardian to a Final Account.

ACKNOWLEDGMENT.

Remarks.

An acknowledgment, is the act of the grantor going before a competent officer, and declaring the instrument to be his act and deed, and desiring the same to be recorded as such. The certificate of the officer on the instrument that such a declaration has been made to him, is also called an acknowledgment. The acknowledgment is indispensable, before the instrument can be put upon record. Below will be found the law relating to the officer before whom the acknowledgment must be made.

In Pennsylvania, before a judge of the Supreme Court, the Courts of Common Pleas, the District Courts, or before any Mayor or Alderman, or Justice of the Peace of the Commonwealth, or before the Recorder of the City of Philadelphia.

When made out of the state, and within the United States, the acknowledgment may be before one of the judges of the Supreme or District Courts of the United States, or before any one of the judges or justices of the Supreme or Superior Courts, or courts of Common Pleas of any state or territory within the United States; and so certified under the hand of the said judges, and the seal of the court.

Commissioners appointed by the Governor of Pennsylvania, residing in either of the United States or the District of Columbia, are also authorized to take acknowledgment of deeds. When made out of the United States, the acknowledgment may be before any consul or vice-consul of the United States, duly appointed for and exercising consular functions in the state, kingdom, county or place where such an acknowledgment may be made, and certified under the public or official seal of such consul or vice-consul of the United States. Act of January 16th, 1827. By the act of May 28th, 1715, S. 4, deeds made out of the province [state] may be proved by the oath or solemn affirmation of one or more of the witnesses thereunto, before one or more of the justices of the peace of this province [state], or before any mayor or chief magistrate or officer of the cities, towns, or places, where such deed or conveyances are so proved. But by construction it is now established that a deed acknowledged before such officer is valid, although the act declared it shall be proved. 1 Pet. R. 433. The certificate of the acknowledgment of a married woman must state, 1st, that she is of full age; 2d, that the contents of the instrument have been made known to her; 3d, that she has been examined separate and apart from her husband; and, 4th, that she executed the deed of her own free will and accord, without any coercion or compulsion of her husband. When lands are situated in any other state, care should be taken by the purchaser to see that the acknowledgment is in accordance with the laws of that state in which such lands are situated. Many persons are careless with regard to this matter, and such carelessness may involve them in a law suit, if not entirely the loss of such real estate. For the law of the several states relating to the officer before whom the acknowledgment must be made, I would refer the reader to Bouvier's Law Dictionary, under the title "Acknowledgment."

Acknowledgment of a Deed, &c., by one person.

Erie County, *ss.*

Before me, the subscriber, one of the Justices of the Peace in and for the said county, personally came the above-named John Jones, who in due form of law acknowledged the above Indenture [letter of attorney, release, assignment, &c., as the case may be] to be his act and deed, to the end that the same might be recorded as such.

In testimony whereof, I have hereunto set my hand and seal this tenth day of January, A. D. one thousand eight hundred and forty five.

JOHN KELLOGG.

Acknowledgment by Husband and Wife.

Lancaster County, *ss.*

Before me, the subscriber, one of the Justices of the Peace in and for the said county, personally came the above-named John Jones and Mary his wife, who in due form of law acknowledged the above Indenture to be their act and deed, and desired that the same might be recorded as such.

The said Mary being of full age and by me examined separate and apart from her said husband, and the contents of the foregoing indenture being first made fully known to her, declared that she did voluntarily and of her own free will and accord, seal, and as her act and deed deliver the same, without any coercion or compulsion of her said husband. In testimony whereof, I have hereunto set my hand and seal this tenth day of January, A. D. one thousand eight hundred and forty five.

JOHN SMITH.

* *An Affidavit where a Deed has not been acknowledged, but proved by a subscribing witness.*

Chester County, *ss.*

Be it remembered, that on the tenth day of January, A. D. one thousand eight hundred and forty five, before me, the subscriber, one of the Justices of the Peace in and for the said county, personally came John Parke, of Auburn, in said county, yeoman, one of the subscribing witnesses to the execution of the above indenture, and being duly sworn [or affirmed] upon his oath [or affirmation] according to law, doth depose and say, that he did see John Jones, the grantor above named, sign and seal, and as his act and deed, deliver the above indenture, deed, or conveyance, for the uses and purposes therein mentioned: and that he did also see William Sankey subscribe his name thereunto as the other witness of such sealing and delivery, and that the name of this deponent thereunto set and subscribed as a witness, is of this deponent's own proper hand-writing. JOHN PARKE.

Sworn [or affirmed as the case may be] and subscribed the day and year aforesaid, before me. Witness my hand and seal.

JOHN CORRY, *Justice of the Peace.*

Another Affidavit, where a Deed has not been acknowledged.

City of Philadelphia, *ss.*

Be it remembered, that on the tenth day of January, in the year of our Lord one thousand eight hundred and forty five, before me, James Law, Esquire, one of the Aldermen of the said city, personally came Albert Whitman, of said city, and on his solemn affirmation, according to law, doth depose and say, that he was present and did see William Sankey, of the city of New York, merchant, [the grantor in the within indenture named,] sign, seal, and, as his act and deed, deliver the within written indenture, deed or conveyance, for the uses and purposes therein mentioned: and that the same was so signed, sealed and delivered in the presence and hearing of John Newton, of the city of Philadelphia, merchant, and of this affirmant; and that the name William Sankey set and subscribed to the said indenture, as the party executing the same, is of the proper hand-writing of the said William Sankey, and that the names of John Newton and Albert Whitman, also set and subscribed to the said indenture as the witnesses

* This form of proving deeds is in accordance with the Act of Assembly of Pennsylvania, where deeds are made out of the state. See act of 28th May, 1715. 1 *Smith*, p. 94.

attesting the due execution thereof, are of the respective handwriting of the said John Newton and of this affirmant.

ALBERT WHITMAN.

Affirmed and subscribed the day and year aforesaid, before me. Witness my hand and seal.

JAMES LAW, *Alderman.*

Acknowledgment by virtue of a Letter of Attorney.

Berks County, *ss.*

Before me, the subscriber, one of the Justices of the Peace in and for the said county, personally came the above-named James Hansen, and in his own name and in the names of his constituents, the above-named John Jones and James Jones, in due form of law acknowledged the above-written indenture to be his own act and deed, and the act and deed of his constituents, the said John Jones and James Jones, by him, the said James Hansen, done and executed by virtue of a letter of attorney to him for that purpose granted; to the end that the same might as such be recorded. In testimony whereof I have hereunto set my hand and seal this tenth day of January, A. D. one thousand eight hundred and forty five.

WILLIAM SMITH, *Justice of the Peace.*

Acknowledgment of Sheriff's Deed.

Dauphin County, *ss.*

Be it remembered, that on this tenth day of January, in the year of our Lord one thousand eight hundred and forty-five, in open Court of Common Pleas, held at Harrisburg, in and for the county of Dauphin, before the Judges of said Court, came John Fox, Esquire, Sheriff of said county, and acknowledged the above deed-poll to be his act and deed, and desired that the said acknowledgment of the said deed might be entered of record in the proceedings of the said Court; and the same was thereupon entered accordingly.

In testimony whereof, I have hereunto set my hand, and caused the seal of the said Court to be affixed, the same day and year.

JOHN JOURDON, *Prothonotary.*

Acknowledgment by a Corporation.

City of Philadelphia, *ss.*

Be it remembered, that on the tenth day of January, in the year of our Lord one thousand eight hundred and forty-five, before me, Johu Jay, Esquire, Mayor of the said city, personally appeared Richard Roe, Esquire, President of the above-named Corporation, and, being duly sworn, deposeth and saith, that he was personally present at the execution of the above-written indenture or deed of conveyance, and saw the common seal of the said corporation of "The President, Directors and Company of the Bank of Pennsylvania" duly affixed thereto, and that the seal so affixed thereto is the common and corporate seal of the said "The President, Directors and Company of the Bank of Pennsylvania," and that the above-written indenture or deed of conveyance was duly signed, sealed and delivered by and at and for the act and deed of the said "The President, Directors and Company of the Bank of Pennsylvania," for the uses and purposes therein mentioned; and that the name of this deponent, subscribed to the said deed as President of the said Corporation, in attestation of the due execution and delivery of the said deed, is of this deponent's own proper and respective hand-writing.

RICHARD ROE.

Sworn and subscribed the day and year aforesaid, before me. Witness my hand and seal.

JOHN JAY, *Mayor.*

Acknowledgment by Special Partners.

Lancaster County, *ss.*

Before me, one of the Justices of the Peace in and for said county, personally appeared the above-named A. B., C. D. and E. F., who severally, in due form of law, acknowledged the foregoing certificate as and for theirs, and each of theirs act and deed, to the end that the same might be recorded as such.

Witness my hand and seal, this —— day of ——, A. D. ——.

JOHN GREEN.

Acknowledgment of a Writing in English, with a copy in another language.

Erie County, *ss.*

Before me, John Greene, one of the Justices of the Peace in and for the said county, personally appeared the within named William Smith, who in my presence did acknowledge the foregoing ———, whereof the annexed purports to be a true translation, to be his voluntary act and deed, and by him delivered to the within named John Jay, for the purposes therein mentioned; the name and seal thereunto prescribed and affixed being the proper hand and seal of him the said William Smith.

In testimony whereof, I have hereunto set my hand and seal, this —— day of ——, A. D. ——

JOHN GREEN.

ACQUITTANCE.

Acquittance is an agreement in writing, to discharge a party from an engagement to pay a sum of money; it is evidence of payment. It differs from a release in this, that the latter must be under seal, while an acquittance is not under seal. In Pennsylvania, a receipt, though not under seal, has nearly the same effect as a release. 1 *Rawle R.* 391. 3 *Salk.* 298.

Acquittance for Money received on a Sale.

Know all men by these presents, that I, John Jones, of Erie, in the County of Erie and State of Pennsylvania, do hereby acknowledge myself, upon the day of the date hereof, to have received of William Burns, of Concord, County and State aforesaid, the sum of one hundred dollars, being the last payment, and in full, of five hundred dollars by him paid as the consideration of the purchase of a certain tract of land, situate in Concord aforesaid, and bounded by lands of ——, containing fifty acres of land, be the same more or less, and by me the said John Jones sold and conveyed to the said William Burns. And of the said whole sum of five hundred dollars, and every part and parcel thereof, I, the said John Jones, do by these presents, for me, my heirs, executors and administrators, acquit and discharge the said William Burns, his heirs, executors and administrators, forever.

In testimony whereof, I have hereunto set my hand, this tenth day of January, A. D. 1845.

JOHN JONES.

Acquittance for Money received in part of a Bond.

Received, the first day of January, A. D. 1845, of William Burns, the sum of one hundred dollars, in part payment of the sum of five hundred dollars, due to me by the said William Burns, on his bond dated the first day of January, A. D. 1844.

JOHN JONES.

Acquittance for Interest due on a Bond.

Received, the tenth day of January, A. D. 1845, of William Burns, sixty dollars in full, for one year's interest of one thousand dollars, due to me the tenth day of January, A. D. 1845, on bond of the said William Burns, dated the tenth day of January, A. D. 1844.

JOHN JONES.

AFFIDAVITS AND OATHS.

Remarks.

An affidavit is an oath or affirmation reduced to writing; sworn or affirmed to before some officer who has authority to administer it.

An oath is a solemn promise, by which he who makes it declares that he will tell the truth, the whole truth, and nothing but the truth, in relation to the matter in question; and by which the party who takes it, renounces the mercy or imprecates the vengeance of heaven, if he speaks not the truth. Oaths are taken in various forms, upon the Gospel, by taking the book in hand; by holding up the hand; and by a simple affirmation.

Affidavit,

Where the debt or damages exceed 100 dollars.

John Jones
v.
William Burns } In the Common Pleas of Erie County.

Erie County, *ss.*

Before me, W. K., Esquire, prothonotary of the Court of Common Pleas in and for the county of Erie, personally appeared John Jones, the plaintiff above named, who being duly sworn according to law, deposeth and saith, that he doth truly believe that the debt due by William Burns, the defendant above named, to him the said John Jones, exceeds the sum of one hundred dollars. [Or that the damage sustained by him, the said John Jones, from William Burns, the defendant in the above action, exceeds, &c.]

JOHN JONES.

Sworn and subscribed the —— day of ——, before me.

W. K.

☞ If a suit is brought in the Court of Common Pleas, without the above affidavit being previously filed, and the plaintiff recovers less than $100, he shall recover no costs.

Affidavit to an Account.

York County, *ss.*

On the tenth day of January, A. D. 1845, before me, the subscriber, one of the Justices of the Peace, in and for the said county, personally came A. B. of ——, and being duly sworn according to law, deposeth and saith, that the above account as stated, is just and true, that the above sum of —— dollars is now justly due and owing to this deponent by the above-named C. D., and that the said A. B. never received the same, or any part thereof, either directly or indirectly, nor any other person for him, by his order, consent or direction, or to his knowledge, and further saith not.

A. B.

Sworn and subscribed before me, the day and year aforesaid.

WILLIAM PATTERSON.

General form of an Affidavit to a Petition, &c.

Adams County, *ss.*

Before me, the subscriber, one of the Justices of the Peace, in and for the said county, personally appeared John Jones above named, who being duly sworn according to law, doth depose and say that the facts set forth in the above petition, [or as the case may be,] are true to the best of his knowledge and belief.

John Jones.

Sworn and subscribed before me, this 10th day of January, A. D. 1845.

JOHN CLINE.

Affidavit on an Appeal from an Award of Arbitrators.

Berks County, *ss.*

Before John King, Prothonotary of the Common Pleas of the county aforesaid, appeared John Jones, the defendant in the above case, who being duly sworn, doth depose and say, that it is not for the purpose of delay that the appeal in the above case is entered, but because he firmly believes injustice has been done him, and that he has a just and legal defence to the plaintiff's demand, the nature and character of which is, [here set forth the ground of defence,] and further saith not.

John Jones.

Sworn and subscribed the 15th day of January, A. D. 1845.

JOHN KING, *Prothonotary.*

An Affidavit of Defence.

John Doe *v.* Richard Roe } In the Common Pleas of Centre County, of January Term, 1845, No. 36.

Before John Pacher, Prothonotary of the Common Pleas of Centre County, personally appeard Richard Roe, the defendant above named, who being duly sworn according to law, doth depose and say, that he has a just and legal defence to the whole of the plaintiff's demand in the above suit, [or so much to which a defence is made,] the nature and character of which is, [here state the facts on which the defence is founded in a clear manner, so that it may be an answer to the plaintiff's demand,] and further saith not. RICHARD ROE.

Sworn and subscribed the 15th day of January, A. D. 1845.
JOHN PACHER, *Prothonotary.*

Affidavit of the service of Notices, &c.

Cumberland County, *ss.*

Before me, the subscriber, one of the Justices of the Peace in and for the said county, personally appeared Alfred King, who being duly sworn, doth depose and say, that he served the within —— on John Jones, within named, on the tenth day of January, A D. one thousand eight hundred and forty-five, by leaving a true and attested copy thereof, at his dwelling-house in Carlisle, in the presence of an adult member of his family.

ALFRED KING.

Sworn and subscribed this 10th day of January, 1845.
JOHN DOE.

Affidavit of Administrators, Executors, or a Guardian to a final Account.

Erie County, *ss.*

Before me, the subscriber, one of the Justices of the Peace in and for the said county, personally appeared John Duncan and James Jones, administrators aforesaid, [or executors or guardian, as the case may be], who doth depose and say that the above stated account is just and true, to the best of their knowledge and belief. JOHN DUNCAN,
JAMES JONES.

Sworn and subscribed, this 10th day of January, A. D. 1845.
THEODORE RYMAN.

Affidavit of an Alien on Petition to become a Citizen.

Franklin County, *ss.*

I, John Sampson, above mentioned, being sworn in open court, do declare and say, that the facts stated in the above petition are true; that I was a resident in the United States prior to and on the —— day of ——, A. D. ——, and have continued to reside within the same; that I will support the Constitution of the United States; that I do hereby renounce and relinquish any title or order of nobility to which I am or hereafter may be entitled, and that I do absolutely and entirely renounce and abjure all allegiance and fidelity to any foreign prince, potentate, state or sovereignty whatever, and particularly to the Queen of Great Britain [or as the case may be] of whom I was before a subject.

Affidavit of a Citizen on the application of an Alien.

Franklin County, *ss.*

John Richards, a citizen of the United States, being duly sworn according to law, saith that he is well acquainted with the within named petitioner, John Sampson; that the said John Sampson was residing within the limits and under the jurisdiction of the United States, between the —— day of ——, A. D. —— and the —— day of ——, A. D. ——, and has continued to reside therein, and that he is a man of good moral character, attached to the principles of the Constitution of the United States, and well disposed to the good order and happiness of the same.

Affidavit where a Witness to a Deed is deceased or absent.

Washington County, *ss.*

Be it remembered, that on the tenth day of January, A. D. one thousand eight hundred and forty-five, before me, the subscriber, one of the Justices of the Peace in and for said county, personally appeared Richard Sill, of full age, who being duly sworn, according to law, doth depose and say, that he is well acquainted with the hand-writing of Alfred King, one of the subscribing witnesses to the within ——, having frequently seen him write, and that he verily believes that the name of the said Alfred King, signed to the same as one of the attesting witnesses, is the proper hand-writing of the said Alfred King, who is now absent, [or deceased, as the case may be]. RICHARD SILL.

Sworn and subscribed before me, the day and year aforesaid.

JOHN THOM.

Affidavit of Partner under the limited partnership law.

Allegheny County, *ss.*

Before me, the subscriber, one of the Justices of the Peace in and for the said county, personally appeared the above-named John Duncan, one of the general partners of the firm of——, referred to in the preceding agreement, and being duly sworn, did depose and say, that the several sums of money specified therein to have been contributed by each of the special partners therein, named to the common stock, to wit: the sum of——, &c. &c., have been so contributed, and actually, and in good faith paid in cash. Sworn, &c. JOHN DUNCAN.

An Affidavit to sustain a Writ of Certiorari.

Westmoreland County, *ss.*

John Stewart, above named, maketh oath and saith that it is not for the purpose of delay, that he applies for the above-mentioned writ of Certiorari, but that the proceedings proposed to be removed, are to the best of his knowledge unjust and illegal, and, if not removed, will oblige the said——to pay more money than is justly due, and further saith not. JOHN STEWART.

Sworn and subscribed before me, this 10th day of January, 1845.
JAMES MARSHALL, *Proth'y.*

An Affidavit on an Appeal from the Orphan's Court to the Supreme Court.

In the matter of the estate of——

Lancaster County, *ss.*

John Jones, being duly sworn, doth depose and say, that his appeal entered this day, from the sentence or appeal of the Orphan's Court [specifying the nature thereof] is not intended for delay, but because he verily believes that injustice has been done him. JOHN JONES.

Sworn, &c.

Affidavit of the Publication of Notice.

Bucks County, *ss.*

A. B. *v.* C. D. In the Common Pleas of—— county of—— Term, 1844. No. ——.

E. F., being duly sworn according to law, saith that he is the publisher of a weekly newspaper in——, called the——, and that the above notice was published in said newspaper for—— weeks, ending the —— day of——. E. F.

Sworn and subscribed before me, this 10th day of January, A. D. 1845.

ISAAC LIGHTNER, *Justice of the Peace.*

Affidavit by Wife, in Action by Husband and Wife for Work by her before Marriage.

Philadelphia City, *ss.*

H. F., the wife of A. B. of the city of Philadelphia, dry goods merchant, being duly sworn (or affirmed) according to law, deposes and says, that C. D. is justly and truly indebted to the said A. B. and this deponent in five hundred dollars, for work heretofore done by this deponent whilst she was sole and unmarried, for the said C. D. at his request. H. F.

Sworn and subscribed before me, this 10th day of January, 1845.

JOHN JAY, *Justice of the Peace.*

Affidavit to support a Writ of Domestic Attachment.

Allegheny County, *ss.*

A. B. *v.* C. D. A. B., the plaintiff above named, being duly sworn, according to law, saith, that C. D., the defendant in the above suit, is now justly indebted to him, the said plaintiff, in the sum of —— dollars, and —— cents, for divers goods, wares, and merchandize, sold and delivered by him to the said defendant at his request on the —— day of ——, A. D. 1844. That the said defendant kept a store in —— street, in the —— of ——, and on or about the —— day of ——, absconded or departed from his usual place of abode, or secreted himself (as the case may be, *see* 1 *Miles, p.* 75) with intent to defraud his creditors, as the deponent verily believes. That the said defendant has not left in this county a clear freehold estate sufficient to pay his debts, and further saith not. A. B.

Sworn and subscribed before me this 10th day of January, 1845.

JOHN HIGHLANDS, *Justice of the Peace.*

Affidavit on an Appeal.

Mercer County, *ss.*

In the matter of the —— of A. B. of —— in the —— of ——. C. D., being duly sworn according to law, saith, that the appeal made in this case is not for the purpose of delay, but because he verily believes that injustice has been done him. C. D.

Sworn and subscribed this 10th day of January, A. D. 1845.

JOHN STEWART, *Justice of the Peace.*

Affidavit by executor or administrator of his Cause of Action.

Jefferson County, *ss.*

A. B., of ——, executor, &c., (or Administrator, &c.,) of C. D., deceased, maketh oath and saith, that E. F. is justly and truly indebted to this deponent as *executor* as aforesaid, in the sum of —— dollars for —— to the said E. F. by the said C. D. in his life time delivered, as appears by the books of the said C. D., and as this deponent verily believes. A. B.

Sworn and subscribed before me this 10th day of January, A. D. 1845. JOHN JAY, *Justice of the Peace.*

Common form of Oath by kissing the Book.

You do swear that, &c. ——. So help you God.

Oath of a Witness on a Trial.

You do swear, that the evidence which you shall give to the court and jury, in this issue joined, wherein A. B. is plaintiff and C. D. is defendant, shall be the truth, the whole truth, and nothing but the truth. So help you God.

*Oath of voir dire.**

You do swear, that you will true answers make to all such questions as shall be asked you by the court, touching the matter now before them. So help you God.

Form of Oath by lifting up the right hand.

You do swear, by Almighty God, the searcher of all hearts, that you will, &c. ——, and that as you shall answer to God at the great day.

Form of Affirmation.

You do solemnly, sincerely and truly declare and affirm, that, &c. ——

☞ According to the laws of Pennsylvania, only such "as conscientiously refuse to take an oath," can be admitted to affirm. *See Read's Digest, 2.*

* Where a party prays, upon a trial at law, that a witness may be sworn as to whether he will gain or lose by the matter in controversy, this is called a *voir dire;* and if it appears that the witness is disinterested, his testimony is allowed, otherwise not. 3 Blackstone's Com. 332.

Oath of Foreman of a Grand Jury.

You do swear, that as foreman of this grand inquest you will diligently inquire, and true presentment make, as well of all such matters and things as shall be given you in charge, as of those things which you shall know to be presentable here —— the Commonwealth's counsel, your fellows' and your own, you shall keep secret —— you shall present no one for envy, hatred, malice or ill will; neither shall you leave any one unpresented through fear, favour, affection, reward, gain, or any hope thereof —— but you shall present all things truly as they shall come to your knowledge, to the best of your understanding. So help you God.

Oath of the other Jurors.

You, and each of you, do swear, that the same oath which your foreman hath taken to observe and keep on his part, you and every of you will well and truly observe and keep on your part. So help you God.

Oath of Traverse Jury in the Civil Courts.

You, and every of you, do swear, that you will well and truly try the issue joined between A. B. plaintiff, and C. D. defendant, and a true verdict give according to the evidence, unless dismissed by the court, or the cause be withdrawn by the parties. So help you God.

Another form of Oath of Traverse Jury in the Criminal Courts.

You do swear, that you will well and truly try, and true deliverance make, between the commonwealth of Pennsylvania and the prisoner at the bar, whom you shall have in charge, and a true verdict give according to the evidence. So help you God.

Oaths of Referees under the Act of 1810.

You, and each of you, do —— that you will well and truly try all matters here in variance between —— plaintiff, and —— defendant, according to the best of your judgment and the evidence that shall be laid before you. So help, &c.

Oaths of Referees in Trespass.

You, and each of you, do —— that you will justly and truly assess the damages [if any] here alleged to have been sustained by —— against ——, according to the best of your judgment and the evidence which shall be laid before you. So help, &c.

Oath of Referees in Trover and Conversion.

You, and each of you, do —— that you will justly and truly assess the value of the property in dispute between —— plaintiff, and —— defendant, according to the best of your judgment, and the evidence which shall be laid before you. So help, &c.

Oaths of Jurors in proceedings to recover Possession after sale by Sheriff.

You, and each of you, do —— that you will well and truly inquire of and concerning the premises in this summons mentioned, and assess such damages [if any] as the complainant hath sustained thereby. So help, &c.

Oath of Claimant of land sold by Sheriff, in proceedings to deliver possession under the Act of 16th June, 1836.

I, A. B., do ——, that I verily believe that I am legally entitled to hold the premises in dispute against the petitioner, that I do not claim the same by, from, or under the defendant, as whose property the same was sold, by title derived to me subsequently to the rendition of the judgment, under which the same were sold, but by a different title, &c. (*as the case may be.*)

Oaths of Jurors under Landlord and Tenant Act of 1825.

You, and each of you, do —— that you will well and truly inquire of and concerning the premises in this precept mentioned, and assess such damages [if any] as the complainant hath sustained thereby.

Oath of Inquest in Partition in the Common Pleas.

You, and every of you, do —— that you will well and truly view and inquire whether the lands and tenements in this writ of partition mentioned, can be divided to and among the parties in the said writ named without prejudice to or spoiling the whole, and if you find that the same can be so divided, that then you will make partition thereof accordingly; but if you find that the same cannot be so divided according to the command of the writ, that then you will make a just valuation and appraisement thereof, according to the best of your knowledge, &c.

Oath of Inquest on Real Estate under Execution.

You, and each of you, do —— that you will true inquiry make whether the rents, issues and profits of the lands, tenements and hereditaments, taken in execution by the sheriff of —— county by virtue of certain writs of fieri facias, which will be laid before you, are of a clear yearly value, beyond all reprizes, sufficient within the space of seven years to pay or satisfy the debts or damages in the said writs respectively mentioned, with costs of suit, and a true inquisition thereof make, according to the best of your judgment, &c.

Oath of Inquest on Writ of Inquiry.

You, and each of you, do —— that you will diligently inquire what damages A. B.; the plaintiff in this writ named; hath sustained against C. D., the defendant in said writ named, as well by occasion of the premises in the said writ specified, as for his costs and charges by him about his suit in that behalf expended, and a true inquisition make, according to law, &c.

Oath of Inquest on Writ of Liberari Facias.

You, and each of you, do —— that you will diligently inquire, and to the best of your knowledge ascertain, the clear yearly value of a messuage, plantation and tract of land, situate, &c., with the appurtenances, in a certain writ of liberari facias, wherein A. B. is plaintiff, and C. D. is defendant mentioned, and a true inquisition thereof make, according to law and the best of your judgment, &c.

Oath of Arbitrators.

You, and each of you, do swear, by Almighty God, the searcher of all hearts, that in this suit, in which A. B. is plaintiff and C. D. is defendant, you will justly and equitably try all matters in variance submitted to you between the parties, and a true award make, according to the evidence, and that as you shall answer to God at the great day.

Oath of Executors or Administrators.

You, and each of you, do swear, by Almighty God, the searcher of all hearts, that as Executors [or administrators as the case may be] of A. B., deceased, you will well and truly administer the goods and chattels, rights and credits, of the said decedent, according to law; and diligently and faithfully regard, and well and truly comply with the provisions of the law relating to collateral inheritances, and that as you shall answer to God at the great day.

☞ A Jew must be sworn on the Old Testament, and with his hat on. 2 *Str.* 821. A Mahometan must be sworn upon the Koran. 2 *Str.* 1104. The evidence of a Gentoo, sworn according to the ceremonies of his own religion, is admissible. 1 *Atk.* 21.

Oath of a Constable attending upon a Jury.

You do swear, that you will keep this jury in some private and convenient place, and remain there in attendance upon them, that you will suffer no one to speak to them, nor speak to them yourself, unless it be to ask them if they have agreed on their verdict. So help you God.

Oath of a Witness to the Grand Jury.

You do swear, that the testimony you shall give to the grand inquest for the body of the county of ——, upon such bills of indictment, whereunto you shall be examined, shall be the truth, the whole truth, and nothing but the truth. So help you God.

Oath of an Attorney-at-law on his admission to the Bar.

You do swear, [or affirm,] that you will support the Constitution of the United States, and the constitution of this commonwealth, and that you will behave yourself in the office of attorney within these courts, according to the best of your learning and ability, and with all good fidelity, as well to the court as to the client, that you will use no falsehood, nor delay any person's cause for lucre or malice.

Oath of Clerk of Markets.

You do swear, that you will well and truly, to the best of your skill and judgment, do and perform all things enjoined and required of you as clerk of the market, by the laws of this state. So help you God.

Oath of Constable.

You do swear, that you will support the Constitution of the United States, and the Constitution of this commonwealth, and perform the duties of the office of constable, for the township of ——, the ensuing year with fidelity, and until you shall be legally discharged. So help you God.

Oath of Overseer of the Poor.

You do swear, that you will support the Constitution of the United States, and the constitution of this commonwealth, and perform the duties of the office of overseer of the poor with fidelity. So help you God.

Oath of Appraisers of goods distrained for rent.

You, A. B., do swear, that you will well and truly, according to the best of your understanding, appraise the goods and chattels of C. D., distrained on for rent, by E. F. So help you God.

☞ This oath the sheriff or constable, who is aiding and assisting in making the distress, is empowered and required to administer.

Oath of Deputy Surveyor.

I, A. B., do swear, [or affirm,] that I will do and perform the duties of the office of deputy-surveyor, with fidelity and impartiality to all men.

Oath of Notary Public.

You do swear, that you shall and will well and faithfully perform the duties of your office of notary public, and that you shall and will support the constitution of the commonwealth of Pennsylvania. So help you God.

Oath of Sheriff and County Commissioners before the selection of Jurors.

You, and each of you, do swear, [or affirm,] that you will use your utmost endeavours and diligence in making an impartial selection of competent persons for jurors during the ensuing year, and that you will not suffer partiality, favour, affection, hatred, malice, or ill-will in any case or respect whatever, to influence you in selecting, drawing or returning of jurors; but that you will, in all respects, honestly conform to the true intent and meaning of the Acts of Assembly, in such case made and provided.

ARTICLES OF AGREEMENTS AND CONTRACTS.

Remarks.

A contract is an agreement upon sufficient consideration to do or not to do a particular thing.

There are agreements by specialty, made by instrument under seal; and agreements without specialty, made by instrument without seal or by parol.

Agreements by seal, are generally of a higher consideration in law than agreements without a seal or by parol; and it is, therefore, advisable in contracts to add a seal.

In effect, there is no difference between an agreement in writing without a seal, and by parol; except that the former can be more easily proved, and is, therefore, to be preferred.

Care should be taken to have the agreement or contract clearly understood and expressed. The want of care is a fruitful source of difficulty and law suits.

To render an agreement complete, six things must concur: there must be, 1st, a person able to contract; 2d, a person able to be contracted with; 3d, a thing to be contracted for; 4th, a lawful consideration; 5th, clear and explicit words to express the agreement; and 6th, the assent of the contracting parties. *Plowd.* 161; *Co. Litt.* 35, b.

Articles of Agreement for the sale of Land.

Articles of agreement, made and entered into the first day of May, in the year of our Lord one thousand eight hundred and forty-four, between John Jones of Erie, in the county of Erie, and State of Pennsylvania of the one part, and William Burns of the same place, of the other part, as follows, to wit:

The said John Jones, for the consideration hereinafter mentioned, doth for himself, his heirs, executors and administrators, covenant, promise, grant and agree, to and with the said William Burns, his heirs and assigns, by these presents, that he, the said John Jones, shall and will, on or before the first day of May, one thousand eight hundred and forty-six, at the proper costs and charges of the said John Jones, his heirs and assigns, by good and lawful deed or deeds, well and sufficiently grant, convey and assure, unto the said William Burns, his heirs and assigns in fee simple, clear of all incumbrances, all that messuage or piece of land situate in Erie aforesaid, and bounded and described as follows, [here describe the premises by its boundaries.]

In consideration whereof, the said William Burns, for himself, his heirs, executors and administrators, doth covenant, promise, and agree, to and with the said John Jones, his heirs and assigns, by these presents, that he, the said William Burns, his heirs, executors and administrators, or some of them, shall and will well and truly pay, or cause to be paid, unto the said John Jones, his executors, administrators or assigns, the sum of one thousand dollars, in manner following, to wit: two hundred dollars on the execution of this agreement, four hundred dollars on the first day of May, one thousand eight hundred and forty-five, and the remaining four hundred dollars, on the first day of May, one thousand eight hundred and forty-six, with annual interest on the whole sum; and the payment of the said several sums of money, is declared to be a condition precedent to the execution of the deed or deeds of conveyance aforesaid, by the said John Jones.

And for the true performance of all and every the covenants and agreements aforesaid, each of the said parties bindeth himself, his heirs, executors and administrators, unto the other, his executors, and administrators and assigns, in the penal sum of two thousand dollars, lawful money of the United States, firmly by these presents. In witness whereof, the said parties to these presents have hereunto set their hands and seals. Dated the day and year first above written.

Signed, sealed and delivered, in the presence of }
JAMES STILES.

JOHN JONES.

WILLIAM BURNS.

Another Agreement for the sale of Land.

Agreement, made and entered into the tenth day of June, A. D. 1844, between John Jones, of Erie, of the one part, and William Burns, of the same place, of the other part; witnesseth, that the said John Jones, in consideration of the sum of one hundred dollars now paid, and two hundred and forty dollars to be paid when a deed is executed, doth grant, bargain, and sell to the said William Burns, his heirs and assigns, all that piece of ground situated in Erie, and bounded as follows, viz: [here describe the premises by its boundaries,] together with all and singular, the appurtenances thereunto belonging, or in any wise appertaining.

And the said parties hereby bind themselves, their heirs, executors, and administrators, for the performance of all and every of the above agreement, as witness their hands and seals this tenth day of June, 1844.

Signed, sealed and de-
livered, in presence of }
JAMES STILES.

JOHN JONES.

WILLIAM BURNS.

Received June 10th, 1844, of William Burns, one hundred dollars, the first payment above mentioned. JOHN JONES.

Another Agreement for the sale of land.

Articles of agreement, made and concluded the tenth day of May, in the year of our Lord one thousand eight hundred and forty-four, between John Jones, of Erie, in the county of Erie and State of Pennsylvania, of the one part, and William Burns, of the same place, of the other part, as follows, to wit: The said John Jones agrees to sell to the said William Burns all that certain messuage or piece of land situated, &c., [here describe the premises,] with the appurtenances, for the sum of five hundred dollars, and will, on or before the fourth day of October next, on the receipt of the said sum of five hundred dollars, at the charges of the said William Burns, execute a proper conveyance thereof, with covenant of general warranty, and against incumbrances, to the said William Burris, his heirs and assigns, and the said William Burns agrees that, on the execution of such conveyance, he will pay the said sum of five hundred dollars to the said John Jones or his assigns.

And it is further agreed, that the conveyance shall be prepared by, and at the expense of the said William Burns, to the approbatlon of the respective counsel of the said John Jones and William Burns, and that all taxes and outgoings in respect of the premises, in the mean time, shall be paid by the said John Jones. And it is further agreed, that the said William Burns shall receive the rents and profits of the premises, from this date, to his proper use.

And it is further agreed, that if the said conveyance shall not be executed, and the purchase money paid, on or before the said fourth day of October next, then the said William Burns shall pay legal interest for the same from this date, unto the said John Jones.

In witness whereof the parties to these presents have hereunto set their hands and seals the day and year first above written.

Sealed and delivered in presence of }

JAMES STILES.

JOHN JONES.

WILLIAM BURNS.

Agreement for the purchase of Cordwood.

It is agreed and concluded upon, by and between John Jones, of Erie, of the one part, and William Burns, of Greene, of the other part, that the said John Jones shall, and doth hereby, sell to the said William Burns all the cordwood that shall arise from the trees and parcels of trees now growing and standing on a certain piece of rough ground, situated &c., [here describe the ground,] after the rate of fifty cents per cord, each cord to be in measure according to the usual measure of cordwood.

And the said John Jones for himself, his heirs, executors and administrators, doth covenant and promise to and with the said William Burns, his executors, administrators and assigns, as follows, viz: That he, the said John Jones, shall and will, at his own proper cost and charges, rank up all the trees and parcels of trees growing and being upon the said piece of land as shall be fit to convert into cordwood as aforesaid.

And also shall and will permit and suffer the said William Burns, his executors or assigns, at his or their own cost and charges, as well to cut and convert the said cordwood into charcoal, at the east end of the said piece of land, whereon the said trees or the greatest part of them now stand, and also to take the turf, dust and earth, from off the said piece of ground, and not elsewhere, with free liberty of carrying away the same wood so converted into charcoal, from off the said premises, the most convenient way leading to the road that leads to ———. And the said William Burns doth hereby for himself, his executors and administrators, covenant and promise to and with the said John Jones, his heirs and assigns, that he, the said William Burns, his executors or administrators, shall and will well and truly pay, or cause to be paid unto the said John Jones, the full and entire sum of fifty cents per cord, for each and every cord measured as aforesaid, on or before the first day of April next. Witness our hands and seals this tenth day of June, A. D. 1844.

Sealed and delivered in presence of } JAMES STILES.

JOHN JONES.

WILLIAM BURNS.

Agreement for Building a House.

Articles of agreement, made and concluded, the first day of August, one thousand eight hundred and forty four, between John Jones, of Mercer, in the county of Mercer, and state of Pennsylvania, of the one part, and William Burns, of the same place, of the other part, as follows, viz: The said John Jones, for the considerations hereinafter mentioned, doth for himself, his executors and administrators, covenant, promise and agree, to and with the said William Burns, his executors, administrators and assigns, that he, the said John Jones, shall and will, within the space of six months from the date hereof, in a good and workmanlike manner, and according to the best of his art and skill, well and substantially erect, build, set up, and finish one house or messuage, at Mercer aforesaid, of the dimensions following, viz: [here describe the House,] and compose the same with such stone or brick, timber, and other materials as the said William Burns, or his assigns, shall find and provide for the same.

In consideration whereof, the said William Burns, doth for himself, his executors and administrators, covenant and promise to and with the said John Jones, his executors, administrators and assigns, well and truly to pay, or cause to be paid, unto the said John Jones, his executors, administrators and assigns, the sum of six hundred dollars, in manner following, viz: Two hundred dollars, part thereof at the beginning of the said work; two hundred dollars more thereof, on the first day of November next; and the remaining two hundred dollars in full for the said work, when the same shall be completely finished.

And also, that he, the said William Burns, his executors, administrators or assigns, shall and will at his and their own proper expense, find and provide all the stone, brick, tile, timber and other materials, necessary for making and building of the said House.

And for the true performance of all and every the covenants and agreements aforesaid, each of the said parties bindeth himself, his heirs, executors and administrators, unto the other, his executors, administrators and assigns in the penal sum of twelve hundred dollars firmly by these presents. In witness whereof, the said parties to these presents have hereunto set their hands and seals, the day and year first above written.

Sealed and delivered in presence of

JAMES STILES.

JOHN JONES.

WILLIAM BURNS.

Agreement for performing Bricklayer's and Plasterer's work in building a House.

It is agreed, this first day of January one thousand eight hundred and forty five, between John Jones, of Pittsburgh, of the one part, and William Burns, of the same place, of the other part, as follows, viz: The said John Jones, for the considerations hereinafter mentioned, doth for himself, his heirs, executors and administrators, covenant, promise and agree, to and with the said William Burns, his executors, administrators and assigns, that he, the said John Jones, his executors, administrators, workmen, or assigns, in sufficient and workmanlike manner, at his and their own charges, with the materials to be for that purpose provided by the said William Burns, shall and will do and perform all the work and workmanship belonging to the bricklayer and plasterer, in and about the erecting and building of one good and substantial new messuage or tenement, in the room and place whereon lately stood a certain house belonging to the said Burns, in Pittsburgh aforesaid, and will build the same in such manner, and with such thickness of walls, height or stories, and such or so many lights, chimneys and conveniences, and in such manner, and will do and perform such ornamental work about the said building, as the said Burns, his executors or assigns, shall order and direct, and that he, the said Jones, will use his utmost care in working up the said Burns' materials for the said building to the most advantage, and will also pay and discharge all his said workmen to be employed in and about the same: and will completely finish all the said work and workmanship belonging to the bricklayer and plasterer for building the said intended messuage, on or before the first day of September next ensuing the date hereof. In consideration of which said works so to be done and performed as aforesaid, he, the said Burns, for himself, his executors, administrators and assigns, doth covenant, promise and agree, to and with the said Jones, his executors, administrators and assigns, by these presents, that he, the said Burns, his executors, administrators and assigns, shall and will well and truly pay, or cause to be paid, unto the said Jones, his executors, administrators, and assigns, for all such work which shall be by him and them done and performed in and about the said building, ornamental work excepted, at and after the rate of —— per yard, for every yard which the said work shall measure, accounting three feet square for every yard, and —— dollars in full for all the said ornamental work to be done and performed as aforesaid: but nothing is to be measured or paid for that is not covered with plaster, nor is any extra charge to be made or allowed, for corners, arches, jams, joints, fire-places, or any other kind of work whatever, usually or at any time rated as extra, but the whole is to be measured as plain; and the said Burns will pay all the said money in manner following, viz: [insert the terms of payment.] In witness whereof, the parties to these presents have hereunto set their hands and seals the day and year first above written.

Sealed and delivered in presence of

JAMES STILES.

JOHN JONES.

WILLIAM BURNS.

Agreement with a Millwright.

Articles of agreement made and concluded the first day of June, A. D. 1844, between John Jones, of Reading, Berks County, Pennsylvania, of the one part, and William Burns, of the same place, of the other part. The said John Jones, for the considerations hereinafter mentioned, doth hereby covenant and agree to and with the said William Burns, in manner following, to wit: That he the said John Jones from the day of the date hereof, for and during the full term of three years, if they the said John Jones and William Burns shall both so long live, shall and will at the now dwelling-house of him, the said William Burns, situated in Reading aforesaid, or at such other place or places, (if by him the said William Burns, from time to time so required, ordered and directed,) work as a journeyman, and well and truly and faithfully serve him the said William Burns, in the business of a millwright, carpenter, joiner, turner, and in all such other arts, mysteries, and work as he, the said John Jones, now is, or shall be any wise capable of doing or performing, during the term aforesaid, and that, according to the best of his, the said John Jones's ability, knowledge, and judgment therein: and that he, the said John Jones, during the continuance of the said term, shall yearly work and perform the trade or business aforesaid for him, the said William Burns, in manner as follows, viz: from the twenty-second day of March to the twenty-second day of September, from the hours of six in the morning to six in the evening, and from the twenty-second day of September to the twenty-second day of March, from daylight to daylight, and that daily, (sickness, Sundays, Christmas, New-Year's day, the fourth day of July, and such days as he may be lawfully required to muster as a militia-man, and usual hours of breakfast and dinner, only allowed and excepted.) And further, that he, the said John Jones, during the term aforesaid, shall not at any time absent himself from such service of the said William Burns, nor work, do, or perform any part of the said trade or business aforesaid, for the use or benefit of any other person or persons whomsoever, without the consent of the said Burns, first had in writing for that purpose. And the said William Burns doth hereby covenant, promise, and agree to and with the said John Jones, that he, the said William Burns, shall and will well and truly pay, or cause to be paid unto the said John Jones, for his said services, the sum of thirty dollars per month, and board him during the said time.

Witness our hands and seals, the day and year aforesaid.

Sealed and delivered in presence of }

JAMES STILES.

JOHN JONES. [L.S.]

WILLIAM BURNS. [L.S.]

Agreement on a sale of Wheat.

It is this day agreed, by and between John Jones, of Butler, Butler county, Pennsylvania, and William Burns of the same place, as follows: the said John Jones, in consideration of two hundred bushels of wheat, sold to him this day by the said William Burns, and by him agreed to be delivered to the said John Jones, free of all charges, on or before the first day of January next, shall and will pay, or cause to be paid, to the said William Burns, or his assigns, within three months after such delivery, the sum of one hundred and fifty dollars. And the said William Burns, in consideration of the agreement aforesaid, of the said

John Jones, doth promise and agree, on or before the first day of January next aforesaid, at his own proper expense, to send in and deliver to the said John Jones, or his assigns, the said two hundred bushels of wheat, so sold him as aforesaid, and that he, the said William Burns, shall and will warrant the same to be good, clean, and merchantable grain.

Witness our hands and seals this tenth day of June, A. D. 1844.

Witness present,

JAMES STILES.

JOHN JONES.

WILLIAM BURNS.

An Agreement for the sale and delivery of Coal.

Memorandum of agreement, made this day between John Jones and William Burns, both of Pittsburgh, as follows: that he, the said William Burns, for the consideration hereinafter mentioned, hath sold, and by these presents doth agree, to deliver to the said John Jones, at his furnace in Pittsburgh, free of all charges and expenses whatsoever, one hundred tons of coal, from time to time, between the date of these presents, and the first day of January next, in such quantities, and at such times, as the said John Jones shall require, and the whole to be delivered on or before the said first day of January; and the said John Jones agrees to pay to the said William Burns therefor, the sum or price of —— per ton, the one-half to be paid in such wares as are manufactured at the furnace of the said John Jones, and the remaining half in cash, on the first day of January next.

Witness our hands and seals this first day of November, A. D. 1844.

Witness present,

JAMES STILES.

JOHN JONES.

WILLIAM BURNS.

An Agreement for letting a House.

It is agreed, this tenth day of March, A. D. 1845, between John Jones, of Erie, Erie county, Pennsylvania, of the one part, and William Burns, of the same place, of the other part, as follows: the said John Jones doth let unto the said William Burns, all that certain house and lot of ground situate [here describe the premises], for one year from the first day of April next, and for such longer time after the expiration of the said one year, as both the said parties shall agree, and until the end of three months after notice shall be given by either of the said parties, to the other of them, for leaving the said premises, at, and for the yearly rent of one hundred dollars, to be paid quarterly, on the first days of July, October, January and April, by even and equal portions, which said yearly rent, payable quarterly, as aforesaid, the said William Burns doth hereby, for himself, his executors and administrators, covenant and agree to pay the said John Jones, his executors, administrators and assigns, accordingly, for so long a time as he shall hold and enjoy the said premises as aforesaid, and until the end of the said three months next after notice shall be given by either of the said parties, to the other of them, for leaving the said premises as aforesaid.

Witness our hands and seals, the day and year first above written.

Witness present,

JAMES STILES.

JOHN JONES. [L.S.]

WILLIAM BURNS. [L.S.]

Agreement between a Housekeeper and his Lodger.

It is agreed, by and between A. F., of —— and C. D. of ——, as follows, viz.: The said A., in consideration of the rent hereinafter mentioned and agreed to be paid to him, hath let to the said C., two rooms, up one pair of stairs forwards, part of the now dwelling-house of the said A. F. situated in ——, together with the furniture at present standing therein; that is to say, two tables, &c. To hold to the said C. D., for the term of three years, to commence from the first of April next, at the yearly rent of fifty dollars, to be paid quarterly, to wit, on the first days of July, October, January, and April.

The said C. D., in consideration hereof, agrees to pay to the said A. F., or his assigns, the aforesaid yearly rent of fifty dollars, at the times above limited for payment thereof; and at the end of the term, or in case of any default in payment, shall and will, on request of the said A. F., or his assigns, immediately yield and deliver up to him or them, the peaceable and quiet possession of the said room, together with the whole furniture, he, from the first entrance thereon there found and possessed, in good and sufficient order and condition, reasonable wear and tear only excepted.

In witness, &c.

For the Sale of a parcel of Trees growing, and liberty to cut down and carry them away, &c.

Articles of agreement, indented, &c. between John Jones of ——, of the one part, and William Burns, of ——, merchant, of the other part, in manner following, that is to say:

The said John Jones, in consideration of fifty dollars, to him in hand paid, at ——, by the said William Burns, the receipt whereof is hereby acknowledged, and in consideration of the further sum of fifty dollars, to be paid by the said William Burns, his executors or administrators, as hereunder is mentioned, hath granted, bargained, and sold, and by these presents doth grant, bargain, and sell, unto the said William Burns, his executors, administrators, and assigns, one hundred of the oak trees, now standing and growing in and upon the farm called Brookland, in the county of ——, now in the tenure of John Jay, which the said William Burns, his executors or assigns, shall think fit to choose, together with the tops and bark of and belonging to the said one hundred trees hereby sold. And the said John Jones for himself, his executors, administrators, and assigns, doth covenant, promise, and agree to and with the said William Burns, his executors, administrators, and assigns, by these presents, that at all, or any time or times, until the ——, which will be in the year of our Lord ——, he, the said William Burns, his executors, workmen, servants, or assigns, shall and may have free liberty of ingress, egress, and regress, into and from all or any part of the lands and grounds belonging to the farm aforesaid, with horses, carts, and carriages, to take, fell, cut down, and carry away the said one hundred trees, and the tops and bark thereof, to and for his and their own use and uses; and like liberty to dig saw-pits in convenient places in the said grounds, and therein to saw, cut out, and convert all, or so many of the said trees as he or they shall think fit, for the better conveniency or carriage thereof. And the said William Burns, for himself, his executors, administrators, and assigns, doth covenant, promise and agree, to and with the said John Jones, his executors, administrators and assigns, by these presents, as followeth: that is to say, that within the time aforesaid, he, the said William Burns, his executors, administrators, workmen, or assigns, will choose out, and at his and their own charge fell, cut down, and carry away, the said one hundred trees so sold to him as aforesaid; and in consideration and in full for the purchase thereof, shall and will truly pay, or cause to be paid, unto the said John Jones, his executors, administrators, or assigns, the sum of one hundred dollars, in the manner following, viz: —— part thereof on the —— next ensuing the date of these presents, and the remaining sum of ——, on the —— next following. In witness, &c.

An Agreement with a Manager.

Articles of agreement made and entered into the tenth day of March, in the year of our Lord one thousand eight hundred and forty five, between John Jones, of Harrisburg, in the county of Dauphin, and State of Pennsylvania, of the one part, and William Burns, of the same place, of the other part, as follows, viz: The said John Jones, for the consideration hereinafter mentioned, doth covenant and agree, well, truly, and faithfully, to serve the said William Burns, his heirs and assigns, as his book-keeper, overseer and manager, at his furnace in Harrisburg, wherein he is skilled, from this tenth day of March, A. D. 1845, for and during the term of one year, next ensuing, and fully to be completed, and ended, during which term, he, the said John Jones, shall and will be ready at all times, to render just and true accounts unto the said William Burns, of all work, matters and things to be done and performed at the furnace aforesaid; and shall not, nor will, at any time during the said term, wilfully neglect or depart from the said service or employment; nor do or cause, or wilfully suffer to be done, or caused, any act or thing whatsoever, to the prejudice of the said William Burns, his heirs or assigns, in his furnace aforesaid; but on the contrary, shall order and direct all workmen, servants and persons, employed in the furnace aforesaid, to do their work, service and duty, to the utmost of his skill, knowledge and ability, and for the most profit and advantage of the said owner.

And the said William Burns, for himself, his heirs and assigns, doth covenant and agree, to and with the said John Jones, his executors, administrators and assigns, by these presents, that he, the said William Burns, shall and will well and truly pay, or cause to be paid unto the said John Jones, for his services aforesaid, the just and full sum of six hundred dollars, over and besides finding and providing for him, the said John Jones, sufficient meat, drink, washing and lodging, during the said term: and also, shall and will, at his own proper cost and charges, supply the said John

Jones with all things needful and necessary, for carrying on the work of the said furnace.

And, for the true performance of all and every the covenants and agreements aforesaid, each of the said parties bindeth himself, his heirs, executors and administrators, unto the other, his executors, administrators and assigns, in the penal sum of twelve hundred dollars, firmly by these presents. In witness whereof, the parties to these presents have hereunto set their hands and seals, the day and year first above written.

Sealed and delivered in presence of

JAMES STILES.

JOHN JONES.

WILLIAM BURNS.

Agreement or Articles of co-partnership between Partners.

Articles of agreement, made and concluded, the first day of May, in the year of our Lord one thousand eight hundred and forty four, between John Jones, of Lancaster, in the county of Lancaster, and State of Pennsylvania, of the one part, and William Burns, of the same place, of the other part.

The said parties have agreed, and by these presents do agree, to associate themselves in the art and trade of buying, selling, vending and retailing, all sorts of wares, goods and commodities, belonging to the trade or business of merchandise; which said co-partnership shall continue from the date of these presents, for and during, and to the full end and term of four years, next ensuing.

And, to that end and purpose, he, the said John Jones, hath, the day of the date of these presents, delivered in as stock, the sum of five thousand dollars, and the said Williams Burns, the sum of five thousand dollars, to be used, laid out, and employed, in common between them, for the management of the said business to their general advantage.

And it is hereby agreed between the said parties, each for himself respectively, and for his own particular part, and for his respective executors and administrators, doth covenant, promise, and agree, each with the other of them, his respective executors and administrators, in manner following, that is to say:

That they shall not, nor will not, at any time hereafter, exercise, or follow the said trade, or any other, during the said term, to their private benefit and advantage, but shall and will, from time to time, and at all times, during the said term, (if they shall so long live,) do their best endeavours, to the utmost of their skill and ability; for their mutual advantage, with the stock as aforesaid, and the increase thereof.

And also, that they shall and will, during the said term, discharge equally between them, the rent of the premises which they shall rent, or hire, for the managing of the trade or business aforesaid.

And that all such profit, gain and increase as shall arise, by reason of the said joint business, shall be equally and proportionably divided between them, share and share alike. And also, all losses, as shall happen in the said business, by bad debts, ill commodities, or otherwise, shall be paid and borne equally between them.

And further, it is agreed between them, that there shall be kept, during the said term, and joint business, perfect, just and true books of accounts, wherein each of the said co-partners shall enter and set down, as well all the money by him received and expended, in and about the said business, as also all commodities and merchandise by them bought and sold, by reason and on account of the said co-partnership, and all other matters and things in any wise belonging or appertaining thereto, so that either of them may, at any time, have free access thereto.

And also, that the said co-partners, once in three months, or oftener, if need shall require, upon the request of any one of them, shall make and render each to the other, or to the executors and administrators of each other, a true and perfect account of all profits and increase by them made, and of all losses sustained; and also of all payments, receipts, disbursements, and all other things whatsoever, by them made, received and disbursed, acted, done and suffered, in the said co-partnership; and the account so made, shall and will clear, adjust, pay and deliver, each unto the other, at the time of making such account, their equal shares of the profit so made, as aforesaid.

And at the end of the said term of four years, or other sooner determination of these presents (be it by the death of one of the said parties or otherwise), they, the said co-partners, each to the other, or in case of the death of either of them, the surviving party, to the executors or administrators of the party deceased, shall and will make a true and final account of all things, as aforesaid, and in all things well and truly adjust the same; and also, that upon making such account, all and every the stocks and stocks, as well as the gain and increase thereof, which shall appear to be remaining, shall be equally parted and divided between them, the said co-partners, their executors or administrators, share and share alike.

In witness whereof, the said parties to these presents have hereunto set their hands and seals the day and year first above written.

Sealed and delivered in presence of }

James Stiles.

JOHN JONES.

WILLIAM BURNS.

Agreement or Articles of copartnership between an active and silent Partner.

Articles of agreement, made and concluded, the tenth day of June, one thousand eight hundred and forty four, between John Jones, of the city of Philadelphia, of the one part, and William Burns, of the same place, of the other part, as follows, to wit:

First. The said John Jones and William Burns have joined, and by these presents, do join themselves together as copartners, under the name and firm of John Jones & Co., for the purpose of carrying on, in the city aforesaid, the dry goods, grocery, and hardware business, and for the buying, selling and retailing of goods, wares and merchandise, belonging to the said trade or business, which said copartnership is to continue for the term of six years from the date hereof, unless sooner dissolved by death or otherwise.

Second. The said William Burns agrees to furnish to the said copartnership, a sufficient stock of suitable goods, wares and merchandise, for commencing said business, not exceeding in amount one thousand dollars, to be charged to the said copartnership at first cost, and from time to time, as such stock shall be reduced, by sales or otherwise, to renew and replace the same upon the like terms.

Third. The said John Jones agrees, that he will not, without the express consent of the said William Burns, purchase nor procure on account of, or for the purpose of the said copartnership, any goods, wares or merchandise, in the line of the said joint business, from any other person than the said William Burns, or in any other way than is provided for in the foregoing articles; unless the said William Burns, by his consent in writing, shall authorize the said John Jones so to do.

Fourth. The said John Jones further agrees, that he will take upon himself the sole care and management of the said joint business, will attend to sales, keep accurate accounts of all transactions relating to the said joint business, and will devote his care, labour and diligence exclusively to the superintendence thereof.

That he will, from time to time, as often as required by the said William Burns, remit to him all moneys received from such sales, on the joint account, after deducting all necessary expenses in the prosecution of the said business to advantage; and that he will further, whenever required by the said William Burns, exhibit to him all books and accounts in relation thereto.

Fifth. The said John Jones further agrees, that he will not, during the said term of six years, use, exercise, or follow the said business, for his own private benefit or advantage; but that he will, at all times, during the continuance of the said copartnership, do his best endeavours for their joint benefit and advantage.

Sixth. It is further agreed, by and between the parties aforesaid, that all gain, profits and increase, as shall arise from the said joint business, shall from time to time, during the said term, be equally divided between them, share and share alike; and also, that all losses that shall happen to their said joint trade, by bad debts, or otherwise, shall be paid and borne equally between them.

Lastly. It is further agreed, that at the end of the said term of six years, or upon a sooner termination of the said copartnership, by death or otherwise, the stock and profits which may then be on hand, and all other the property of the said copartnership, shall, after the payment of all debts by the said copartnership, be equally divided between the said John Jones and William Burns, or if either of them be dead, between the survivor and the legal representatives of the party deceased.

In witness whereof, the said parties to these presents, have hereunto set their hands and seals, the day and year first above written.

Sealed and delivered in presence of

JAMES STILES.

JOHN JONES.

WILLIAM BURNS.

Agreement on articles of Copartnership between two Tradesmen.

Articles of agreement, made and concluded the first day of January, A. D. one thousand eight hundred and forty-five, between John Jones, of Pittsburgh, in the county of Allegheny and State of Pennsylvania, of the one part, and William Burns, of the same city, county and state aforesaid, of the other part. In the first place, the said John Jones and William Burns have agreed, and by these presents do agree, to become copartners together in the art or trade of painting, and all things thereto belonging, and also in buying, selling, vending, and retailing all sorts of wares, goods and commodities, belonging to the said trade of painting; which said copartnership, it is agreed, shall continue from ——, for and during, and unto the full end and term of ten years, from thence next ensuing, and fully to be completed and ended. And to that end and purpose, he the said John Jones, hath the day of the date of the presents delivered in as stock, the sum of ——, and the said William Burns, the sum of ——, to be used, laid out, and employed, in common between them, for the management of the said trade of painting, to their utmost benefit and advantage. And it is hereby agreed between the said parties, and the said copartners each for himself respectively, and for his own particular part, and for their respective executors and administrators, doth covenant, promise, and agree, each with the other of them, his respective executors and administrators, by these presents, in manner and form following, that is to say:

That they, the said copartners, shall not nor will not at any time hereafter, use, exercise, or follow, the trade of painting aforesaid, or any other trade whatsoever, during the said term, to their private benefit and advantage; but shall and will, from time to time, and at all times during the said term, (if they shall so long live,) do their and each of their best and utmost endeavours, in and by all means possible to the utmost of their skill and power, for their joint interest, profit, benefit, and advantage: and truly employ, buy, sell, and merchandize, with the stock as aforesaid, and the increase thereof in the trade of painting aforesaid, without any sinister intention or fraudulent endeavours whatsoever. And also, that they, the said copartners, shall and will, from time to time, and at all times hereafter, during the said term, pay, bear, and discharge, equally between them, the rent of the shop, which they, the said copartners, shall rent or hire for the joint exercising or managing the trade aforesaid. And that all such gain, profit, and increase, that shall come, grow, or arise, for or by reason of the said trade or joint business as aforesaid, shall be from time to time during the said term, equally and proportionably divided between them, the said copartners, share and share alike. And also, that all such losses as shall happen in the said joint trade, by bad debts, ill commodities or otherwise, without fraud or covin, shall be paid and borne equally and proportionably between them. And further, it is agreed by and between the said copartners, that there shall be had and kept from time to time, and at all times during the said term and joint business and copartnership together as aforesaid, perfect, just, and true books of accounts, wherein each of the said copartners shall duly enter and set down, as well all money by him received, paid, expended, and laid out, in and about the management of the said trade, as also all wares, goods, commodities, and merchandizes, by them, or either of them, bought and sold by reason or means, or upon account of the said copartnership, and all other matters and things whatsoever to the said joint trade, and the management thereof in any wise belonging or appertaining, which said books shall be used in common between the said copartners, so that either of them may have free access thereto without any interruption of the other. And also, that they, the said copartners, once in three months, or oftener if need shall require, upon the reasonable request of one of them, shall make, yield and render each to the other, or to the executors and administrators of each other, a true, just, and perfect account of all profits and increase, by them or either of them made, and of all losses by them or either of them sustained, and also of all payments, receipts, disbursements, and all other things whatsoever, by them made, received, disbursed, acted, done, or suffered, in the said copartnership and joint business as aforesaid; and the same account so made shall and will clear, adjust, pay, and deliver, each unto the other at the time of making such account, their equal shares of the profits so made as aforesaid: And at the end of the said term of ten years, or other sooner determination of these presents, (be it by the death of one of the said partners, or otherwise,) they, the said copartners, each to the other, or in case of the death of either of them, the surviving party, to the executors or administrators of the party deceased, shall and will make a true, just, and final account of all things as aforesaid, and divide the profits aforesaid, and in all things well and truly adjust the same, and that also upon the making of such final account, all and every the stock and stocks, as well as the gains and increase thereof, which shall appear to be remaining, whether consisting of money, wares, debts, &c., shall be equally parted and divided between them, the said copartners, their executors or administrators, share and share alike.

In testimony whereof, the said parties to these presents have hereunto set their hands and seals, the day and year first above written.

Sealed and delivered in presence of }

JAMES STILES.

JOHN JONES.

WILLIAM BURNS.

Agreement, or Articles for special or limited Partnership.

This is to certify, to all to whom these presents shall come, that we, whose names are hereto subscribed, to wit, John Jones, of ——, merchant, William Burns, of ——, engineer, &c., have entered into a limited partnership, for the business of mining and transporting of mineral coal within the state of Pennsylvania, under and by virtue of an Act of the General Assembly of the said commonwealth, passed the 21st March, 1836, entitled, "An Act relative to limited partnerships," and all and singular the supplements thereto, upon the terms, conditions, and liabilities hereinafter set forth, to wit:

1. The said partnership is to be conducted under the name or firm of Jones & Jay.

2. The general nature of the business intended to be transacted by the said firm or partnership, is the mining of mineral coal and transporting the same, &c., (*describing the character of the projected business.*)

3. The general partners in the said firm are, John Jones, resident in ——, John Jay, residing in ——, &c., and the special partners are William Burns, residing in ——, John Gray, residing in ——, &c.

4. Each of the special partners has contributed to the common stock of said firm, the amount now herein set forth, to wit: William Burns has so contributed the amount of $——, John Gray has so contributed, &c.

5. The said partnership is to commence immediately, at and after the making and signing of this certificate, and is to terminate on the —— day of ——, A. D. 18—.

Witness our hands and seals, this —— day of ——, A. D. one thousand eight hundred and forty-four.

Dissolution of Partnership.

Whereas, by agreement made the tenth day of August, A. D. 1842, John Jones and William Burns, of the city of Pittsburgh, did enter into copartnership, for the purpose of carrying on the business of merchandizing, for the term of two years.

And whereas, the said John Jones, wishing to discontinue and decline the joint partnership, entered into as aforesaid, he, the said John Jones, hath proposed to his said partner, William Burns, a dissolution, to which proposition the said William Burns hath assented.

The parties, therefore, mutually consent and agree, by these presents, that the said partnership heretofore existing between them, be this day dissolved, and it is accordingly dissolved.

And, it is further stipulated, and agreed mutually between them, that William Burns do take the entire stock of goods and merchandize now on hand, belonging to the partnership, at a valuation to be set upon the same by three competent persons mutually appointed to value the same, and that he also have power to collect the debts now due to the partnership, and to recover all and any part of the same, in the name of the firm, by suits at law or otherwise. And that finally, the said William Burns do pay over to the said John Jones, or his legal representatives, the full share and profits, which shall appear to be due to the said John Jones, in six months from the date hereof.

Witness our hands and seals, this tenth day of August, A. D. 1844.

Sealed and delivered in presence of }

JAMES STILES.

JOHN JONES.

WILLIAM BURNS.

Covenants and clauses to be inserted in Partnership Contracts when desired.

Not to trust any one whom the copartner shall forbid.

And, that neither of the said parties shall sell or credit any goods or merchandise belonging to the said joint trade, or to any person or persons, after notice in writing from the other of the said parties, that such person or persons are not to be credited or trusted.

Not to be bound, or endorse Bills.

And that neither of the said parties shall, during this copartnership, without the consent of the other, enter into any deed, covenant, bond, or judgment, or become bound as bail or surety, or give any note, or accept or endorse any bill of exchange, for himself and partner, with or for any person whatsoever, without the consent of the other first had and obtained.

Neither party to assign his Interest.

And, it is agreed between the said parties, that neither of them shall, without the consent of the other obtained in writing, sell or assign his share or interest in the said joint trade, to any person or persons whatsoever.

Parties to draw Quarterly.

And that it shall be lawful for each of them to take out of the cash of the joint stock, the sum of one hundred dollars quarterly, to his own use, the same to be charged on account; and neither of them shall take any further sum for his own separate use, without the consent of the other in writing; and any such further sum, taken with such consent, shall draw interest after the rate of six per cent., and shall be payable together with the interest due, within sixty days after notice in writing given, by the other of the said parties.

An agreement to continue a Partnership by indorsement on the old Articles.

We, the within named John Jones and William Burns, do by these presents, endorsed, declare and mutually covenant and agree, unto and with each other, his and their executors and administrators, to continue the joint trade and partnership within mentioned, for the further term of three years, if both of us shall so long live, to be accounted for, from the expiration of the five years within limited for the continuance of the same, with the joint stock, and under, and subject to the several covenants and agreements within expressed and contained.

In witness whereof, we have hereunto set our hands and seals, the tenth day of January, A. D. one thousand eight hundred and forty-five.

Sealed and delivered in presence of }

JOHN STILES.

JOHN JONES. 

WILLIAM BURNS. 

An agreement in relation to Party Walls.

This agreement, made the tenth day of January, A. D. one thousand eight hundred and forty-five, between John Jones, of Erie, in the county of Erie and State of Pennsylvania, of the one part, and William Burns, of Erie, in the county and state aforesaid, of the other part, witnesseth:

That whereas, the said John Jones is seised or possessed of a certain lot or piece of ground situate in Erie aforesaid, and described as follows: [here insert the description of the land of the party of the first part] and whereas, the said William Burns is seised or possessed of a certain other lot or piece of ground situate in Erie aforesaid, and described as follows: [here insert the description of the land of the party of the other part,] adjoining and contiguous to the said before-mentioned and described lot of ground of him the said John Jones; and whereas, the said William Burns has lately erected on his own lot aforesaid, and along the division line between the above-mentioned lots, a brick tenement or building, of the length of —— feet, and of the height of —— stories, the —— end of which tenement is at the distance of —— feet, from the ——, front of the said lots, or —— street aforesaid. [Add here any other matter necessary to explain the transaction.] Now this indenture witnesseth, that the said William Burns doth hereby covenant, promise, grant and agree, that the said John Jones, his heirs and assigns aforesaid, shall and may at all times hereafter, have the full and free liberty and privilege of joining to the said —— wall of the said brick tenement, as well below as above the surface of the ground, and along the whole length or any part of the length thereof, any building which he or they, or any of them, may desire, or have occasion to erect on the said lot along the division line aforesaid, and to use and enjoy the said wall or any part thereof, as a wall of the building or buildings so to be erected, and to sink the joists of such building or buildings into the wall aforesaid to the depth of —— inches and no further. Provided always, nevertheless, and on this express condition, that the said John Jones, his heirs and assigns as aforesaid, before proceeding to join any other buildings to the said wall, and before making any use thereof, or breaking into the same, shall pay, or secure to be paid, unto the said William Burns, his heirs and assigns aforesaid, the full moiety, or one half part of the value of the said wall, or so much thereof as shall be joined or used as aforesaid, which value shall be fixed and assessed by ——.

In witness whereof, we have hereunto set our hands and seals this —— day of ——, A. D. ——.

Agreement for renewing a Policy of Insurance by Indorsement.

By agreement of the parties, the within policy is renewed for —— years, from the period within mentioned, for the expiration thereof, upon the terms and considerations within mentioned and contained.

This renewal expires on the —— day of ——, A. D. ——, at —— o'clock.

Sealed with the seal of the corporation and of the parties, this —— day of ——, A. D. ——.

AMICABLE ACTION.

There is, in Pennsylvania, a mode of instituting suits, without a service by sheriff, by an amicable agreement, signed by the parties or their attorneys, and filed in the prothonotary's office. When entered, such action is considered as if it had been adversely commenced, and the defendant had been regularly summoned. It saves the expense of the original writ, and the sheriff's fee for serving it. The writ, however, is supposed in law to be filed. A case may be stated for the opinion of the court in this way, or a judgment entered. When a judgment is entered in this way, the cause of action should always be expressed in the agreement, and it should be attested by two witnesses. The same stay of execution is allowed in this, as in other cases brought in the usual way. The lien of judgments may also be revived by amicable agreement.

Amicable Agreement to institute a Suit.

John Jones *vs.* William Burns. } In the Common Pleas of Jefferson county, of May Term, 1845. No. ——.

Summons in case, [or as the claim may be.]

It is hereby agreed, that the above action be entered with the same effect as if a summons returnable on the first Monday in May, 1845, [or whatever time may be the regular return day of the court where such agreement may be made,] had been regularly issued, served personally on the said defendant, and duly so returned.

JOHN JONES,
WILLIAM BURNS.

Signed, sealed and delivered in presence of us, }

JOHN STILES,
JOHN ROE.

An Agreement to revive a Lien.

John Jones *vs.* William Burns. } In the Court of Common Pleas of Huntingdon County, of May Term, 1845. No. 100.

Amicable action to revive and continue the lien for the term of five years, of judgment No. 45, of May term, 1840.

It is hereby agreed, that the Prothonotary of Huntingdon county enter the above amicable action upon the records of the Court of Common Pleas of the county aforesaid, as of No. 100 of May term, 1845, and that a judgment be forthwith entered thereon, in favour of the plaintiff above named, and against the defendant above named. And that the judgment aforesaid, No. 45, of May term, 1840, be revived, according to the Act of Assembly, with costs.

Witness our hands and seals, this —— day of ——, A. D. one thousand eight hundred and forty-five.

JOHN JONES,
WILLIAM BURNS.

Signed, sealed and delivered in presence of

JOHN STILES,
JOHN DOE.

For Judgment, after rule of Reference entered.

A. B. *vs.* C. D. } In the Common Pleas of —— County, of —— Term, A. D. ——. No. —.

And now, January ——, A. D. ——, it is hereby agreed, by and between the parties to the above suit, that the choosing (or "meeting," *if they have chosen*), of arbitrators be dispensed with, and that a judgment be entered thereon in favour of the plaintiff, and against the defendant above named, for the sum of —— dollars debt, besides costs of suit, with release of all errors, and with stay of execution according to law.

Witness our hands, the day and year above written.

To waive Inquisition and Condemnation of Land taken in Execution.

And now ——, A. D. ——, the undersigned being the defendant named in the within writ of *fieri facias*, and the owner at the time of the issuing of said writ of the real estate levied on by virtue thereof, do hereby dispense with and waive the inquisitiou thereon, and agree that the same shall be sold by the sheriff of —— county, upon the present writ of *fieri facias* before the return day thereof, and without any further writ from the court for that purpose.

Witness my hand, the —— day of ——, A. D. ——.

APPLICATION FOR WARRANTS.

Application for taking out a Warrant by a Settler for Lands settled on.

John Jones, of the township of Derry, in the county of York, applies for three hundred acres of land, situate in said township and county, adjoining lands of John Ebaugh on the east, William Jones on the south, George Gary on the west, and Adam Ebaugh on the north; on which tract he has made an actual settlement and improvement.

JOHN JONES.

To the Surveyor General.

Affidavit and Certificate for Land settled on.

York County, *ss.*

Before us, the subscribers, two of the Justices of the Peace in and for said county, personally came Jonas Gray, a disinterested witness, and being sworn, agreeably to law, did depose and say that, to his certain knowledge, the above-described tract of land was first improved in the month of July, 1800, and not before; that grain has been raised thereon, and that the said John Jones and family are now settled and reside on the same tract of land, and has continued to reside thereon ever since the first day of June, 1804, [or as the case may be.]

JONAS GRAY.

Sworn and subscribed, this 22d day of Sept., 1845, before us,

TIMOTHY TUTTLE,
DAVID ROYCE.

Affidavit and Certificate for Land improved but not settled.

York County, *ss.*

Before us, the subscribers, two of the Justices of the Peace in and for said county, personally came John Roe, a disinterested witness, who, being sworn according to law, did depose and say that, to his certain knowledge, the land above described was first improved in the month of May, 1800, and not before, [or as the case may be.]

JOHN ROE.

Sworn and subscribed this 10th day of January, A. D. 1845, before us,

TIMOTHY TUTTLE,
DAVID ROYCE.

Affidavit and Certificate for unimproved Land.

York County, *ss.*

Before us, the subscribers, two of the Justices of the Peace in and for said county, personally came James Goodman, a disinterested witness, who, being sworn according to law, did depose and say that, to his certain knowledge, the land described in the above application is unimproved, and, as he verily believes, not heretofore claimed by any other person, [or as the case may be.]

JAMES GOODMAN.

Sworn and subscribed this 10th day of January, A. D. 1845, before us,

WILLIAM DUNN,
JAMES DUNLAP.

Affidavit of Applicant for Lands prior to the last purchase of 1784, (*under the act of* 13*th April*, 1807.)

York County, *ss.*

Before me, the subscriber, a Justice of the Peace in and for said county, personally came John Jones, the above-named applicant, who, being duly sworn according to law, did depose and say that, to the best of his knowledge and belief, no warrant or other office right has issued for the land above described, either in his own name, or in the name or names of any person or persons under whom he claims the same.

JOHN JONES.

Sworn and subscribed, &c.

☞ This last certificate is not necessary in the last purchase.

APPRENTICE.

Remarks.

An apprentice is one who is bound, in due form of law, to a master, and who is to learn from him his art, trade or business, and to serve him during the time of his apprenticeship. 1 B. Com., 426; 2 Kent, Com., 211. The term during which the apprentice is to serve, is called his apprenticeship. This contract is generally entered into by indenture or deed, and is to continue no longer than the minority of the apprentice.

A master is bound to instruct his apprentice by teaching him, bona fide, the knowledge of the art of which he has undertaken to teach him the elements. He ought to watch over the conduct of the apprentice, giving him prudent advice and showing him a good example, and fulfilling towards him the duties of a father, as, in his character of master, he stands in loco parentis. He is also required to fulfil all the covenants he has entered into by the indenture. He cannot abuse his authority, either by bad treatment, or by employing his apprentice in menial employments, wholly unconnected with the business he has to learn. He cannot dismiss his apprentice, except by application to a competent tribunal, upon whose decree the indenture may be canceled.

An apprentice is bound, on his part, to obey his master in all his lawful commands, take care of his property, and promote his interest, endeavour to learn his trade or business, and perform all the covenants in his indenture, not contrary to law. He cannot leave his master's service during the term of the apprenticeship. Bouvier's Law Dict., vol. i. p. 85. For further information on this subject, see 2 Kent, Com., p. 211, &c.

In Pennsylvania, the Courts of Quarter Sessions, and the Mayor's Courts, have jurisdiction in apprentice cases, and can rescind the contract and cancel the indentures.

A writing without seal, is not an indenture of apprenticeship within the meaning of the act of 1770. Exparte Ruggles, 10 S. and R. 416.

An infant under seven years of age, may be bound apprentice in any art, mystery, occupation or labour, with the assent of his parent, guardian or next friend, under this act. Burtzman *vs.* Bunnell, 5 Wh. 128. It seems that the consent of the parent or guardian (if there be one) must be had in every case of binding, except where the infant is a charge. And the word or in the first section of the act of 1770, must be construed so as to effectuate the general intent and policy of the legislature. Com. *vs.* Vanlear, 1 S. and R. 250. Com. *vs.* Jones, 3 S. and R. 158.

It is not necessary that the person who consents as next friend to the minor, should have received an appointment as such from legal authority. Roach's case 1, Ash. 27.

An indenture executed by a minor, with the consent of his sister as next friend, was held valid. Ibid.

An indenture of apprenticeship executed by an infant, without the consent of his parent or guardian, is not binding on the infant. Guthrie *vs.* Murphy, 4 W. 80.

The father of an infant cannot bind him as an apprentice without his consent; and it is necessary that the infant should become a party to, and execute the indenture. Com. *vs.* Moore, 1 Ash. 123. An apprentice who has been bound in another state, to learn any trade or occupation, cannot be taken out of the state, unless such removal is provided for in the indenture, or arises from the nature of the contract, as in the case of seafaring men, &c. Com. *vs.* Edwards, 6 Binn. 202, S. P. Com. *vs.* Deacon, 6 S. and R. 526.

The court will discharge an apprentice for acts of the master injurious to his mind and morals; as for compelling him to work on Sundays. Com. *vs.* St. Germans, 1 Br. 24.

A habeas corpus may issue for the body of an apprentice on the petition of his master, and the court may order the apprentice to be delivered to his master. Com. *vs.* Beck, 1 Br. 277.

Indenture of Apprenticeship.

This indenture, made the first day of May in the year of our Lord one thousand eight hundred and forty four:—witnesseth, That Thomas Jones, the son of John Jones, of Reading, in the County of Berks, and State of Pennsylvania, (by and with the consent and advice of his said father, testified by his becoming a party hereto,) hath bound and put himself, and by these presents doth bind and put himself, apprentice to William Burns, of Reading, county and state aforesaid, tanner, after the manner of an apprentice to dwell with and serve the said William Burns [if it is intended to continue the apprenticeship after the death of the master, or to authorize him to assign the apprentice to another master, here insert the words, *his executors, administrators and assigns*], from the day of the date hereof, for and during and until the full end and term of seven years, thence next ensuing, and fully to be completed and ended; during which term the said apprentice his said master faithfully shall serve, and that honestly and obediently in all things, as a dutiful apprentice ought to do.

And the said William Burns [here, if intended as above, insert the words, *his executors, administrators and assigns*], shall teach and instruct, or cause to be taught and instructed, the said apprentice, in the art, trade and mystery of a tanner, and shall send and keep the said apprentice at a school taught by some competent teacher, for three months at least, in each and every year, and shall and will find and provide for the said apprentice, sufficient school books, meat, drink, apparel, washing and lodging, during the said term; and at the expiration thereof, shall and will give his said apprentice two suits of apparel, one whereof shall be new. In witness whereof, the said parties have hereunto set their hands and seals the day and year first above written.

Sealed and delivered in presence of }

JAMES STILES.

WILLIAM BURNS.

THOMAS JONES.

JOHN JONES.

Another form of Indenture of Apprenticeship.

This indenture, made the first day of May, in the year of our Lord one thousand eight hundred and forty four:—witnesseth, That John Jones, of the city of Pittsburgh, hath put and placed, and by these presents, doth put and bind out his son Thomas Jones, and the said Thomas Jones doth hereby put, place and bind out himself as an apprentice to William Burns, of the city of Pittsburgh, to learn the art, trade or mystery of a carpenter and house joiner; the said Thomas Jones, after the manner of an apprentice, to dwell with and serve the said William Burns from the date hereof until the tenth day of October, one thousand eight hundred and forty nine, at which time the said apprentice, if he should be living, will be twenty-one years of age. During all which time or term, the said apprentice, his said master faithfully shall serve, and that honestly and obediently, in all things, as a dutiful apprentice ought to do.

And the said William Burns, on his part, doth hereby covenant, promise and agree, to teach and instruct the said apprentice, or cause him to be taught and instructed, in the art, trade or mystery of a carpenter and house joiner, and also to send and keep the said apprentice, for three months at least, in each and every year, at some school taught by a competent teacher; and shall well and faithfully find and provide for the said apprentice, good and sufficient school books, meat, drink, clothing, lodging, and other necessaries fit and convenient for said apprentice, during the term aforesaid, and at the expiration thereof, shall give unto the said apprentice two suits of wearing apparel, one of which shall be new.

In testimony whereof, the said parties have hereunto set their hands and seals the day and year first above written.

Sealed and delivered in presence of }

JAMES STILES.

JOHN JONES.

WILLIAM BURNS.

THOMAS JONES.

Indenture of Apprenticeship by Overseers of the Poor.

This indenture, made the tenth day of October, in the year of our Lord one thousand eight hundred and forty-four:—witnesseth, That John Jones and William Burns, overseers of the poor, of the county of Crawford, have put and placed, and by virtue of an act of this state, entitled, "An Act for the relief of the Poor," do hereby, with the approbation and consent of James Price and Charles Dunn, Esquires, two of the justices of the peace, for the said county, put and place Sarah Brown, a poor child of township of Mead, apprentice to Thomas Cole, of the same place, with him to dwell and serve, from the day of the date hereof, until the full end and term of seven years, during all which term the said Sarah Brown her said master faithfully shall serve in all lawful business, according to her power and ability, and honestly and obediently in all things demean and behave herself towards her said master, and all his during the said term: and the said Thomas Cole doth covenant and agree for himself, his executors and administrators, to and with the said John Jones and William Burns, overseers as aforesaid, and their successors, for the time being, and every of them, by these presents, as follows: That he, the said Thomas Cole, the said Sarah Brown shall and will teach and instruct, or cause to be taught and instructed, in sewing, spinning, knitting, housewifery, and in reading, writing and branches of common school education; and shall and will, during the said term, find, provide, and allow her sufficient meat, drink, apparel, lodging and washing, and all other necessaries; and also, shall and will so provide for the said Sarah Brown, that she be not in any wise a charge or chargeable to the said township, or to the inhabitants of the same, but from all charges concerning her shall and will save the said township, and the inhabitants thereof, harmless and indemnified during the said term; and, at the expiration thereof, shall and will, at his own charge, give and allow the said Sarah Brown two suits of apparel, one whereof shall be new.

In witness whereof, the said parties to these presents have hereunto set their hands and seals, the day and year first above written.

Sealed and delivered in presence of

JAMES STILES.

JOHN JONES.

WILLIAM BURNS.

THOMAS COLE.

☞ The overseers of the poor are authorized, with the consent and approbation of two or more magistrates, to put out as apprentices all poor children, whose parents are dead, or by the said magistrates found unable to maintain them. Act of 13th June, 1836. The officers of the House of Refuge also have the power to bind out any who are sentenced to that place. Their custom is, to bind out its inmates to trades, as soon as sufficiently reformed.

Approbation of the Apprenticeship of Paupers.

We, the subscribers, justices of the peace, in and for the county of ——, do hereby approve and consent to the execution of the indentures of apprenticeship in the case of the within named A. B., a pauper, the term of which is to expire on the —— day of ——, A. D. one thousand eight hundred and ——.

ARBITRATION AND AWARD.

Remarks.

Arbitrators are so called because they have generally an arbitrary power. Their sentences are called awards.

An arbitration is a reference and submission of a matter in dispute concerning property or a personal wrong, to the decision of one or more persons as arbitrators.

Arbitrations are either voluntary or compulsory. The voluntary, are those made by mutual consent; and the compulsory, are where either party has a right to enter a rule of reference without the consent of the other. Before the revised Act of 1836, a variety of modes of arbitration existed in Pennsylvania. 1st. Are those made by mutual consent, in which the parties select the arbitrators, and bind themselves by bond to abide their decision; these are made without any rule of court. 3 Bl. Com. 16. 2d. Those which are made in a cause depending in court, by a rule of court, before trial; these are arbitrations at common law, and the award is enforced by attachment. Kyd on Awards, 21. 3d. Those which are made by virtue of the statute 9 & 10 Will. 3, c. 15, by which it is agreed to refer a matter in dispute not then in court, to arbitrators, and agree that the submission be made a rule of court, which is enforced as if it had been made a rule of court. Kyd on Awards, 22. 4th. Those made under the Act of Assembly of 1705. 5th. Those made under the Act of 1806.

The provisions of the Acts of 1705 and 1810, and the English statutes above mentioned, have been incorporated into the revised Act of 1836. The Act of 1806 is still in force, but seldom do arbitrations take place under it, by reason of the difficulty and danger of enforcing the awards under it. The most usual methods of arbitrations at this time in Pennsylvania, are those made by mutual consent, in which the parties select the arbitrators, and bind themselves by bond to abide their decision, or else by the Act of Assembly, of 16th June, 1836, (Pamph. Laws, p. 715), which provides for either voluntary or compulsory arbitrations, Either party may, in a civil suit or action, or his attorney, may enter at the prothonotary's office, a rule of reference under the said Act of 1836, wherein he shall declare his determination to have arbitrators chosen, on a certain day to be mentioned therein, not exceeding thirty days thereafter, for the trial of all matters in variance in the suit between the parties, provided that the plaintiff shall not enter such rule, until he files a declaration or statement of his cause of action. A copy of this rule is to be served on the opposite party, his agent or attorney, at least fifteen days before the day fixed for the appointment of arbitrators. On the day appointed, they meet at the prothonotary's and endeavour to agree upon arbitrators; if they cannot, the prothonotary makes out a list on which are inscribed the names of a number of citizens, and the parties alternately strike each one of them from the list, beginning with the plaintiff, until there are but the number agreed upon, or fixed by the prothonotary left, who are to be the arbitrators. The time of meeting is then agreed upon by the parties, or appointed by the prothonotary, provided that the time of meeting shall not be less than ten, nor more than twenty days after their appointment. The party by whom the rule of reference shall have been entered, must procure from the prothonotary a certified copy of the record, and serve a copy of the same on each of the arbitrators, and also on the opposite party, giving ten days notice previous to the day of meeting. At the time fixed for the meeting, the arbitrators are sworn or affirmed, justly and equitably to try all matters in variance submitted to them, and proceed to hear and determine the case. Their award is filed in the office of the prothonotary, and has the effect of a judgment, subject, however, to an appeal, which may be entered at any time within twenty days after the filing of such award. For further particulars, see Pamphlet Laws of 1836, p. 715.

Under Act of 1836. *Agreement to refer.*

John Jones
vs.
William Burns. } In the Court of Common Pleas of Erie county, No. 37 of August Term, 1844.

And now, September 10th, 1844, the said John Jones and William Burns, under the provisions of the Act of Assembly of 16th June, 1836, do hereby agree to submit all matters in controversy in our said suit to Daniel Stone, Samuel Dean and Thomas Brown, mutually chosen by us, and furthermore agree, that our submission to such award or umpirage be made a rule of and in said court, and hereby respectively bind ourselves to submit to, and be finally concluded by, the award or umpirage of said referees, or a majority of them.

Witness our hands and seals.

Sealed and delivered in presence of

JAMES STILES,
CHARLES COLE.

JOHN JONES.

WILLIAM BURNS.

Erie County, *ss.*

Before me, the subscriber, prothonotary of the Court of Common Pleas of Erie County aforesaid, in the said court, personally came on this —— day of ——, James Stiles, who being duly sworn [or affirmed], did depose and say, that he was witness to the execution of the above agreement, and saw said John Jones and William Burns severally sign and seal the same as their act and deed.

JAMES STILES.

Sworn and subscribed in open court before me.

Awards of Arbitrators, in Debt or Case.

And now, the tenth day of October, A. D. 1844, at Erie, the arbitrators within named being all present, [or if two only are present, say, "Daniel Stone and Samuel Dean, two of the arbitrators within named, being present, and proof having been made, that due notice of the time and place of meeting was given to Thomas Brown, the other arbitrator, who was absent, and James Burns having been duly appointed to fill the vacancy,"] and all being duly sworn, [or affirmed,] and having heard the evidence and allegations of the parties, do award in favour of the plaintiff the sum of one hundred dollars [or "no cause of action," as the case may be.]

(Signed by the arbitrators, or a majority of them.)

Award in Replevin for Rent.

And now, the tenth day of October, A. D. 1844, at Erie, the arbitrators within named being all present, and all being duly sworn, and having heard the evidence and allegations of the parties, do award that there is due to the avowant, John Jones, from the plaintiff, William Burns, the sum of sixty dollars, for rent in arrear, due the first day of July, 1844, and that the value of the goods distrained is seventy-five dollars.

Award in Replevin, when property is to be returned.

And now, the —— day of ——, A. D. ——, at Erie, the arbitrators within named being all present, and all being duly sworn according to law, and having heard the evidence and allegations of the parties, do award in favour of the defendant in replevin, and direct that the plaintiff in replevin return the property distrained, and —— dollars damages for detention.

ASSIGNMENT.

An assignment, in common parlance, signifies the transfer of all kinds of property, real, personal and mixed, and whether the same be in possession or in action; as a general assignment.

In a more technical sense, it is usually applied to the transfer of a term of years; but it is more properly used to signify a transfer of some particular estate or interest in lands. The proper technical words of an assignment, are, assign, transfer and set over; but the words grant, bargain and sell, or any other words which will show the intent of the parties to make a complete transfer, will amount to an assignment.

Assignment of Dower by the Heir.

This indenture, made the first day of May, in the year of our Lord one thousand eight hundred and forty-four, between Thomas Jones, son and heir of John Jones, late of the city of Lancaster, of the one part, and Ellen Jones, widow and relict of the said John Jones, of the other part:—

Whereas, the said John Jones was in his lifetime at the time of his death, seized in his demesne as of fee, of and in divers lands and tenements in the city of Lancaster, in the county of Lancaster, and State of Pennsylvania, which, upon the decease of the said John Jones, descended unto the said Thomas Jones: Now, this indenture witnesseth, that the said Thomas Jones hath endowed and assigned, and by these presents, doth endow and assign, unto the said Ellen Jones, the third part of the said lands and tenements, to wit: All that messuage [here describe the premises,] to have and to hold unto the said Ellen Jones, for and during the natural life of the said Ellen Jones, in severalty by mites and bounds, in the name of the dower, and in recompense and satisfaction of all the dower which the said Ellen Jones ought to have, of or in the said lands and tenements which were of the said John Jones in his lifetime.

In witness whereof, the said parties to these presents have hereunto set their hands and seals, the day and year first above written.

Sealed and delivered in presence of

JAMES STILES.

THOMAS JONES.

ELLEN JONES.

Assignment of a Deed.

Know all men by these presents, that John Jones, the grantee within named, and Ellen his wife, for and in consideration of the sum of two hundred dollars, to them in hand paid by William Burns, of Carlisle, Cumberland county, Pennsylvania, at and before the ensealing and delivery hereof, the receipt whereof is hereby acknowledged, have granted, bargained, sold, assigned and set over unto the said William Burns, his heirs and assigns, all that the within mentioned messuage, tenement and tract of land containing fifty acres more or less, together with all and singular the rights, members and appurtenances whatsoever thereunto belonging or in any wise appertaining; and the reversions and remainders, rents, issues and profits thereof; to have and to hold the said messuage, tenement or tract of land, hereby granted and assigned, or mentioned, or intended so to be, with the appurtenances, unto the said William Burns, his heirs and assigns, to the only proper use and behoof of the said William Burns, his heirs and assigns, forever. And the said John Jones and his heirs, the said hereby granted and assigned premises, with the appurtenances unto the said William Burns, his heirs and assigns, against the said John Jones and his heirs, and against all and every other person or persons whomsoever, lawfully claiming, or to claim, by, from or under him, them or any of them, shall and will warrant and forever defend by these presents.*

* Assignments of deeds, and all other instruments of writing, in order to be recorded, must be acknowledged in the same manner as a deed. Assignments

In witness whereof, the said parties to these presents have hereunto set their hands and seals, this first day of May, A. D. 1844.

JOHN JONES.

ELLEN JONES.

Assignment of a Lease.

Know all men by these presents, that I, the within named John Jones, for and in consideration of the sum of fifty dollars, to me in hand paid, by William Burns, of Lancaster, in the county of Lancaster, and State of Pennsylvania, at and before the ensealing and delivering hereof, the receipt whereof I do hereby acknowledge, have granted, assigned and set over, and by these presents do grant, assign and set over, unto the said William Burns, his executors, administrators and assigns, the within indenture of lease, and all that messuage described therein, with the appurtenances; and also all my estate, right, title, term of years yet to come, claim and demand whatsoever, of, in, to or out of the same; to have and to hold the said messuage and appurtenances unto the said William Burns, his executors, administrators and assigns, for the residue of the term within mentioned, under the yearly rents and covenants, within reserved and contained, on my part and behalf to be done, kept and performed.

In witness whereof, I have hereunto set my hand and seal, this tenth day of March, A. D. 1844.

JOHN JONES.

Another Assignment.

Memorandum of assignment, this fourth day of June, 1844.

The within named John Jones hath this day assigned and made over unto William Burns, of Erie, all and singular the hereditaments and premises in the within written lease described

of deeds ought, in general, to be discouraged, on account of the difficulty of getting them properly upon record.

and granted, with the whole of his estate and interest. As witness his hand and seal.

JOHN JONES.

Assignment of a Debt.

Know all men by these presents, that I, John Jones, of Erie, in the county of Erie and State of Pennsylvania, in consideration of the sum of one hundred dollars, now justly due and owing by me to William Burns, of Erie aforesaid; and, for the better securing the payment of the same to the said William Burns, have bargained, sold, assigned and transferred to him all that debt or sum of one hundred dollars, which is now due and owing to me from James Stiles, of Meadville, for goods sold and delivered by me to the said James Stiles or his order, before the day of the date hereof; and all my right, title, interest, claim and demand, of, in and to the said debt or sum of one hundred dollars, or any part thereof; to hold to the said William Burns, his executors, administrators and assigns, from henceforth to his own proper use, benefit and behoof forever.

In witness whereof, I have hereunto set my hand and seal, this tenth day of May, A. D. 1844.

JOHN JONES.

Assignment of a Judgment.

Know all men by these presents, that I, John Jones, of Reading, in the county of Berks and State of Pennsylvania, in consideration of the sum of two hundred dollars to me in hand paid by William Burns, of Reading aforesaid, have granted, bargained, transferred, assigned and made over, unto the said William Burns, his executors, administrators and assigns, a certain judgment by me recovered in the County Court of Common Pleas of Berks, in the State of Pennsylvania, at August term last, against James Stiles, of ——, for the sum of two hundred dollars debt or damages, and the sum of twenty dollars costs of suit; together with all the benefit and advantages that may be obtained thereby. And I do hereby grant to him, the said William Burns, his executors, administrators and assigns, full power to recover the same to his own and their own use.

In witness whereof, I have hereunto set my hand and seal, this tenth day of October, 1844.

JOHN JONES.

Assignment of Moneys due upon Account.

Know all men by these presents, that I, John Jones, of Harrisburg, in consideration of the sum of one hundred dollars to me in hand paid, by William Burns, of the same place, do hereby assign and set over, unto the said William Burns, to his own proper use, without any account to be given for the same, the sum of one hundred and thirty dollars, and all other sum or sums of money that are remaining due and payable upon and by virtue of the annexed account of moneys due to me by James Stiles, and all my right, title, interest and demand in and to the same; and to give and grant unto the said William Burns full power and authority to demand and receive the same to his own use; and upon the receipt thereof, to give discharges for the same, or any part thereof. And I, the said John Jones, do hereby covenant and agree to and with the said William Burns, that the said sum of one hundred and thirty dollars is justly due and owing, and that I have not received or discharged the same or any part thereof.*

In witness whereof, I have hereunto set my hand and seal, this tenth day of June, A. D. 1844.

JOHN JONES.

Assignment of a Mortgage.

Know all men by these presents, that I, John Jones, the mortgagee within named, for and in consideration of the sum of one thousand dollars to me in hand paid by William Burns, of Butler, in the county of Butler, and State of Pennsylvania, at and before the ensealing and delivery of these presents, the receipt whereof is hereby acknowledged, have granted, bargained, sold, assigned and set over, and by these presents do grant, bargain, sell, assign and set over, unto the said William Burns, his heirs and assigns, the within named indenture of mortgage, and all that messuage,

* An account of this kind is called a *chose in action*; and must be sued for in the name of the *assignor*, for the use of the *assignee*.

with the appurtenances therein mentioned and described; together with the rights, members and appurtenances thereunto belonging, and all my estate, right, title and interest therein; to have and to hold all and singular the premises hereby granted and assigned, or mentioned or intended so to be, unto the said William Burns, his heirs and assigns forever; subject, nevertheless, to the right and equity of redemption, of the within named James Stiles, his heirs and assigns, in the same.

In witness whereof, I have hereunto set my hand and seal, this first day of October, 1844.

Sealed and delivered }
in presence of }
JAMES STONE.

JOHN JONES.

Assignment of a Bond where the Assignor is liable.

For a valuable consideration, to me in hand paid by William Burns, of Pittsburgh, I do hereby assign and set over the within obligation, and all moneys due and to become due thereon, unto the said William Burns, his executors, administrators and assigns; and in case the same cannot be recovered of the within named Daniel Stone, then I do promise and agree to pay the amount thereof, together with all charges thereupon accruing unto the said William Burns, his executors, administrators or assigns.

Witness my hand and seal, this first day of August, A. D. 1844.

Witnesses present:
JAMES STILES,
DAVID DEAN.

JOHN JONES.

Assignment of a Bond where the Assignor is not liable.

For a valuable consideration, to me in hand paid, by William Burns, of Pittsburgh, I do hereby assign and set over the within obligation, and all moneys due and to become due thereon, unto the said William Burns, his executors, administrators and assigns; and in no case holding myself responsible for the recovery or payment of the same; but the risk and losses, if any, to be borne by the said William Burns, his executors, administrators, or assigns.

Witness my hand and seal, this tenth day of October, A. D. 1844.

Witness present,

JAMES STILES,
DAVID DEAN.

JOHN JONES.

Short form of Assignment where the Assignor is liable.

For value received, I do assign and set over the within obligation, and all moneys due thereon, unto William Burns, his executors, administrators and assigns, hereby guaranteeing the payment thereof, in case of default being made by the within-named Samuel Stone.

Witness my hand and seal, this tenth day of May, A. D. 1844.

Witness present,

JAMES STILES,
DAVID DEAN.

JOHN JONES.

Assignment where the Assignor is not liable.

For value received, I do hereby assign and set over the within obligation, and all moneys due thereon, unto William Burns, his executors, administrators or assigns, not holding myself liable for the payment of the same; the losses, if any, and the recovery thereof, to be wholly at the risk of the said William Burns.

Witness my hand and seal, this tenth day of May, A. D. 1844.

Witness present,

JAMES STILES,
DAVID DEAN.

JOHN JONES.

Note.—There must be two subscribing witnesses to either of the foregoing assignments of bonds.

Assignment of a Note, where the Assignor is liable.

For value received, I assign the within note to William Burns, this tenth day of June, one thousand eight hundred and forty-four, and guarantee the collection of the same.

JOHN JONES.

Assignment, where the Assignor is not liable.

Without any recourse to me had, I assign, for a valuable consideration, the within note to William Burns; it being the express understanding of the parties, that he takes it at his own risk, and frees me from all responsibilities. JOHN JONES.

Assignment of an Apprentice.

Know all men by these presents, that I, John Jones, for divers good causes and considerations, have assigned and set over, and by these presents, (as far as I lawfully may or can,) do assign and set over the within indenture and the apprentice therein named unto William Burns, his executors, administrators and assigns, for the residue of the term within mentioned: he and they performing all and singular, the covenants therein contained, on my part to be kept and performed, and indemnifying me from the same.*

In witness whereof, I have hereunto set my hand and seal, this tenth day of August, A. D. 1844.

JOHN JONES.

Assignment of a Servant.

In consideration of the sum of seventy-five dollars, to me in hand paid, by William Burns, of Philadelphia, I do hereby assign and set over the within named servant, to serve the said William Burns, his executors, administrators and assigns, for the residue of the term within mentioned.†

Witness my hand and seal, this tenth day of October, A. D. 1844.

JOHN JONES.

* This assignment cannot be made unless the indenture extends to assigns; and then not without the consent of all the parties therein named, which must be in writing, and certified before a Justice of the Peace.

† This must be done before a Justice of the Peace.

Assignment of Shares in a Company.

For value received, I, John Jones, of Pittsburgh, assign the whole of my right, title and interest of, in and to ten shares in the Monongahela Bridge Company of Pennsylvania, to William Burns, of Allegheny city, and constitute him, his assigns and substitutes, my attorney and attorneys, with full power to receive in his or their name or names, certificates for the said shares, hereby obliging myself at his or their request, to do all necessary matters and things, for the more effectually transferring the said shares to him or them.

Witness my hand and seal, this tenth day of June, A. D. 1844.

JOHN JONES.

Acknowledged before me, a Notary Public for the Commonwealth of Pennsylvania, this twelfth day of June, 1844.

JAMES DEAN.

Assignment of a Policy of Insurance.

Having sold and conveyed the premises within mentioned to A. B., of ——, his heirs and assigns forever, I do hereby for and in consideration of the sum of —— dollars, to me in hand paid by the said A. B., assign and transfer the within policy of insurance to him, his executors, administrators and assigns. The said A. B., by subscribing this assignment, making himself responsible for all the covenants to which I have bound myself by the within policy.

Witness our hands and seals, this tenth day of January, A. D. one thousand eight hundred and forty-five.

J. D.

A. B.

ATTESTATION.

Attestation in contracts and evidence, is the act of witnessing an instrument of writing, at the request of the party making the same ; and subscribing it as a witness.

Where there are Interlineations or Erasures in Instruments of Writing.

Signed, sealed and delivered, by the within named John Jones, the words, "*and his heirs and assigns*," (or whatever they may be), having been previously interlined in the tenth and eighteenth lines, in presence of us.

By a Blind Person.

The above-written instrument was signed, sealed and delivered by the above-named John Jones, and he being blind, the same was carefully and deliberately read over to him, in presence of us.

Where there are Erasures.

Signed, sealed and delivered by the within named John Jones, the words "——," having been previously stricken out of the tenth line, and the words "——" interlined in the same.

BILLS.

Remarks.

There are bills of various kinds. A bill of exchange is defined to be an open letter of request from, and order by, one person on another, to pay a sum of money therein mentioned to a third person, on demand, or at a future time therein specified. 2 Bl. Com. 466; Bayl. on Bills, 1; Chit. on Bills, 1. The party to a bill of exchange, is the drawer, or he who makes the order. The drawee, is the person to whom it is addressed. The acceptor, is he who accepts the bill. The payee, is the party to whom, or in whose favour the bill is made. The endorser, is he who writes his name on the back of a bill. The indorsee, is one to whom a a bill is transferred by indorsement; and the holder, is in general any one of the parties who is in possession of the bill, and entitled to receive the money therein mentioned.

Foreign bills of exchange consist, generally, of several parts. A party who has engaged to deliver a foreign bill, is bound to deliver as many parts as may be requested. 2 Pardess, n. 342. The several parts of a bill of exchange are called a set; each part should contain a condition that it shall be paid, provided the others remain unpaid.

The whole set make but one bill. Bills of exchange are either foreign or inland. Foreign, when drawn by a person out of, on another in the United States, or *vice versa*, or by a person in a foreign country, on another person in another foreign country; or by a person in one state on another in another of the United States. 2 Pet. R. 589; 10 Pet. R. 572; 12 Pick. 483; 15 Wen. 527; 3 Marsh (Kty.) R. 488; Leigh's R. 37; 4 Wash. C. C. Rep. 148; 1 Whart. Dig. Tit. Bills of Exchange. There is, however, some conflicting decisions whether a bill drawn by a person in one state on another in another of the United States is a foreign bill: for which, see 5 John. R. 384; but the current of decisions makes them foreign bills. The principal difference between foreign and inland bills, is, that the former must be protested, and the latter need not. 6 Mod. 29; 2 B. & A. 656; Chit. on Bills, (Ed. of 1836,) p. 14.

Bill of Sale of Goods and Chattels.

Know all men by these presents, that I, John Jones, of the borough of Reading and State of Pennsylvania, in consideration of the sum of one hundred dollars to me in hand paid by William Burns, of the same place, at and before the ensealing and delivering of these presents, the receipt whereof I do hereby acknowledge, have bargained, sold, released, granted and confirmed, and by these presents do bargain, sell, release, grant and confirm unto the said William Burns, all the goods, household stuff and implements of household, and all other goods and chattels whatsoever, mentioned and expressed in the schedule hereunto annexed,* now remaining and being in the house lately occupied by me in Reading aforesaid, to have and to hold all and singular the said goods and chattels, &c., and every of them, by these presents bargained, sold, released, granted and confirmed unto the said William Burns, to his only proper use and behoof, his heirs, executors, administrators and assigns forever.

In witness whereof, I have hereunto set my hand and seal, this tenth day of May, one thousand eight hundred and forty-four.

Witness present,

JAMES STILES.

JOHN JONES. [L.S.]

* A schedule must be annexed to this instrument, setting forth at large every article intended to be conveyed to the said William Burns, which must be signed by the said John Jones; and I would here remark that a bill of sale is not considered good against creditors, where the personal property is retained in the possession of the original owner.

Bill of Sale of goods and Stock, in consideration of Maintenance, &c.

This indenture, made the tenth day of May, one thousand eight hundred and forty-four, between John Jones, of Pittsburgh, of the one part, and William Burns, of the same place, of the other part, witnesseth, that the said John Jones, in consideration of the covenants hereinafter mentioned, on the part of him, the said William Burns, to be performed, and for the further consideration of one dollar to him in hand paid by the said William Burns, he, the said John Jones, hath granted, bargained and sold, and by these presents doth grant, bargain and sell, unto the said William Burns, all and singular, the stock, goods, household stuff, and implements of household, and all other goods and chattels whatsoever mentioned and expressed in the schedule hereunto annexed, [*see note to the first bill of sale*], now remaining and being in the dwelling-house now occupied by me, and upon the farm on which said dwelling-house stands: to have and to hold all and singular, the said stock, goods, and chattels, &c., and every of them, by these presents bargained, sold and confirmed unto the said William Burns, to his only proper use and behoof, his heirs, executors, administrators, and assigns forever.

And the said William Burns, in consideration of the premises, doth hereby for himself, his heirs, executors and administrators, covenant and agree to and with the said John Jones, his executors and administrators, that he the said William Burns, his executors and administrators, shall and will at his and their costs and charges, maintain and keep the said John Jones, during his natural life, with good and sufficient meat, drink, wearing apparel, washing and lodging, at his, the said William Burns' own dwelling-house, and also, that the said William Burns, his executors and administrators, shall pay and allow unto the said John Jones yearly and every year, during his natural life, the sum of twenty-five dollars for spending money; the same to be paid to the said John Jones, at four equal quarterly payments, to be computed from this day.

In witness whereof, the parties to these presents have hereunto set their hands and seals, the day and year first above written.

Sealed and delivered in presence of }

JAMES STILES.

JOHN JONES. [L. S.]

WILLIAM BURNS. [L. S.]

Bill of Sale of a Vessel.

To all to whom these presents shall come, greeting: Know ye, that I, John Jones, of Philadelphia, owner of the sloop or vessel called the William Penn, of the burthen of one hundred and ninety tons, or thereabouts, for and in consideration of the sum of six hundred dollars, to me in hand paid, before the ensealing and delivery of these presents, by William Burns, of the same place, the receipt whereof I do hereby acknowledge, have bargained and sold, and by these presents do bargain and sell, unto the said William Burns, his executors, administrators and assigns, the said sloop or vessel, together with the mast, bowsprit, sails, boats, anchors, cables, and all other necessaries thereunto appertaining and belonging. To have and to hold the said sloop or vessel, and appurtenances thereunto belonging, unto him, the said William Burns, his executors, administrators and assigns, to their sole and only proper use, benefit and behoof forever. And I, the said John Jones, have, and by these presents, do promise, covenant and agree for myself, my heirs, executors and administrators, to and with the said William Burns, his executors and administrators, to warrant and defend the title to the said sloop or vessel, and all the other before-mentioned appurtenances, against all and every person and persons whomsoever.

In testimony whereof, I have hereunto set my hand and seal, this tenth day of May, one thousand eight hundred and forty-four.

Sealed and delivered in presence of }

JAMES STILES.

JOHN JONES.

A set of Bills of Exchange.

No. 190 Ex. £215 Stg.

Philadelphia, May 10, 1844.

Sixty days after sight of this, my first of exchange, (second and third of the same tenor and date not paid,) pay to Messrs. Wilmer, Cohen & Co., or order, two hundred and fifteen pounds sterling, and charge the same, without further advice, to

JOHN JONES.

Messrs. Smith, Lee & Co., London. }

Second.

No. 190 Ex. £215 Stg.

Philadelphia, May 10, 1844.

Sixty days after sight of this my second of exchange, (first and third of the same tenor and date not paid,) pay to Messrs. Wilmer, Cohen & Co., or order, two hundred and fifteen pounds sterling, and charge the same, without further advice, to

JOHN JONES.

Messrs. Smith, Lee & Co.,
London.

Third.

No. 190 Ex. £215 Stg.

Philadelphia, May 10, 1844.

Sixty days after sight of this my third of exchange, (first and second of the same tenor and date not paid,) pay to Messrs. Wilmer, Cohen & Co., two hundred and fifteen pounds sterling, and charge the same, without further advice, to

JOHN JONES.

Messrs. Smith, Lee & Co.,
London.

Domestic Bill of Exchange.

$500

Pittsburgh, June 10, 1844.

Three days after sight, pay to the order of William Burns, five hundred dollars, value received, without further advice, which charge to the account of Yours, &c.

JOHN JONES.

Messrs. Robinson & Co.,
Philadelphia.

☞ Possession of a bill of exchange is evidence of an authority to demand payment of its contents. 1 Dal. 193. But there is a distinction between bills endorsed specially, and in blank. Possession of the latter proves property; but bills specially indorsed, do not pass by delivery; and, therefore, possession does not prove property in them. 2 Dal. 146; 1 Yeates, 94.

A bill of exchange made payable without the words "or order" or "assigns" or some other words of negotiability, is not indorsable over, so as to enable the indorsee to sue the acceptor in his own name. 1 Dal. 194.

Draft.

$550\frac{50}{100}$

Pittsburgh, May 10, 1844.

Sir,

At ten days sight, pay to the order of William Burns, Esq., Cashier of the Bank of North America, five hundred and fifty dollars and fifty cents, for account of Yours, &c.

JOHN JONES.

Mr. Samuel Stone, Philadelphia.

☞ If Mr. Stone accepts, he indorses on the back or across the face of the draft, these words, "*Accepted—May* 15, 1844. *Samuel Stone.*" The bank then collects. If negotiated through an individual, he may deposit it in bank for collection.

Note to Bank.

$500

Pittsburgh, January 10, 1845.

Ninety days after date, I promise to pay to William Burns, or order, at the Exchange Bank, five hundred dollars, without defalcation, for value received. JOHN JONES.

☞ The one to whom this note is payable, viz: William Burns, if he transfers it, or wishes to get it discounted at the bank, becomes the first indorser, and if discounted, the last indorser checks the money. To make an indorser liable on his indorsement, the instrument must be commercial paper, for the indorsement of a bond or single bill will not, by itself, create a responsibility. 13 Serg. & Rawle, 311.

Check.

No. 1.

Pittsburgh, January 14, 1844.

Cashier of the Exchange Bank, pay to William Burns, or bearer, five hundred dollars. DANIEL WARD.

$500

Due Bill.

$100 50

Upon settlement this day, with John Jones, I acknowledge to be due and owing to him by me, the sum of one hundred dollars and fifty cents. JAMES HUNTER.

Promissory Note.

$100

Lancaster, May 10, 1844.

For value received, I promise to pay to William Burns, or order, the sum of one hundred dollars, on the first day of June next, with interest. JOHN JONES.

Judgment Note.

For value received, I promise to pay William Burns, of Carlisle, or order, one hundred dollars, with interest, on the tenth day of January next. And further, I do hereby empower any attorney of the Court of Common Pleas, of Cumberland County, or any other Court of Record of Pennsylvania, or elsewhere, to appear for me, and after a declaration filed, thereupon to confess a judgment against me, for the above sum as of last, next, or any other subsequent term, with cost of suit, release of errors, &c., with stay of execution until the said tenth day of January next.

Witness my hand and seal, at Carlisle, this tenth day of January, A. D. one thousand eight hundred and forty-five.

Signed, sealed and delivered
in presence of

JAMES STILES.

JOHN JONES.

A Note with Security, or for two or more Persons.

We, or either of us, [or jointly and severally,] promise to pay to Eliphalet Betts, or order, on the first day of June next, one thousand dollars, with interest, for value received.

JOHN JONES.
WILLIAM BURNS.

Meadville, Pa., January 10th, 1845.

A Note on Demand.

For value received, I promise to pay Jared Tuttle, or order, on demand, one hundred dollars, without defalcation.

JOHN JONES.

Mercer, Pa., January 10th, 1845.

☞ If a seal is added to a note, it is not barred by the Statute of Limitations, which prevents the recovery of a simple contract debt, unless suit be brought, or a fresh promise of payment made within six years.

BONDS.

Remarks.

A bond or obligation, is a deed whereby the obligor obliges himself, his heirs, executors and administrators, to pay a certain sum of money to another at a day appointed. If this be all, the bond is called a single bond; but there is generally a condition added, that if the obligor does some particular act, the obligation shall be void, or else shall remain in full force and virtue. 2 Bl. Com. 340. The penal sum in a bond, is the sum which is usually double the amount of the real debt, and which is designed to cover interest, cost, and other contingencies. All that can be recovered of a penal sum, are interest, cost, and other contingencies; but care should be taken to distinguish between a penalty and liquidated damages. It is difficult, in some cases, to distinguish between the two, but our courts, in general, have inclined to consider the sum reserved by such agreement to be a penalty, rather than as stipulated damages, whenever it is sufficiently clear a penalty was intended.

A bond was given in the sum of $1000, with condition for the extinguishment, within nine months from the date, of incumbrances on certain property then sold by the obligor to the obligee: Held, that the sum mentioned, was in the nature of a penalty; and not to be considered as stipulated damages. Robeson *v.* Whitesides, 16 S. & R. 320.

If an agreement contain a penalty, the party may bring debt for the penalty, and can recover no more; or he may bring covenant, and recover more or less damages than the penalty. Martin *v.* Taylor, 1 W. C. C. R. 1.

If the obligation of a bond be possible at the time of making it, but afterwards becomes impossible by the act of God, then the penalty is saved.

A bond in Pennsylvania, may be transferred under Act of Assembly, by indorsement under hand and seal, in the presence of two witnesses; and in such case the assignee may bring suit in his own name.

The assignee of a bond takes it at his own peril. He stands in the same place as the obligee, so as to let in every defalcation which the obligor had against the obligee at the time of the assignment on notice of the assignment. The only intent of the act being to enable the assignee to sue in his own name, and prevent the obligee from releasing after assignment. 5 Binney, 232; 2 Bin. 165; 1 Dallas, 27. But see 2 Dal. 398; 4 Dal. 371; 17 S. & R. 287; 1 Penna. R. 262; 1 Rawle, 227. This rule, however, is subject to one qualification. If the assignee, when he is about to take the assignment, calls upon the obligee to know whether the whole money is due, and the obligor tells him it is a good bond, but is entirely silent as to any claim of his against the bond, he can never after open his mouth against the demand of the assignee. 1 Bin. 433. See also 3 Yeates, 350; 16 S. & R. 18; 1 Penn. R. 24; *Ibid.* 476. Where there is a penal bond with several payments at different times, and the obligor fails to meet any one payment as it becomes due, the obligee can declare on the penalty, and take a judgment on the whole of the real debt mentioned in the bond, with stay of execution on the several payments, until such payment should become due, as by the conditions of the bond. An instrument under seal, is not barred by the Statute of Limitations. As, for instance, at the expiration of twenty years, without the payment of interest on a bond or other acknowledgment of its existence, satisfaction is to be presumed; but if a single day less than twenty years has elapsed, the presumption of satisfaction from mere lapse of time, does not arise. This is evidently an artificial and arbitrary distinction, but it is sanctioned by immemorial usage. The conditional part of some bonds is only inserted, but it is only in those cases where the first part is like any other bond, or some particular one referred to.

Common form of Bond.

Know all men by these presents, that I, John Jones, of Erie, in the county of Erie and State of Pennsylvania, am held and firmly bound unto William Burns, of Meadville, in the county of Crawford, and state aforesaid, in the sum of one thousand dollars, [this amount is called the penal sum, and is usually double the amount of the real debt,] lawful money of the United States, to be paid to the said William Burns, or his certain attorney, executors, administrators or assigns; to which payment well and truly to be made and done, I do bind myself, my heirs, executors and administrators, and every of them, firmly by these presents: sealed with my seal, and dated the tenth day of May, Anno Domini, one thousand eight hundred and forty-four.

The condition of this obligation is such, that if the above

bounden John Jones, his heirs, executors, administrators, or any of them, shall and do well and truly pay or cause to be paid unto the above-named William Burns, his executors, administrators or assigns, the just and full sum of five hundred dollars, lawful money aforesaid, with legal interest for the same, on or before the twenty-first day of January next, without fraud or further delay, then this obligation to be void and of none effect, or else to be and remain in full force and virtue.

Signed, sealed and delivered }
in presence of }

JAMES STILES.

JOHN JONES.

Judgment Bond.

Know all men by these presents, that I, John Jones, of the city of Pittsburgh, am held and firmly bound unto William Burns, of the same place, in the sum of one thousand dollars, lawful money of the United States, to be paid to the said William Burns, or his certain attorney, executors, administrators or assigns; to which payment well and truly to be made and done, I do bind myself, my heirs, executors and administrators, and every of them, firmly by these presents: sealed with my seal, and dated the tenth day of May, Anno Domini, one thousand eight hundred and forty-three.

The condition of this obligation is such, that if the above bound John Jones, his executors, administrators, or any of them, shall and do well and truly pay, or cause to be paid, unto the above-named William Burns, his executors, administrators or assigns, the just and full sum of five hundred dollars, lawful money aforesaid, in manner following, that is to say, one hundred dollars on the tenth day of May, one thousand eight hundred and forty-five; two hundred dollars on the tenth day of May, one thousand eight hundred and forty-six, and the remaining two hundred dollars on the tenth day of May, one thousand eight hundred and forty-seven, with annual interest on the whole sum, without fraud or further delay, then this obligation to be void, or else to be and remain in full force and virtue.

And further, I do hereby empower any attorney of any of the courts of record, of this state or elsewhere, to appear for me, and after one or more declarations filed for the above penalty, thereupon to confess judgment or judgments against me, as of the last, next, or any subsequent term, with stay of execution on each and every payment, until such payment respectively falls due, and with release of errors, &c.

Signed, sealed and delivered } in presence of us

JAMES STILES.
THOMAS BROWN.

JOHN JONES.

Bond from one to two.

Know all men by these presents, that I, John Jones, of Lancaster, in the county of Lancaster, and state of Pennsylvania, am held and firmly bound unto William Burns and Charles Dean, of the same place, in the sum of one thousand dollars, lawful money of the United States, to be paid to the said William Burns and Charles Dean, or one of them, or to their certain attorneys, executors, administrators or assigns, to which payment well and truly to be made and done, I do bind myself, my heirs, executors and administrators, and every of them, firmly by these presents; sealed with my seal, and dated the first day of June, Anno Domini, one thousand eight hundred and forty-four.

The condition of this obligation is such, that if the above bound John Jones, his executors or administrators, do and shall well and truly pay or cause to be paid, to the above-named William Burns and Charles Dean, or either of them, their or either of their executors, administrators or assigns, the just and full sum of five hundred dollars, lawful money aforesaid, the legal interest for the same, on or before the first day of June, Anno Domini, one thousand eight hundred and forty-five, without fraud or further delay, then this obligation to be void, or else to be and remain in full force and virtue.

Signed, sealed and delivered, } in presence of

JAMES STILES.

JOHN JONES.

Bond from two to one.

Know all men by these presents, that we, John Jones and William Burns, of Reading, in the county of Berks, and State of Pennsylvania, are held and firmly bound unto Charles Dean, of the same place, in the sum of one thousand dollars, lawful money of the United States, to be paid to the said Charles Dean, or his certain attorney, executors, administrators or assigns; to which payment well and truly to be made and done, we do bind ourselves and each of us by himself, [if one of the obligors be a woman, write "*by him and herself,*"] for and in the whole, our heirs, executors, administrators, and each of us, firmly by these presents; sealed with our seals, and dated the first day of January, Anno Domini, one thousand eight hundred and forty-four.

The condition of this obligation is such, that if the above bound John Jones and William Burns, or either of them, their or either of their executors or administrators, do and shall well and truly pay, or cause to be paid, to the said Charles Dean, his executors, administrators or assigns, the just and full sum of five hundred dollars, lawful money aforesaid, with legal interest for the same, on or before the first day of January, Anno Domini, one thousand eight hundred and forty-five, then this obligation to be void, or else to be and remain in full force and virtue.

Signed, sealed and delivered in presence of

JAMES STILES.

JOHN JONES.

WILLIAM BURNS.

Bond of Indemnity to Bail.

Know all men by these presents, that I, John Jones, of Doylestown, in the county of Bucks and State of Pennsylvania, am held and firmly bound unto William Burns, of Reading, in the county of Berks, and state aforesaid, in the sum of one thousand dollars, lawful money of the United States, to be paid to the said William Burns, or his certain attorney, executors, administrators or assigns; to which payment well and truly to be made and done, I do bind myself, my heirs, executors, administrators, and every of them, firmly by these presents: Sealed with my seal, and dated the first day of June, Anno Domini, one thousand eight hundred and forty-four.

Whereas the above-named William Burns, at the special instance and request of the above-bound John Jones, together with the said John Jones and Thomas Brown, of Reading aforesaid, is bound to Charles Dean, sheriff of the county of Berks, in the penal sum of five hundred dollars, lawful money of the United States, conditioned for the appearance of the said John Jones before the judges of the Court of Common Pleas at Reading, in and for the county of Berks, on the first Monday of August next, to answer Richard Dale, in a plea of *trespass on the case*, [*or as the plea is expressed in the bail bond*,] as by the said in part recited bond or obligation and condition thereunder written, may more fully appear: *Now the condition* of this obligation is such, that if the above-bound John Jones do and shall appear according to the condition of the said bond, or obligation, and as the law in such cases requires, and if the said John Jones, his heirs, executors and administrators, shall also from time to time, and at all times hereafter, save harmless and indemnify him, the said William Burns, his executors and administrators, and his and their goods and chattels, lands and tenements, of, and from all damages, sum and sums of money, costs and charges whatsoever, which he, they, or any of them, shall, or may at any time or times hereafter sustain, or be put unto, by reason or means of the said William Burns being bound for the appearance of the said John Jones, as aforesaid, then this obligation to be void, or else to be and remain in full force and virtue.

Signed, sealed and delivered }
in presence of }

JAMES STILES.

JOHN JONES. [L. S.]

Refunding bond to executors, on payment of Legacy.

Know all men by these presents, that we, John Jones, of Erie, in the county of Erie and State of Pennsylvania, legatee under the last will and testament of Thomas Brown, deceased, and Charles Dean, of Erie aforesaid, are held and firmly bound unto Richard Dale and Abel Stone, executors of the last will and testament of the said Thomas Brown, deceased, in the sum of five hundred dollars, lawful money of the United States, to be paid to the said Richard Dale and Abel Stone, or to their certain attorney, executors, administrators or assigns; to which payment well and truly to be made and done, we do bind ourselves and each of us by himself, for and in the whole, our heirs, executors and administrators, and every of them firmly by these presents: Sealed with our seals, and dated the first day of May, Anno Domini, one thousand eight hundred and forty-four.

Whereas the said Thomas Brown, by his said last will and testament, bearing date the tenth day of March, one thousand eight hundred and forty-three, did give and bequeath unto the said John Jones, a certain legacy of two hundred and fifty dollars, [*or "one equal fourth part of his personal estate after the payment of debts," or as the case may be,*] as by the said in part recited will, duly proved and remaining on record in the register's office, at Erie, appears. Now the condition of this obligation is such, that if any part, or the whole of the said legacy, shall at any time after payment thereof to the said John Jones, appear to be wanting to discharge any debt or debts, legacy or legacies, which the said executors shall not have other assets to pay; then and in such case, if the said John Jones, his heirs, executors or administrators, shall and do return the said legacy, or such part thereof as shall be necessary for the payment of the said debts, or the payment of a proportional part of the said legacies, then this obligation shall be void and of none effect, or else shall be and remain in full force and virtue.

Signed, sealed and delivered in presence of

JAMES STILES.

JOHN JONES.

WILLIAM BURNS.

Refunding bond, given by distributee under approval of court, (Sec. 41 *and* 57 *of Act of* 24*th of Feb.*, 1834, *"relating to executors and administrators.")*

Know all men by these presents, that we, John Jones and William Burns, are held and firmly bound unto the Commonwealth of Pennsylvania, in the sum of five hundred dollars, lawful money, to be paid unto the said commonwealth, her certain attorney or assigns, to which payment well and truly to be made, we bind ourselves, and each of us, our heirs, executors, and administrators, jointly and severally, firmly by these presents: Sealed with our seals, dated the tenth day of May, in the year of our Lord one thousand eight hundred and forty-four. Whereas, Abel Brown, administrator of the estate of Charles Dean, deceased, has presented to the Orphans' Court of Allegheny county, a statement of all demands against said estate, which have been made known to him, and after deducting the amount thereof from the assets in his hands, together with such further sum as may be necessary to pay the interest and costs of suit of such as may be in dispute, and such as he may deem it his duty to dispute, he is desirous of making distribution of the residue under the direction of the said Orphans' Court, and whereas the said John Jones is entitled to two hundred and fifty dollars, and the said William Burns has been approved of by the said court, as security for the said John Jones.

Now the condition of this obligation is such, that if any debt or demand, other than as hereinbefore alluded to be recovered against the estate of the said Charles Dean, or otherwise be duly made to appear, which the said Abel Brown shall not have other assets to pay, then and in such case, if the said John Jones shall and do return and refund the said sum of two hundred and fifty dollars, or such rateable part thereof as may be necessary for the payment of such debt or demand, then this obligation shall be void and of none effect, or else shall be and remain in full force and virtue.

Signed, sealed and delivered }
in presence of }

JAMES STILES.

JOHN JONES.

WILLIAM BURNS.

Bond of Guardian at his appointment.

Know all men by these presents, that we, John Jones, and William Burns, both of Erie, in the county of Erie, and State of Pennsylvania, are held and firmly bound to the Commonwealth of Pennsylvania, in the sum of —— dollars, lawful money, to be paid to the said commonwealth, her certain attorney or assigns; to which payment well and truly to be made and done, we do bind ourselves, our heirs, executors and administrators, and each of us, firmly by these presents: Sealed with our seals, and dated the —— day of —— one thousand eight hundred and ——.

The condition of this obligation is such, that if the above bounden John Jones, guardian of Thomas Brown, a minor child of Charles Brown, late of Erie, deceased, shall at least once in every three years, and at any other time when required by the Orphans' Court for the county of Erie, render a just and true account of the management of the property and estate of the said minor, under his care, and shall also deliver up the said property, agreeably to the order and decree of the said court, or the directions of law, and shall in all respects faithfully perform the duties of guardian of the said Thomas Brown, then the above obligation shall be void; otherwise it shall be and remain in full force and virtue.

Signed, sealed and delivered }
in presence of }

JAMES STILES.

JOHN JONES.

WILLIAM BURNS.

Bond by Executor, on application to Orphans' Court for an order to sell or mortgage Real Estate.

Know all men by these presents, that we, John Jones and William Burns, of the township of Wayne, and county of Erie, are held and firmly bound to the Commonwealth of Pennsylvania, in the sum of one thousand dollars, lawful money, to be paid to the said commonwealth: to which payment well and truly to be made, we do bind ourselves, our heirs, executors and administrators, and each of us, firmly by these presents. Sealed with our seals, and dated the —— day of —— one thousand eight hundred and ——.

The condition of this obligation is such, that if the above bounden John Jones, executor of the last will and testament of Thomas Brown, late of Concord, deceased, shall and do faithfully execute the powers committed to him by the Orphans' Court of the county of Erie, for selling [or mortgaging] the real estate of the said decedent, and shall make a faithful appropriation of the proceeds of such sale [or mortgage] according to his duty, and in such manner as the said court shall legally decree, then the above obligation to be void, or else to be and remain in full force and virtue.

Signed, sealed and delivered }
in presence of }

JAMES STILES.

JOHN JONES.

WILLIAM BURNS.

Bond by Administrator, on application to Orphans' Court for an order to sell or mortgage Real Estate.

Know all men by these presents, &c., [as in the last preceding bond] The condition of this obligation is such, that if the above-bounden John Jones, administrator of all and singular, the goods and chattels, lands and tenements, which were of Thomas Brown, late of Erie, deceased, shall and do faithfully, &c., [as in the last preceding condition.]

Bond by Guardian, on application to Orphans' Court for an order to sell or mortgage Real Estate.

Know all men by these presents, &c., [as in the bond next preceding the last.]

The condition of this obligation is such, that if the above-bounden John Jones, guardian of Charles Brown, a minor child of Thomas Brown, late of Erie, deceased, shall and do faithfully, &c., [as in the condition next preceding the last.]

Conditional part of a Bond for the performance of Covenants.

The condition of this obligation is such, that if the above-bound John Jones, his heirs, executors or administrators, shall and do in all things, well and truly observe, perform, fulfil and keep all and singular, the covenants, grants, articles, clauses, provisoes, conditions and agreements whatsoever, which on the part of the said John Jones, are, or ought to be observed, performed, fulfilled and kept, comprised and mentioned in certain Indentures of Lease, bearing even date herewith, and made, or mentioned to be made, between the said John Jones, of the one part, and the above-named William Burns, of the other part, according to the purport, true intent and meaning of the same, then this obligation to be void, or else to be and remain in full force and virtue.

Conditional part of a Bond to execute a Conveyance.

The condition of this obligation is such, that if the above-bound John Jones, shall and do, on or before the first day of May next ensuing the date hereof, or in case of his death before that time, if the heir or heirs of the said John Jones, within six months next after his decease, (if such heir or heirs shall be then of full age, or if within age, then within six months after such heir or heirs shall be of full age,) shall and do, upon the reasonable request, and at the proper cost and charges in the law, of the said William Burns, his heirs or assigns, make, execute and acknowledge, or cause to be made, executed and acknowledged, all and every such act or acts, deed or deeds, conveyance or conveyances whatsoever, which shall be needful or necessary, for conveying, assuring, establishing and confirming unto the said William Burns, his heirs and assigns, a good, pure, absolute, and indefeasible estate of inheritance, in fee simple, clear of all incumbrances, of, and in a certain messuage, situated in the town of Beaver, Beaver county, Pennsylvania, and bounded and described as follows, to wit: [*here describe the premises by its boundaries*] with the appurtenances; and if in the mean time, and while and until the same deed or deeds shall be executed, the said John Jones, his heirs and assigns, shall and do permit and suffer the said William Burns, his heirs and assigns, peaceably and quietly to have, hold and enjoy the same messuage, piece or parcel of land, then this obligation to be void, or else to be and remain in full force and virtue.

Conditional part of a Bond to leave money to a Wife.

Whereas, a marriage is intended to be shortly had and solemnized between the above-bound John Jones and Anne Brown, (daughter of the above-named Thomas Brown:) Now the condition of this obligation is such, that if (after the said intended marriage) the said Anne Brown, shall happen to survive the said John Jones (her intended husband), then and in such case, if the heirs, executors or administrators of him, the said John Jones, shall and do, within the space of six months next after his decease, well and truly pay, or cause to be paid, unto her, the said Anne, or her assigns, the sum of two thousand dollars, to and for her own proper use and benefit, and to be at her own free and absolute disposal, without any manner of account to be given by her, for or concerning the same, then this obligation to be void, or else to be and remain in full force and virtue.

Conditional part of a Bond to permit a Wife to make a Will.

Whereas, a marriage is intended to be shortly had and solemnized between the above-bound John Jones and the said Anne Brown: Now the condition of this obligation is such, that if, after the said intended marriage, the said John Jones shall and do permit and suffer the said Anne Brown to make her last will and testament in writing, and in and by the same, at her will and pleasure, to bequeath, or otherwise dispose of all such household furniture, wearing apparel, or other goods or chattels whatsoever, whereof she is now possessed; and if the said John Jones, his executors or administrators, shall and do on request to him or them made, well and truly deliver, or cause to be delivered unto the legatee or legatees named in the said will, their legal representatives or assigns, all such goods and chattels, as shall be to them respectively bequeathed, by the said will, according to the directions thereof, then this obligation to be void, or else to be and remain in full force and virtue.

Conditional part of a Bond to maintain Parents.

Whereas, the said John Jones, and Mary his wife, by Indenture bearing even date herewith, have granted and confirmed unto the said William Jones, in fee, a certain messuage situated, &c., [*here describe the premises as in the deed,*] with the appurtenances, the said William Jones having agreed to maintain them, the said John Jones and Mary his wife (his father and mother) during their natural lives, or the life of the survivor of them: Now the condition of this obligation is such, that if the above-bound William Jones, his heirs, executors, administrators or assigns, shall and do well and sufficiently maintain, support and keep the said John Jones and Mary his wife, during their natural lives, and the life of the survivor of them, with good and sufficient meat, drink, apparel, washing, lodging, and attendance in sickness and in health; and also pay unto them, him or her, the sum of forty dollars yearly, during the term aforesaid, then this obligation to be void, or else to be and remain in full force and virtue.

Another to maintain Parents.

Whereas, the said John Jones and Mary his wife, by Indenture bearing even date herewith, have granted and confirmed unto the said William Jones, in fee, a certain messuage situated, &c., [*here describe the premises as in the deed,*] with the appurtenances, the said William Jones having agreed to maintain them, the said John Jones and Mary his wife (his father and mother), during their natural lives, and the life of the survivor of them : Now the condition of this obligation is such, that if the said William Burns, his heirs, executors, administrators or assigns, shall and do allow the said John Jones and Mary his wife, and the survivor of them, the sole use of the house [*or room*] which they now occupy, on the premises, with the necessary privileges in the kitchen and cellar, and shall and do deliver or cause to be delivered unto the said John Jones yearly, and every year, during the joint lives of the said John Jones and Mary his wife, the following articles in good order, and at proper seasons to wit: [here mention the articles,] and in case of the death of either of them, shall and do deliver unto the survivor of them, the articles aforesaid, and shall and do provide and keep for them, and the survivor of them, a good riding horse and milk cow, to be changed as often as need be, and feed and pasture the same, in like manner with his or their own, then this obligation to be void; but if default shall be made in any of the articles aforesaid, then to be and remain in full force and virtue.

A conditional part of a Bond to keep a person during life.

The condition of this obligation is such, that whereas, the above-bound John Jones, for and in consideration of a competent sum of money, as well as the sum of one dollar to him in hand paid, by the above-named William Burns, has agreed and undertaken to keep the said William Burns, during his natural life; if, therefore, the said John Jones, his executors, administrators or assigns, do and shall from time to time, and at all times hereafter, during the life of the said William Burns, well and sufficiently maintain and keep, or cause to be well and sufficiently maintained and kept, the said William Burns, in the house of him the said John Jones, with meat, drink, clothes, and all other things necessary and convenient, then this obligation to be void, or else to be and remain in full force and virtue.

A conditional part of a Bond to execute a Conveyance at a time to come, and that the obligee receive the profits.

The condition of this obligation is such, that if the above-bound John Jones, his heirs, executors or administrators, do and shall, upon and at the request of the said William Burns, his heirs or assigns, on or before the first day of May, next ensuing the date hereof, convey and assure, or cause to be conveyed and assured unto the said William Burns, his heirs and assigns, or to such other person and persons, and to his and their heirs, as the said William Burns shall nominate and appoint, and to such uses as he shall direct, a messuage or tenement, situated &c., [*here describe the premises by boundaries*,] now in the possession of Charles Dean, by such conveyances and assurances in the law, as by the said William Burns or his heirs, or by his or their counsel learned in the law, shall be reasonably devised or advised, and required, freed and discharged of and from all incumbrances whatsoever, except, &c. And also, if the said John Jones, his heirs, and assigns, or either of them do and shall, until such a conveyance and assurance be made and executed as aforesaid, permit and suffer the said William Burns, his heirs and assigns, peaceably and quietly to have, receive and take to his and their own proper use and uses, the rents, issues and profits of all and singular the premises, and every part and parcel thereof, without any manner of let, suit, trouble, disturbance, hindrance or denial of the said John Jones, his heirs and assigns, or any of them, or of any other person or persons whatsoever, by his or their, or any of their means, right, title or procurement, then this obligation to be void, or else to be and remain in full force and virtue.

A conditional part of a Bond for service of an Apprentice.

Whereas, Thomas Jones, son of the above-bound John Jones, by Indenture of Apprenticeship bearing even date with the above-written obligation, hath bound and put himself apprentice to the above-named William Burns, with him to dwell and abide, from the day of the date hereof, unto the full end and term of five years, thence next ensuing, and fully to be completed and ended, as by the said Indenture may more fully appear.

Now the condition of this obligation is such, that if the said Thomas Jones shall well and truly serve and dwell with the said William Burns, after the manner of an apprentice, during all the said term of five years, according to the true intent and meaning of the said Indenture, and shall behave himself honestly and obediently towards the said William Burns, [*his executors, administrators, or assigns,*] as a good and dutiful apprentice ought to do, during the said term, then this obligation to be void, or else to be and remain in full force and virtue.

A conditional part of a Bond of an Attorney to account to his Constituent.

Whereas, by letter of Attorney bearing date the tenth day of June, Anno Domini one thousand eight hundred and forty four, the said William Burns hath duly authorized and empowered the above-bound John Jones to recover and receive divers debts and sums of money to the use of the said William Burns, as by the said Letter of Attorney more fully and at large appears. Now the condition of this obligation is such, that if the above-bound John Jones shall and do account for and pay unto the said William Burns, his executors, administrators, or assigns, all such sum or sums of money as he shall from time to time receive, by virtue of the said Letter of Attorney, (the reasonable commissions and expenses of the said John Jones for recovering and receiving the same, being first deducted therefrom,) then the above obligation to be void, or else to be and remain in full force and virtue.

Conditional part of a Bond of a Treasurer of a Company.

Whereas, the above-bounden John Jones has been chosen treasurer of the Erie and Waterford Turnpike Road Company, and by reason whereof, he will receive into his hands divers sums of money, goods and chattels, and other things, the property of the said Company: Now the condition of this obligation is such, that if the said John Jones, his executors or administrators, at the expiration of his said office, upon request to him or them made, shall make and give unto such auditor or auditors, as shall be appointed by the said Company, a just and true account of all such sum or sums of money, goods and chattels, and other things, as have come into his hands, charge or possession, as treasurer aforesaid, and shall and do pay and deliver over, to his successor in office, or any other person duly authorized to receive the same, all such balances or sums of money, goods and chattels, and other things, which shall appear to be in his hands, and due from him to the said Company, then this obligation to be void, or else to be and remain in full force and virtue.

Conditional part of a Bond to a Mother of a Bastard Child.

The condition of this obligation is such, that if the above-bound John Jones, his heirs, executors, administrators, or any of them, shall and do well and truly pay, or cause to be paid, unto the above-named Mary Burns, or to her certain attorney, executors, administrators or assigns, the just and full sum of one dollar lawful money as aforesaid, weekly, and every week until a certain male bastard child, born of the body of her the said Mary Burns, begotten by him the said John Jones, arrives at the age of seven years, if the said child should so long live, the first payment to be made on the eighth day of May, instant, [*if given pursuant to the judgment of the Court of General Quarter Sessions of the Peace, add the following words: "According to the sentence of the Court of General Quarter Sessions of the Peace, of Berks County, held August Sessions,* 1844,"] then this obligation to be void, or else to be and remain in full force and virtue.

Conditional part of a Bond of Indemnity to Surety in a Bond.

The condition of this obligation is such, that whereas the above-named William Burns, at the special instance and request of the above-bounden John Jones, and for his only debt, duty, matter and cause, together with him, the said John Jones, are held and firmly bound unto a certain Thomas Dale, of Harrisburg, in and by one obligation, bearing even date herewith, in the penal sum of one thousand dollars, lawful money as aforesaid, conditioned for the true payment of five hundred dollars, like money, on or before the tenth day of October, next ensuing the date of the said obligation and condition thereof, relation being thereunto had appears. If, therefore, the said John Jones, his heirs, executors or administrators, shall and do on or before the said tenth day of October, well and truly pay, or cause to be paid, unto the above-named Thomas Dale, or his certain attorney, executors, administrators or assigns, the aforesaid debt or sum of five hundred dollars, with interest, in discharge of the said recited obligation, and also, shall and do from time to time, and at all times hereafter, well and sufficiently save, defend, keep harmless and indemnify the said William Burns, his heirs, executors and administrators, and his and their goods and chattels, lands and tenements, of and from the said obligation, and of and from all actions, suits, payments, costs, charges and damages, for or by reason thereof, then this obligation to be void, or else to be and remain in full force and virtue.

Conditional part of Bond of Indemnity to Bail in Bail Bond.

The condition of this obligation is such, that whereas the above-named William Burns, at the special instance and request of the above-bound John Jones, in and by one obligation, bearing date the tenth day of June, Anno Domini one thousand eight hundred and forty-four, became bound unto Thomas Dale, Esq., High Sheriff of the county of Berks, in the sum of four hundred dollars, conditioned for the appearance of the said John Jones before the Court of Common Pleas, to be held at Reading, the fourth day of August next, as by the said recited obligation and condition thereof, relation being thereunto had, appears.

If, therefore, the said John Jones shall appear according to the said obligation, and as the law requires; and also shall and do from time to time, and at all times hereafter, well and sufficiently save, defend, keep harmless, and indemnify the said William Burns, his heirs, executors and administrators, and his and their goods and chattels, lands and tenements, of and from the said obligation, and of and from all actions, suits, payments, costs, charges and damages, for or by reason thereof, then this obligation to be void, or else to be and remain in full force and virtue.

Conditional part of a Bond of Indemnity to Special Bail.

The condition of this obligation is such, that whereas the above-named William Burns, at the special instance and request of the above-bound John Jones, became special bail for the said John Jones, in a certain action of trespass [*debt, or as the case may be*] at the suit of Daniel Stone, in the Court of Common Pleas, of the county of Erie, as by the recognisance of bail, on record in the said court, relation being thereunto had, appears. If, therefore, the said John Jones shall appear according to the condition of the said obligation, and as the law requires; and also, shall and do from time to time, and at all times hereafter, well and sufficiently save, defend, keep harmless, and indemnify the said William Burns, his heirs, executors and administrators, and his and their goods and chattels, lands and tenements, of and from the said obligation, and of and from all actions, suits, payments, costs, charges and damages, for or by reason thereof, then this obligation to be void, or else to be and remain in full force and virtue.

Conditional part of Bond of Indemnity to Bail in Recognizance.

The condition of this obligation is such, that whereas the above-named William Burns, at the special instance and request of the above-bound John Jones, standeth bound for the said John Jones, to the commonwealth of Pennsylvania, in the sum of five hundred dollars conditioned for the appearance of the said John Jones, at the next Court of General Quarter Sessions of the Peace, to be held at Mercer, in and for the county of Mercer, aforesaid, to answer to such matters and things as shall then and there be objected against him on the Commonwealth's behalf, [*or to answer a certain indictment preferred against him, for &c.,*] and also that the said John Jones shall in the mean time keep the peace and be of good behaviour towards all the citizens of the Commonwealth, and especially towards James Stiles, as by the said recognizance, relation being thereunto had, appears. If, therefore, the said John Jones shall appear, according to the condition of the said obligation, and as the law requires; and also, shall and do from time to time, and at all times hereafter, well and sufficiently save, defend, keep harmless and indemnify the said William Burns, his heirs, executors and administrators, and his and their goods and chattels, lands and tenements, of and from the said obligation, and of and from all actions, suits, payments, costs, charges and damages, for or by reason thereof, then this obligation to be void, or else to remain in full force and virtue.

Conditional part of a Bond of Indemnity to surety in an Administration Bond.

The condition of this obligation is such, that whereas the above-named William Burns, at the special instance and request of the above-bound John Jones, in and by a certain obligation, bearing date the tenth day of May, one thousand eight hundred and forty-four, hath become bound together with the said John Jones, unto Thomas Brown, Esq., register for the probate of wills and granting letters of administration in and for the county of Lycoming aforesaid, in the sum of one thousand dollars, for the due administration of all and singular the goods and chattels, rights and credits, which were of James Stiles, late of ——, who died intestate, &c., as by the said recited obligation and condition thereof, remaining in the Register's office at Williamsport, relation being thereunto had, appears. If, therefore, the said John

Jones, administrator as aforesaid, shall and do well and truly administer all and singular, the goods and chattels, rights and credits which were of the aforesaid James Stiles, according to law, and do and perform every other act and acts, matters and things, on the part and in behalf of the said John Jones, to be done and performed, according to the true intent and meaning of the condition of the said recited obligation; and also shall and do from time to time, and at all times hereafter, well and sufficiently save, defend, keep harmless and indemnify the said William Burns, his heirs, executors and administrators, and his and their goods and chattels, lands and tenements, of and from all actions, suits, payments, costs, charges and damages, for or by reason thereof, then this obligation to be void, or else to remain in full force and virtue.

Conditional part of a Bond of Indemnity to Executor on payment of a Legacy.

The condition of this obligation is such, that whereas William Burns, by his last will and testament, bearing date the tenth day of May, one thousand eight hundred and forty, did bequeath unto James Jones, the son of the above-bound John Jones, a certain legacy of two hundred dollars, &c. And whereas, the said Thomas Brown, at the request of the said John Jones, hath paid the said legacy unto him for the use and benefit of his said son, who is a minor, under the age of twenty-one years. If, therefore, the said John Jones, his heirs, executors or administrators, shall cause and procure the said James Jones, the son, on his arrival at the age of twenty-one years, to release the legacy aforesaid, unto the said Thomas Brown; and also, shall and do from time to time, and at all times hereafter, well and sufficiently save, defend, keep harmless and indemnify, the said Thomas Brown, his heirs, executors and administrators, and his and their goods and chattels, lands and tenements, of and from the said obligation, and of and from all actions, suits, payments, costs, charges and damages, for or by reason thereof, then this obligation to be void, or else to be and remain in full force and virtue.

Conditional part of a Bond of Indemnity to save harmless on paying Rent.

The condition of this obligation is such, that whereas the above-named John Jones, by indenture of lease, bearing date the tenth day of March, one thousand eight hundred and forty-four, hath demised and to farm let, unto the said William Burns, all that messuage [*describe the premises as in the lease*]. To hold the same to the said William Burns, for the term of one year, paying

&c., [*as in the lease,*] as in and by the said indenture appears. And whereas a certain Thomas Dale claims title to the premises aforesaid, with the appurtenances. If, therefore, the said John Jones shall and do from time to time, indemnify the said William Burns, his heirs, executors and administrators, and his and their goods and chattels, lands and tenements, of and from the claim of the said Thomas Dale, and of and from all actions, suits, payments, costs, charges and damages, for or by reason thereof, then this obligation to be void, or else to be and remain in full force and virtue.

Conditional part of a Bond of Indemnity against Claim for Dower.

The condition of this obligation is such, that whereas the above-bound John Jones, by indenture bearing date the first day of May, one thousand eight hundred and forty-two, hath granted, bargained and sold unto the above-named William Burns, all that certain messuage or piece of land situate, &c., [*describe the premises,*] with the appurtenances, to hold the same to him, his heirs and assigns forever, as by the said indenture, relation being thereunto had, appears. If, therefore, the said John Jones, his heirs, executors and administrators, shall and do from time to time, and at all times hereafter, well and sufficiently save, keep harmless and indemnify the said William Burns, his heirs, executors and administrators, and his and their goods and chattels, lands and tenements, of and from the dower, or thirds which Mary Jones, the wife [*or mother, &c.,*] of the said John Jones, shall or may claim in the premises, and of and from all actions, suits, payments, costs, charges and damages, for and by reason thereof, then this obligation to be void, or else to be and remain in full force and virtue.

Conditional part of a Bond of Indemnity for a Bond mislaid or lost.

The condition of this obligation is such, that whereas the above-named John Jones, in and by a certain obligation bearing date on or about the first day of May last past, became bound unto the above-named William Burns in the sum of two hundred dollars, conditioned for the payment of one hundred dollars, which said obligation has been since lost or mislaid; and whereas, the said John Jones hath fully satisfied and paid the said sum of one hundred dollars, with interest due on the said obligation, the receipt whereof, the said William Burns doth hereby acknowledge, and thereof, and from every part thereof, and all actions, suits and demands, concerning the same, acquit and forever discharge the said John Jones, his heirs, executors and administrators, by these presents. If, therefore, the said William Burns, his heirs, executors and administrators, shall and do deliver up the said obligation, when it shall be found, to the said John Jones, his heirs, executors or administrators, to be canceled; and until the same shall be so delivered up and canceled, save, defend, keep harmless and indemnify, the said John Jones, his heirs, executors and administrators, and his and their goods and chattels, lands and tenements, of and from the said obligation, and of and from all actions, suits, payments, costs, charges and damages, for or by reason thereof, then this obligation to be void, or else to be and remain in full force and virtue.

Bond to the County for a Bastard Child.

Know all men by these presents, that we, John Jones and William Burns, of the township of Greenwich, in the county of Berks, and state of Pennsylvania, are held and firmly bound unto James Dean and Daniel Stone, Overseers of the poor of the county aforesaid, for the time being, in the just and full sum of five hundred dollars, lawful money of the United States, to be paid to the said Overseers of the poor, or to either of them, or either of their certain attorneys, successors or assigns, to which payment well and truly to be made and done, we do bind ourselves, jointly and severally, our heirs, executors and administrators, and every of them firmly by these presents: Sealed with our seals, and dated the tenth day of May, one thousand eight hundred and forty-four.

The condition of this obligation is such, that whereas Mary Ware, of Bern, in the county aforesaid, single woman, is now pregnant with child, [*or hath lately been delivered of a male bastard child, in the township aforesaid,*] and hath charged the said John Jones with being the father thereof; if, therefore, the said John Jones shall and do from time to time, and at all times hereafter well and sufficiently save, defend, keep harmless and indemnify the said James Dean and Daniel Stone, and their successors, overseers of the poor of the said county, for the time being, and also all the inhabitants thereof, of and from all expenses, costs, charges and damages whatsoever, which shall or may hereafter happen or accrue, for or by reason or means of the birth, maintenance, education or bringing up of the said child, [*or of such child or children wherewith the said Mary Ware now goeth,*] and of and from all actions, suits, troubles and demands whatsoever, touching or concerning the same, then this obligation to be void, or else to be and remain in full force and virtue.

Bond to refund Money on failure of Contract.

Know all men by these presents, that we, John Jones and William Burns, of Carlisle, in the county of Cumberland and State of Pennsylvania, are held and firmly bound unto Daniel Stone and James Dean, trustees [*or if not incorporated, say "members"*] of the first Associate Reformed Presbyterian Congregation of Carlisle, county and state aforesaid, in the sum of two thousand dollars, lawful money of the United States, to be paid to the said Daniel Stone and James Dean, or to their certain attorney, successors or assigns, in trust for the said congregation, to which payment well and truly to be made and done, we do bind ourselves, jointly and severally, our heirs, executors and administrators, and every of them firmly by these presents: Sealed with our seals, and dated the tenth day of October, one thousand eight hundred and forty-four.

Whereas the said John Jones, for the consideration of one thousand dollars, to him in hand paid, or secured to be paid, did make, finish and sell unto the said congregation an organ [*clock, or other article*], which he has delivered and placed in the said church. Now the said John Jones doth hereby for himself, his heirs, executors and administrators, warrant the said organ to be good in each and every respect, and to remain good and sufficient for the term of five years.

Now, the condition of this obligation is such, that if the said organ shall, within the time aforesaid, prove defective or insufficient, in the opinion of any three competent artists or mechanics, who shall be disinterested, and if the said John Jones, his heirs, executors or administrators, shall repair, amend and render the same good and sufficient in all its parts, or, if he shall pay or make full satisfaction unto the said congregation, for the consideration money aforesaid, and save, keep harmless and indemnify the said congregation, on account of the said organ, or any matter concerning the same, then the above obligation to be void, or else to be and remain in full force and virtue.

Replevin Bond to Sheriff by Plaintiff.

Know all men by these presents, that we, John Jones and William Burns, are held and firmly bound unto Thomas Brown, Esq., High Sheriff of the county of Allegheny, in the just and full sum of five hundred dollars, lawful money of the United States, to be paid to the said Thomas Brown, Esq , his certain attorney, executors, administrators or assigns, to which payment well and truly to be made and done, we do bind ourselves and each of us, our and each of our heirs, executors, administrators and every of them, jointly and severally, firmly by these presents: Sealed with our seals, and dated the first day of June, Anno Domini one thousand eight hundred and forty-four.

The condition of this obligation is such, that whereas the above-bound John Jones having obtained a certain writ of replevin, issued out of the Court of Common Pleas of the said county, tested at Pittsburgh, the twenty-second day of May, A. D. 1844, against a certain Daniel Stone, of the county aforesaid, commanding the said sheriff, that he should replevy and cause to be delivered to the said John Jones, one black horse, &c. [*describe the property as in the writ*]. Now if the above-bound John Jones shall and will prosecute his suit against the said Daniel Stone with effect, and shall and will make return of the said goods, if return of the same shall be adjudged, and shall and will also, from time to time, and at all times hereafter, well and sufficiently keep, save harmless and indemnify the above-named sheriff and his officers, and his and their heirs, executors and administrators, and every of them, of and from all suits, costs and charges whatsoever, that shall and may accrue to him or them, by reason of the replevy and delivery aforesaid, that then this obligation shall be void, or else to be and remain in full force and virtue.

Sealed and delivered in presence of }

JAMES STILES.

JOHN JONES.

WILLIAM BURNS.

Property Bond in Replevin, to Sheriff by Defendant.

Know all men by these presents, that we, &c. [*as in the replevin bond to sheriff by plaintiff*]. The condition of this obligation is such, that whereas John Jones having obtained a certain writ of replevin, issued out of the Court of Common Pleas of Allegheny county, tested at Pittsburgh, the twenty-second day of May, A. D. 1844, against the above-bound Daniel Stone, of the county aforesaid, commanding the said sheriff that he should replevy, and cause to be delivered to the said John Jones, one black horse, &c. [*as in writ of replevin*].

And whereas, the said Daniel Stone hath claimed property in the said black horse, &c., wherefore, delivery of the said black horse, &c., cannot be made. Now, if the above-bound Daniel

Stone shall and do well and truly deliver up the said black horse, &c., to the said John Jones, if the property thereof shall be adjudged in the said John Jones, and shall and do well and truly abide by the judgment of the said court in all things relating to the premises, and shall also save, keep harmless and indemnify the said sheriff in the premises, then this obligation to be void, or else to be and remain in full force and virtue.

Bond of Indemnity in case of Foreign Attachment.

Know all men by these presents, &c. [*as in the replevin bond to sheriff by plaintiff*].

The condition of this obligation is such, that whereas in and by a certain writ of attachment, issued out of the Court of Common Pleas of Union County, tested at New Berlin, the tenth day of May, Anno Domini 1844, commanding the said sheriff that he should attach Daniel Stone, by all and singular, the goods and chattels, lands and tenements, in whose hands or possession soever the same might be found in his bailiwick, &c., to answer John Jones in a plea of trespass on the case, &c., which said writ is returnable the first Monday of August next ensuing.

Now, if the said John Jones shall and will save harmless and indemnify the above-named Thomas Brown, sheriff as aforesaid, and his officers, and every of them, for or by reason of his or their executing the said writ, as therein he is commanded, and if the said John Jones shall and will prosecute his said plea against the said Daniel Stone, with effect according to law, and abide the judgment and award of said court, then this obligation shall be void, or else to be and remain in full force and virtue.

Bond of Indemnity upon Levy and Sale.

Know all men by these presents, that we, &c. [*as in the replevin bond*]. The condition of this obligation is such, that whereas a writ of *fieri facias* has lately issued out of the Court of Common Pleas of the county of Lancaster, tested at Lancaster, the tenth day of June, Anno Domini one thousand eight hundred and forty-four, directed to the above-named Thomas Brown, sheriff of the said county, at the suit of the said John Jones, against Daniel Stone, commanding him, the said sheriff, to cause to be levied of the goods and chattels, lands and tenements, of the said Daniel Stone, in his bailiwick, the sum of five hundred dollars, which was lately adjudged to the said John Jones, as well for his damages, as for his costs and charges by him about his said suit in that behalf expended. And whereas the said sheriff does not certainly know what are the goods and chattels, or effects of the said Daniel Stone: if, therefore, the said John Jones, his heirs, executors and administrators, shall and do from time to time, and at all times hereafter, indemnify and save harmless the above-named Thomas Brown, sheriff as aforesaid, and his officers, and his and their heirs, executors and administrators, and every of them, and his and their goods and chattels, lands and tenements, of and from all manner of suits, action and actions, damages, costs or charges whatsoever, that shall or may accrue to him or them, or either or any of them, on account of his or their levying upon, or levying upon and selling, by the direction of him, the said John Jones, and by force of the said writ, the goods and chattels of any person or persons whatsoever, as, or supposing them to be the goods and chattels of the said Daniel Stone, then this obligation to be void, or else to be and remain in full force and virtue.

Conditional part of a Bond of Indemnity for the payment of an Annuity during life.

Whereas the above-bound John Jones, on the day of the date of the above-written obligation, hath had and received to his own use, of and from the above-named William Burns, the sum of one thousand dollars, the receipt whereof, he, the said John Jones, doth hereby acknowledge, for consideration whereof, he, the said John Jones, hath agreed to pay unto the said William Burns one annuity or clear yearly sum of one hundred dollars, during his natural life, to be paid in manner hereafter to be mentioned. Now, the condition of this obligation is such, that if the above-bounden John Jones, his heirs, executors or administrators, or any of them do, and shall yearly and every year, during the natural life of the above-named William Burns, well and truly pay, or cause to be paid, to him, the said William Burns, or his assigns, the clear yearly sum of one hundred dollars, by quarterly payments, on the four following days of payment, in the year, that is to say, the first days of January, April, July and October, in each year, by even and equal portions, the first payment thereof to begin and be made on the first day of January next ensuing the date of the above-written obligation, then this obligation to be void; but if default shall happen to be made of or in any of the said quarterly payments, or any part thereof, on any or either of the said quarterly days on which the same ought to be paid as aforesaid, then the same shall stand and remain in full force and virtue.

Sealed and delivered in presence of }

James Stiles.

JOHN JONES.

Conditional part of a Bond of Indemnity to discharge incumbrances.

The condition of this obligation is such, that whereas the above-bound John Jones, by indenture bearing even date herewith, hath granted, bargained and sold unto the above-named William Burns, a certain messuage or piece of land, situate, &c., [*describe the premises as in the deed,*] with the appurtenances. And whereas the piece of land is subject to the lien of a judgment in favour of Daniel Stone, against the said John Jones, in the Court of Common Pleas of Union County, for two hundred dollars besides interest and costs: if, therefore, the said John Jones do and shall, on or before the first day of May, one thousand eight hundred and forty-five, pay and satisfy the said judgment, interest and cost in full, and procure such satisfaction to be entered of record in said court, and do and shall from time to time, and at all times hereafter, well and sufficiently save, keep harmless and indemnify the said William Burns, his heirs, executors, administrators, of and from the said judgment, and of and from all actions, suits, payments, costs, charges and damages, for or by reason thereof, then this obligation to be void, or otherwise to be and remain in full force and virtue.

Conditional part of a Bond to indemnify Indorsers.

The condition of this obligation is such, that whereas the said William Burns and Daniel Stone, at the special instance and request of the above-bound John Jones, did indorse for the said John Jones, a certain promissory note dated the tenth day of May, 1844, for the payment of six hundred dollars, payable at the Exchange Bank in the city of Pittsburgh, ninety days after date; also, one other note dated the twenty-second day of May, 1844, for the payment of five hundred dollars, payable at the Exchange Bank in the city of Pittsburgh, ninety days after date thereof, both which said notes were indorsed by them for the accommodation of the said John Jones. If, therefore, the said John Jones shall and do from time to time, and at all times hereafter, well and sufficiently save, defend, keep harmless and indemnify the said William Burns and Daniel Stone, their heirs, executors, administrators, and their goods and chattels, lands and tenements, of and from the said liabilities as indorsers, as aforesaid, or for the removal of the said notes by indorsing other paper for that purpose, for the said John Jones, and of and from all actions, suits, payments, costs, charges and damages, for or by reason thereof, then this obligation to be void, or else to be and remain in full force and virtue.

Conditional part of a Bond for payment of Money after a person's death.

The condition of the above-written obligation is such, that if the above-bound John Jones, his heirs, executors or administrators, do and shall well and truly pay, or cause to be paid, unto the above-named William Burns, his executors, administrators or assigns, the sum of one thousand dollars, within the space of six months next after the decease of Charles Doe, otherwise to remain in full force and virtue.

Conditional part of a Bond of Indemnity by an Executor who retains Money in his hands directed by the Will to be put out at Interest.

Whereas A. A., late of ——, late husband of the above-named B. A., by his last will and testament in writing, bearing date on or about the —— day of ——, did, amongst divers other pecuniary legacies, give unto the said B. A., and to the above-bounden G. F. (by the description, &c.) and to the survivors of them, and to the executors and administrators of such survivor, the sum of —— dollars, upon trust, to place the same out in bank stock, and to pay and apply the interest and process thereof, for and towards the maintenance and education of all and every the children of his niece S. F. by her said husband, J. F., in such shares and proportions as his said niece should direct, until her said children should attain their respective ages of twenty-one years; and then in trust to pay to the said children, and to the survivor or survivors of them, the said sum of —— dollars, or the produce thereof, at their respective ages of twenty-one years, equally between them, share and share alike; and of his said will, did constitute and appoint his said wife, B., and his nephew-in-law J. F., executrix and executor, as by the said will duly proved in the register's office of the county of ——, relation being thereunto had, will appear: and whereas the said S. F. had, at the time the testator made his said will, and still hath five children living by her said husband, J. F.; that is to say, A., B., C., D., and E., all still under age: and whereas the said J. F. and S. L. have requested the said J. F. to retain in his hands, out of the said testator's estate, the said legacy of —— dollars, so given to them, the said B. A. and J. F. as aforesaid, until they shall severally become entitled to receive their proportions of the same, which the said B. A. hath agreed to, or the said J. F. and S. L. indemnifying her therein, (as hereinafter is mentioned;) now the condition of this obligation is such, that if the above-bounden J. F., his heirs, executors or administrators, do and shall well and truly pay, or cause to be paid, unto the said A., B., C., D. and E., children of the said J. F., by the said J. F., or to the survivor or survivors of them, the said legacy or sum of —— dollars, so given to the said B. A. and J. F., by the recited will, in trust for them as aforesaid, when and as they shall respectively attain the age of twenty-one years, in the proportions and according to the directions of the said recited will, and do and shall, from time to time, and at all times hereafter, well and sufficiently save harmless, and keep indemnified, the said B. A., her heirs, executors and administrators, and her and their goods and chattels, lands and tenements, of, from, and against all losses, costs, charges, damages and expenses which she or they shall or may bear, pay, sustain, or be put unto, for or by reason or means of the said legacy or sum of —— dollars, not being placed out upon bank stock, according to the directions contained in the said recited will, or for or by reason or means of any other matter, cause, or thing whatsoever relating to the said legacy;. then, &c.

Bond of a Constable, for faithful Performance, &c.

Know all men, &c., That we are held and firmly bound unto the Commonwealth of Pennsylvania, in the sum of, &c. &c.

Whereas the above-bounden A. B. has been duly elected and returned to the Court of Quarter Sessions of the Peace of the County of ——, as constable of the township of —— in the said county for the ensuing year, which election has been approved and confirmed by the said court.

Now the condition of this obligation is such, that if the said A. B. shall and do, from time to time, and at all times during his continuance in office, justly and faithfully discharge the duties appertaining to the office of constable, according to law, then this obligation to be void, otherwise to be and remain in full force and virtue.

Conditional part of a Bond, to leave Money to a Wife.

Whereas a marriage is intended shortly to be had and solemnized between the above-bounden J. C. and H. B., (the mother of the above-named G. B. and S. B.;) now the condition of the above obligation is such, that if (after the said intended marriage) the said H. shall happen to survive the said J., her intended husband, then, and in such case, if the heirs, executors or administrators of him, the said J., shall and do, within the space of six months next after his decease, well and truly pay, or cause to be paid unto her, the said H., or her assigns, the sum of one thousand dollars, to and for her own proper use and benefit, and to be at her own free and absolute disposal, without any manner of account to be given by her for or concerning the same, then the obligation to be void and of none effect, or else to remain in full force and virtue.

Conditional part of a Bond to indemnify lessee on payment of Rent.

The condition of this obligation is such, that whereas the above-named A. B., by indenture of lease, bearing date the —— day of ——, hath demised and to farm let unto the said C. D., all that messuage, &c. To hold the same to the said C. D. for the term of —— years paying —— (as in the lease) as in and by the said indenture appears. And whereas a certain E. F. claims title to the premises aforesaid, with the appurtenances, if, therefore, the said A. B. shall and do from time to time indemnify the said C. D., his heirs, executors and administrators, and his and their goods and chattels, lands and tenements, of and from all actions, suits, payments, costs, charges and damages for or by reason thereof; then, &c.

Conditional part of a Bond for payment of an Annuity during the life of a Feme Covert.

Whereas the above-named A. A. hath contracted and agreed with the above-bounden H. H. for the purchase of a clear annuity or yearly sum of ——, payable to him, the said A. A., his executors, administrators or assigns, during the life of M. M., the wife of T. M., of ——, at or for the price or sum of ——, which said sum of, the said A. A. hath advanced and paid to the said H. H., at or before the sealing and delivery of the above obligation, the receipt whereof the said H. H. doth hereby acknowledge, and thereof, and of and from every part thereof, doth acquit, exonerate, release and forever discharge the said A. A., his heirs, executors and administrators, and every of them by these presents: The condition of this is such, that if the said H. H., his heirs, executors or administrators, do and shall well and truly pay, or cause to be paid, unto the said A. A., his executors, administrators or assigns, the annuity or clear yearly sum of —— dollars, by half yearly payments on the —— day of ——, and the —— day of ——, in every year during the life of the said M. M., by yearly portions, clear of all deductions on any account or pretence whatsoever; the first half yearly payment thereof to be made on the —— day of —— next, and also a proportionable part of the said annuity, or clear yearly payment of —— for or in respect of so many days as shall have elapsed from the last half yearly day of payment next preceding the decease of the said M. M., up to the day of her death; then the said obligation to be void. But if default shall be made of, or in payment of the said annuity or clear yearly sum of ——, or any part thereof, at the days or times aforesaid, or any of them, then the said obligation to be and remain in full force, virtue, and effect.

Conditional part of a Bond of Indemnity, on paying Money to a Person who had not taken out Letters of Administration.

Whereas the above-named —— stands indebted to the estate of C. B., of ——, deceased, in the sum of —— dollars: And whereas the said C. B. was at the time of his death indebted to E. W., by bond in the sum of —— dollars, principal money, with a great arrear of interest for the same; and whereas the said C. B. made his last will and testament in writing, and thereof appointed the said E. W. sole executor, who, in compassion to the above-bound B. B., the widow and relict of the said C. B., she being left in indigent circumstances with seven children, hath given up to her the said bond for her own benefit, but declines proving the said will: And whereas the principal money and interest due on the said bond, are more than the effects of the said C. B. amount to, and the above-bound A. A. and B. B. have requested the said —— to pay her, the said B. B., the sum of —— dollars, due from them to the estate of her said late husband, without obliging her to take out letters of administration of the goods and chattels of her said late husband with his will annexed, as the same will exhaust great part of the said sum of —— dollars, and there being no other debt or effects of her said late husband to get in, the said —— have agreed to comply with such request on the said A. A. and B. B. indemnifying them for so doing: And whereas the said —— have accordingly on the day of the date hereof, paid the said B. B. the said sum of —— dollars, the receipt whereof she doth hereby acknowledge. Now, therefore, the condition of this obligation is such, that if the said A. A. and B. B., or either of them, their or either of their heirs, executors or administrators, do and shall, from time to time, and at all times hereafter, well and sufficiently save, defend, keep harmless and indemnify the said ——, and their ——, and their goods and chattels, lands and tenements, of, from and against all losses, costs, charges, damages and expenses which they shall or may bear, pass, sustain or be put unto, for or by reason or reasons of their having paid the said B. B., the said sum of —— dollars, and from them to the estate of the said C. B., as aforesaid, or any matter, cause or thing relating thereto, then, &c.

Bond to suffer a Wife to live apart from her Husband.

Know all men, &c. Whereas, J. B., the wife of the above-bounden B. B., doth now live separate and apart from her said husband, and follows the trade or employment of making and selling ——, and the said B. B. hath agreed that his said wife shall have and receive all benefit arising thereby, or of any other trade or business which she shall think fit to follow, to and for her own separate use and support; wherewith he, the said B. B., is not to intermeddle, or have any profit or advantage from; so as she, the said J. B., doth not and shall not contract any debt or debts, whereof, or by means whereof, the person or effects of her said husband, shall or may be sued, charged or incumbered, by any means whatsoever: Now the condition of this obligation is such, that if the said B. B. do and shall, from time to time, during the space of —— years now next ensuing, (if the said J. B. shall so long live,) permit and suffer the said J. B., his wife, to live separate and apart from him, and to have and receive all benefit, profit and advantage arising, or which shall arise by her said trade or business of making and selling ——, or any other trade or business which she shall follow or employ herself in during the said term, to and for her own separate use, support and maintenance, without any account, suit, trouble or molestation whatsoever; and without acting, doing or causing or permitting to be done, any act, matter or thing whatsoever, whereby or wherewith, or by any means or occasion whereof, the said J. B., his wife, shall or may be molested or incumbered by any ways or means whatsoever, and also if the said B. B., his executors or administrators of his or their goods or chattels, lands or tenements, shall, at any time hereafter, during the said term of —— years, be sued, attached, or otherwise charged and incumbered, for or by reason or means of any debt or debts, which his said wife hath or shall, or may contract: then in either of the said cases this obligation to be void, or else to remain in full force and virtue.

Bond to suffer a Wife to live apart, to have all her Effects and to behave quietly to her.

Know all men, &c. Whereas M., the wife of the said R. R., hath for several years last past lived separate and apart from the said R. R., her husband, and hath, during all the said time, maintained and provided for herself and I., the daughter of the said R. R., without any expense to the said R. R., and whereas, it is agreed between the said R. R. and the said M., his wife, that the said M., the wife of the said R. R., shall and may at all times hereafter, live separate and apart from the said R. R., and also that the said M. R. shall and may have, hold and enjoy to her sole and separate use all such moneys, goods and effects as the said M. R. is now possessed of, or shall or may at any time or times hereafter, get or acquire, or which shall be given or bequeathed to her by any person or persons whatsoever, without any hindrance, molestation, or interruption of or by him, the said R. R. And whereas the said R. R. hath also agreed to behave himself peaceably and quietly towards the said M. R., his wife, and the said J. R., his daughter, and not to molest, assault, disturb or do any bodily hurt or injury to them, or either of them: Now the condition of this obligation is such, that if the above-bounden R. R. shall and do, from time to time, and at all times hereafter, during the term of his natural life, permit and suffer the said M. R., his wife, and the said J. R., his daughter, (in case they or either of them shall so long happen to live,) to live separate and apart from the said R. R., without any molestation, disturbance or interruption of or by him, the said R. R., and also if the said R. R., his executors or administrators, shall and do at all times hereafter, permit and suffer the said M. R., his wife, to have, hold, and enjoy to her sole and separate use, all and every the moneys, goods, chattels and effects, whereof the said M. R. is now possessed, and also all and every the moneys, goods, chattels and effects which the said M. R. shall or may at any time or times hereafter get or acquire, or which shall or may be given or bequeathed to the said M. R., by any person or persons whatsoever, without any hindrance, molestation or interruption of or by him the said R. R.; and also, if the said R. R. shall and do, from time to time, and at all times hereafter, demean and behave himself peaceably and quietly towards the said M. R., his wife, and the said J. R., his daughter, and each of them, and shall not, nor in any manner whatsoever, molest, assault, disturb, or do any bodily hurt or injury to the said M. R., his wife, and the said J. R. his daughter, or either of them, then this obligation to be void; but if default shall be made in performance of all or any of the conditions above specified, then this obligation is to remain in full force and virtue.

NOTE.—*These bonds cannot be made to the woman herself, but to some person for her use.*

CASE STATED.

Remarks.

A case stated, is an agreement in writing, between a plaintiff and defendant, that the facts in dispute between them are true as therein stated. The facts being thus agreed upon, it is left for the court to decide for which party is the law.

As no writ of error lies on a judgment rendered on a case stated, it is usual in the agreement to insert a clause, that the case stated shall be considered in the nature of a special verdict, or to agree expressly that either party may sue out a writ of error. See 8 S. & R. 529.

The following will answer as a form for such an agreement.

A. B. vs. C. D. } In the Common Pleas of ——, county of ——. Term A. D. ——. No. ——.

And now, January 6th, A. D. ——, it is hereby agreed by and between the parties to the above suit that the following case be stated for the opinion of the court in the nature of a special verdict. A. B. the plaintiff above named, &c., (*here state the facts agreed upon.*)

If the court be of opinion that ——, then judgment to be entered for the plaintiff, but if not, then judgment to be entered for the defendant. The costs to follow the judgment, and either party reserving the right to sue out a writ of error therein.

A. B.
C. D.

CAVEAT.

Remarks.

A caveat is the name of a notice given by a party having an interest in the same, to some officer not to do an act till the party giving the notice shall have been heard; as a caveat to the Register of Wills, not to permit a will to be proved, or not to grant letters of administration, until the party shall have been heard. A caveat is also sometimes made, to prevent a patent for inventions being issued.

A Caveat against the Probate of a Will.

To Thomas Moorhead, Jr., Esq., Register of Wills for the County of ——, State of Pennsylvania.

I, A. B., one of the heirs (or as the case may be), of C. D., late of the —— of ——, deceased, do hereby caveat and protest against the probate of any last will and testament or instrument in the nature thereof, being or pretending to be the testament and last will of the said C. D., until examination thereof in the proper court, and the decree of the said court be therein pronounced.

Witness my hand this —— day of ——, A. D. ——.

A. B.

Caveat against granting Letters of Administration.

To Thomas Moorhead, Jr., Esq., Register of Wills for the County of ——, State of Pennsylvania.

I, A. B., being interested in the personal estate of C. D., late of the —— of ——, deceased, do hereby caveat and protest against granting letters of administration therein to —— or any other person, until the examination of his or their right thereto before the proper tribunal be had, and the decision of the said tribunal therein be given.

Witness my hand this —— day of —— A. D. ——.

A. B.

CERTIORARI.

Certiorari is the name of a writ issued from a superior court directed to one of inferior jurisdiction, commanding the latter to certify to the former the record in the particular case.

Certiorari to a Justice of the Peace.

The Commonwealth of Pennsylvania to A. B., one of our Justices of the Peace, in and for the county of Crawford, greeting: We being willing, for certain causes, to be certified of a certain plea of ——, between C. D., plaintiff, and E. F., defendant, before you depending, do command you that the plea aforesaid, with all things touching the same, before our judges at Meadville, at our county Court of Common Pleas, there to be held for the county of Crawford, the —— day of May next ensuing. So full and entire, as before you they remain, you certify and send together with this writ, that we may further cause to be done, therefore, that which of right, and according to our laws and constitution, ought.

Witness the Honourable G. C., President Judge of the said court, the —— day of ——, A. D. 1845.

Return of Magistrate to be indorsed on the Writ.

To the honourable, the judges within named, the plea within mentioned, with all things touching the same so fully and entire, as before me they remain, I hereby respectfully certify and send, as within I am commanded, together with the writ.

A. B., *Justice of the Peace.*

COGNOVIT ACTIONEM.

Remarks.

A cognovit is a written confession of an action by a defendant, subscribed but not sealed, and authorizing the plaintiff to sign judgment, and issue execution, usually for a sum named. It is given after the action is brought, in order to save expense. A *cognovit actionem*, is an acknowledgment and confession of the plaintiff's cause of action against the defendant, to be just and true. 3 Ch. Pr. 664. Sometimes the defendant confesses the one part of the plaintiff's alleged claim, and denies the rest.

Cognovit in action of Debt.

A. B. *vs.* C. D } In the Common Pleas of ——, county of ——. Term A. D. ——, No. ——.

I confess the debt in this cause, and that the plaintiff hath sustained damages to the amount of six cents on occasion of the detaining thereof, besides his costs and charges in this behalf to the amount of —— dollars, (or, to be taxed by the prothonotary) and in case I make default in the payment of the said debt, damages and costs aforesaid, on the —— day of —— next, the plaintiff shall be at liberty to enter up judgment for the said debt (or sum of —— dollars) and costs as aforesaid; and also the costs of entering up such judgment and of suing out execution therefor, and shall be at liberty thereupon forthwith to issue execution for the same.

And I do hereby agree to withdraw the pleas pleaded by me (if the defendant have pleaded) and undertake not to appeal or bring any writ of error, or do any other matter or thing whereof the plaintiff may be delayed in entering up his judgment, and bring out execution upon default made as aforesaid. Dated this —— day of ——, A. D. ——.

Cognovit in Assumpsit.

A. B. *vs.* C. D. } In the Common Pleas of ——, county of ——. Term A. D. ——, No. ——.

I confess this action, and that the plaintiff hath sustained damages to the amount of —— dollars, besides his costs and charges, in his behalf, to be taxed by the prothonotary. And in case I shall make default in the payment of the sum of —— dollars (being the debt in this action), together with the said costs on the —— day of —— next, the plaintiff shall be at liberty to enter up judgment for the said sum of —— dollars and costs as aforesaid, and sue out execution thereon for the same, together with the amount of official fees, sheriff's poundage, costs of levying, and all other incidental expenses.

And I do hereby agree to withdraw the plea by me pleaded to this action, and undertake not to bring any writ of error in this cause, or do any other matter or thing whereby the plaintiff may be delayed in entering judgment, and suing out execution upon default made as aforesaid.

Witness my hand this —— day of ——, A. D. ——.

NOTE.—If the cognovit be but for part of the plaintiff's claim, say:

I confess that I owe to the above-mentioned plaintiff —— dollars, parcel of the debt by him in his declaration in this action demanded. And that he hath, &c., &c.

COMMISSION.

If a party wishes to procure the testimony of witnesses beyond the limits of the state, a rule must be taken upon interrogatories filed, and a commission for that purpose issued. Some variation exists in the rules of court, in the several judicial districts of this Commonwealth, but the following will answer for some of them, and others can change to suit their practice. Any competent person may be appointed commissioner.

Caption to Interrogatories on a Commission.

John Doe *vs.* Richard Roe. } In the Common Pleas of Chester County, of May Term, A. D. 1844. No. 12.

Interrogatories to be exhibited, John Jones and William Burns, witnesses to be produced, sworn or affirmed, and examined, on the part of the plaintiff, [or defendant, as the case may be,] in the above cause, before commissioners to be named in a commission to be issued out of the said court to the —— of ——.

Interrogatory first.—Do you know the parties above named, or either, or which of them?

Interrogatory second.—And so on.

At the foot say: Commissioner on the behalf of the plaintiff, [or defendant, as the case may be,] John Jay, Esq., of the —— of ——, in the state of ——.

Caption to Cross Interrogatories to the same.

Cross interrogatories to be exhibited to John Jones and William Burns, witnesses to be produced, sworn or affirmed, and examined on the part of the plaintiff, [or defendant, as the case may be,] in the above cause, before commissioners to be named in a commission to be issued of the said court to the state of ——.

Cross interrogatory first.—Do you know, &c.

Cross interrogatory second, &c. &c.

Commissioner on behalf of the defendant [or plaintiff] above named, John Lyttle, Esq., of the —— of ——, in the state of ——.

Rule for a Commission.

John Doe vs Richard Roe. } In the Common Pleas of Chester County, of May Term, 1845. No. 12.

Enter rule in the above case, on behalf of the —— for commission to ——, of —— on —— days' notice.

A. B., Attorney for ——.

To W. K., Prothonotary of Chester County. }

Commission to examine Witnesses.

—— *County, ss.* The Commonwealth of Pennsylvania to ——, greeting:

Know ye that in confidence of your prudence and fidelity we have appointed you, and by these presents do give unto you (or any two or three of you, as the case may be), full power and authority in pursuance of an order made in our county court of Common Pleas in and for the county of Chester, in a certain cause there depending, where A. B. is plaintiff, and C. D. is defendant, to call before you (or any two of you) so that there be one on the part of the plaintiff, and one on the part of the defendant, at a certain day and place by you for that purpose to be appointed, all and every person and persons who may be named to you (if mutual say) as well on the part of the plaintiff as on the part of the defendant, or either of them; (if exparte say) or the part of the said —— against the said ——, as witnesses in the said cause.

And there and then to examine each of the said witnesses on their oaths, or affirmations, touching the premises, and reduce their testimony to writing. And when you shall have so done, you are to send the same before us in our county court of Common Pleas aforesaid, together with the interrogations, and the answers thereunto under the hands and seals (or of two or three as the case may be). In testimony whereof, we have caused the seal of our court to be hereunto affixed.

Witness the Hon. J. P., President Judge of the said court, the —— day of ——, A. D. ——.

After the commission is issued, the following are suitable instructions to the commissioner or commissioners for taking said depositions.

Justices of the Peace are also empowered to issue commissions to take depositions to be read in causes depending before them.

Letter of Instruction to Commissioners.

WESTCHESTER, January 20, 1845.

SIR:—

Herewith you will receive a commission issued by the Court of Common Pleas of Chester county, authorizing you to examine witnesses in a certain cause depending in the said court, wherein A. B. is plaintiff, and C. D. defendant, upon the interrogatories annexed to the commission, and for your guidance you will carefully pursue the following instructions.

All the commissioners [if there be more than one], named in the commission, shall have notice of the time and place of executing it. And if any of them do not act, let the fact that they were notified, or could not be notified, and the reason of their not acting, be stated. Having agreed upon the time and place of meeting, you will proceed to execute the commission in the following manner:

I. The acting commissioner will examine the witnesses separately, after publicly administering to them the following oath or affirmation:

"You do swear, by Almighty God, the searcher of all hearts, that the answers which shall be given by you to the interrogatories proposed to you, shall be the truth, the whole truth, and nothing but the truth, and that as you shall answer to God at the great day."

The oath shall be administered by the witness holding up his right hand, or laying his hand upon and kissing the Gospels.

Or if the witness shall declare that he has conscientious scruples against taking an oath, or swearing in any form, he shall be permitted to make his affirmation in the following form: "You do solemnly, sincerely and truly declare and affirm, that, &c.," omitting the words, "and that as you shall answer to God at the great day," and instead say, "and this you affirm."

II. The general style and title of the depositions must be drawn up in the following manner.

"Depositions of witnesses produced, sworn [or affirmed] and examined, on the —— day of ——, in the year of our Lord one thousand eight hundred and forty-four, at the house of J. S., the commissioner, in the —— of ——, in the county of —— and state of ——, by virtue of a commission issuing out from the Court of Common Pleas of the county of Chester, in the state of Pennsylvania, to the said J. S. directed, for the examination of witnesses in a certain cause depending in said court, wherein A. B. is plaintiff, and C. D. is defendant."

"N. O., of the —— of ——, merchant, aged —— years, or thereabouts, being produced, sworn [or affirmed] and examined, on behalf of the plaintiff A. B., [or defendant, as the case may be,] deposeth as follows:"

"1. To the first interrogatory on the part of the said plaintiff, he answers as follows:" [here insert the witness's answer.]

"2. To the second interrogatory on the part of the said plaintiff, he answers as follows:" and so on throughout.

III. If there be cross-interrogatories, go on thus:

"1. To the first cross-interrogatory on the part of the defendant, he answers as follows:" and so on throughout.

All the interrogatories and cross-interrogatories in the commission must be put to the witness, and his answer written out. If he cannot answer, let him say, *he knoweth not.*

IV. When the witness has finished his deposition, let him subscribe his name at the bottom of each page, and the acting commissioner will certify as follows:

Examination taken, reduced to writing, and by the witness subscribed and sworn to, this —— day of ——, 1844.
J. S., *Commissioner.*

V. If any papers or exhibits are produced and proved, they must be annexed to the depositions in which they are referred to, and endorsed by the acting commissioner in this manner:

"At the execution of a commission for the examination of witnesses between A. B. plaintiff, and C. D. defendant, this paper writing was produced and shown to N. O., and by him deposed unto at the time of his examination, and is the document referred to by him as the paper marked B. before

"J. S., *Commissioner.*"

VI. The acting commissioner will sign his name at the bottom of each page of the depositions and exhibits.

VII. If an interpreter is employed, the commissioner will administer to him the following oath:

"You do swear, by almighty God, the searcher of all hearts, that you will truly and faithfully interpret the oath and interrogatories to be administered to N. O., a witness now to be examined, out of the English language into the —— language, and that you will truly and faithfully interpret the answers of the said N. O. thereto, out of the —— language into the English language, and that as you shall answer to God at the great day."

Let the deposition be subscribed by the interpreter as well as the witness, and certified by the commissioner as follows:

Examination taken, reduced to writing, subscribed by the witness, and by the sworn interpreter, and sworn to by the witness, this —— day of —— 1844, before
J. S., *Commissioner.*

VIII. Having in this manner examined all the witnesses produced, you will please fasten the depositions and exhibits to the commission, passing some tape through and connecting the whole; and you will then make the following endorsement upon the commission; the execution of this appears in a certain schedule hereunto annexed; to which you will subscribe your name.

Thus prepared and executed, the whole must be folded and enclosed in an envelop, sealed with your seal; you will then write your name across or by the side of the seals, and address the whole thus: "To G. H., Esquire, Prothonotary of Chester County, Westchester, Pennsylvania, care of M. R." Or if issued from a Justice's court, thus: "To R. P., Esquire, Justice of the Peace, Westchester, Chester County, Pennsylvania."

IX. When the commission is thus executed, made up and directed, it must be returned in the manner specified in the direction on the commission, if there be any.

If there be no direction on the commission specifying the manner in which it is to be returned, then it must either be delivered to the court by the commissioner personally, or else be forwarded by some person coming to this place, or else placed in the nearest post-office.

In case of returning the commission by mail, it is to be deposited by the commissioner in the nearest post-office, he making the following endorsement thereon.

"Deposited in the post-office at —— this —— day of ——, 1844, by me." J. S., *Commissioner.*

Interrogatories to Garnishee in Foreign Attachment.

A. B. *vs.* C. D., garnisheee of E. F.	In the court of Common Pleas of ——, county of ——. Term, 18—. No. ——. Scire facias to garnishee.

Interrogatories to G. H., the garnishee above named.

First.—Do you know C. D., of whom you are the garnishee in a foreign attachment, issued at the suit of the above-named plaintiff?

Second.—Have you had any commercial or other transactions with the said C. D.? If yea, what was the state of your accounts with the said C. D. on the —— day of ——, A. D. ——? Annex a copy of each account to your answer hereto.

Third.—Was there or was there not a balance in your hands in favour of the said C. D., on the —— day of ——, A. D. ——, or at any time since, up to the time of your answering these interrogatories? If yea, state the amount particularly.

Fourth.—Had you in your possession any goods or merchandize, money or effects of any nature whatever, belonging to the said C. D., on the —— day of ——, A. D. ——, or at any time since? If yea, state the nature, quantity and value of said goods and merchandize.

Fifth.—Were you not on the —— day of —— indebted to the said C. D. in some (and in what) way, and in what amount, or have you not since (and where and how) became so indebted?

Interrogatories to Witness in proceedings for Divorce.

A. B. by her next friend, C. D. *vs.* E. F.	}	In the Common Pleas of —— county, of —— Term, A. D. 18—. No. ——.

Interrogatories to be exhibited to witnesses who may be produced, sworn (or affirmed) and examined on the part of the libellant in the above case.

First.—Do you know the parties, libellant and respondent above-named, or either of them? and how long have you known them, and when, and where, and which of them?

Second.—Were you present at their marriage? If so, when, where and by whom were they married? Have or have not the respondent and the libellant lived and cohabited together as man and wife? State your knowledge herein fully, circumstantially, and at large.

Third.—Do you or do you not know whether the said respondent, C. D., has wilfully and maliciously deserted and absented himself from the habitation of the said libellant, A. B., without any, or if any, what reasonable cause? If aye, whether such desertion has been persisted in by the said respondent for the space of two years or more, or for any other and for what time, and whether the respondent still continues to persist therein? *If the charge be ill-treatment say*, Whether the said respondent, C. D., has or has not by cruel and barbarous treatment endangered the life of the said libellant, A. B., and has he or has he not offered such indignities to her person as to render her condition intolerable and her life burdensome, and thereby forced her to withdraw herself from his house and family? *If the charge be adultery say*, Whether or no the respondent above-named has committed adultery? If so, when, where, and with whom? State the circumstances fully and at large.

Fourth.—Do you know any thing further favourable to the libellant? If so, state the same fully, as if you had been thereto particularly interrogated.

COMPOSITION.

Composition in contracts, means an agreement made upon a sufficient consideration, between a debtor and creditor, by which the creditor accepts a part of the debt due to him, in satisfaction of the whole. Montagu on Com. 1; 3 Co. 118; 1 Str. 426, &c.

General form of Composition with Creditors.

To all to whom these presents shall come, we whose names are here under written and seals affixed, creditors of A. B., of ——, send greeting: Whereas the said A. B. doth justly owe and is indebted unto us his said several creditors, in divers sums of money; but by reason of many losses, great hindrances, and other damages happened unto the said A. B., he is become utterly unable to pay and satisfy us our full debts, with such goods, wares and merchandizes as he hath, which we, the said creditors, are unwilling to accept of, or any ways to intermeddle with the same; and, therefore, we, the said creditors, have resolved and agreed to undergo a certain loss, and to accept of ten cents for every dollar owing by the said A. B. to us, the several and respective creditors aforesaid, to be paid in full satisfaction and discharge of our several and respective debts: Now know ye, that we, the said creditors of the said A. B., do for ourselves severally and respectively, and for our several and respective heirs, executors and administrators, covenant, promise, compound and agree, to and with the said A. B., his executors and administrators, and to and with every of them by these presents, that we, the said several and respective executors administrators and assigns, shall and will accept, receive and take of and from the said A. B., his executors and administrators, for each and every dollar that the said A. B. doth owe and is indebted to us, the said several and respective creditors, the sum of ten cents, in full discharge and satisfaction of the several debts and sums of money that the said A. B. doth owe and stands indebted unto us, the said creditors respectively; so that the said sum of ten cents to be paid for each and every dollar that the said A. B. doth owe and standeth indebted unto us the said several and respective creditors, be paid unto us, the said several and respective creditors, our several and respective executors, administrators or assigns, within the time or space of six months next after the date of these presents: And we, the said several and respective creditors, do severally and respectively, for ourselves, our several and respective heirs, executors, administrators and assigns, covenant, grant, promise and agree, to and with the said A. B., his executors and administrators, that he, the said A. B., his executors, administrators and assigns, shall and may, from time to time, and at all times within the said term or space of six months next ensuing the date hereof, assign, sell, or otherwise dispose of his said goods and chattels, wares and merchandizes, at his and their own free will and pleasure, for and towards the payment and satisfaction of the said ten cents for every dollar the said A. B. doth owe and is indebted as aforesaid, unto us, the said respective creditors: And that neither we, the said several and respective creditors, or any of us, nor the executors, administrators, or assigns of us, or any of us, shall or will, at any time or times hereafter, sue, arrest, molest, trouble, imprison, attach or condemn the said A. B., his executors or administrators, or his or their goods and chattels, for any debt or other thing now due and owing to us, or any of us, his respective creditors aforesaid, so as the said A. B., his executors or administrators, do well and truly pay, or cause to be paid unto us, his said several and respective creditors, the said sum of ten cents for every dollar he doth owe and standeth indebted unto us respectively within the said time or space of six months next ensuing the date hereof. In witness whereof, the parties to these presents have hereunto set their hands and seals, the tenth day of December, A. D. one thousand eight hundred and forty-four.

A. B. 

C. D. 

E. F. 

G. H. 

A Deed of Composition of Debts by Partners.

To all to whom these presents shall come; we whose names and seals are hereunto subscribed and set, creditors of R. C. and C. R., of Harrisburg, send greeting:

Whereas the said R. C. and C. are, and do stand jointly indebted unto us, the said creditors, in divers sums of money, which they are willing to satisfy and pay as far as they are able: Now know ye, that we, the said creditors who have hereto subscribed our names and affixed our seals, finding that the said R. C. and C. R. are by losses and otherwise disabled to pay our full debts, do severally and respectively agree, and bind ourselves, our heirs, executors and administrators unto the said R. C. and C. R. by these presents, to accept and take of them, the said R. C. and C. R., their executors or administrators, after the proportion or rate of —— cents in the dollar, in full satisfaction of all such debts and sums of money as they jointly owe to us and every of us respectively, the same to be paid at four equal payments on the days following, that is to say, the —— day of ——, &c, so as the said R. C. and C. R. (for the more sure and better payment of the several sums of money aforesaid, in recompense and satisfaction of our and every of our said several debts as aforesaid), their executors or administrators, do before the —— day of —— become jointly and severally bound, with sufficient sureties unto us and every of us respectively by obligation in due form of law to be made, sealed and delivered to each and every of us, and to each and every of our use and uses, by the appointment of us, and each of us.

Provided, always, that neither these presents nor any thing herein contained, shall bind us, any or either of us, who have hereunto subscribed our names and put our seals, unless all and every of the creditors aforesaid shall have sealed and executed the same ——, on or before the —— day of —— next ensuing. In witness, &c.

CONDITIONS OF SALE.

Conditions of sale, are the terms upon which the vendor of property by auction, proposes to sell it; the instrument containing these terms, when reduced to writing or printing, is also called the conditions of sale.

It is always prudent and advisable, that the conditions of sale should be printed and put up in a conspicuous part of the auction room. When the terms are fully exposed, they are binding on both parties, and nothing that was said at the time of sale, to add to or to vary such printed conditions, will be of any avail. 1 H. Bl. 289; 12 East, 6; 6 Ves. 330; 15 Ves. 521. Babington on Auctions, 233 to 243.

Conditions of Sale of Lands.

The conditions of the present sale of the property of A. B. in the township of Franklin, and county of Erie, are as follows, to wit:

1. That the highest bidder shall be declared the purchaser, and if dispute shall arise between two or more bidders, the estate shall be immediately put up again.

2. That no person shall advance at any one bidding, less than —— dollars, or retract his or her bidding.

3. That the purchaser shall pay immediately after the sale, to the seller, [or auctioneer, as the case may be,] a deposit of —— dollars, in part of the purchase-money, and sign an agreement for the payment of the remainder, on or before the —— day of ——, 1845, upon having a good title made to him.

4. The purchaser shall have a proper conveyance, at his own expense, on payment of the remainder of the purchase-money, and possession will be given on completion of the purchase, [of such part as is in hand,] and the purchaser will be entitled to the rents and profits, from the —— day of ——, A. D. ——. But if, from any cause, the remainder of the purchase-money shall not be paid on the —— day of ——, the purchaser shall pay interest for the same, at the rate of six per cent. per annum, from that day to the day of payment; but, nevertheless, this stipulation to be without prejudice to the vendor's right to insist on the performance of this condition.

5. That all attested copies of deeds that shall be required by the purchaser, shall be prepared at his own expense.

Lastly. Upon failure of complying with the above conditions, the money deposited shall, at the expiration of the time before limited, become forfeited to the vendor, who then shall be at full liberty, with or without notice, to resell the estate; and if on such resale, there should be any deficiency, the purchaser at this sale neglecting to comply with these conditions, shall make good such deficiency to the vendor, and all expenses attending such resale. [Add, if thought needful: "But in case the vendor cannot make out a good title, the deposit money shall be returned by the vendor to the purchaser, with interest for the same, from the day of payment, to the day of repayment thereof."]

Agreement following Conditions.

It is hereby declared and agreed, by and between A. B., the vendor of the estate mentioned in the above conditions, and C. D., the purchaser, that the said C. D. has become the purchaser of the premises so sold, at the sum of ——, and that the sum of —— has been paid down by the said C. D. to the said A. B. by way of deposit, and in part of the said purchase-money. And that the said conditions of sale shall be taken as the terms of agreement for the said sale and purchase, respectively, and be observed and fulfilled by the said A. B. and C. D. respectively, in all things. As witness their hands, this tenth day of December, A. D. 1844.

A. B., *Vendor.*
C. D., *Purchaser.*

Witnesses,
E. F.
G. H.

Receipt at the foot of Conditions.

Received of C. D. of, &c., being the purchaser of the premises mentioned in the foregoing conditions, the sum of —— dollars, as the deposit, and in part of the purchase-money for the said premises, subject to the conditions of sale, before stated. Witness my hand, &c.

Form of a Vendue Article.

The conditions of the present sale, held at Strasburg in the county of Lancaster, are as follows, to wit:

1. The highest and best bidder shall be deemed the purchaser.
2. All purchases, taken singly, which do not amount to — dollars, to be cash.
3. One or more purchases, which amount to —— dollars each, and upwards, shall be entitled to —— days' credit, provided notes, with approved security, be given for the amount thereof.
4. No cash goods to be removed, until first paid for.
5. No goods, which entitle the purchaser to credit, can be removed, until notes, as aforesaid, be first given.
6. Any person or persons purchasing goods at the present sale, who do not comply with these conditions, must give up the goods before the sale is over, and stand gainer or loser (as the case may be) on exposing them to sale a second time.

Given under my hand, this tenth day of December, A. D. 1844.

A. B.

Another.

The conditions of sale of certain goods, sold by Public Vendue, by the subscriber, executor of the estate of C. D. deceased, are as follows, to wit:

1. The highest and best bidder shall be deemed the purchaser.
2. Any person buying an article or articles, at the present Vendue, to the amount of —— dollars, and upwards, shall be entitled to —— days' credit, by giving a note, with approved security (if required) for the amount, before the goods be removed.
3. All purchases, taken collectively, which do not amount to —— dollars, must be paid for before the removal of the goods.
4. Any person or persons who may purchase goods at the present sale, must either keep the goods, subject to the above restric-

tions, or return them before the sale is adjourned, and be gainer or loser by a second sale, (as the case may be).

Given under my hand, this tenth day of December, A. D. 1844.

A. B.

DEEDS.

Remarks.

Several things are essential to a deed, viz: Writing on paper or parchment; signing and sealing, and delivery.

A written or printed seal is good in Pennsylvania. It is also required, that in every deed there be persons able to contract and be contracted with, for the purpose intended by the deed; and also, a thing or subject-matter to be contracted for; all of which must be expressed by sufficient names and terms. The consideration may be either a *good* or a *valuable* one. A *good* consideration is such as that of blood, or natural love and affection, as when a man grants an estate to a near relation; being founded on motives of generosity, prudence or natural duty.

A *valuable* consideration is such as money, marriage or the like, which the law esteems an equivalent given for the grant, and is therefore founded in motives of justice. Deeds made upon good consideration only, are considered as merely voluntary, and are frequently set aside in favour of creditors and *bona fide* purchasers. 2d vol. Blackstone, chap. 20, p. 297.

When a deed has been acknowledged before a magistrate, appointed by law to take and certify the acknowledgment, in order that the deed may be recorded, the parties have no right to make the most trifling alteration. Moore *vs.* Brickham et al., 4 Binn. 1.

If a deed be altered after delivery, the alteration destroys the deed as to the party who altered it, but does not destroy the estate. If it contains covenants, the party altering it loses all remedy upon them, but the title is not divested. Withers *vs.* Atkinson, 1 Watts, 236.

All writings, sealed and delivered, are in law deeds; but in common acceptation, a deed is a conveyance of land.

If the grantor have a wife, she must sign and acknowledge the deed, in accordance with that kind of acknowledgment inserted for husband and wife; otherwise she may, after the death of her husband, claim her dower, or the use of one-third, during her natural life. An interlineation, if made after the execution of the deed, will avoid it, though in an immaterial point; nor is it presumed to have been made before; the presumption is the contrary, unless otherwise proved. Morris *vs.* Vanderen, 1 Dal. 67. Prevost *vs.* Gratz, 1 P. C. C. 369.

If a deed should be interlined, or a word erased, let a note be made of it, and witnessed by the witnesses. For which see "attestation."

Common Form of a Deed.

* This indenture, made the first day of January, in the year of our Lord one thousand eight hundred and forty-five, between John Jones, of the city of Pittsburgh, in the state of Pennsylvania, iron-monger, and Mary his wife, of the one part, and William Burns, of Birmingham, in the county of Allegheny, and state aforesaid, of the other part. † Witnesseth, that the said John Jones and Mary, his wife, for and in consideration of the sum of six hundred dollars, to them in hand paid by the said William Burns, at and before the ensealing and delivering hereof, the receipt whereof they do hereby acknowledge, and thereof acquit and forever discharge the said William Burns, his heirs, executors and administrators, have granted, bargained, sold, aliened, released and confirmed, and by these presents, do grant, bargain, sell, alien, release and confirm unto the said William Burns, and to his heirs and assigns, all that certain messuage or tenement and tract of land, situated in Fayette township, in the county of Allegheny and state aforesaid, bounded as follows, viz: Beginning at a birch, thence by land of Samuel Stone, south one hundred perches to a beech, thence by land of Thomas Brown, east eighty perches to a post, thence by land of same, north one hundred perches to a sugar-tree, thence by land of Charles Dean, west eighty perches to the place of beginning, containing fifty acres, neat measure. ‡ It being the same premises, [or part of the same] which Richard Rice, and Mary his wife, by Indenture bearing date the tenth day of June, A. D. one thousand eight hundred and thirty-two, for the consideration therein mentioned, did grant and confirm unto the said John Jones (party hereto), his heirs and assigns forever; as in and by the said in part recited indenture, recorded in the office for recording of deeds, at Pittsburgh, in and for the county of Allegheny, in Deed Book M., vol. 2, page 341, &c., relation being thereunto had, more fully and at large, appears. [Here may be inserted the whole chain of title, which is not actually required, but desirable.] Together with all and singular, other the houses, out-houses, buildings, barns, stables, ways, woods, waters, water-courses, rights, liberties, privileges, hereditaments and appurtenances, whatsoever thereunto belonging, or in any-wise appertaining, and the reversions and remainders, rents, issues and profits thereof; and also, all the estate, right, title, interest, property, claim and demand whatsoever, of them, the said John Jones, and Mary his wife, in law, or equity, or otherwise howsoever, of, in, to, or out of the same.

* This part of the deed is called the *premises*, and may be enlarged if necessary.

† This part is called the *testatum*, which is followed by a description of the estate conveyed.

‡ This is the *recital*, containing a general exposition of the chain of former titles.

* To have and to hold the said messuage or tenement and tract of fifty acres of land, hereditaments and premises, hereby granted or mentioned, or intended so to be, with the appurtenances, unto the said William Burns, his heirs and assigns, to the only proper use and behoof of the said William Burns, his heirs and assigns forever. † And the said John Jones, and Mary his wife, for themselves, their heirs, executors and administrators, do covenant, promise, grant and agree, to and with the said William Burns, his heirs and assigns, by these presents, that they, the said John Jones, and Mary his wife, and their heirs, the said above-mentioned and described messuage or tenement, and tract or piece of land, hereditaments and premises, hereby granted, or mentioned, or intended so to be, with the appurtenances, unto the said William Burns, his heirs and assigns, against him, the said John Jones and his heirs, and against all and every other person and persons whomsoever, lawfully claiming or to claim the same or any part or parcel thereof, [‡ by, from or under them, or any of them,] shall and will warrant and forever defend, by these presents.

In witness whereof, the said parties to these presents have hereunto set their hands and seals, dated the day and year first above written.

Signed, sealed and delivered }
in presence of }

James Bond.

JOHN JONES.

MARY JONES.

Allegheny County, *ss.*

Before me, the subscriber, one of the Justices of the Peace in and for the said county, personally came the above-named John Jones and Mary his wife, who in due form of law acknowledged the above indenture to be their act and deed, and desired that the same might be recorded as such. The said Mary, being of full age, and by me duly examined separate and apart from her said husband, and the contents of the foregoing indenture being first made fully known to her, declared that she did voluntarily, and of her own free will and accord, seal, and as her act and deed,

* This is called the *habendum*, which defines the limits of the estate.

† This part is called the warranty, and may be varied in its form and extent.

‡ This, leaving out the words in brackets, is a *general warranty*, and the words included in brackets, if retained, makes it a *special warranty*.

deliver, the same without any coercion or compulsion of her said husband. In testimony whereof, I have hereunto set my hand and seal, this first day of January, A. D. one thousand eight hundred and forty-five.

JAMES BOND.

Deed with full Covenants.

This indenture, made the tenth day of January, in the year of our Lord one thousand eight hundred and forty-five, between John Jones, of Concord, in the county of Erie and state of Pennsylvania, of the one part, and William Burns, of the same place, of the other part; Witnesseth, that the said John Jones, for and in consideration of the sum of five hundred dollars, lawful money of the United States, to him in hand paid by the said William Burns, at and before the ensealing and delivering hereof, the receipt whereof he doth hereby acknowledge, and thereof acquit and forever discharge the said William Burns, his heirs, executors and administrators, by these presents, have granted, bargained, sold, aliened, released and confirmed, and by these presents doth grant, bargain, sell, alien, release and confirm, unto the said William Burns, and to his heirs and assigns, all that certain messuage or tenement, and tract of land situate, &c., [*here describe the premises and recite former titles.*] Together with all and singular the houses, out-houses, buildings, barns, stables, ways, woods, waters, water-courses, rights, liberties, privileges, hereditaments and appurtenances, whatsoever thereunto belonging, or in anywise appertaining, and the reversions and remainders, rents, issues and profits thereof; and also, all the estate, right, title, interest, claim and demand whatsoever of him, the said John Jones, in law or equity, or otherwise howsoever, of, in, to, or out of the same.

To have and to hold the same, with the appurtenances, unto the said William Burns, and to his heirs and assigns, in fee simple forever. And he, the said John Jones, for himself, his heirs, executors and administrators, doth hereby covenant, promise and agree, to and with the said William Burns, and his heirs and assigns, that he, the said John Jones, is now the owner of the said premises, and is seised of a good and indefeasible estate of inheritance therein, and that he hath full right and power to sell and convey the same in fee simple absolute; that the said premises are free and clear of all incumbrances; that the said William Burns, his heirs and assigns, may forever hereafter have, hold, possess and enjoy the same, without any suit, molestation or interruption, by any person whatsoever, lawfully claiming any right therein; and that he, the said John Jones, and all persons hereafter claiming under him, will at any time hereafter, at the request and expense of the said William Burns, his heirs or assigns, make all such further assurances for the more effectual conveying of the said premises, with the appurtenances, as may be reasonably required by him or them: And that he, the said John Jones, and his heirs, will warrant and defend the said premises, with the appurtenances, unto the said William Burns, and his heirs and assigns forever.

In witness whereof, the said party of the first part hath hereunto set his hand and seal, the day and year first above written.

Sealed and delivered in presence of }

JAMES STILES.

JOHN JONES.

Deed by Attorney.

This indenture, made the —— day of ——, in the year of our Lord one thousand eight hundred and forty-five, between Samuel Lewis, of the city of Pittsburgh, and Mary, his wife, of the first part, by James Langdon, their attorney in fact, specially constituted by power of attorney bearing date the —— day of ——, A. D. 1844, and recorded in the office for recording deeds in and for the county of ——, in deed book O, page 244, reference being thereunto had, appears, and John Jones, of the borough of Erie, in the County of Erie and State of Pennsylvania, of the second part, witnesseth, &c., [as in the common form, and conclude as follows.] In witness whereof, the said party of the first part, by James Langdon, their attorney-in-fact, have hereunto set their hands and seals the day and year first above written.

Sealed and delivered in presence of }

JAMES STILES.

SAMUEL LEWIS.

MARY LEWIS.

By their Attorney,
JAMES LANGDON.

A Deed without Covenants.

This indenture, made the tenth day of January, in the year of our Lord one thousand eight hundred and forty-five, between A. B., of, &c., of the first part, and C. D., of, &c., of the second part, Witnesseth, that the said party of the first part, for and in consideration of the sum of fifty dollars, to him in hand paid by the said party of the second part, the receipt whereof is hereby acknowledged, hath bargained and sold, and by these presents doth bargain and sell, unto the said party of the second part, and to his heirs and assigns forever, all, &c. [*Here describe the property.*] Together with all and singular, the hereditaments and appurtenances thereunto belonging, or in any wise appertaining; and the reversion and reversions, remainder and remainders, rents, issues and profits thereof; and also, all the estate, right, title, interest, claim or demand, whatsoever of him, the said party of the first part, either in law or equity, of, in and to, the above bargained premises, and every part and parcel thereof: To have and to hold to the said party of the second part, his heirs and assigns, to the sole and only proper use, benefit and behoof of the said party of the second part, his heirs and assigns forever. In witness, &c.

Quit Claim Deed.

Know all men by these presents, that I, John Jones, of the borough of Reading, in the County of Berks, and State of Pennsylvania, for and in consideration of the sum of one thousand dollars, to me in hand paid, or secured to be paid, by William Burns, of the city of Lancaster, and state aforesaid, the receipt whereof is hereby acknowledged, hath granted, bargained, sold, remised and quit claimed, and by these presents doth grant, bargain, sell, remise and quit claim, unto the said William Burns, and to his heirs and assigns forever, all that, &c. [Here describe the premises.] Together with all and singular the hereditaments and appurtenances thereunto belonging, or in any wise appertaining, and the reversions, remainders, rents, issues and profits thereof; and all the estate, right, title, interest, claim or demand whatsoever, of me, the said John Jones, either in law or equity, of, in and to the above bargained premises:

To have and to hold the same to the said William Burns, and to his heirs and assigns forever. In witness whereof, &c.

Deed by Executors.

This indenture, made the second day of October, in the year of our Lord one thousand eight hundred and forty-four, between Abraham Brown and Charles Davis, of, &c., executors of the last will and testament of Edward Fraley, late of, &c., of the one part, and George Hughes, of, &c., of the other part: Whereas the said Edward Fraley, by virtue of divers good conveyances and assurances in law, duly had and executed, became in his lifetime seised in his demesne as of fee (amongst other lands), of and in a certain messuage or tenement and tract of land, situate in the township of Moyamensing, in the county of Philadelphia aforesaid, containing one hundred acres, be the same more or less, and being so thereof seised, made his last will and testament in writing, bearing date the fourth day of May, A. D. one thousand eight hundred and forty-three, wherein and whereby, amongst other things, he ordered that the whole of his real estate should be sold by his executors thereinafter named, of which said will he appointed Abraham Brown and Charles Davis executors, as in and by the said recited will, since his decease duly proved, and remaining in the register's office at Louisville, recourse being thereunto had, appears. Now this indenture witnesseth, that the said Abraham Brown and Charles Davis, executors as aforesaid, for and in consideration of the sum of two thousand dollars, to them in hand paid by the said George Hughes, at and before the sealing and delivery hereof, the receipt whereof is hereby acknowledged, have granted, bargained, sold, aliened, released and confirmed, and by these presents, by force and virtue of the said last recited will, do grant, bargain, sell, alien, release and confirm unto the said George Hughes, all that above-mentioned and described messuage, &c., bounded and described as follows: Beginning, &c., [here describe the premises.]

Together with all and singular the houses, out-houses, buildings, barns, stables, ways, woods, waters, water-courses, rights, liberties, privileges, hereditaments and appurtenances whatsoever thereunto belonging or in any wise appertaining, and the reversions and remainders, rents, issues and profits thereof: And also all the estate, right, title, interest, property, claim and demand whatsoever of the said Edward Fraley, at and immediately before the time of his decease, in law or equity, or otherwise howsoever, of, in, to or out of the same. To have and to hold the said messuage or tenement and tract of one hundred acres of land, hereditaments and premises hereby granted or mentioned, or intended so to be, with the appurtenances, unto the said George Hughes, his heirs and assigns, to the only proper use and behoof of the said George Hughes, his heirs and assigns forever. And the said Abraham Brown and Charles Davis, executors aforesaid, for themselves, their heirs, executors and administrators, do severally and not jointly, nor the one for the other, or for the act or deed of the other, but each for his own acts only, covenant, promise, grant and agree, to and with the said George Hughes, his heirs and assigns, by these presents, that they, the said Abraham Brown and Charles Davis, have not heretofore done or committed any act, matter or thing whatsoever, whereby the premises hereby granted, or any part thereof, is, are or shall or may be impeached, charged or encumbered, in title, charge, estate or otherwise howsoever. In witness whereof, &c.

☞ This covenant is generally inserted in deeds given by executors.

Deed by Executors under a special authority in a Will.

To all persons to whom these presents shall come, we, A: B., C. D. and E. F., of ——, executors of the last will and testament of G. H., late of ——, deceased, send greeting. Whereas the said G. H., to enable his executors to make an equal division of his estate, according to his said will, did therein and thereby authorize them to make sale of, and convey all his real estate, either at public or private sale, as to them should seem meet, and to make good and sufficient deeds of bargain and sale thereof, to the purchasers and their heirs and assigns, and in and by the said will did appoint us, the said A. B., C. D. and E. F., executors thereof.

Now know ye, that by virtue of the power and authority aforesaid, and in consideration of the sum of ——, to us paid by K. L. and M. N., of ——, the receipt whereof we do hereby acknowledge, we have granted, bargained, sold and conveyed, and do hereby grant, bargain, sell and convey to the said K. L. and M. N., their heirs and assigns forever, a certain parcel of land, situate, &c. To have and to hold the granted premises to the said K. L. and M. N., their heirs and assigns, as tenants in common, and not as joint tenants. And we, the said A. B., C. D. and E. F., for ourselves, our heirs, executors and administrators, covenant with the said K. L. and M. N., their heirs and assigns as aforesaid, that the said G. H. died seised of the granted premises, that they are free from all incumbrances done or suffered by us or either of us, and that we will, and our heirs, executors and administrators, shall warrant and defend the same to the said K. L. and M. N., their respective heirs and assigns, against the lawful claims and demands of all persons claiming by, from or under the said G. H., or us or either of us. In witness, &c.

Deed Poll.

To all people to whom these presents shall come, A. B., of the city of Lancaster, in the State of Pennsylvania, widow and relict of J. B., late of the same place, Esq., deceased, E. B., of the same place, merchant, eldest son and heir-at-law of the said deceased, F. B , of the borough of Norristown, in the State of Pennsylvania aforesaid, gentleman, another of the sons of the said deceased, and

J. S, of the borough of Norristown aforesaid, gentleman, and M., his wife, late M B., daughter of the said deceased, (who are the only heirs of the said deceased,) send greeting.

Whereas, &c. [Recite the title of the said A. B., deceased, to the premises intended to be conveyed. See recitals.]

Now know ye, that the said J. B., E. B., F. B., and J. S. and M. his wife, for and in consideration of the sum of two thousand dollars, lawful money of the United States, to them in hand paid by I. N., of the city of Philadelphia, aforesaid, at and before the sealing and delivery hereof, the receipt whereof they do hereby acknowledge, and thereof acquit and for ever discharge the said I. N., his heirs, executors, and administrators, by these presents, have granted, bargained, sold, released, and confirmed, and by these presents do grant, bargain, sell, release, and confirm, unto the said I. N., his heirs and assigns, all that messuage or tenement, &c.

Together with all and singular the buildings, improvements, ways, woods, waters, water-courses, rights, liberties, privileges, hereditaments, and appurtenances whatsoever, thereunto belonging, or in any wise appertaining, and the reversions and remainders, rents, issues, and profits thereof; and also all the estate, right, title, interest, property, claim, and demand whatsoever, of them, the said A. B., &c., in law or equity, or otherwise howsoever, of, in, to, or out of the same.

To have and to hold the said messuage or tenement, and lot or piece of ground, hereditaments and premises, hereby granted, or mentioned or intended so to be, with the appurtenances, unto the said I. N., his heirs and assigns, to the only proper use and behoof of the said I. N., his heirs and assigns, for ever; subject to the payment of the arrearages of the principal and interest (if any) due to the Commonwealth of Pennsylvania for patenting the same. In witness, &c.

Deed Poll on disfranchising a Member of a Company.

To all to whom these presents shall come, the master, wardens, and society, of the art and mystery of Carpenters of the city of ———, send greeting: Know ye, that we, for divers good causes and considerations, have acquitted, released, and discharged, and by these presents, for us and our successors, do acquit, release, and discharge, Andrew Bryan, of ——, of and from his freedom in the said society or company, and of and from all other offices, duties, charges, payments, and things whatsoever relating thereto, or whereto he now stands engaged by virtue of any charters, by-laws, ordinances, or other matter or thing whatsoever; and so as of and from the same, he shall and may at all times hereafter be fully and absolutely discharged by these presents. In witness whereof, we have hereunto caused to be set the seal of our society, this —— day of ——, in the year of our Lord one thousand eight hundred and forty-four.

Deed Poll for Unpatented Lands, with Clause of Special Warranty.

Know all men by these presents, that A. B., of Blockley township, in the County of Philadelphia and State of Pennsylvania, joiner, and H., his wife, for and in consideration of the sum of four hundred dollars, to them in hand paid by C. D., of Moyamensing township, in the county and state aforesaid, at and before the sealing and delivery hereof, the receipt whereof is hereby acknowledged, have granted, bargained, sold, released and confirmed, and by these presents, do grant, bargain, sell, release, and confirm unto the said C. D., his heirs and assigns, all their estate, right, title, interest, property, claim, and demand whatsoever, of, in, to, or out of a certain tract or parcel of land, situate, &c., containing one hundred acres, be the same more or less, surveyed or intended to be surveyed, by virtue of a warrant for the same, bearing date the first day of July, one thousand seven hundred and ninety-six, granted to the said A. A. as by the said warrant remaining filed in the Surveyor General's Office, recourse being thereunto had, appears.

Together with all and singular the rights, members, and appurtenances thereunto belonging, or in any wise appertaining; and the reversions and remainders, rents, issues, and profits thereof: To have and to hold the said tract of land, hereditaments, and premises, hereby granted, or mentioned or intended so to be, with the appurtenances, unto the said C. D., his heirs and assigns, to the only proper use and behoof of the said C D., his heirs and assigns for ever, subject to the payment of the arrearages, if any, due to the Commonwealth for patenting the same.

And the said A. B. and his heirs, the said hereby granted premises, unto the said C. D., his heirs and assigns, against him the said A. B. and his heirs, and against all and every other person and persons whatsoever, lawfully claiming or to claim by, from, or under him, them, or any of them, shall and will warrant and for ever defend, by these presents. In witness whereof, &c.

Deed for Lands sold by Administrators by order of Orphans' Court in Partition.

This indenture, made the —— day of ——, between John Jones and William Burns, administrators of all and singular the goods and chattels, rights, and credits, which were of William Dickson, late of ——, yeoman, deceased, of the one part, and John Smith, of ——, gentleman, of the other part: Whereas the said William Dickson was, in his lifetime, lawfully seised in his demesne as of fee, of and in a certain plantation and tract of land, situated in ——, and bounded and described as follows, that is to say: Beginning at ——, containing, &c., with the appurtenances, and being so thereof seised as aforesaid, died intestate. And whereas at an Orphans' Court held at ——, in and for the county of —— aforesaid, the —— day of ——, upon the petition of John Dickson, eldest son and heir at law [or, as the case may be] of the said William Dickson, praying the court to award an inquest, to make partition of the said real estate of the said intestate in the said petition mentioned, to and among his children and representatives, in such manner and in such proportions, as by the laws of Pennsylvania is directed and appointed, if such partition could be made without prejudice to or spoiling the whole, otherwise to value and appraise the same, the said inquest was awarded by the court, according to the prayer of the said petitioner. Whereupon a writ of partition or valuation issued out of the said court, bearing test the —— day of ——, to the sheriff of the said county directed, commanding him to summon an inquest, to make partition of the said real estate to and among the children and representatives of the said intestate, according to law, if such partition could be thereof made without prejudice to and spoiling the whole; but if such partition could not be thereof made as aforesaid, then to value and appraise the same: And that the partition or valuation so made, he should distinctly and openly have before the judges of the said court at ——, the —— day of —— then next. At which day, before the judges aforesaid, the sheriff of the said county, to wit, C. M., Esq., made return of the said writ, with a schedule thereunto annexed, by which schedule or inquisition, under the hand and seal, as well of the said sheriff as of the inquest therein named, it appears by the oaths and affirmations of the said inquest, that the real estate in the said writ mentioned, could not be parted and divided to and among the parties therein named, without prejudice to or spoiling the whole thereof: And therefore the inquest aforesaid, upon their oaths or affirmations aforesaid, had valued and appraised the same at the sum of —— dollars, which return and valuation were, on motion, confirmed by the court. And whereas all the heirs and legal representatives of the said William Dickson, having severally and respectively refused to take the said plantation and tract of land, at the valuation aforesaid, the said court did, upon the application of the said John Dickson, [or as the case may be,] grant a rule upon all the heirs and legal representatives of the said intestate, to show cause at an Orphans' Court to be held at ——, in the county of ——, the —— day of —— then next, why the said real estate should not be sold according to the act of General Assembly, in such case made and provided, at which said time and place legal notice of the aforesaid rule being proved to have been duly given to all the heirs and legal representatives of the said intestate, and no cause being shown why the said real estate should not be sold as aforesaid; the said court did then and there make an order commanding the said John Jones and William Burns, administrators as aforesaid, to expose the aforesaid plantation and tract of land of the said intestate, to public sale, on the premises, upon the —— day of —— then next, upon the terms in the said order directed. In pursuance whereof, the said administrators having first given sufficient security according to law, for the faithful execution of the power committed to them, did on the day, and at the place in the said order directed, expose the premises therein mentioned to sale, by public vendue, and sold the same to the said John Smith, at and for the sum of three thousand dollars, he being the highest bidder, and that the highest and best price bidden for the same; which sale on return thereof made to the judges of the same court, on the —— day of —— last past, was confirmed, and it was considered and adjudicated by the said court, that the said plantation and tract of land with the appurtenances, so sold as aforesaid, should be transferred and vested in the said John Smith, as fully as the said William Dickson, held the same at his decease, subject and liable to the payment of the purchase-money, according to the terms prescribed in the said order, as by the records and proceedings of the same court, remaining at ——, aforesaid, relation thereunto being had, will more fully and at large appear. Now this indenture witnesseth, that the said John Jones and William Burns, administrators as aforesaid, for and in consideration of the said sum of three thousand dollars to them in hand paid by the said John Smith at and before the ensealing and delivery hereof, the receipt and payment whereof they do hereby acknowledge, and thereof acquit and for ever discharge the said John Smith, his heirs, executors, and administrators, have granted, bargained, sold, aliened, released and confirmed, and by these presents (by virtue of the powers and authorities to them given by the aforesaid order of Orphans' Court, and pursuant to the directions thereof) do grant, bargain, sell, alien, release and confirm, unto the said John Smith, his heirs and assigns, all that the above-mentioned and described plantation and tract of land, with the appurtenances: together with all and singular the buildings, improvements, ways, woods, waters, water-courses, rights, liberties, privileges, hereditaments, and appurtenances whatsoever, thereunto belonging or in anywise appertaining, and the reversions and remainders, rents, issues, and profits thereof; and also, all the estate, right, title, interest, property, claim, and demand whatsoever of the said William Dickson in his lifetime, at and immediately before the time of his decease, of, in, to, or out of the same: To have and to hold the said plantation and tract of land, hereditaments and premises, hereby granted, or mentioned, or intended so to be, with the appurtenances, unto the said John Smith, his heirs and assigns, to the only proper use, benefit, and behoof of the said John Smith, his heirs and assigns forever. And the said John Jones and William Burns do severally, but not jointly or the one for the other, or for the act or deed of the other, but each for his own act only, covenant, promise, grant, and agree to and with the said John Smith, his heirs and assigns, by these presents, that they, the said John Jones and William Burns have not, nor hath either of them done, committed, or wittingly or willingly suffered to be done or committed any act, matter, or thing whatsoever, whereby the premises aforesaid, or any part thereof is, are, or shall or may be impeached, charged or incumbered in title, charge, or estate or otherwise howsoever. In testimony whereof, the said parties to these presents have hereunto set their hands and seals, dated the day and year first above written.

Sealed and delivered in presence of us,

JOHN JAY,
ALFRED KING.

JOHN JONES.

WILLIAM BURNS.

Deed by Administrators, by order of Court, to satisfy debts, &c.

This indenture, made the tenth day of September, in the year of our Lord one thousand eight hundred and forty-four, between John Jones and William Burns, administrators of all and singular the goods and chattels, rights and credits which were of William Dickson, late of, &c., yeoman, who died intestate, of the one part, and John Smith, of, &c., of the other part: Whereas, &c. [Here recite the former title] By force and virtue of which said last recited indenture, or of some other good conveyances and assurances in the law duly had and executed, the said John Jones became in his life time lawfully seised in his demesne, as of fee, of and in the premises aforesaid, with the appurtenances; and being so thereof seised, died intestate; after whose death, to wit, at an Orphans' Court, held at ——, in and for the county of ——, the tenth day of August, one thousand eight hundred and forty-four, upon the petition of John Jones and William Burns, the administrators aforesaid, stating to the said court that the personal estate of the said deceased was not sufficient for the payment of the debts of the said intestate, [or say, not sufficient for the maintenance and education of the minor children of the said intestate, as the case may be,] and prayed the court to direct a sale to be made of the above described messuage, &c., it was considered and ordered by the said court that the premises aforesaid should be sold at public sale on the twenty-second day of February then next, for the purpose aforesaid, and that a report of the proceedings thereof be made to the next Orphans' Court, to be held for the said county, after such sale.

In pursuance of which said order, the said John Jones and William Burns, administrators as aforesaid, after having given due public and timely notice of the time and place of sale, did, on the day and time therein mentioned, expose the premises aforesaid to sale, by public vendue or outcry, and sold the same to John Smith, for the sum of one thousand dollars, lawful money of the United States, he being the highest bidder, and that the best price bidden for the same; which sale, on report thereof made to the judges of the said court, was, on the fifth day of April following, by them confirmed. And it was considered and adjudged by the said court, that the same should be and remain firm and stable forever, as by the records and proceedings of the said court, relation being thereunto had, will at large appear.

Now this indenture witnesseth, that the said John Jones and William Burns, for and in consideration of the said sum of one thousand dollars, to them in hand paid by the said John Smith, at and before the ensealing and delivering hereof, the receipt whereof they do hereby acknowledge, and thereof acquit and forever discharge the said John Smith, his heirs, executors and administrators, by these presents have granted, bargained, sold, released and confirmed, and by these presents, in pursuance and by virtue of the said order of court, do grant, bargain, sell, release and confirm unto the said John Smith, and to his heirs, assigns, all that, the said messuage, &c., bounded and described as follows: Beginning, &c. [Here describe the premises.] Together with all and singular other the houses, out-houses, buildings, barns, stables, ways, woods, waters, water-courses, rights, liberties, privileges, hereditaments and appurtenances whatsoever thereunto belonging, or in any wise appertaining, and the reversions and remainders, rents, issues and profits thereof: And also all the estate, right, title, interest, property, claim and demand whatsoever of the said William Dickson, at and immediately before the time of his decease, in law or equity, or otherwise howsoever, of, in, to or out of the same. To have and to hold the said messuage or tenement and tract of one hundred and fifty acres of land, hereditaments and premises hereby granted or mentioned, or intended so to be, with the appurtenances, unto the said John Smith, his heirs and assigns, to the only proper use and behoof of the said John Smith, his heirs and assigns forever.

And the said John Jones and William Burns, administrators aforesaid, for themselves, their heirs, executors and administrators, do severally and not jointly, nor the one for the other, or for the act or deed of the other, but each for his own acts only, covenant, promise, grant and agree, to and with the said John Smith, his heirs and assigns, by these presents, that they, the said John Jones and William Burns, have not heretofore done or committed any act, matter or thing whatsoever, whereby the premises hereby granted, or any part thereof, is, are or shall or may be impeached, charged or incumbered, in title, charge, estate or otherwise howsoever. In witness whereof, &c.

A Deed by an Administrator, of Land which his Intestate had bound himself to convey.

To all people to whom, &c., A. B., of ——, administrator of the goods and estate which were of C. D., late of ——, deceased, sends, greeting: Whereas (*here recite the agreement of the intestate to convey, and that the administrator had obtained permission, &c.*) Now know ye, that by virtue of the authority and license aforesaid, and in order to fulfil and perform all things in the above-mentioned contract or agreement on the part of the said A. B., to be performed, in consideration of the sum of ——, to me paid by the said C. D., the receipt, &c., and in consideration that the said C. D. hath performed and fulfilled all things in the above-recited contract or agreement, on his part to be performed and fulfilled, I, the said A. B., have granted, bargained, sold, conveyed, released and confirmed, and do hereby, &c., to the said C. D., his heirs and assigns forever, the said, &c., with the appurtenances; to have and to hold the same to the said C. D., his heirs and assigns, to his and their use forever, &c.

☞ This deed will not pass the widow's right to dower, unless she join in the conveyance.

Sheriff's Deed on a Venditioni.

To all people to whom these presents shall come, J. H. B., Esq., High Sheriff of the county of ——, in the Commonwealth of Pennsylvania, sends greeting: Whereas by a writ of *fieri facias*, to me directed, bearing date the ninth day of May last past, I was commanded, that of the goods and chattels, lands and tenements of J. S., &c., in my bailiwick, I should cause to be levied, &c. [*as in the fieri facias.*] And that I should have those moneys before the judges at ——, at a Court of Common Pleas, there to be held for the said county of ——, the fifth day of August then next, to render to the said C. H., for his debt and damages aforesaid, and that I should have then and there that writ. At which day, I, the said sheriff, made return to the said Judges, that by virtue of the said writ to me directed, I had seized and taken in execution, a certain messuage, &c., which remained in my hands unsold for want of buyers; so that I could not have the moneys, in the said writ mentioned, at the day and place therein contained, as by the said writ I was commanded: And that the residue of the execution of the said writ was contained in a certain schedule thereunto annexed; by which schedule or inquisition it appears, on the oaths and affirmations of the inquest therein named, that the rents, issues and profits of the said messuage, &c., were not of a clear yearly value sufficient, beyond all reprizes, within the space of seven years, to satisfy the debt and damages in the said writ mentioned: Wherefore, by a certain other writ of *venditioni exponas*, issued out of the said court, bearing date the sixth day of August last past, I, the said sheriff, was commanded that the said messuage, &c., with the appurtenances, so by me seised and taken in execution, I should expose to sale: And that I should have those moneys before the said judges at ——, at the Court of Common Pleas, there to be held the fourth day of November then next, to render to the said C. H. for his debt and damages aforesaid.

In pursuance whereof, I, the said sheriff, having given due and timely notice of the time and place of sale, did, on Friday, the eighth day of November, expose the premises aforesaid to sale, by public vendue or outcry, and sold the same to I. R., of, &c., for the sum of one thousand dollars, he being the highest bidder, and that the best price bidden for the same. Now know ye, that I, the said sheriff, for and in consideration of the aforesaid sum of one thousand dollars, to me in hand paid by the said I. R., at and before the ensealing and delivering hereof, the receipt whereof I do hereby acknowledge, have granted, bargained and sold, and by these presents, according to the directions of the said last recited writ, and by force and virtue thereof, do grant, bargain and sell, unto the said I. R., his heirs and assigns, all that the said messuage, &c., together with all and singular the buildings, improvements, rights, members and appurtenances whatsoever thereunto belonging, or in anywise appertaining, and the reversions and remainders, rents, issues and profits thereof; and also all the estate, right, title, interest, property, claim and demand whatsoever of him the said I. S., of, in, to or out of the same: To have and to hold the said messuage, &c., hereditaments and premises, hereby granted or mentioned, or intended so to be, with the appurtenances, unto the said I. R., his heirs and assigns, to his and their only proper use and behoof forever; for such estate, and under such rents and conditions, as the said I. S. had and held the same, at and immediately before the taking thereof in execution, according to the form and effect of the laws and usages of this Commonwealth, in such case made and provided. In witness whereof, I, the said sheriff, have hereunto set my hand and seal.

Dated the fifth day of November, one thousand eight hundred and forty-four.

Sheriff's Deed upon a Levari Facias.

To all people to whom these presents shall come, H. S., Esq., High Sheriff of the county of ——, in the Commonwealth of Pennsylvania, sendeth greeting: Whereas by a writ of Levari Facias, issued out of the county Court of Common Pleas, of the county of ——, bearing test at ——, the —— day of —— last past, to the said sheriff directed, he was commanded that without any other writ of the lands and tenements of A. N., late of ——, widow, in his bailiwick, to wit of a certain messuage, &c., [as in the writ], and that he should have those moneys before the judges at ——, at the county Court of Common Pleas, there to be held for the said county of ——, the —— day of —— then next, to render to the said S. P., for his debts and damages aforesaid: And whereas the said sheriff having given due and legal notice of the time and place of sale of the said messuage, &c , did on Monday the —— day of ——, expose the same to sale by public vendue or outcry, and sold the same to J. L., of ——, for the sum of ——, he being the highest bidder, and that the highest and best price bidden for the same: Now know ye, that the said sheriff, for and in cousideration of the aforesaid sum of ——, to him in hand paid by the said J. L., at and before the ensealing and delivery hereof, the receipt whereof he doth hereby acknowledge, hath granted, bargained and sold, and by these presents, according to the directions of the said recited writ, and by force and virtue thereof, doth grant, bargain and sell unto the said J. L., his heirs and assigns, all that the said messuage, &c., together with all and singular the buildings, improvements, rights, members and appurtenances whatsoever thereunto belonging or in anywise appertaining, and the reversions and remainders, rents, issues and profits thereof, and also all the estate, right, title, interest, property, claim and demand whatsoever of her, the said A. N., of, in, to or out of the same: To have and to hold the said messuage, &c., hereditaments and premises hereby granted or mentioned, or intended to be so, with the appurtenances, unto the said J. L., his heirs and assigns, to his and their only proper use and behoof forever for such estate, and under such rents and conditions as the said A. N., had and held the same at and immediately before the taking thereof in execution, but for no larger or greater estate than she, the said A. N., then and there had and held the same, according to the form and effect of the laws and usage of this commonwealth, in such case made and provided. In witness whereof, the said sheriff hath hereunto set his hand and seal, the —— day of ——.

Deed of Guardian for Lands sold by order of Orphans' Court.

This indenture, made the tenth day of May, A. D. one thousand eight hundred and forty-four, between P. C., guardian, legally appointed by the Orphans' Court of the county of ——, of the estate of S. M., a minor son of J. M., late of ——, blacksmith, deceased, of the one part, and E. G , of ——, gentleman, of the other part: Whereas by force and virtue of certain good conveyances and assurances in the law, duly had and executed, the said J. M. became in his lifetime lawfully seized in his demesne as of fee, of and in a certain plantation and tract of land, situate in, &c., and bounded and described as follows: [*here describe the premises,*] with the appurtenances, and being so thereof seised, died intestate, [*or if the deceased made a will, add the following after the word seised,* "made his last will and testament in writing, bearing date the —— day of ——, wherein and whereby (among other things) he did give and devise the said plantation and tract of land unto his said son S. M., and his heirs, as in and by the said in part recited will (since his decease duly proved and remaining in the register's office at ——,) reference being thereunto had, appears,"] and whereas at an Orphans' Court held at —— aforesaid, in and for the said county, upon the petition of the said S. M., the said P. C. was duly appointed guardian of the estate of the said S. M. during his minority; and it appearing to the said court that the said S. M. was not possessed of a personal estate adequate to his maintenance and education, the said court did then and there make an order empowering the said P. C. to make public sale of the said plantation and tract of land, the estate of the said S. M., for the purposes aforesaid, and to make a title thereto to the purchaser, and did direct the said sale to be held on the premises, upon the —— day of —— then next. In pursuance whereof, the said P. C., having first given bond with sufficient surety to the said court, according to the act of assembly, for the faithful discharge of the trust thus committed to him, did on the day and at the place in the said order directed, expose the premises therein mentioned to sale by public vendue, and sold the same to the said E. G., at and for the sum of ——, he being the highest bidder, and that the highest and best price bidden for the same, which sale, on report thereof made to the judges of the said court on the ——, was confirmed by the said court, and it was considered and adjudged by the said court, that the same should be and remain firm and stable forever, as by the records and proceedings of the same court, reference thereunto being had, will fully appear. Now this indenture witnesseth, that the said P. C., for and in consideration of the sum of ——, to him in hand paid by the said E. G , at and before the ensealing and delivery hereof, the receipt and payment whereof he doth hereby acknowledge, and thereof acquit and forever discharge the said E. G., his heirs, executors and administrators, by these presents, hath granted, bargained, sold, aliened, released and confirmed, and by these presents (by virtue of the powers and authorities to him given by the aforesaid order of Orphans' Court, and pursuant to the directions thereof) doth grant, bargain, sell, alien, release and confirm unto the said E. G , his heirs and assigns, all that the above-mentioned and described plantation and tract of land, with the appurtenances: Together with all and singular the houses, out-houses, buildings, barns, stables, ways, woods, waters, water-courses, rights, liberties, privileges, hereditaments and appurtenances whatsoever thereunto belonging or in any wise appertaining, and the reversions and remainders, rents, issues and profits thereof: And also all the estate, right, title, interest, property, claim and demand whatsoever of the said J. M. in his lifetime at and immediately before the time of his decease, of, in, to or out of the same: To have and to hold the said plantation and tract of land, hereditaments and premises, hereby granted or mentioned, or intended so to be, with the appurtenances, unto the said E. G., his heirs and assigns, to the only proper use, benefit and behoof of the said E. G , his heirs and assigns forever. And the said P. C. doth covenant, promise, grant and agree to and with the said E G., his heirs and assigns, by these presents, that he, the said P. C., hath not done, committed, or wittingly or willingly suffered to be done or committed, any act, matter or thing whatsoever, whereby the premises aforesaid, or any part thereof, is, are or shall or may be impeached, charged or incumbered in title, charge or estate, or otherwise howsoever. In witness whereof, &c.

Deed of Trust or Assignment for the benefit of Creditors.

This indenture, made the fourth day of July, Anno Domini one thousand eight hundred and forty-four, between A. B. of the borough of Reading, in the county of Berks, and state of Pennsylvania, of the one part, and C. D. of the same place, of the other part: Whereas the said A. B , owing to sundry losses and misfortunes, is at present unable to discharge his just debts, and is willing to assign all his property for the benefit of his creditors: —

Now this indenture witnesseth, that the said A. B. as well in consideration of the premises, and for the purpose of making a just distribution of his estate and effects among his creditors, as also of the sum of one dollar, to him in hand paid, by the said C. D., the receipt whereof is hereby acknowledged, hath granted, bargained, sold, assigned, transferred and set over, and by these presents doth grant, bargain, sell, assign, transfer and set over unto the said C. D., his heirs and assigns, all that certain messuage, &c. [Here describe the lands, tenements, &c. intended to be conveyed.]

And also all his goods, chattels and effects, and property of every kind, real, personal and mixed: to have and to hold, receive and take the same to the said C. D., his heirs and assigns, to the proper use and behoof of the said C. D., his heirs and assigns for ever.

In trust, however, and to the intent and purpose that he, the said C. D., shall and do as soon as convenient, sell and dispose of all the lands, tenements, goods and chattels of him, the said A. B., and collect and recover all the outstanding claims and debts to him due, and with the moneys arising therefrom, after deducting his reasonable costs and charges, shall and will pay the creditors of the said A. B. their respective demands in full, if there shall be sufficient assets to satisfy the whole; and if there are not sufficient assets to satisfy all the demands in full, then pro rata according to the amount of their respective demands, without preference as between individuals.

And should any part or portion of said trust property or funds remain after fully complying with the trusts aforesaid, then the said C. D. shall deliver over and re-convey the same unto the said A. B., his heirs, executors, administrators and assigns.

In testimony whereof, the said party to these presents hath hereunto set his hand and seal, the day and year first above written.

A. B.

[Acknowledged as other deeds.]

The following deed to trustees for the use of a wife, is such an one as is made to secure a certain quantity of land to the use and control of the wife, and which can be held by her against the creditors of the husband; provided it is paid for out of her own estate, or even if paid for by the funds of the husband, if such husband is not embarrassed by debts at the time of making the trust estate.

Deed to a Wife by intervention of Trustees.

This indenture, made the tenth day of May, in the year of our Lord one thousand eight hundred and forty-four, between John Jones of the city of Philadelphia and state of Pennsylvania, and Mary his wife, of the one part, and William Burns, of Lancaster, in the county of Lancaster and state aforesaid, of the other part: Witnesseth, that the said John Jones and Mary his wife, for and in consideration of the sum of five hundred dollars, lawful money of the United States, to them in hand paid by the said William

Burns, for the uses and upon the trusts hereinafter mentioned, at and before the ensealing and delivery hereof, the receipt whereof they do hereby acknowledge, and thereof for ever acquit and discharge the said William Burns, have granted, bargained, sold, aliened, enfeoffed, released and confirmed, and by these presents, do grant, bargain, sell, alien, enfeoff, release, and confirm, unto the said William Burns, his heirs and assigns for ever, all that certain piece or parcel of land, situated, &c., [here describe the premises] together with all and singular the buildings and improvements, to the same belonging, or in anywise appertaining, and the reversions and remainders, rents, issues and profits thereof. To have and to hold the said piece or parcel of land, with the appurtenances, hereby granted or intended so to be, unto the said William Burns, his heirs and assigns forever: in trust, nevertheless, and for the uses following and none other, that is to say, for the sole and separate use of Anna Brown, the wife of Thomas Brown, of Lancaster, county and state aforesaid, for and during her natural life, and so as she alone, or such person as she shall appoint, shall take and receive the rents, issues and profits thereof, and so as her said husband shall not in anywise intermeddle therewith; and from and after the decease of the said Anna Brown, in trust for the use of the heirs of the body of the said Anna Brown, by the said Thomas Brown begotten, or to be begotten, forever, with power to the said William Burns to sell and convey in fee simple, the whole or any part of the aforesaid premises and appurtenances, to any person or persons, and for such sum or sums of money as the said Anna Brown by writing under her hand and seal, and duly acknowledged at any time during her natural life, may appoint and direct. And the said John Jones and Mary his wife, for themselves, their heirs, executors and administrators, do covenant, promise, grant and agree, to and with the said William Burns, his heirs and assigns, by these presents, that they, the said John Jones and Mary his wife, and their heirs, the said above-mentioned and described piece or parcel of land, with the appurtenances, unto the said William Burns, his heirs and assigns, against him, the said John Jones and his heirs, and against all and every other person and persons whomsoever, lawfully claiming or to claim the same, or any part thereof, [*by, from or under him, them or any of them,] shall and will warrant and forever defend, by these presents.

In witness whereof, &c.†

* See note at the conclusion of the first deed.

† The acknowledgment for this deed is in the same form as any other.

Deed from same Trustee by direction of the Wife to sell her Trust Estate.

This indenture, made the —— day of ——, A. D. one thousand eight hundred and forty-five, between William Burns, trustee of the hereafter-mentioned and described premises, for the use of Anna Brown, wife of Thomas Brown, of the first part, and Samuel Stone, of ——, of the second part: Witnesseth, that the said William Burns, by the appointment and direction of the said Anna Brown, given under her hand and seal, duly acknowledged, for the sum of five hundred dollars, lawful money of the United States, to him in hand paid by the said Samuel Stone, for the use of the said Anna Brown, at and before the ensealing and delivery hereof, the receipt whereof he doth hereby acknowledge, and thereof acquit and forever discharge the said Samuel Stone, hath granted, bargained, sold, released and confirmed, and by these presents doth grant, bargain, sell, release and confirm unto the said Samuel Stone, his heirs and assigns, all that piece or parcel of land, situate, &c.: [here describe the premises] together with all and singular the buildings, improvements, rights, liberties, privileges, hereditaments and appurtenances whatsoever thereunto belonging or in anywise appertaining, and the reversions and remainders, rents, issues and profits thereof, and also all the estate, right, title, interest, property, claim and demand whatsoever of him, the said William Burns, in law or equity, or otherwise howsoever, of, in and to the same; to have and to hold the said piece or parcel of land hereby granted or mentioned, or intended so to be, with the appurtenances, unto the said Samuel Stone, and to his heirs and assigns forever. And the said William Burns, for himself, his heirs, executors and administrators, doth hereby covenant, promise and agree, to and with the said Samuel Stone, his heirs and assigns, by these presents, that he, the said William Burns, and his heirs, the said above-mentioned and described premises with the appurtenances, unto the said Samuel Stone, his heirs and assigns, against him, the said William Burns and his heirs, and against all and every other person and persons whomsoever, lawfully claiming or to claim the same or any part thereof, by, from or under him, them or any of them, shall and will warrant and forever defend, by these presents. In witness whereof, I have hereunto set my hand and seal the day and year first above written.

Sealed and delivered in presence of

JAMES STILES.

WILLIAM BURNS.

This may certify that I, Anna Brown, the wife of Thomas Brown, do hereby appoint and direct William Burns, trustee of the aforesaid property for my use, to sell and convey as before described, the premises within mentioned: And that I have received on the day of the date of the above indenture, five hundred dollars in full of the consideration money therein mentioned.

Witness my hand and seal the day and date of the above indenture.

Witness present,

JAMES STILES.

ANNA BROWN.

Lancaster County, *ss.*

Be it remembered that on the —— day of ——, A. D. one thousand eight hundred and forty-five, before me, the subscriber, one of the justices of the peace in and for the said county, personally came the above-named William Burns, trustee of the premises herein described, for the use of Anna Brown, and by her appointment and direction, acknowledged the above indenture to be his act and deed, and desired that the same might be recorded as such.

Also, on the day and date aforesaid, personally came Anna Brown, above named, and acknowledged the above certificate of appointment and direction to be her act and deed, and desired that the same might be recorded as such.

In testimony whereof, I have hereunto set my hand and seal, the day and year aforesaid.

JAMES STILES, *J. P.*

Deed of Marriage Settlement of a Wife's Fortune (consisting of Lands, Goods, &c.,) to her use as a separate and distinct Estate.

An indenture of three parts, made, &c., between A. B., of ——, of the first part, C. D., &c., of the second part, and E. F. and G. H., (trustees) of the third part. Whereas the said C. D. is seised to her and her heirs forever, of all that messuage or tenement, situate, lying and being in ——: And whereas a marriage is intended shortly to be had and solemnized between the said A. B. and the said C. D., upon the contract of which marriage the said A. B. hath agreed, that if the same shall take effect, then, notwithstanding the said marriage, he, the said A. B, his executors, administrators or assigns, shall not and will not intermeddle with, or have any right, title or interest, either in law or equity, in or to any part of the rents, issues and profits of the said messuage,

&c., but the same shall remain, continue and be to the said C. D., or to such uses as the said C. D. shall think fit and appoint: Now this indenture witnesseth, that for the making the said agreement effectual in law, and for the preserving the rents, &c., of the messuage, &c., to and for the separate use of the said C. D., and so that the same shall not be in the power or disposal of the said A. B., he, the said A. B., doth for himself, &c., covenant, &c., to and with the said E. F. and G. H., (trustees) and the survivor of them, and the executors and administrators of the survivor of them, by these presents, that notwithstanding the said intended marriage shall take effect, all the rents of the messuage, &c., which shall, from time to time, become due and payable to her, the said C. D., by virtue of, &c., aforesaid, and also the interest, due or to grow due for, &c.; and also the reversion and reversions of the said messuage, &c., shall be accounted, reckoned and taken as and be a separate and distinct estate, of and from the estate of him, the said A. B., and be in no wise liable or subject to him, or to the payment of any of his debts, but with the profits or increase, that shall hereafter be gotten, gained or made of the same, be ordered, disposed and employed, to such person and persons, and to and for such use and uses, intents and purposes, and in such manner and form as are hereinafter mentioned and declared, (that is to say,) that the ready money arising or accruing out of the said separate and distinct estate before mentioned, shall, from time to time, be placed out at interest on such securities as she, the said C. D., shall think fit; which securities, during the coverture, shall be taken and made in the names of the said E. F. and G. H., (the trustees) or the survivor of them, or in the name or names of such other person or persons, as she, the said C. D., shall order and appoint, in trust for her, the said C. D. And that all the said separate and distinct estate, before declared and allotted for the said C D. as aforesaid, and the produce and increase thereof, shall be had, taken, held, possessed and enjoyed by such person and persons, and for such use and uses, as the said C. D. shall at any time or times hereafter, during her life, limit, devise, order or dispose of the same, or any part thereof, either by her last will and testament in writing whatsoever, signed with her hand in the presence of two or more credible witnesses.

—— And the said A. B. doth for himself, his heirs, &c , covenant, &c. to and with the said E. F. and G. H., (trustees,) &c., by these presents, in manner following, that is to say, that if the said intended marriage shall take effect, he, the said A. B., shall and will permit and suffer the said C. D. to give, grant and dispose of her said separate estate, as she shall think fit in her lifetime, and to make such will or other writing as aforesaid, and thereby to give, order, devise, limit and appoint her said separate estate to any person or persons, for any trust, use, intent or purpose whatsoever; and that he, the said A. B., shall and will permit and suffer such will, hereafter to be made by the said C. D., to be duly proved by the executors in such will named or to be named, and probate of such will to be had and taken, as is usual; and that the person or persons, to whom the said C. D. shall give or dispose any part of her said separate estate by her will, or any other writing that shall be signed, sealed and executed by her in the presence of two or more credible witnesses as aforesaid, shall and lawfully may, peaceably and quietly have, hold, use, occupy, possess and enjoy the same, according to the true meaning of such gift, devise or appointment, without any let, denial, hindrance or interruption of or by the said A. B., his executors, administrators or assigns, or any of them.

And also that it shall and may be lawful to and for the said E. F. and G. H., &c., at any time from and after the said intended marriage shall take effect, to commence any action or suit, in law or equity, in the names of the said A. B. and C. D., his intended wife, against any person or persons, for the recovery of any sum or sums of money, due or to grow due to the said C. D., on her separate estate as aforesaid; and that the said A. B. shall not and will not release or discharge any such action or suit, nor receive, release or discharge any sum or sums of money now due or hereafter to grow due to the said C. D. from her said separate estate as aforesaid, without the special license and consent of them, the said E. F. and G. H., &c., in that behalf, first had and obtained in writing under their, or some of their hands and seals, but he, the said A. B., shall and will avow, justify and maintain all lawful actions and suits, that shall and may be so commenced for the recovery of the premises, and that he, the said A. B., shall and will, as often as thereto desired by the said E. F. and G. H., or the survivor of them, join with the said C., his now intended wife, in any receipt, release, discharge or acquittance necessary to be given on receiving any moneys, due or to grow due to the said C., as aforesaid. And further, that he, the said A. B., shall and will, from time to time, and at all times, from and after the said intended marriage shall take effect, upon every reasonable request, and at the proper costs and charges of the said E. F. and G. H., (the trustees,) or, &c., make, do and execute, all and every such further act and acts, thing and things, for the better settling, recovering and receiving, the moneys, goods and estate of the said C. D., allotted and declared for her separate use, benefit and disposal as aforesaid, as by the said E. F. and G. H., or, &c., or their, or any of their counsel learned in the law, shall be reasonably devised, advised or required. Provided always, and it is declared, concluded and agreed, by and between all, &c., that they, the said E. F. and G. H., &c., shall and may, from time to time, reimburse, satisfy and pay himself and themselves out of the said estate, all such necessary and reasonable charges as they shall sustain or be put to by reason of their being made parties to these presents, or transacting any thing pursuant thereto: And that neither of them, the said E. F. and G. H., shall be any ways accountable for the act of the other, or liable to make good any more of the estate than what shall really and *bona fide* come into his hands or custody. Provided also, and it is declared, concluded and agreed, by and between the said parties to these presents, that the said A. B., his executors and administrators, shall, from time to time, and at all times hereafter, be indemnified and saved harmless, out of the separate estate of the said C. D., of and from all manner of costs, charges, damages or trouble, that he or they shall or may sustain, incur or be put unto, for or by reason of the said A. B.'s joining or being a party in any action or suit for recovering any part of the separate estate of her, the said C., as aforesaid, or any other account whatsoever, relating to the said separate estate. In testimony whereof, &c.

Deed of a Water-course.

This indenture, made the tenth day of May, in the year of our Lord one thousand eight hundred and forty-five, between A. B., of, &c., of the one part, and C. D., of, &c., of the other part: Whereas the said A. B. and C. D., at the time of the sealing and delivering of these presents, are respectively seised in fee of and in two contiguous tracts, pieces, or parcels of land, with the appurtenances, in the township of Cumru aforesaid: and whereas there is a dam and race, or water-course, built, erected and made, in and upon a certain run or stream of water (called Angelica) within the land of the said A. B., for watering, overflowing, and improving of meadow ground thereon. Now this indenture witnesseth, that the said A. B., for divers good causes and considerations, and more especially for and in consideration of the sum of one dollar, to him in hand paid by the said C. D. at or before the ensealing and delivery hereof, the receipt whereof he doth hereby acknowledge, hath granted, bargained, sold, released and confirmed, and by these presents doth grant, bargain, sell, release and confirm unto the said C. D., and to his heirs and assigns, all the water of the said run or stream of water, to be led and conveyed from the said dam, along the race or water-course aforesaid, into the said land of the said C. D. for the space of three days in every week, to wit: From Wednesday evening at sunset, to Saturday evening at sunset, from the first day of May to the first day of November, yearly, and every year, for the watering, overflowing, and improving of meadow ground on the land of the said C. D., together with free ingress, egress and regress, to and for the said C. D., his heirs and assigns, and his and their workmen, with horses, carts and carriages, at all convenient times and seasons, through the land of the said A. B., his heirs and assigns, in and along the banks of the said dam and race, or water-course, for the amending, cleansing and repairing the same, with liberty and privilege, for that purpose, to dig and take stones and earth from the adjacent land of the said A. B., when and as often as need be, or occasion may require: to have and to hold, all and singular the premises and privileges hereby granted, or mentioned, or intended so to be, with the appurtenances, unto the said C. D., his heirs and assigns, to the only proper use and behoof of the said C. D., his heirs and assigns forever; he or they paying one moiety or half part of the expenses, which from time to time may accrue, in supporting, cleansing and repairing the dam and water-course aforesaid. In witness, &c.

Deed of an Alley or Passage.

This indenture, made the first day of June, in the year of our Lord one thousand eight hundred and forty-five, between A. B. of, &c, of the one part, and C. D. of, &c., of the other part: Witnesseth, that the said A. B., for and in consideration of the sum of one hundred dollars, lawful money of the United States, unto him well and truly paid, by the said C. D., at and before the ensealing and delivering hereof, the receipt whereof is hereby acknowledged, hath granted, bargained and sold, and by these presents doth grant, bargain and sell unto the said C. D. and to his heirs and assigns, the free and uninterrupted use, liberty and privilege of, and passage in and along, a certain alley or passage, of five feet in breadth by eighty feet in depth, extending out of and from Penn street, in the said borough, along the east side of the present messuage, dwelling-house and lot of the said C. D., together with free ingress, egress and regress, to and for the said C. D., his heirs and assigns, his and their tenants and under tenants, occupiers or possessors, of the said C. D.'s messuage and ground, contiguous to the said alley or passage, at all times and seasons, forever hereafter, into, along, upon, and out of the said alley, in common with him, the said A. B., his heirs and assigns, tenants or occupiers of the said A. B.'s messuage and ground, adjacent to the said alley: to have and to hold all and singular the privileges aforesaid to him, the said C. D., his heirs and assigns, to the only proper use and behoof of him, the said C. D., his heirs and assigns forever, in common with him, the said A. B., his heirs and assigns, as aforesaid; subject nevertheless to the moiety or equal half part of all necessary charges and expenses which shall from time to time accrue, in paving, amending, repairing and cleansing the said alley. In witness whereof, &c.

A Gift of Lands, by Deed.

This indenture, made, &c., between E. F., of ——, of the one part, and G. H., son of the said E. F., of the other part: Witnesseth, that the said E. F., as well for and in consideration of the natural love and affection which he, the said E. F., hath and beareth unto the said G. H., as also for the better maintenance, support, and livelihood of him, the said G. H., hath given, granted, aliened, enfeoffed, and confirmed, and by these presents doth give, grant, alien, enfeoff, and confirm unto the said G. H., his heirs and assigns, all that messuage, &c , together with all and singular the hereditaments and appurtenances thereunto belonging, or in any-wise appertaining; and the reversion and reversions, remainder and remainders, rents, issues, and profits thereof, and all the estate, right, title, interest, property, claim, and demand whatsoever, of him, the said E. F., of, in, and to the said messuage, tenements, and premises, and of, in, and to every part and parcel thereof, with their and every of their appurtenances: to have and to hold the said messuage, tenements, hereditaments, and all and singular the premises hereby granted and confirmed, or mentioned, or intended so to be, with their and every of their appurtenances, unto the said G. H., his heirs and assigns, to the only proper use and behoof of him, the said G. H., his heirs and assigns forever. And the said E. F., for himself, his heirs, executors and administrators, doth covenant, grant, and agree, to and with the said G. H., his heirs and assigns, by these presents, that he, the said G. H., his heirs and assigns, shall, and lawfully may, from time to time, and at all times hereafter, peaceably and quietly have, hold, use, occupy, possess, and enjoy the said messuage, farm, lands, tenements, hereditaments, and premises hereby granted and confirmed, or mentioned, or intended to be hereby granted and confirmed, with their and every of their appurtenances, free, clear, and fully discharged, or well and sufficiently saved, kept harmless, and indemnified of, from, and against all former and other gifts, grants, bargains, sales, jointures, feoffments, dowers, and estates, and of, from, and against all former and other titles, troubles, charges, and incumbrances whatsoever, had, done, or suffered, or to be had, made, done, or suffered by him the said E F., his heirs or assigns, or any other person or persons, lawfully claiming, or to claim, by, from, or under him, them, or any of them. In witness, &c.

Deed of Partition.

This indenture, made, &c. [Here insert the parties.] Whereas the said A. B. and C. D. now stand seised in fee simple, as tenants in common, of and in a certain tract or parcel of land, situated in Moyamensing township aforesaid, adjoining lands of L. M., N. O., P. Q , containing one hundred acres, with the appurtenances. Now this indenture witnesseth, that the parties to these presents have agreed to make, and by these presents do make, a full, just, and equal partition and division between them, of and in the aforesaid tract of land, according to their respective shares and interests therein, in manner following, that is to say: that the said A. B. and his heirs, shall have all that piece or allotment of land, part of the said tract, beginning, &c., containing, &c.

Together with the messuages, edifices, buildings, and improvements, on the said described piece of land, and all the ways, woods, waters, water-courses, rights, liberties, privileges, hereditaments, and appurtenances whatsoever thereunto belonging, or in anywise appertaining, and the reversions and remainders, rents, issues and profits thereof. To hold and enjoy the same unto the said A. B., his heirs and assigns forever, in severalty, as his and their full part, share, and dividend, of and in all and singular the premises: And the said C. D. doth, by these presents, for him and his heirs, give, grant, allot, assign, set over, release and confirm, unto the said A. B. and to his heirs and assigns forever, the said described piece or allotment of land, with the appurtenances, to have and to hold to him, the said A. B., his heirs and assigns, to the only proper use and behoof of him, the said A. B., his heirs and assigns forever, in severalty.

And the said C. D. and his heirs shall have all that piece or allotment of land, (residue of the said tract,) beginning, &c., containing, &c., together with the messuages, edifices, buildings, and improvements, on the said described piece of land, and all the ways, woods, waters, water-courses, rights, liberties, privileges, hereditaments and appurtenances whatsoever thereunto belonging, or in anywise appertaining, and the reversions and remainders, rents, issues and profits thereof. To hold and enjoy the same unto the said A. B., his heirs and assigns forever, in severalty, as his and their full part, share and dividend, of and in all and singular the premises, and the said C. D. doth, by these presents, for him and his heirs, give, grant, allot, assign, set over, release and confirm, unto the said A. B. and to his heirs and assigns forever, the said described piece or allotment of land, with the appurtenances, to have and to hold to him, the said A. B., his heirs and assigns, to the only proper use and behoof of him, the said A. B, his heirs and assigns forever, in severalty.

And the said C. D. for himself, his heirs, executors and administrators, doth covenant, promise and grant, to and with the said A. B., his heirs and assigns, and every of them, by these presents, that he, the said A. B., his heirs and assigns, shall or lawfully may from time to time, and at all times hereafter, forever, freely, peaceably and quietly, have, hold, occupy, possess and enjoy the said last-described piece or allotment of land, containing, &c., with the appurtenances, and receive and take the rents, issues and profits thereof, without the let, suit, trouble, molestation, interruption, or denial of him, the said A. B., his heirs or assigns, or of any other person or persons whatsoever, lawfully claiming, or to claim, by, from or under him, them or any of them, or by or with his, their, or any or either of their acts, means, consent, privity or procurement. [Here insert the same covenant as the last, from A. B. to C. D.]

In witness whereof, the said parties have hereunto set their hands and seals, dated the day and year above written.

☞ There must be two of these indentures drawn alike, and each of the parties must sign both.

Deed of Rent-Charge.

This indenture, made the first day of May, in the year of our Lord one thousand eight hundred and thirty-seven, between C. B. of, &c., of the one part, and A. B., of the same place, yeoman, father of the said C. B., of the other part: Witnesseth, that the said C. B., for divers good causes and considerations, and especially for and in consideration of the sum of one dollar, to him in hand paid, by the said A. B., at and before the ensealing and delivering hereof, the receipt whereof he doth hereby acknowledge, hath given, granted and confirmed, and by these presents doth give, grant and confirm, unto the said A. B., his executors, administrators and assigns, one annuity or yearly rent-charge, of two hundred dollars, lawful money of the United States, to be received, taken, had and issuing out of all that messuage, &c. [here describe the premises,] which the said A. B. and M., his wife, by deed, under their hands and seals, bearing date, &c., granted unto the said C. B. in fee, with all and singular the hereditaments and appurtenances thereunto belonging, and every part and parcel thereof.

To have and to hold the said annuity, or yearly rent-charge of two hundred dollars, unto the said A. B., his executors, administrators and assigns, for, and during the natural life of the said A. B. and M. his wife, the father and mother of the said C. B. and the life of the survivor of them; payable, and to be paid, in and upon the first day of January, first day of April, first day of July, and first day of October, in each and every year, by even and equal portions: And, if it shall happen, that the said annuity or yearly rent-charge of two hundred dollars, or any part thereof, shall be behind, and unpaid, in part or in the whole, by the space of thirty days, next after either of the days or times of payment, whereon the same should, or of right ought to, be paid as aforesaid, *then*, and so often, and at all times thereafter, it shall and may be lawful to and for the said A. B., his executors, administrators and assigns, into the above premises, or into any part thereof, to enter and distrain, for the said annuity, or yearly rent-charge, and the distress and distresses, then and there found and taken, to take, lead, drive, carry away and impound, and the same so impounded, to detain and keep, at the proper risk and charges of the said C. B., his heirs and assigns, for the space of five days.

And if within the same space of five days, payment and satisfaction of the said annuity, or yearly rent-charge, be not made, then, and at any time thereafter, the same distress and distresses to expose and sell, by public auction or vendue, for the best price that may be gotten, and after the said annuity or yearly rent-charge, and the arrearages thereof, be fully paid and satisfied, together with the costs and charges thereabout, the overplus, if any there be, to return to the said C. B., his executors, administrators and assigns: And the said C. B., for himself, his heirs, executors and administrators, doth covenant, promise, grant and agree, to and with the said A. B., his heirs, executors, administrators and assigns, by these presents, that the said C. B., his heirs and assigns, shall and will well and truly pay, or cause to be paid, unto the said A. B., his executors, administrators and assigns, the said annuity, or yearly rent-charge, of two hundred dollars, above-mentioned, in and upon the several days and times above-mentioned, in manner and form above expressed, according to the true intent and meaning of these presents.

Provided always, nevertheless, that if the said C. B., his heirs or assigns, shall and do allow the said A. B. and M. his wife, and the survivor of them, the sole use of the room [or house] which they now occupy, on the premises, with the necessary privileges in the kitchen and cellar, and shall and do deliver, or cause to be delivered, unto the said A. B. yearly, and every year, during the joint lives of the said A. B. and M. his wife, the following articles, in good order, and at proper seasons, to wit: [Here mention the articles.] And, in case of the death of either of them, shall and do deliver unto the survivor of them, one-half of the articles aforesaid, and shall and do provide and keep for them, and the survivor of them, a good riding horse and milk cow, to be changed as often as need be, and feed and pasture the same, in like manner with his, or their own, then and in such case, he, the said C. B., his heirs, executors, administrators and assigns, shall pay, or cause to be paid, unto the said A. B., his executors, administrators and assigns, the sum of ten cents only, (if demanded,) in and upon each of the days and times aforesaid; while the provisions and accommodations aforesaid, are duly found, given and delivered, according to the true intent and meaning of these presents, in lieu and instead of the full quarterly payment of fifty dollars, which shall then be due. In witness whereof, &c.

Deed of Release.

To all people to whom these presents shall come: A. B., C. D., E. F., and G. his wife, of, &c., send greeting: [Here insert the recitals.]

Now know ye, that the said A. B., C. D., E. F. and G. his wife, for and in consideration of the sum of five hundred dollars, to them in hand paid by the said I. S., at and before the ensealing and delivering hereof, the receipt whereof they do hereby acknowledge, and thereof acquit and forever discharge the said I. S., his heirs, executors and administrators, by these presents have, and each and every of them hath, remised, released and for ever quit claim, and by these presents do, and each and every of them doth, remise, release and for ever quit claim unto the said I. S., and to his heirs and assigns, all the estate, and estates, shares, purparts and dividends, right, title, interest, property, claim, and demand whatsoever, of them, the said A. B., C. D., &c., in law or equity, or otherwise howsoever, of, in, to, or out of, all that messuage or tenement, plantation and tract of land, situate, lying and being in the township of Oley aforesaid, (in the actual possession and seisin of the said I. S. now being) bounded and limited as follows, viz. Beginning, &c.

Together with all and singular other the buildings, improvements, rights, members, and appurtenances whatsoever, thereunto belonging, or in anywise appertaining, and the reversions and remainders, rents, issues and profits thereof: To have and to hold all and singular the premises hereby remised and released, or mentioned or intended so to be, with the appurtenances, unto the said I. S., his heirs and assigns, to the only proper use and behoof of the said I. S., his heirs and assigns, forever:

So that neither the said A. B., C. D., E. F. and G. his wife, nor their heirs, nor any other person or persons whosoever, lawfully claiming, or to claim, by, from or under them, or any of them, shall or may, at any time or times hereafter, have, claim, challenge or demand any estate, right, title or interest, of, in, to or out of the said messuage, &c., hereditaments and premises, hereby remised and released, or mentioned or intended so to be, with the appurtenances, or any part or parcel thereof; but thereof and therefrom shall and will be utterly excluded, and for ever debarred, by these presents. In witness, &c.

Deed of Exchange of Lands.

This indenture, made the —— day of ——, between John Smith, of ——, of the one part, and James Black, of ——, of the other part: Witnesseth, that the said John Smith hath given and granted, and by these presents, doth give and grant, unto the said James Black, one field or close of freehold land called or known by the name of ——, &c., with all and every of their appurtenances, situated, lying and being in ——, in the county of ——, &c. [*describe the premises*], for and in exchange of, and for all the lands, tenements and hereditaments of the said James Black, called or known by the name of —— in —— aforesaid, in the said county of ——, bounded and described as follows, [*describe the premises*]. To have and to hold the said field or close, with the appurtenances, to the said James Black, his heirs and assigns forever, for and in exchange of and for the said lands, tenements and hereditaments, called —— with the appurtenances: And the said John Smith doth covenant, &c. [*add such covenants as may be agreed upon*].

And the said James Black hath likewise on his part given and granted, and by these presents doth fully, freely and absolutely, give and grant unto the said John Smith, his heirs and assigns, all those lands, tenements and hereditaments, aforesaid, with the appurtenances, called or known by the name of ——, situate, lying, and being in —— aforesaid, in the said county of ——. To have and to hold the said lands, tenements and hereditaments, &c., to the said John Smith, his heirs and assigns, forever, for and in exchange of and for the said field or close of land ——, &c. Provided always, nevertheless, and these are upon this condition, and it is the true intent and meaning of the parties hereunto, that if it shall happen that either of the said parties to these presents, their executors, administrators or assigns, shall at any time hereafter during the said respective terms above granted, by colour or means of any former or other gift, grant, bargain or sale, or otherwise howsoever, be ousted or evicted of and from the possession of either of the said messuages or tenements, and other the premises, so respectively granted in exchange, as aforesaid, or any part thereof, then and in such cases, these presents, and every matter and thing therein contained, shall be utterly void and of none effect, and then and thenceforth it shall, and may be lawful to and for the party or parties so ousted or evicted, into his or their said former messuage or tenement and premises, with all and singular the appurtenances to re-enter, and the same to have again, repossess, and enjoy, as of his and their former estate or estates: any thing herein contained to the contrary thereto in any wise notwithstanding. In witness, &c.

Deed of Confirmation.

Know all men by these presents, that I, John Jones, of Carlisle, in Cumberland county and state of Pennsylvania, in consideration of the sum of one hundred dollars, to me in hand paid by William Burns, the receipt whereof is hereby acknowledged, have granted, bargained, sold, ratified and confirmed, and by these presents do grant, bargain, sell, ratify and confirm, unto the said William Burns, his heirs and assigns forever, all the estate which I have in the messuage with the appurtenances in Newville, in the county aforesaid, now in the possession and occupation of the said William Burns: To have and to hold the same unto him, the said William Burns, and his heirs and assigns forever. In witness whereof, &c.

Covenant of Warranty.

And the said John Jones, for himself, his heirs, executors and administrators, doth hereby covenant, promise, grant and agree, to and with the said William Burns, his heirs and assigns, by these presents, that he, the said John Jones and his heirs, the said above-mentioned and described messuage and tract of land, hereditaments and appurtenances, hereby granted or mentioned, or intended so to be, unto the said William Burns, his heirs and assigns, against him, the said John Jones, and his heirs, and against all and every other person and persons whomsoever, lawfully claiming or to claim the same or any part thereof, [*by, from or under him, them or any of them,] shall and will warrant and forever defend by these presents.

Covenant for Quiet Enjoyment.

And the said Thomas Martin, for himself, his heirs, executors and administrators, doth covenant, promise, grant and agree, to and with the said John Brady, his heirs and assigns, by these presents, that he, the said John Brady, his heirs and assigns, shall and lawfully may, from time to time, and at all times hereafter, peaceably and quietly have, hold, use, occupy, possess and enjoy the said messuage or tenement, &c., hereditaments and premises, hereby granted or mentioned, or intended so to be, with the appurtenances, without the lawful let, suit, hindrance or molestation of the said Thomas Martin, his heirs or assigns, or of any other person or persons whatsoever, by or with his, their or either of their act, means, consent, privity or procurement.

Covenant for further Assurance.

And further, that he, the said Thomas Martin, and his heirs, and all and every other person or persons lawfully claiming, or to claim, by, from or under him, them, or any of them, shall and will from time to time, and at all times hereafter, upon the reasonable request, and at the proper cost and charges in the law of the said John Brady, his heirs and assigns, make, do and execute, or cause to be made, done and executed, all and every such further and other lawful reasonable act or acts, deed or deeds, device and devices in the law, whatsoever, for the further, better, more perfect

* This, without the words in brackets, is a *general warranty*, that is to say, a warranty against all the world; but with the words in brackets, it is a *special warranty*, that is to say, a warranty against the grantor and his heirs only.

and absolute assurance and confirmation of the said messuage or tenement, &c., hereditaments and premises hereby granted or mentioned, or intended so to be, with the appurtenances, unto the said John Brady, his heirs and assigns, as by him or them, or by his or their counsel learned in the law, shall be reasonably advised, devised, or required.

Covenant against Incumbrances.

And the said John Jones, for himself, his heirs, executors and administrators, doth covenant, promise, grant and agree, to and with the said William Burns, his heirs and assigns, by these presents, that he, the said John Jones, hath not heretofore done, committed, or wittingly or willingly suffered to be done or committed, any act, matter or thing whatsoever, whereby the premises hereby granted, or any part thereof, is, are or shall or may be impeached, charged or incumbered, in title, charge, estate or otherwise howsoever.

Joint Covenant of two or more, to one Person.

And the said A. B., C. D. and E. F., for themselves, their heirs, executors and administrators, and for every of them, do covenant, promise, grant and agree, &c.

Joint and Several Covenant of two or more, to one Person.

And the said A. B., C. D. and E. F., for themselves, their heirs, executors and administrators, and for every of them, do jointly and severally covenant, promise, grant and agree, &c.

A Several Covenant of two or more.

And the said A. B., C. D. and E. F., for themselves severally and respectively, and for their several and respective heirs, executors and administrators, and not jointly, or the one for the other, or others of them, or for the heirs, executors or administrators, acts or deeds of the others of them, but each and every of them for himself only, and for his heirs, executors and administrators, acts and deeds only, do covenant, promise, grant and agree, &c.

DEPOSITION.

Remarks.

Deposition is the testimony of a witness reduced to writing in due form of law, taken by virtue of a commission or other authority, of a competent tribunal. It should be written by the officer, before whom the deposition is taken, or by the witness himself, but never in the hand-writing of the attorneys concerned in the cause, or the parties, or their agents. The hours, between which the depositions are to be taken, are generally named, and they cannot legally be taken at any other time, unless it should be by consent; all of which should appear. The rules of court of the several judicial districts of this Commonwealth, regulate the modes and time of service, in taking depositions.

By an Act of Assembly of the 26th February, 1831, Pamph. L. p. 1292, in all cases where a deposition is to be taken upon a commission, or on a rule of court, or from a justice of the peace, the individual authorized to take the deposition may issue a subpœna for any witness named, and compel his attendance by attachment, or commit him to prison if he refuses to testify. Rules of court generally provide, that either party may at any time enter a rule to take the depositions of witnesses, upon reasonable notice to the opposite party. Where a witness resides beyond the limits of the state, a commission may be issued upon interrogatories filed, for which see title Commission.

Caption of Deposition under a Rule of Court.

Deposition of witnesses produced, sworn and examined by me, the —— day of ——, A. D. ——, at my office, at ——, between the hours of —— A. M., and —— P. M., by virtue of the annexed rule of court of ——, for the examination of witnesses in a certain cause then depending, wherein A. B. is plaintiff, and C. D. is defendant.

E. F., aged —— years or thereabouts, of ——, being produced, sworn and examined, on the part of the ——, deposeth as follows, &c.

A Deposition in the hand-writing of the Witness.

Deposition of A. B., a citizen of the state of ——, residing in the —— of ——, aged ——, reduced to writing by himself to serve as evidence in the case of C. D. *vs.* E. F., in the Circuit Court of the United States, for ——.

I, the said A. B., being duly sworn according to law, do depose and say as follows, &c.

DEPUTATION.

Deputation to a Deputy Register.

To all people to whom these presents shall come, I, —— Register for the Probate of Wills and granting Letters of Administration in and for the county of ——, and commonwealth of Pennsylvania, send greeting:

Know you that, reposing especial trust and confidence in the prudence, integrity and abilities of ——, I have appointed and deputed, and do hereby appoint and depute him, the said ——, to be Deputy Register for the said county, with power to officiate in the Register's office of the said county, in my absence, and take Probate of Wills, grant Letters of Administration, and to do whatsoever else by the laws of the state appertains to my said office. Hereby ratifying, allowing and holding for firm all and whatsoever my said deputy may lawfully do in the premises by virtue of this deputation.

In testimony whereof, I have hereunto set my hand and affixed the seal of said office, the —— day of ——, A. D. ——.

DISCHARGE.

Remarks.

A discharge is the act by which a person in confinement under some legal process, or held on accusation of some crime or misdemeanour, is set at liberty. The writing containing the order for his being so set at liberty, is also called a discharge.

Discharge of Insolvent Debtor from Arrest.

A. B.
vs.
C. D.

Discharge C. D., the defendant above-named, he having given bond to the said plaintiff, with surety approved by me, the subscriber, President Judge of the Court of Common Pleas of the county of ——, agreeably to the provisions of an Act of Assembly, passed on the —— day of ——, A. D. ——, on paying jail fees, if any be due.

Witness my hand, this —— day of ——, A. D. ——.

[*This may be endorsed on the execution.*]

Discharge of Prisoner charged with a Criminal Offence.

Discharge out of your custody the body of A. B., if detained for no other cause than that mentioned in my warrant of the —— day of —— last past. I having taken sureties for his appearance at the next Court of General Quarter Sessions of the peace, to be held at the county aforesaid, to answer the complaint therein mentioned. And for your so doing, this shall be your sufficient warrant.

Given under my hand and seal, the —— day of ——, A. D. ——.

INTEREST.

Remarks.

Interest in Pennsylvania is six per cent.

Interest is to be determined by the law of the place at which the contract is to be executed; and where no rate is stipulated, the parties are presumed to have contracted in reference to the law of the place of performance, whether it be statutory or customary. Archer *vs.* Dunn, 2 W. & S. 364–5. Where the contract is made in another state, the interest allowed in that state may be given. Jeffray *vs.* Dennis, 2 W. C. C. R. 253.

So where a note was given in China, payable eighteen months after date, without any stipulation respecting interest, the court allowed the Chinese interest of one per cent. per month, from the expiration of the eighteen months. Cowqua *vs.* Lauderbrun, 1 W. C. C. R. 521.

If any person in this state shall receive or take more than legal interest, he shall forfeit the money and other things lent; one-half thereof to the governor for the support of government, and the other half to the person who shall sue for the same. See Act of 2d March, 1723; 1 Smith, p. 156.

Every payment made on any obligation drawing interest, is construed to be a payment on the interest, and the balance on the principal. Compute, for instance, the interest on the principal up to the time of the first payment. If the said first payment is more than the interest due at the time of payment, add the interest with the principal, and deduct the amount of said payment. Then cast the interest upon the balance to the second payment, add and deduct in the same way as before, and so on through all the payments.

If, however, the payment or payments be less than the interest due at the time of payment, the above rule will not apply, but the payment will be applied on the interest; and the amount of interest still remaining due cannot be added to the principal, to increase the amount upon which interest is to accrue. In short, if interest is not collected, the one to whom it is due cannot get interest on it, as that would be construed to be compound interest.

The following mode of calculating interest is correct, when the payment is more than the amount of interest accrued at the time of such payment. A bond was given by A. B. to C. D. for $1000, dated 1st of January, 1840, and payable in five equal annual instalments, payable on the 1st of January, in each and every year, with interest on the whole sum from date of bond.

On the same is endorsed as follows: 1st January, 1841, is paid $260; 1st January, 1842, $248; 1st January, 1843, $236; 1st January, 1844, $224; and on the 1st of January, 1845, $212.

Original sum on the bond - - - - -	$1000 00
Interest from 1st January, 1840, till the 1st of January 1841, on $1000, when the first payment was made - - - - - -	60 00
	1060 00
Deduct the payment made 1st January, 1841, of -	260 00
Leaving due after first payment - - -	800 00
Interest on $800 from the 1st of January, 1841, till the 1st of January, 1842. It being one year - - - - - - -	48 00
	848 00
Deduct payment of 1st January, 1842, of - -	248 00
Remaining due after second payment - -	600 00
Interest on $600 from 1st January, 1842, till 1st January, 1843. It being one year - -	36 00
	636 00
Deduct payment of 1st January, 1843, of - -	236 00
Remaining due after third payment - - -	400 00
Interest on $400 from the 1st of January, 1843, till the 1st of January, 1844. It being one year -	24 00
	424 00
Deduct payment of 1st January, 1844, of - -	224 00
Remaining due after fourth payment - -	200 00
Interest on $200 from 1st January, 1844, till 1st January, 1845. It being one year - -	12 00
	212 00
Deduct payment of 1st January, 1845, of - -	212 00

The following is a calculation of interest where several of the payments made, did not amount to as much as the interest due at the time those payments were made. A bond was given by A. B. to C. D. for $1000, dated 1st January, 1840, and payable in five equal annual instalments, payable on the 1st of January, in each and every year, with interest on the whole sum from date of bond. On the same is endorsed as follows: 1st January, 1841, paid $30; 1st January, 1842, $40; 1st January, 1843, $50; and on the 1st January, 1844, $260. See how much remains due 1st January, 1845.

Original bond for - - - -		$1000 00
Paid 1st January, 1841,	$30	
" " 1842,	— 40	
" " 1843,	— 50	
Three payments added	120	
Interest on $1000 from 1st January, 1840, till the 1st of January, 1844, when $260 was paid. It being 4 years - - - -		240 00
		1240 00
Deduct the three payments added above, and amounting to - - - -		120 00
		1120 00
Deduct also payment of 1st January, 1844, of -		260 00
		860 00
Interest on $860 from 1st January, 1844, till 1st January, 1845. It being one year - -		51 60
Remaining due 1st January, 1845, - -		$911 60

AN INTEREST TABLE,

Showing the interest on sums from $10 to $5,000 for 15 days, for 1 month, and for 1 year, at six per cent.

		cts.			cts.			cts.
$ 10	15d.	2½	$ 10	1m.	5	$ 10	1y.	60
20	“	5	20	“	10	20	“	1 20
30	“	7½	30	“	15	30	“	1 80
40	‘	10	40	“	20	40	“	2 40
50	‘	12½	50	“	25	50	“	3 00
60	‘	15	60	“	30	60	“	3 60
70	‘	17½	70	“	35	70	“	4 20
80	‘	20	80	“	40	80	“	4 80
90	‘	22½	90	“	45	90	“	5 40
100	‘	25	100	“	50	100	“	6 00
200	“	50	200	“	1 00	200	“	12 00
300	‘	75	300	“	1 50	300	“	18 00
400	“	$ 1 00	400	“	2 00	400	“	24 00
500	“	1 25	500	“	2 50	500	“	30 00
1000	“	2 50	1000	“	5 00	1000	“	60 00
2000	“	5 00	2000	“	10 00	2000	“	120 00
3000	“	7 50	3000	“	15 00	3000	“	180 00
4000	“	10 00	4000	“	20 00	4000	“	240 00
5000	“	12 50	5000	“	25 00	5000	“	300 00

INTEREST PER DAY.

$ 100	1 day	1⅔	cents.	$ 2000	1 day	33⅓	cents.
200	“	3⅓	“	3000	“	50	“
300	“	5	“	4000	“	66⅔	“
400	“	6⅔	“	5000	“	83⅓	“
500	“	8⅓	“	6000	“	$1 00	“
600	“	10	“	7000	“	1 16⅔	“
700	“	11⅔	“	8000	“	1 33⅓	“
800	“	13⅓	“	9000	“	1 50	“
900	“	15	“	10,000	“	1 66⅔	“
1000	“	16⅔	“	20,000	“	3 33⅓	“

A TABLE,

Showing the number of days from any day in the month to the same day in any other month throughout the year.

	January.	February.	March.	April.	May.	June.	July.	August.	September.	October.	November.	December.
January,	365	31	59	90	120	151	181	212	243	273	304	334
February,	334	365	28	59	89	120	150	181	212	242	273	303
March,	306	337	365	31	61	92	122	153	184	214	245	275
April,	275	306	334	365	30	61	91	122	153	183	214	244
May,	245	376	304	335	365	31	61	92	123	153	184	218
June,	214	245	273	304	334	365	30	61	91	122	153	183
July,	184	215	243	274	304	335	365	31	62	92	123	153
August,	153	184	212	243	273	304	334	363	31	61	92	122
September,	122	153	181	212	242	273	303	334	365	30	61	91
October,	92	123	151	182	212	243	273	304	335	365	31	61
November,	61	92	120	151	181	212	243	273	304	334	365	30
December,	31	61	90	121	151	182	212	243	274	304	335	365

EXPLANATION.—How many days are there from the 10th of January to the 10th of June?

Look for January in the column at the *left hand*, then seek for June along the line to the *right*, and you will find the number of days to be 151.

Inventory.

A true and perfect inventory, and just appraisement, of all and singular, the goods and chattels, rights and credits, which were of William Dickenson, late of the township of Springfield, in the county of Erie, and Commonwealth of Pennsylvania, yeoman, deceased, at the time of his death, to wit:

		Dolls.	cts.
Cash - - - - - - -		500	00
Wearing apparel - - - - -		80	00
Goods bequeathed to the widow, viz: - -			
3 cows - - -	$40 00		
1 bureau, dining table, 6 chairs and 3 portraits and frames - -	$125 00		
4 beds and bedding - -	95 00		
1 large Bible - - -	10 00		
		270	00
1 two-horse wagon - - - -		50	00
1 Buggy do - - - - -		100	00
Plough and harrow - - - -		12	00
3 horses - - - - - -		180	00
12 cows - - - - - -		150	00
Grain in the ground, about twenty-five acres of wheat - - - - -		250	00
Bonds and notes - - - - -		740	00
Book debts - - - - -		100	50
		2432	50

Taken and appraised by us, the first day of January, A. D. one thousand eight hundred and forty-five.

JOHN DOE,
RICHARD ROE.

Erie County, *ss.*

On the first day of January, A. D. 1845, before me, the subscriber, one of the Justices of the Peace, in and for the said county, came the above-named John Doe and Richard Roe, who being duly sworn [or affirmed, as the case may be] according to law, do declare, that the above inventory contains a just and true appraisement of the goods and chattels, rights and credits, which were of the said William Dickenson deceased, so far as the same came to their knowledge. JOHN DOE.
RICHARD ROE.

Sworn and subscribed before me the day and year aforesaid,

JOHN NICHOLSON, *Justice of the Peace.*

Remarks.

In taking the inventory as aforesaid, it shall be the duty of the executor or administrator, if the decedent shall have left a widow or children, who were residing with him at the time of his decease, and there is reason to believe the estate insufficient to pay his debts, exclusive of such articles as may be by law exempted from levy or sale, upon an execution against a debtor, to keep separate and distinct therein, an account of all such articles as are exempted from levy or sale; and the same shall not be sold, but suffered to remain for the use of such widow and children, without further account thereof. Act of 24th February, 1834, Pamph. L. p. 70. The articles which are exempt in Pennsylvania from execution, and which are mentioned as above stated, to remain for the use of the widow and children, without further account thereof, are as follows, to wit: Household utensils, not exceeding in value thirty dollars. The necessary tools of a tradesman, not exceeding in value thirty dollars. All wearing apparel of the defendant and his family. Four beds, and the necessary bedding. A spinning-wheel and reel. A stove, with the pipe of the same, and necessary fuel for three months. One cow, two hogs, also six sheep, with the wool thereof, or the yarn or cloth manufactured therefrom, and feed sufficient for the said cow, hogs and sheep, from the first day of November, until the last day of May. Any quantity of meat not exceeding two hundred pounds, twenty bushels of potatoes, ten bushels of grain, or the meal made therefrom. Any quantity of flax not exceeding ten pounds, or the thread or linen made therefrom. All Bibles and school books in the use of the family. In the above inventory, should be included all bonds, notes, and other evidences of debt, also all other claims and demands for money, or any other personal property owned or held by the decedent at the time of his decease shall, as far as the same may be known to his executors or administrators, be included in the inventory to be made and returned as aforesaid. If personal property or assets of any kind, not contained in the inventory made and returned as aforesaid, shall afterwards come to the possession or knowledge of the executor or administrator, he shall take an inventory thereof, and return the same into the office of the proper register, within four months from the time of the discovery thereof. See Act of 24th Feb., 1834, Pamph. L. p. 70. Executors and administrators of every decedent shall immediately after the granting of letters testamentary, or of administration to them, cause notice thereof to be given in one newspaper, published at, or near the place where such decedent resided, once a week during at least six successive weeks, together with their names and places of residence, and in every such notice they shall request all persons having claims or demands against the estate of the said decedent to make known the same to them without delay. See Act of 24th February, 1834, Pamph. L. p. 70.

The executors or administrators of a decedent (who resided in Pennsylvania at the time of his decease,) must file an inventory in the register's office of the county, within thirty days from the time of administration granted, and also make a settlement thereof in one year, or when legally required.

The appraisers of an estate cannot charge respectively to exceed one dollar per day, for every day while diligently employed in making the appraisal. When any executor or administrator shall sell, at public auction or vendue, any of the personal estate of the decedent, he shall, within thirty days thereafter, file in the office of the register having jurisdiction, a just and true account of the articles so sold, and the prices and purchasers thereof. See Act of Assembly, 24th Feb., 1834.

All debts owing by any person within this state, (Pennsylvania,) at the time of his decease, shall be paid by his executors or administrators, so far as they have assets, in the manner and order following, viz: 1. Funeral expenses, medicine furnished and medical attendance given during the last illness of the decedent, and servants' wages not exceeding one year. 2. Rents not exceeding one year. 3. All other debts, without regard to the quality of the same, except debts due to the commonwealth, which shall be last paid.

No executors or administrators shall be compelled to pay any debt of the decedent, except such as are by law preferred in the order of payment to rents, until one year be fully elapsed from the granting of the administration of the estate. Same Act of Assembly.

For the mode of settling an account on final settlement, see Administrators, Executors or Guardian's accounts as the case may be.

LANDLORD AND TENANT.

Remarks.

A landlord is one who rents or leases real estate to another.

A tenant is one who holds or possesses lands or tenements by any kind of title, either in fee, for life, for years, or at will. A tenant for life is one to whom lands or tenements are granted, or to which he derives by operation of law a title for the term of his own life, or for that of any other person, or for more lives than one. He is called tenant for life, except when he holds the estate by the life of another, when he is called tenant *per autre vie*. 2 Bl. Com. 84. A tenant for years is one to whom another has let lands, tenements and hereditaments, for a term of certain years, or for a lesser definite period of time; and the lessee enters thereon. 2 Bl. Com. 140.

A tenant at will is when lands or tenements are let by one man to another, to have and to hold to him at the will of the lessor, by force of which the lessee is in possession. In this case the lessee is called a tenant at will. Every lease at will must be at the will of both parties. Co. Litt. 55; 2 Bl. Com. 145.

Tenants in common are such as hold by several and distinct titles, but by unity of possession. 2 Bl. Com. 191.

Warrant of Landlord to distrain for Rent.

Chester County, *ss.*

To A. B., constable of the township of ——, in the county of Chester.

Whereas by an agreement made in writing the tenth day of March, in the year of our Lord one thousand eight hundred and forty-four, between C. D. and E. F., both of the township of ——, in the County of Chester, farmers, the said C. D. did demise and lease unto the said E. F., a certain plantation and tract of land, for the term of one year, to commence on the first day of April next after the date of the said agreement, subject to the conditions in the same agreement mentioned, he, the said E. F., yielding and paying therefor unto the said C. D., the yearly rent of two hundred dollars in equal quarterly payments: And whereas the first two quarters of the said term have since expired, and one quarter's rent amounting to fifty dollars yet remains due and unpaid. These are therefore to authorize and require you to distrain the goods and chattels of the said E. F., lying and being upon the said demised premises, or wherever the same goods and chattels may be found within the space of thirty days next ensuing the conveying away or carrying off such goods and chattels from the said demised premises, and proceed to sell the same according to law, for the best price that can be gotten, returning the overplus, if any, to the said E. F., after payment of the said rent, and all legal costs and charges of such distress. And for so doing this shall be your warrant.

Witness my hand and seal at —— township aforesaid, the tenth day of October, in the year of our Lord one thousand eight hundred and forty-four.

C. D.

Notice of Distress.

To E. F., of the township of ——, in the County of Chester.

Take notice, that by the authority and on behalf of your landlord, C. D., I have this day distrained the several goods and chattels specified in the schedule hereunto annexed, in your house and barn at the township aforesaid, for fifty dollars, arrearage of rent due to him, the said C. D. And if you do not pay the said rent so due and in arrear as aforesaid, or replevy the same goods and chattels according to law, within five days hereafter, I shall, after the expiration of the said five days from the date hereof, cause the said goods and chattels to be appraised and sold, according to the act of General Assembly in such case made and provided.

Given under my hand the tenth day of October, Anno Domini one thousand eight hundred and forty-four.

A. B., *Constable of* —— *township.*

Schedule.

An inventory of the several goods and chattels distrained by me, A. B., constable of the township of ——, in the County of Chester, the tenth day of October, Anno Domini one thousand eight hundred and forty-four, in the house and barn of E. F., of the same township, by the authority and on behalf of C. D., of the township aforesaid, for fifty dollars arrear of rent due to him, the said C. D.

In the house.	In the barn.
One clock,	Twenty bushels of wheat,
One bureau, &c.	Ten bushels of rye, &c.

A copy of the above notice and schedule was this day delivered to the said E. F., [or "was this day left at the mansion house of the said E. F.,"] in my presence.

October 10, 1844. J. S.

Proceedings under the Act of 3*d April,* 1830.

Notice to remove in 15 (*or* 30) *days.*

You have hereby notice to quit, within fifteen [or thirty*] days from the date of this notice, the premises situated, &c., which I have leased to you, reserving rent, (you having neglected or refused to pay the amount so reserved, as often as the same has grown due according to the terms of our contract, and there being no goods on the premises, adequate to pay the rent so reserved, except such articles as are exempt from levy and sale, by the laws of this commonwealth,) or I shall proceed against you as is by law directed. A. B.

To C. D.

* Where the lessee shall neglect or refuse to pay rent reserved, as often as the same may grow due, according to the terms of the contract, and where there are no goods on the premises adequate to pay the said rent so in arrear, except such articles as are exempt from levy and sale, by the laws of the commonwealth, it shall and may be lawful for the lessor to give the lessee notice to quit the premises within *fifteen days* from the date of the notice, if such notice is given on or after the first day of April, and before the first of September, and within *thirty days* from the date thereof, if given on or after the first of September, and before the first day of April. Act of 3d April, 1830.

If, after notice, the lessee does not leave the premises within the fifteen (or thirty) days, or pay the rent, the lessor may make complaint on oath, to two Justices of the Peace, and have the tenant ejected.

Landlord's Affidavit or Complaint.

County of ——, *ss.*

On the —— day of ——, in the year 1844, personally appeared before us, two of the Justices of the Peace in and for the said county, A. B., who being sworn [or affirmed] according to law, saith that the premises, situate, &c., [here describe the premises,] were leased to a certain C. D., reserving rent, that the said rent is in arrear and unpaid, that there are not goods and chattels on the said premises adequate to pay and satisfy the said rent, except such as are by law exempt from levy and sale, and that the said lessee was, on the —— day of ——, notified in writing to quit the said premises within fifteen [or thirty] days from that date, but has nevertheless, refused to surrender and deliver up possession of the said premises.

Sworn, &c.

Form of Appraisement.

An appraisement of the several goods and chattels distrained by A. B., constable of the township of ——, the tenth day of October, Anno Domini one thousand eight hundred and forty-four, in the house and barn of E. F., of the same township, by the authority and on behalf of C. D., of the township aforesaid, for fifty dollars, arrear of rent due to him the said C. D.

In the house.		In the barn.	
One clock valued at	$15	Twenty bushels of wheat valued at	$20
One Bureau	10	Ten bushels of Rye	5

Appraised by us, after having been duly sworn according to law, the 16th day of October, A. D. 1844.

S. M.
P. R.
Appraisers.

☞ Appraisers must be sworn, for form of which, see "oath of appraisers of goods distrained for rent."

Notice of Sale.

Will be sold by public vendue on Tuesday, the twenty-fourth day of October, instant, at the house of G. H. in —— township, in the county of Chester, the following goods and chattels distrained for rent, as the property of E. F., of the said township, that is to say, one clock, one bureau, twenty bushels of wheat, ten bushels of rye, &c., &c. Due attendance will be given and the terms of sale made known by

A. B.
Constable of —— township.

Proceedings against Tenant holding over.

Notice to quit after expiration of the term.

Sir—Take notice, that as the term for which the plantation or tract of land situate in ——, &c., [or messuage and tenement, &c.] now occupied by you, and which was demised by me to you for the term of one year, expired on the —— day of ——, 1845. And as I am desirous to have again and repossess the said premises, you are hereby required to remove from and leave the same.

A. B.

April 10, 1845.
To C. D.

Notice to quit at the expiration of the term.

Sir—Take notice, that as the term for which the messuage and tenement, with the appurtenances, situate in, &c., now in your possession, which was leased by me to you, for the term of two years, will expire on the —— day of ——, 1845, and as I am desirous to have again and repossess the said premises, upon the determination of the said lease, you are hereby required to remove from and leave the same at the expiration of the term aforesaid.

A. B.

December 20, 1844.
To C. D.

☞ The above notice to tenant to quit, must be served at least three months previous to any further proceedings being instituted to eject him. If, at the expiration of three months after notice to quit, the tenant still refuses to deliver possession of the premises, the following proceeding may be instituted to eject him.

Complaint to two Justices.

To E. F. and G. H., Justices of the Peace in and for the county of ——.

The complaint of A. B. most respectfully sets forth, that he is owner of a certain messuage or tenement with the appurtenances, situate in, &c., and was in possession thereof on the —— day of ——, A. D. ich time he demised the said premises to a certain C. D., by a written lease bearing date the day and year aforesaid, for the full term of one year, from that day, which said term was fully ended on the —— day of ——, A. D. 1845; the said A. B. being desirous, upon the determination of said lease, to have again and repossess his estate, for that purpose did, on the —— day of ——, last past, require the said C. D. to remove from and leave the same, and the said C. D. hath hitherto refused, and still doth refuse, to comply therewith; that three months having elapsed since the service of the said notice, he makes this his complaint, that such proceedings may be taken by you as are directed by the Act of Assembly in such case made and provided.

A. B.

Sworn and subscribed before me, this —— day of ——, 1845. J. P.

LEASE.

Remarks.

A lease is a contract for the possession and profits of lands and tenements on one side, and a recompense of rent or other income on the other; 4 Bac. Abr. 4; or else it is a conveyance of lands and tenements to a person for life, or years, or at will; in consideration of a return of rent or other recompense. Cruise's Dig., title Leases.

Lease.

This indenture, made the tenth day of May, in the year of our Lord one thousand eight hundred and thirty-seven, between A. B., of, &c., of the one part, and C. D., of, &c., of the other part: Witnesseth, that the said A. B., for and in consideration of the yearly rent and covenants hereinafter mentioned and reserved, on the part and behalf of the said C. D., his executors, administrators and assigns, to be paid, kept and performed, hath demised, set, and to farm let, and by these presents doth demise, set and to farm let, unto the said C. D., his executors, administrators and assigns, all that messuage and lot of ground, situate, lying and being in the city of Philadelphia aforesaid, bounded northward, &c. Together with all and singular, &c.: To have and to hold the said messuage and lot of ground, and all and singular the premises hereby demised, with the appurtenances, unto the said C. D., his executors, administrators and assigns, from the first day of May next ensuing the date hereof, for and during the term of seven years thence next ensuing, and fully to be completed and ended, yielding and paying for the same unto the said A. B., his executors, administrators and assigns, the yearly rent or sum of one hundred dollars in four equal quarterly payments of twenty-five dollars each, the first of which to be made on the first day of May next.

And the said C. D., for himself, his heirs, executors and administrators, doth covenant, promise and agree, to and with the said A. B., his heirs, executors, administrators and assigns, by these presents, that he, the said C. D., his heirs, executors and administrators, or some of them, shall and will well and truly pay or cause to be paid, unto the said A. B., his heirs, executors, administrators or assigns, the said yearly rent of one hundred dollars, hereby reserved, on the several days and times hereinbefore mentioned and appointed for the payment thereof, according to the true intent and meaning of these presents. And the said A. B., for himself, his heirs, executors and administrators, doth covenant, promise, grant and agree, to and with the said C. D., his executors, administrators and assigns, by these presents, that he, the said C. D., his executors, administrators and assigns, (paying the rent and performing the covenants aforesaid,) shall and lawfully may peaceably and quietly, have, hold, use, occupy, possess and enjoy the said demised premises, with the appurtenances, during the term aforesaid, without the lawful let, suit, trouble, eviction, molestation or interruption of the said A. B., his heirs or assigns, or any other person or persons whatsoever. In witness whereof, the said parties, &c.

A Lease for years, of a House and Lands, with exceptions and Special Covenants, &c.

This indenture, made the first day of January, A. D. one thousand eight hundred and forty-five, between A. A., of Norristown, in the County of Montgomery, of the one part, and B. B, of the same place, of the other part: Witnesseth, that the said A. A., for and in consideration of the yearly rent of five hundred dollars, payable half yearly, at the expiration of every six months from the leasing of said premises, and also the covenants hereinafter mentioned and reserved to be paid, kept and performed by the said B. B, his executors, administrators and assigns, which the said B. B. doth hereby covenant to pay and perform, hath demised, set and to farm let, and by these presents doth demise, set and to farm let, unto the said B. B., his executors, administrators and assigns, all that messuage, tenement or farm house, late in the possession of E. B., with the appurtenances, situate in ——, together with all and singular the yards, gardens, orchards, lawns, edifices and buildings thereunto belonging, and also all those several closes, pieces or parcels of arable land, meadow, pasture, wood and wood-ground, containing by estimation —— acres, (be they more or less, lying and being in ——, to the said messuage, tenement or farm house belonging, and therewith held, used, occupied and enjoyed, as part and parcel thereof.)

Except, and always reserving, out of this present lease unto the said A. A., his heirs and assigns, all timber and timberlike trees, and all other trees whatsoever, but the fruit trees for their fruit only, and the pollard trees for their lops and tops only, which now are, or at any time or times hereafter shall be standing, growing, and being in, upon and about the said leased premises, or any part thereof, with free liberty of ingress, egress and regress to and for the said A. A., his heirs and assigns, servants and workmen, from time to time, and at all times during the term hereby leased, the same to fell, stock up, cut down, hew and carry away, in and through the said leased premises or any part thereof, (doing no wilful hurt or damage to the grain or grass of the said B. B., his executors, administrators and assigns,) at all times during the term hereby leased, and free liberty to enter into and upon the said premises, and every part thereof, to view the condition of the repairs thereof.

And also that he, the said B. B., his heirs, executors, administrators or assigns, shall not, nor will, at any time during this present lease, crop or sow above two years together, any of the arable lands and closes, hereby leased, but every third year permit the same to lie fallow and unsown. And that it shall and may be lawful to and for the said A. A., his heirs and assigns, with servants, horses, ploughs, carts and other necessaries, at —— day next preceding the expiration of this present lease, to enter upon such closes and grounds, parcel of the said hereby leased premises, as then ought to lie fallow and unsown, and the same to plough, fallow and manure, and to have the grass, herbage, sheep walks and sheep commons thereof, and also to enter upon the dung which shall then be in the yard or yards, and at the same time to have the dung in the hen house, and also to have some convenient place in the said dwelling house for his and their servants to lodge and diet in, and some convenient place to lay hay and chaff in, and some convenient stable for their horses to stand and be in, without extinguishment of any of the yearly rent hereinbefore reserved, and without giving or making any allowance or satisfaction for the same.

And further, that the said B. B., his executors, administrators and assigns, shall not, at any time or times, during the last two years of the said term, sell, give away, or otherwise dispose of any of the straw which shall be growing and arising upon the said leased premises. And the said B. B., his executors, administrators or assigns, shall not, nor will, at any time or times during the time hereby leased, lop, top, shred or cut any of the trees or spring wood belonging to the said leased premises, but such pollard trees and spring wood, as have been usually lopped and cut by former and other tenants, and those only of twelve years growth, and the lops which shall arise and come therefrom, carry into the said hereby leased messuage or farm-house, there to be spent by way of fire-bote, and not to be sold or disposed of in any other way whatsoever, and shall not nor will, at any time or times during this lease, inordinately burn or waste any of the fire-wood which is so allowed to be spent by way of fire-bote as aforesaid, and shall keep the said pollard trees, as also all the fruit trees and spring wood from all wilful or negligent hurt or waste. In witness whereof, the said parties have hereunto set their hands and seals the day and year first above written.

Signed, sealed and delivered }
in presence of }

ALEXANDER HILANDS.

A. A.

B. B.

Short Lease of a House.

Agreed the —— day of ——, in the year of our Lord one thousand eight hundred and ——, between N. B., of —— township, in the County of —— and State of Pennsylvania, merchant, of the one part, and S. W., of the same place, carpenter, of the other part, as follows: The said N. B. doth let unto the said S. W., his heirs and assigns, a certain lot of land whereon is erected a stone dwelling and stable, situate in the township aforesaid, and now occupied by D. D., adjoining lands of C. L., for the term of one year, from the first day of April next, for the yearly rent of —— dollars, to be paid in four equal quarterly payments, viz., on the first days of July, October, January and April, which said yearly rent the said S. W. doth hereby for himself, his executors and administrators, covenant and agree to pay unto the said N. B., his heirs, executors and assigns. And at the expiration of the said term, or sooner, he, the said S. W., his heirs and assigns, shall and will quietly and peaceably surrender and yield up the said demised premises, with the appurtenances, unto the said N. B., his heirs and assigns, in as good order and repair as the same now are, reasonable wear, tear and casualties which may happen by fire or otherwise only excepted. In witness whereof, we have hereunto set our hands and seals the day and year above written.

Witness present,

S. W.

N. B.

Lease of a Farm.

This indenture, made the —— day of ——, in the year of our Lord one thousand eight hundred and ——, between S. S., of the township of ——, in the County of ——, and State of Pennsylvania, of the one part, and W. J., of —— township, county and state aforesaid, of the other part: Witnesseth, that the said S. S., for and in consideration of the yearly rent and covenants hereinafter mentioned and reserved, on the part and behalf of the said S. S., his heirs, executors and administrators, to be paid, kept and performed, hath demised, set, and to farm let, and by these presents doth demise, set, and to farm let, unto the said W. J., his heirs and assigns, all that certain messuage or tenement, tract, piece or parcel of land, situate in the township of —— aforesaid adjoining lands of A. E., J. S., S. J. and others, and now in the tenure of T. T., containing —— acres, together with all and singular the buildings, improvements and other the premises hereby demised, with the appurtenances. To have and to hold the same unto the said W. J., his heirs and assigns, from the first day of April next ensuing the date hereof, for and during the term of —— years, thence next ensuing, and fully to be completed and ended; the said W. J. yielding and paying for the same unto the said S. S., his heirs and assigns, the yearly rent or sum of —— dollars, on the —— day of —— in each and every year during the term aforesaid. [If the rent is to be paid in produce, after the words, *fully to be completed and ended,* say as follows, or as the agreement may be: "The said W. J. yielding and paying thereout unto the said S. S., his heirs and assigns, the yearly rent as follows: one half of all the winter grain, one third of all the summer grain raised and growing on the premises, and the sum of twenty dollars in cash, for the meadow grass, the said grain to be delivered by the bushel at the house of the said S. S., in good order and in proper season."] And at the expiration of the said term or sooner determination thereof, he, the said W. J., his heirs and assigns, shall and will quietly and peaceably surrender and yield up the said demised premises with the appurtenances, unto the said S. S., his heirs and assigns, in as good order and repair as the same now are, reasonable wear, tear and casualties which may happen by fire or otherwise only excepted. In witness whereof, the said parties have hereunto interchangeably set their hands and seals the day and year above written.

Special Covenants in a Lease not to pursue certain occupations.

And also, that he, the said C. D., his executors, administrators and assigns, shall not, nor will, at any time during the continuance of the said term, permit or suffer any person or persons to use or follow, in and upon the premises, or in or upon any part thereof, the trade of a butcher, soap boiler, brewer, distiller, tallow-chandler, dyer, &c. &c., [as the case may be] or any nauseous or offensive business whatsoever, without the license and consent of the said A. B., his heirs, executors, administrators or assigns, first had and obtained in writing, for that purpose.

Clause to be inserted in a Lease to inhabit part of the premises.

And also, that the said C. D., shall and will personally inhabit and occupy the said messuage or farm-house, with the appurtenances, and not shut up or desert the same during the said term.

Clause not to Assign or underlease.

And also, that the said C. D., his executors and administrators, shall not nor will, at any time during the said term, assign or set over, underlease or underlet the premises, or in any other manner part with the possession or occupation of the same, without the special license of the said A. B., his heirs or assigns, in writing under his or their hands and seals, first had and obtained.

Clause to be inserted in a Lease, if required, that Lessor shall pay the taxes.

That he, the said Samuel Smith, his executors, administrators and assigns, shall and will, from time to time, and at all times during the said term hereby granted, well and truly pay or allow out of the rent hereby reserved, all rates, taxes, duties, charges and assessments whatsoever, that shall or may be assessed, charged, rated or imposed on the said hereby demised premises, or any part thereof, and thereof and therefrom save harmless and keep indemnified the said John Jones, his executors, administrators and assigns, and also his and their goods and chattels, lands and tenements.

Clause to insure the premises from Fire, and to rebuild in case of Damage.

And that he, the said Richard Clyde, his executors, administrators and assigns, shall and will, at his and their own proper costs and charges, from time to time sufficiently insure all and every the messuages or tenements, erections or buildings which shall be erected and built upon the said piece or parcel of ground hereby demised, or any part thereof from casualties by fire, during the then remainder of the said term hereby granted, in some or one of the public offices kept for that purpose in ——, and in case the said messuages or tenements, erections or buildings, or any of them, or any part of any of them, shall at any time or times during the said term be burnt down, destroyed, or damaged by fire, shall and will from time to time immediately afterwards rebuild, or well and sufficiently repair the same.

LETTER OF ATTORNEY.

Remarks.

A letter of attorney is a written instrument under seal, by which one or more persons called the constituents, authorize one or more other persons, called the attorneys, to do some lawful act by the latter, for or instead, and in the place of the former. The authority given in the letter of attorney is either general, as to transact all the business of the constituent; or special, as to do some special business, particularly named; as to collect a debt.

It is either revocable or irrevocable. It is revocable when no interest is conveyed to the attorney, or some other person. It is irrevocable, when the constituent conveys a right to the attorney in the matter, which is the subject of it; as when it is given as part security. 2 Esp. R. 565. If the letters of attorney are to be put upon record, they must be acknowledged.

General form of Letter of Attorney to receive Debts.

Know all men by these presents, That I, A. B., of the borough of Reading, in the County of Berks, and State of Pennsylvania, merchant, have made, constituted and appointed, and by these presents do make, constitute and appoint, and in my place and stead put and depute, C. D., of the city of Philadelphia, and state aforesaid, merchant, my true and lawful attorney, for me, and in my name, and for my use, to ask, demand, sue for, recover and receive, all such sum or sums of money, debts, goods, wares, and other demands whatsoever, which is or shall be due, owing, payable and belonging to me, by any manner or means whatsoever, especially, &c. [Here state particularly what the attorney is required to execute.]

Giving and granting unto my said attorney, by these presents, my full and whole power, strength and authority, in and about the premises; to have, use, and take all lawful ways and means, in my name, for the purposes aforesaid; and upon the receipt of any such debts, dues, or sums of money, [as the case may be], acquittances, or other sufficient discharges, for me, and in my name, to make, seal and deliver.

And generally, all and every other act or acts, thing and things, device and devices, in the law, whatsoever, needful and necessary to be done, in and about the premises, for me and in my name, to do, execute and perform, as fully, largely and amply, to all intents and purposes, as I myself might or could do, if personally present; and attorneys one or more under him, for the purpose aforesaid, to make and constitute, and again at pleasure to revoke.

Hereby ratifying, allowing, and holding for firm and effectual, all and whatsoever my said attorney shall lawfully do, in and about the premises, by virtue hereof. In witness whereof, I have hereunto set my hand and seal, this tenth day of January, in the year of our Lord one thousand eight hundred and thirty-seven.

Letter of Attorney to receive Money on a Bond.

Know all men by these presents, that I, A. B., of the borough of Reading, and State of Pennsylvania, hatter, do make, constitute and appoint C. D., of the city of Baltimore, in the State of Maryland, my true and lawful attorney, for me and in my name, to ask, demand and receive from E. F., of the city of Baltimore aforesaid, the sum of three hundred dollars, due unto me, in and by a certain bond or obligation, bearing date the —— day of ——, and upon non-payment thereof, to have, use, and take all lawful ways and means in my name, or otherwise, for the recovery of the same, with the interest thereon, if any be due, by attachment, bill, plaint, arrest or otherwise. In witness whereof, I have hereunto set my hand and seal, this tenth day of May, A. D. one thousand eight hundred and forty-four.

General Letter of Substitution.

To all people to whom these presents shall come: Whereas A. B., of the city of New Orleans, and state aforesaid, merchant, in and by a certain instrument of writing or letter of attorney, bearing date the first day of January, one thousand eight hundred and twenty-nine, did make, constitute and appoint, C. D. to, &c. [as in the original power,] as in and by the said letter of attorney, (recorded, or intended to be recorded, &c.) relation being thereunto had appears. Now know ye, That the said C. D. has made, appointed, substituted, and by these presents, by virtue of the power and authority given to him by the said recited letter of attorney, doth make, appoint, and substitute, E. F., of, &c., to be the true and lawful attorney of the said A. B., the constituent in the foregoing letter of attorney named, to do, execute, and perform, all such acts, deeds, matters and things, as shall and may be requisite and necessary to be done and performed, for effecting the purposes and object in the said letter of attorney contained, as fully and effectually in all respects, and to all intents and purposes, as I myself might or could do in virtue of the power and authority aforesaid, if personally present, hereby ratifying and confirming all and whatsoever my said substitute may lawfully do in virtue hereof. In witness, &c.

Letter of Revocation, &c.

To all people to whom these presents shall come; I, A. B., of, &c., send greeting: Whereas, I, the said A. B., did heretofore, by a certain instrument in writing, or letter of attorney, empower C. D., of, &c., to be my attorney, in my name and for my use, to recover and receive all such moneys, debts and effects whatsoever, as were due, owing or payable unto me, by, &c. [as in the power.] And to do all other matters and things, as fully as I myself might or could do, for that purpose, &c. or to that or the like effect, as by the same writing, relation being thereunto had, at large appears. Now know ye, That I, the said A. B., for divers good causes and valuable considerations me thereunto moving, have revoked, recalled, countermanded, and made void, and by these presents do revoke, recal, countermand, and to all intents and purposes, make null, void and of none effect, the said recited writing, or letter of attorney, and all powers and authorities therein and thereby given and granted; and all other matters and things therein, or in any of them contained; and all acts, matters and things whatsoever, which shall or may be acted, done or performed, by virtue or means thereof in any manner whatsoever: [Here conclude, In witness whereof, &c. But if another attorney is appointed, then continue as follows:]

And further know ye, that I, the said A. B., do by these presents, make, name, constitute and appoint, and in my place and stead, put and depute J. R., of, &c., to be my true and lawful attornew, irrevocable, for me and in my name, &c., [proceed as in a common letter of attorney].

Letter of Attorney to receive Dividends of Stock.

Know all men by these presents, That I, A. B., of the city of Lancaster, and State of Pennsylvania, brewer, do make, constitute and appoint, C. D., of the city of Washington, in the District of Columbia, Esquire, my true and lawful attorney, for me and in my name, to receive the dividends which are or shall be payable, according to law, on all the stock standing in my name, in the books of the Treasury of the United States, [or in the books of the Loan Office, or Bank of, &c., as the case may be] with the power also, to make and substitute an attorney or attorneys under him, for that purpose; and to do all lawful acts requisite for effecting the premises; hereby ratifying and confirming all that my said attorney, or his substitutes, shall lawfully do, by virtue hereof. In witness, &c.

To receive the back Pay of a Deceased Soldier.

Know all men by these presents, That I, Mary Bond, administratrix of all and singular the goods and chattels, rights and credits, which were of Abel Bond, late a private in the fourth company and sixth regiment of infantry of the army of the United States, deceased, who died intestate, have made, constituted and appointed, and by these presents, do make, constitute and appoint, John Wilson, of the county of Dauphin and State of Pennsylvania, Esquire, my true and lawful attorney, for me and in my name and for my use, to ask, demand and receive, from the proper officer of the United States authorized to settle and pay all such sum or sums of money or arrearages of pay due and coming unto my late husband, the said Abel Bond, deceased, giving and granting unto my said attorney my whole strength and power in the premises, hereby ratifying and confirming all that my said attorney shall lawfully do by virtue hereof. In witness, &c.

To Receive a Legacy.

To all people to whom these presents shall come; I, Daniel Brown, of, &c., and Sarah my wife, (late Sarah Wilson,) one of the daughters and legatees named in the last will and testament of Hugh Wilson, late of, &c., deceased, send greeting: Whereas, the said Hugh Wilson, in and by his last will and testament, bearing date the second day of February, A. D. 1829, did, amongst other things, give and bequeath unto his said daughter, the sum of five hundred dollars, payable in six months after his decease, [or did give and bequeath to her an equal share of his estate, as the case may be.] And of his said will appointed James Freeman, executor, as in and by the said will duly proved, and remaining in the register's office at Sunbury, in and for the county of Northumberland, relation being thereunto had, appears.

Now know ye, That I, the said Daniel Brown, and Sarah my wife, have made, constituted and appointed, and by these presents do make, constitute and appoint, Charles Davis, of the borough of Easton, in the county of Northampton, our true and lawful attorney, for us and in our names, and for our use, to ask, demand, sue for, recover, and receive, of and from the said James Freeman, executor as aforesaid, or in whose hands soever the same may be found, the said legacy or bequest mentioned in the said will, and also all such other sum or sums of money, debts, goods, wares, and demands whatsoever, which are or shall be due, owing, payable, and belonging to us by any means whatsoever, for or on account of her full share, part, or dividend of the estate aforesaid. Giving and granting, &c. [as in the first letter of attorney.]

Letter of Attorney to convey Lands.

Know all men by these presents, that I, A. B., of, &c., have made, constituted and appointed, and by these presents do make, constitute and appoint, and in my place and stead put and depute C. D., of, &c., my true and lawful attorney, for me, and in my name, place and stead, to grant, bargain and sell all that messuage, &c., [here describe the premises] with the appurtenances; and all my estate, right, title and interest therein, unto such person or persons, and for such price or prices, as he shall think proper; and also, for me and in my name, place and stead, and as my proper act and deed, to sign, seal, deliver and acknowledge, all such deed or deeds of conveyance, as shall be necessary for the absolute granting and assuring of the premises, unto the purchaser or purchasers, in fee simple. Giving, &c. [as in the first letter of attorney.]

To Acknowledge a Deed.

Know all men by these presents, That I, the within-named A. B., do hereby nominate and appoint C. D., E. F. and G. H., all of Washington county, in the State of Virginia, or any one of them, my true and lawful attorneys, for me, and in my name, to acknowledge the within deed, and the lands and tenements therein mentioned, to be the estate and property of the within-named I. K. In witness, &c.

Short Letter of Attorney to transfer Stock.

Know all men by these presents, that I, A. B., of, &c., do make, constitute and appoint, C. D., of, &c., my true and lawful attorney, for me and in my name, to transfer and assign unto E. F., ten shares of stock, in the Exchange Bank of Pittsburgh, standing in my name, in the books of said bank; and to do all necessary acts, and to make the necessary acquittances to effect the premises, hereby ratifying and confirming all my said attorney shall lawfully do, by virtue hereof. In witness, &c.

From the President and Directors of a Corporation, to collect Debts.

Know all men by these presents, that we, the President, Directors and Company, of the —— Bank, for us and our successors, have made, constituted and appointed, and do, by virtue hereof, make, constitute and appoint, A. B., of ——, Gent., C. D., of ——, Esq., and E. F., of ——, Gent., jointly, or any two of them, whereof the said A. B. to be one, our sufficient and lawful attorneys, for us and in our name and to our use, to demand, recover and receive, all and singular the sum and sums of money now due, payable, and coming unto us, or our successors, by virtue of any mortgages, promissory notes, contracts or engagements, in deed, or in law, now in being, from any person or persons whatsoever: Hereby giving and granting to our said attorneys, and to any two of them, whereof the said A. B. to be one, full power and authority to institute and pursue unto final judgment and execution, any process or suit, processes or suits, which our said attorneys or any two of them, whereof the said A. B. to be one, shall deem expedient; and in such suit or process, suits or processes, for us to appear, and us to represent before any court or courts having jurisdiction, and therein to plead for us, and all stipulations or other requisites, in any such suit or process, in our name and behalf, to make, allow and establish, at their discretion or at the discretion of any two of them, whereof the said A. B. to be one to submit to arbitration or any compromise whatsoever, any matter in dispute; and of all receipts, due acquittances, in our name and stead, as our deed or deeds, to make, seal and deliver. Hereby ratifying and confirming whatever our said attorneys, or any two of them, whereof the said A. B. to be one, may lawfully do, by virtue hereof, in the premises.

In testimony whereof, we, W. W., President, and X. Y. and Z., Directors of the said Bank, hereunto duly authorized by a vote of the said company, pursuant to the act incorporating the said company, have subscribed our names, and by the hands of the said W. W., affixed the seal of the said bank, this sixth day of ——.

A short Letter of Attorney to deliver possession of Lands.

Know all men, &c., —— for me, and in my name and stead, to enter into all those messuages, lands, tenements, &c., situate in ——, and after such entry, in my name and stead, to deliver peaceable possession and seisin of and in the said messuages, lands, tenements and hereditaments, and their appurtenances, to E. F., of ——, yeoman, or his heirs, or to his or their attorney, to his and their use, according to the form, tenour and effect of a certain deed, by me to the said E. F. made, the date whereof is, &c., as by inspection thereof will more fully appear; and generally to do all and every act and acts, thing and things whatsoever, necessary to making quiet entry and giving peaceable possession and seisin as aforesaid: Hereby ratifying, &c. In testimony, &c.

A general Letter of Attorney, to receive Debts.

Know all men by these presents, That I, A. B., &c., have made, constituted and appointed, and by these presents do make, &c., C. D., &c., my true and lawful attorney, for me and in my name, and to my use, to ask, demand, sue for, recover and receive of E. E., &c., all and every such sum and sums of money, debts and demands whatsoever, as now are due and owing unto me, the said A. B., by and from the said E. E.; And in default of payment thereof, to have, use, and take, all lawful ways and means, in my name, or otherwise, for the recovery thereof, by attachment, arrest, or otherwise, and to compound and agree for the same: And on receipt thereof, acquittances, or other sufficient discharges, for the same, for me and in my name, to make, seal and deliver: And to do all lawful acts and things whatsoever, concerning the premises, as fully in every respect, as I myself might or could do, if I were personally present; and an attorney or attorneys under him, for the purposes aforesaid, to make, and at his pleasure to revoke; hereby ratifying, allowing and confirming all and whatsoever my said attorney shall, in my name, lawfully do, or cause to be done, in and about the premises, by virtue of these presents. In witness, &c.

NOTE.—If there are two attorneys, say, —— B., &c., and C., &c., jointly, and either of them severally, to be my true and lawful attorneys and attorney, for me, &c.

From one to his Wife, to receive Wages, &c.

I, T. B., —— do constitute and appoint my wife, A. R., my true and lawful attorney, for me, and in my name, and for my use, to ask, demand and receive, of and from all and every person and persons whatsoever, as well all such sum and sums of money as now are, or which shall or may at any time hereafter become due and owing to me for wages; from (any ship or ships to which I now do or may belong;) as also all and other moneys now due, or to become due and owing to me by any other ways or means whatsoever; and upon non-payment either of the whole or of any part of the said pay, I do hereby authorize and empower my said wife to bring a suit or suits in law, in my name, for the recovery thereof.

In witness whereof, I have hereunto set and affixed my hand and seal, this —— day of, &c.

To receive Principal and Interest of the Public Debt.

Know all men by these presents, That I, G. C., of ——, do make, constitute and appoint, J. R., of ——, my true and lawful attorney, for me and in my name, to receive the dividends which are or shall be payable according to law, on the [here describe the stock] standing in my name, in the books of the Treasurer of the United States, [or the commissioner of the loans, —— as the case may be] from the —— day of —— to the —— day of ——, with power also to make and substitute an attorney or attorneys under him for that purpose, and to do all lawful acts requisite for effecting the premises, hereby ratifying and confirming all that my said attorney or his substitute shall lawfully do by virtue hereof. In witness whereof, &c.

A Letter of Attorney to make Partition.

Know all men, &c., that I, A. B., &c., have made, constituted and appointed, C. D., &c., my true, &c., attorney for me, and in my name and behalf, to make partition and division with the other heirs of my late father, deceased, of his estate, real and personal, and my share and part of his personal estate, to accept and receive: and upon any partition or division to enter upon, and take possession of any lands, tenements or hereditaments, which may be set off to me as my share and purpart of the real estate aforesaid: and to enter into any covenant or agreement respecting my share and purpart of his estate, real or personal, which my said attorney shall think reasonable and for my interest; and in my name and for my use, to demand, sue for, recover, receive, and take possession of all and singular lands, tenements and hereditaments, sum and sums of money, goods and chattels, withheld from me, to which I am entitled, and which I may lawfully claim from the heirs, executors or administrators of my said father, or any other person or persons whatsoever. (*Add a power to appear before courts*, &c., *a power of substitution, and a covenant to ratify*, &c.) In witness, &c.

To Attorney at Law to appear to suit for Defendant.

Know all men by these presents, that I, A. B., of the city of Lancaster, do hereby make, appoint and constitute C. D., Esq., of the borough of Meadville, my good and lawful attorney, in law and in fact, to appear for me in a certain plea, pending in the Court of Common Pleas, wherein E. F. is plaintiff, and I, the said A. B., am defendant; and take defence, and use all lawful ways and means, in my name, therein, in as full and effectual a manner as I could do, if personally present in the said court; hereby confirming and sanctioning whatsoever my said attorney in the said plea, touching the defence thereof, may do, according to law, in the premises. Witness my hand and seal, this tenth day of January, one thousand eight hundred and forty-five.

A. B.

By Plaintiff to institute a Suit.

Know all men by these presents, that I, A. B., of the city of Pittsburgh, do hereby make, constitute and appoint C. D., Esq., of the city of Philadelphia, my good and lawful attorney, in law and in fact, to institute for me, and in my name, a plea of —— against a certain E. F., in a proper and convenient court of law; and the same to conduct to trial and judgment in as speedy a manner, as the said C. D. reasonably can; and to conduct the prosecution of the said suit or action so to be brought; and use all lawful ways and means, in my name therein, in as full and effectual a manner as I, the said A. B. could do, if personally present; hereby confirming and sanctioning whatsoever my said attorney, in the said plea, touching the prosecution thereof, may do, according to law, in the premises. Witness my hand and seal, this tenth day of December, one thousand eight hundred and forty-four.

A. B.

By Plaintiff, to conduct Suit already brought.

Know all men by these presents, that I, A. B., of the borough of Carlisle, do hereby make, constitute and appoint C. D., Esq., of Erie, my good and lawful attorney, in law and in fact, to appear for me, in a certain plea or action, commenced and pending in the Erie County Court of Common Pleas, wherein I, the said A. B., am plaintiff, and a certain E. F., is defendant; and to conduct the prosecution of the said plea or action, so as aforesaid brought; and use all lawful ways and means, in my name therein, in as full and effectual a manner as I could do, if personally present; hereby confirming and sanctioning whatsoever my said attorney in the said plea, touching the prosecution thereof, may do according to law, in the premises. Witness, &c.

LETTERS OF LICENSE.

Remarks.

A letter of license is an instrument or writing made by creditors to their debtor, by which they bind themselves to allow him longer time than he had a right to, for the payment of his debts; and that they will not arrest or molest him in his person or property, till after the expiration of such additional time.

Letter of License from Creditors.

Know all men by these presents, that we, who have hereunto set our hands and seals, creditors of S. R., of the city of Philadelphia, grocer, taking into consideration, that by reason of losses and misfortunes, he, the said S. R., has not at present wherewith to pay and satisfy us our several debts, do therefore, upon the request of him, the said S. R., severally and respectively agree, and bind ourselves, our heirs, executors and administrators, to accept and take of him, the said S. R , all such debts and sums of money as he doth owe unto us, and every of us, respectively, by *four* even and equal payments or portions, that is to say: The first payment to be made in one year, now next ensuing the date hereof; the second payment in two years now next ensuing; the third payment in three years now next ensuing; and the last payment or residue of such debts to be made within four years now next ensuing.

And we do further severally and respectively agree, not to arrest, sue, implead, attach or prosecute, by any manner of ways, or means whatsoever, the said S. R., or his goods or effects, unless default shall happen to be made, in payment of the debts aforesaid, on the several days and times above limited, under forfeiture and loss of such of our debts and sums of money, as we shall so arrest, sue, implead, attach or prosecute. Witness, &c.

LETTERS OF CREDIT.

For Goods.

CARLISLE, MAY 12, 1844.

Messrs. A. & B., Merchants,
Pittsburgh.

Gentlemen,

Please to deliver Mr. C. D., of Amity, or to his order, goods and merchandise, to an amount not exceeding in value in the whole, two hundred dollars; and on your so doing, I hereby hold myself accountable to you for the payment of the same, in case Mr. C. D. should not be able to do so, or should make default, of which default you are required to give me reasonable and proper notice. Your obedient servant,

E. F.

For a limited sum of money.

PITTSBURGH, June 20, 1844.

Sir,

I hereby undertake to guarantee to you, the re-payment of all sums of money which you may advance to C. D., the bearer hereof, not exceeding in the whole five hundred dollars, within one year from the date hereof, with interest.

Yours, &c.

E. F.

To A. B., Philadelphia.

MARRIAGES.

Remarks.

No person is confined to the following form, but is at liberty to use the one most satisfactory to himself, provided that form requires the parties to acknowledge themselves before witnesses to be man and wife. The following requisites are essential, viz: 1st. They must be willing to contract. Those persons, therefore, who have no legal capacity in point of intellect, to make a contract, cannot legally marry, as idiots, lunatics and infants, males under the age of fourteen, and females under the age of twelve; and when minors over those ages marry, they must have the consent of their parents or guardians. 2d. Generally, all persons who are of sound mind, and have arrived to years of maturity, are able to contract marriage. To this general rule, however, there are some exceptions, among which may be mentioned the following. The *previous marriage* of the party to another person, who is still living, and not having been divorced; and *consanguinity* or *affinity* between the parties within the prohibited degree. 3d. The parties must not only be willing and able, but must have actually contracted in due form of law. The common law requires no particular ceremony to the valid celebration of marriage. The consent of the parties is all that is necessary, and as marriage is said to be a contract *jure gentium*, that consent is all that is needful by natural law. If the contract be made *per verba de presenti*, or if made *per verba de futuro*, and followed by consummation, it amounts to a valid marriage, and which the parties cannot dissolve, if otherwise competent; and it is not strictly necessary in Pennsylvania that a clergyman, a magistrate, or other officer should be present, to give validity to the marriage; the consent of the parties may be declared simply before witnesses.

Marriage is a civil contract, which may be completed by any words in the present tense, without regard to form. Hantz *vs.* Sealy, 6 Binn. 405; 8 S. & R. 62; 2 Watts, 9.

Custom, however, will probably always require the marriage ceremony to be performed by a clergyman, a magistrate, or other officer, duly authorized, by reason of the sacredness of the institution. The contract of marriage and the law of divorce, are taken from the Scottish law. See Erskine's Scot. Inst. page 64, &c.

There was an act in Pennsylvania, as early as 1700, for the preventing of clandestine marriages; 1 Smith, p. 21; also a supplement to the same act, 14th Feb., 1730, 1 Smith, p. 180, which are still in force, and to which I would call the attention of those who perform the marriage ceremony.

The provisions of the acts of 1700 and 1730, requiring all marriages to be solemnized in the presence of twelve witnesses, and to be preceded by the publication of banns, are only directory; and a non-compliance with them does not invalidate a marriage. Rodebaugh *vs.* Sanks, 2 W. 9. The acts of 1700 and 1730, to prevent clandestine marriages, are not obsolete in respect to the provision for the publication of banns. Helfenstein *vs.* Thomas, 5 R. 209.

In an action against a clergyman to recover the penalty given by the act of 1730, the burthen of proof lies on the plaintiff, to show that there was no publication of banns. *Ibid.* I take it to be a sound construction of the statute, to hold the minister or justice irresponsible, wherever the parent has actually given his consent, whether in the form of a certificate, or verbal declaration. Rodebaugh *vs.* Sanks, 2 W. 9. Where it appeared that the plaintiff, about a week before the marriage, asked his daughter why she did not get married, and recommended to her to marry I. S., it was held that he could not maintain an action against a clergyman who married her to I. S., although no certificate of consent was produced, and the verbal declarations of the father were not communicated to him. 2 W. 9.

It is not necessary that the plaintiff should show that he has sustained any actual specific damage. It is sufficient that the marriage is an unjustifiable interference with the relation existing between the parent and his offspring, and in that respect a grievance in contemplation of law. Donahue *vs.* Dougherty, 5 R. 124.

It is not a defence to such action that the clergyman misconceived the age of the infant. 5 R. 124.

In debt for the penalty on the supplement to the act against clandestine marriages, the jury must find the whole amount of the penalty. Macklin *vs.* Taylor, 212, 214.

It seems a declaration for the penalty of £50, in such action, must lay the marriage to have taken place without publication; and a declaration against the defendant for joining the parties in marriage, without having a certificate, would be bad; the first section which requires a certificate imposing no penalty. Huston *vs.* Ayres, 346. Only one penalty can be recovered against a justice, or other person for joining two persons in marriage contrary to the act, and, therefore, if the parent of one of the parties has already recovered the penalty, no action can be maintained for it by the parent of the other party. Hill *vs.* Williams, 14 S. & R. 287.

Form for a Marriage Ceremony.

We are gathered together here, in the sight of God, and in the presence of this company, to join together this man and this woman in holy matrimony, which is honourable, and is not, by any, to be entered into unadvisedly or lightly; but reverently, discreetly, advisedly, soberly, and in the fear of God. Into this holy estate, these two persons present come now to be joined. If any one can show just cause, why they may not lawfully be joined together, let him now speak, or else hereafter forever hold his peace.—J. L., wilt thou have this woman to be thy wedded wife, to live together after God's ordinance, in the holy estate of Matrimony? Wilt thou love her, comfort her, honour and keep her, in sickness and in health; and forsaking all others, keep thee only unto her, so long as you both shall live? Answer, "I will."

H. S., wilt thou have this man to be thy wedded husband, to live together after God's ordinance, in the holy estate of Matrimony? Wilt thou obey him, love, honour and keep him, in sickness and in health; and forsaking all others, keep thee only unto him, so long as you both shall live? Answer, "I will." (Join right hands.) Forasmuch as J. L. and H. S. have consented together, in holy wedlock, and have witnessed the same, before God and this company, and have given and pledged their faith each to the other, and have declared the same by joining of hands, I do pronounce them *man* and *wife;* and let no one put asunder those whom God hath joined together.

Certificate of Marriage.

This is to certify, that on the first day of January, in the year of our Lord, one thousand eight hundred and forty-four, before me, J. P., Esquire, one of the Justices of the Peace, in and for the county of Berks, J. L., of the township of Bern, in the said county, yeoman, and H. S., of the borough of Reading, in the county aforesaid, spinster, were legally joined in marriage; each of them being of full age, and declaring themselves free, respectively, from prior engagements, or other lawful impediments. In witness whereof, as well they, the said J. L. and H. S., (she assuming the name of her said husband,) as I, the said justice, and other the witnesses present, have hereunto subscribed our names the day and year aforesaid.

MECHANICS' LIEN.

Remarks.

In nearly all the counties of this commonwealth, mechanics and material men are allowed to file their claims against buildings erected by them, and thus obtain a lien against the building for the amount due to them.

The mechanics' lien law is such by Act of Assembly, and must be strictly pursued. The Act of Assembly of the 16th June, 1836, Pamph. L. p. 695, requires that every person entitled to such lien, shall file a claim or statement of his demand, in the office of the Prothonotary of the Court of Common Pleas of the county in which the building may be situated.

Every claim so filed, must set forth: first, the names of the party claimant, and the owner or reputed owner of the building, and also of the contractor, architect or builder, where the contract of the claimant was made, with such contractor, architect or builder. Second, the amount or sum claimed to be due, and the nature or kind of the work done, or the kind and amount of materials furnished, and the time when the materials were furnished, or the work was done, as the case may be. Third, the locality of the building, and the size and number of the stories of the same, or such other matters of description as shall be sufficient to identify the same. The said act further provides that in every case in which one claim for materials shall be filed by the person preferring the same, against two or more buildings, owned by the same person, the person filing such joint claim shall, at the same time, designate the amount which he claims to be due to him on each of such buildings, otherwise such claim shall be postponed to other lien creditors, and the lien of such claimant shall not extend beyond the amount so designated, as against other creditors having liens by judgment, mortgage, or otherwise. The lien will continue until the expiration of six months after the work shall have been finished, or materials furnished, but no longer, unless a claim be filed within that period of time. Materials furnished for a building, though not used in its erection, constitute a lien. 2 S. & R. 170, 12, *ib.* 303. And although used, if not expressly furnished for the building, no lien is acquired. 16 S. & R.

56. And a lien is not affected by an agreement by the claimant with the owner to receive payment in materials instead of money; 14 S. & R. 33. No lien is acquired where several houses, though adjoining, are erected by the same architect and at the same time, on lots owned by different persons, if the materials are furnished for the whole indiscriminately. 6 S. & R. 512. But otherwise, if the lots are owned by the same person. 5 R. 291. A contractor, being the builder, and a contractor under him, not recognized by the owner, cannot unite as partners in filing a claim for their work against the building. The sub-contractor, in such case, should file a separate claim for his work against the owner and builder with whom he contracted. 8 W. 478. On a claim filed by a mechanic under the act of 1836, one who erected the building, and was the owner at the time the work was done, may be named as contractor; and one who purchased the building after the work was done, but before the filing of the claim, may be joined as owner. 5 Wharton, 366. Where the work done by the plaintiff consisted of the raising of a frame building, which had been previously occupied by a family, and building a basement story of stone under it, it was held that this was not an erection or construction within the act, so as to give the plaintiff a lien. Miller *vs.* Oliver, 8 W. 514.

Form of claim by a House-carpenter, against one who is Owner and Contractor, for Work and Materials for a Building.

John Jones *vs.* William Burns. } In the Court of Common Pleas of Lancaster County, No. 10 of August Term, 1844.

John Jones, house-carpenter, of the county of Lancaster, files this his claim for the payment of one hundred dollars and fifty cents, against all that certain two story brick building, situate in —— street, between —— and —— street, in the city of Lancaster in the said county, containing in front on said —— street, twenty-four feet, and in depth thirty-six feet, and the lot or piece of ground and curtilage appurtenant to said building; the said sum of one hundred dollars and fifty cents, being a debt contracted for work, viz., carpenter's work, &c., and materials, viz: lumber, ironmongery, oils, paints, &c., done and furnished by the said John Jones, within six months last past, for and about the erection and construction of said building and appurtenances, of which the said William Burns was, and is the owner or reputed owner, and at his instance and request, he being the contractor, architect and builder thereof; and the said John Jones claims to have a lien on the said building, and the lot or piece of ground and curtilage appurtenant to the said building from the commencement thereof, for the sum aforesaid, according to the Act of Assembly in such case made and provided: and the said claimant hereto annexes a bill of particulars of the amount of his said debt showing the nature and kind of work done, the kind and amount of materials furnished, and the time when said work and materials were done and furnished. JOHN JONES.

Plaintiff's Bill of Particulars.

William Burns,

To John Jones, Dr.

1844, May 10, To 1 six panel front door - -	$6 00
" " 24, " 8 inside doors and 2 outside back doors at $2 - - - - - -	20 00
" " 26, " Iron hangings for 11 doors, at $1	11 00
" June 24, " $34\frac{2}{3}$ days carpenter's work, finishing inside, at $1 50 - - - - -	52 00
" " " " 30 lbs. nails used in finishing the same, at 5 cents - - - - -	1 50
" " " " 1000 feet lumber used in finishing the same - - - - - -	10 00
Total	$100 50

JOHN JONES.

Form of a claim filed by a House-carpenter against William Burns, owner, and Samuel Dean contractor, for work and materials for a Building.

John Jones
vs.
William Burns & Samuel Dean. } In the Court of Common Pleas of Erie County, No. 9 of February Term, 1844.

John Jones, of the county of Erie, house-carpenter, files this his claim for the payment of the sum of eighty-five dollars and sixty cents, all that certain two story frame building, situate in Holland street, between fifth and sixth streets, in the borough of Erie, in the county aforesaid, containing in front on said Holland street, twenty-four feet, and in depth thirty-two feet, and the lot or piece of ground and curtilage appurtenant to said building; the said sum of eighty-five dollars and sixty cents being a debt contracted for work, viz: carpenter's work, &c., and materials, viz: lumber, paints, oils, &c., done and furnished by the said John Jones, within six months last past, for and about the erection and construction of the said building and appurtenances, of which the said William Burns is owner or reputed owner, and the said Samuel Dean the architect, builder and contractor for the said work and materials, at whose instance and request they were done and furnished as aforesaid: and the said John Jones claims to have a lien on the said building, and lot or piece of ground and curtilage appurtenant to said building, from the time of its commencement, for the sum aforesaid, according to the Act of Assembly in such case made and provided; and said claimant hereto annexes a bill of particulars of the amount of his said debt, showing the nature and kind of work done, the kind and amount of materials furnished and the time when said work was done, and the said materials furnished as aforesaid. JOHN JONES.

(Plaintiff's bill annexed.)

Form of claim filed by a Brickmaker against one who is owner and contractor, for materials furnished for one building.

John Jones *vs.* William Burns. } In the Court of Common Pleas of Erie County, No. 24 of August Term, 1844.

John Jones, brickmaker, of the county of Erie, claims in his own right, a lien for the payment of the sum of two hundred dollars, against all that certain two story brick building, (or messuage and tenement,) situate in French street, between ninth and tenth streets, in the borough of Erie, in the county aforesaid, containing in front on said French street, twenty-four feet, and in depth thirty-two feet, and the lot or piece of ground and curtilage appurtenant to said building; the said sum of two hundred dollars being a debt contracted for materials, viz: bricks furnished by the said John Jones, within six months last past, for and about the erection and construction of the said building, of which the said William Burns was and is the owner or reputed owner, and at his instance and request, he being the contractor, architect and builder thereof; and the said claimant hereto annexes a bill of particulars of the amount of his said debt, showing the kind and amount of materials furnished, and the time when said materials were furnished as aforesaid. JOHN JONES.

Plaintiff's Bill of Particulars.

William Burns,

To John Jones, Dr.

1844, May 20, To 50 thousand brick, at $4 $200 00

JOHN JONES.

Form of claim filed by a Brickmaker against William Burns, owner, and Samuel Dean, contractor, for materials furnished for one building.

John Jones *vs.* William Burns & Samuel Dean. } In the Court of Common Pleas of Erie County, No. 42 of August Term, 1844.

John Jones, brickmaker, of the county of Erie, files this his claim in his own right, for materials, viz: bricks furnished for and about the erection and construction of a certain two story brick building, situate in Ninth street, between State and Peach streets, in the borough of Erie in the county aforesaid, containing in front on said Ninth street, twenty-four feet, and in depth thirty-six feet, of which William Burns was and is the owner or reputed owner, and Samuel Dean the architect, builder and contractor for said materials, furnished by the said John Jones, within six months last past, to said building, at the instance and request of the said Samuel Dean, contractor. This claim is filed as well against said building as against the lot or piece of ground and curtilage appurtenant to the same: and the said John Jones annexes hereto a statement of the particulars of the amount of his said debt, showing the kind and amount of materials furnished, and the time when said materials were furnished.

(Plaintiff's bill annexed.)

Form of claim filed against William Burns, owner, and Samuel Dean, contractor, by a Bricklayer, for work.

John Jones *vs.* William Burns & Samuel Dean.	In the Court of Common Pleas of Erie County, No. 21 of August Term, 1844.

John Jones, bricklayer, of the County of Erie, files this his claim in his own right for work, viz: bricklayer's work, done for and about the erecting and constructing of a certain two story brick building, situate, &c., [here describe the size, situation and boundaries, or other description of the building,] in the township of ——, in the county aforesaid, of which William Burns was and is the owner or reputed owner, and Samuel Dean the architect, builder and contractor for said work, done by the said John Jones, within six months last past, to the said building at the instance and request of the said Samuel Dean, contractor. This claim is filed, as well against the said building, as against the lot or piece of ground and curtilage appurtenant to the same; and the said John Jones annexes hereto a statement of the particulars of the amount of his said debt, showing the nature and kind of work done, and the time when the said work was done, as aforesaid.

(Plaintiff's bill annexed.) JOHN JONES.

Form of claim filed against one who is owner and contractor, by a Bricklayer, for work.

John Jones *vs.* William Burns.	In the Court of ——, for the County of ——, —— Term ——, No. ——.

John Jones, of the County of ——, bricklayer, claims in his own right, a lien for the payment of the sum of —— dollars, against all that certain —— story brick house (or building) situate (describing the situation and size of the building) in the —— of ——, in the county aforesaid, and the lot or piece of ground and curtilage appurtenant to said building: the said sum of —— dollars being a debt contracted for work, viz., bricklaying, &c., done by the said John Jones within six months last past, for and about the erection and construction of the said buildings, of which the said William Burns was and is the owner or reputed owner, and at his instance and request, he being the contractor, architect and builder thereof; and said claimant hereto annexes a bill of particulars of the amount of his said debt, showing the nature and kind of work done, and the time when said work was done, as aforesaid.

(Plaintiff's bill annexed.)

Form of claim filed by a Lumberman against one who is owner and contractor, for lumber furnished for one building.

John Jones *vs.* William Burns.	In the Court of Common Pleas of Erie County, No. 64 of August Term, 1844.

John Jones, lumber-merchant, of the County of Erie, files this his claim for the payment of the sum of one hundred dollars, against all that certain two story frame messuage and tenement, situate in the township of —— in the county aforesaid, on the north side of —— road, containing on said road twenty-four feet, more or less, and in depth about thirty-six feet, [or otherwise describing its situation, boundaries, &c.,] and the lot or piece of ground and curtilage appurtenant to said building; the said sum of one hundred dollars being a debt contracted for materials, viz., lumber, furnished by the said John Jones within six months last past, for and about the erection and construction of the said building, of which the said William Burns was and is the owner or reputed owner, and at his instance and request, he being the contractor, architect and builder thereof; and the said John Jones claims to have a lien for the aforesaid sum of one hundred dollars on the said building and lot or piece of ground and curtilage appurtenant thereto, from its commencement, according to the Act of Assembly in such case made and provided: And said claimant hereto annexes a bill of particulars of the amount of the said debt, showing the kind and amount of materials furnished, and the time when said materials were furnished. JOHN JONES.

(Plaintiff's bill annexed.)

Form of claim filed by a Lumberman against William Burns, owner, and Samuel Dean, contractor, for lumber furnished for one building.

John Jones vs. William Burns & Samuel Dean. } In the Court of Common Pleas of Erie County, No. 34 of May Term, 1844.

John Jones, lumber-merchant, of the County of Erie, files this his claim, for the payment of the sum of two hundred dollars, against all that certain two story frame messuage and tenement, situate in the township of ——, in the county aforesaid, on the south side of the —— road, containing in front on said road thirty feet, more or less, and in depth about twenty-four feet and the lot or piece of ground and curtilage appurtenant to said building; the said sum of two hundred dollars being a debt contracted for materials, to wit, lumber, furnished by the said John Jones within six months last past, for and about the erection and construction of the said building, of which William Burns was and is the owner, and the said Samuel Dean the architect, builder and contractor for the said materials, at whose instance and request they were furnished and provided as aforesaid; and the said John Jones claims to have a lien for the aforesaid sum, on the said building and lot or piece of ground, and curtilage appurtenant to said building, from the commencement of the same, according to the Act of Assembly in such case made and provided; and said claimant hereto annexes a bill of particulars of the amount of the said debt, showing the kind and amount of materials furnished, and the time when said materials were furnished.

(Plaintiff's bill annexed.) JOHN JONES.

Form of claim by a Painter and Glazier, against one who is owner and contractor, for work and materials for one building.

John Jones vs. William Burns. } In the Court of Common Pleas of Erie County, No. 12 of May Term, 1844.

John Jones, painter and glazier, of the County of Erie, files this his claim for the payment of fifty dollars, against all that certain two story frame building, messuage and tenement, situate, [describe the boundaries, &c., according to the other forms,] and the lot or piece of ground and curtilage appurtenant to said building; the said sum of fifty dollars being a debt contracted for work, viz., painting and glazing, and materials, viz., paint, glass, putty, &c. done and furnished by the said John Jones, within six months last past, to, in and about the erection and construction of the said building and appurtenances, of which the said William Burns was and is the owner, or reputed owner, and at his instance and request, he being the contractor, architect and builder thereof:

And the said John Jones claims to have a lien on the said building and lot or piece of ground and curtilage appurtenant to said building, from the commencement thereof, for the sum aforesaid, according to the Act of Assembly in such case made and provided; and said claimant hereto annexes a bill of particulars of the amount of his said debt, showing the nature and kind of work done, the kind and amount of materials furnished, and the time when said work was done and materials furnished. JOHN JONES.

(Plaintiff's bill annexed.)

Form of claim by a Painter and Glazier, against William Burns, owner, and Samuel Dean, contractor, for work and materials for one building.

John Jones *vs.* William Burns & Samuel Dean.	In the Court of Common Pleas of Erie County, No. 24 of May Term, 1844.

John Jones, painter and glazier, of the County of Erie, files this his claim, for the payment of the sum of one hundred dollars, against all that certain two story building, situate in, &c., [describe the building, &c., as in other forms,] and the lot or piece of ground and curtilage appurtenant to said building; the said sum of one hundred dollars being a debt contracted for work, viz., painting and glazing, and materials, viz., paint, glass, putty, &c., done and furnished by the said John Jones within six months last past, to, in and about the erection and construction of the said building and appurtenances, of which the said William Burns was and is the owner or reputed owner, and Samuel Dean, the architect, builder and contractor for the said work and materials, at whose instance and request they were done, furnished and provided as aforesaid; and the said John Jones claims to have a lien on the said building and lot or piece of ground, and curtilage appurtenant to said building, from the commencement thereof, for the sum aforesaid, according to the Act of Assembly in such case made and provided; and said claimant hereto annexes a bill of particulars of the amount of his said debt, showing the nature and kind of work done, the kind and amount of materials furnished, and the time when said work was done and materials furnished.

(Plaintiff's bill annexed.) JOHN JONES.

Form of claim filed by a Brickmaker against one who is owner and contractor, for materials furnished for two or more buildings where the amount claimed is equally divided.

John Jones *vs.* William Burns.	In the Court of Common Pleas of Erie County, No. 24 of May Term, 1844.

John Jones, brickmaker, of the County of Erie, files this his claim for the payment of five hundred dollars, against all those two certain two story brick houses (or buildings), situate in the borough of Erie, in the county aforesaid, on Peach street, between Ninth and Tenth streets, each house being about twenty feet in front on said Peach street, and in depth thirty feet, and the lots or pieces of ground and curtilages appurtenant to said buildings; the said sum of five hundred dollars being a debt contracted for materials, viz., bricks, furnished and provided by the said John Jones, within six months last past, for and about the erection and construction of the said buildings, of which the said William Burns was and is the owner or reputed owner, and at his instance and request, he being the contractor, architect and builder thereof; and the amount claimed to be due on each of the said buildings, for materials furnished and provided as aforesaid, is two hundred and fifty dollars, which the said claimant hereby designates according to the Act of Assembly in such case made and provided, and claims to have a lien for on the said buildings and appurtenances from the commencement of the same; and said claimant hereto annexes a bill of particulars of his said debt, showing the kind and amount of materials furnished, and the time when said materials were furnished as aforesaid. JOHN JONES.

(Plaintiff's bill annexed.)

Form of claim filed by a Brickmaker, against one who is owner and contractor, for materials furnished for two or more buildings, where the amount claimed is unequally divided.

John Jones *vs.* William Burns. } In the —— Court for the County of ——, —— Term, ——, No. ——.

John Jones, brickmaker, of the County of ——, files this his claim for the payment of the sum of —— dollars and —— cents, against all those —— certain brick houses, situate in the —— of ——, in the county aforesaid, in —— street, between —— and —— streets, and the lots or pieces of ground and curtilages appurtenant to said buildings: being a debt contracted for materials, viz., bricks, furnished by the said John Jones within six months last past, for and about the erection and construction of the said buildings, of which the said William Burns was and is the owner or reputed owner, and at his instance and request, he being the architect, contractor and builder thereof; and the said John Jones hereby designates the amount he claims to be due to him for the same on each of the said buildings, as follows, viz., on the northernmost of the said buildings, which is a three story (or as the case may be) brick house, —— feet in front on said —— street, by —— feet in depth, and the lot or piece of ground and curtilage appurtenant to said building, the sum of —— thousand dollars and —— cents; on the southernmost of said buildings, which is a two story (or as the case may be) brick, —— feet in front on said —— street, by —— feet in depth, and the lot or piece of ground and curtilage appurtenant to said building, the sum of —— hundred dollars and —— cents, according to the Act of Assembly in such case made and provided; and claims to have a lien on said building and appurtenances thereto for the same from the time of their commencement; and said claimant hereto annexes a bill of particulars of the amount of his debt, showing the kind and amount of materials furnished, and the time when said materials were furnished as aforesaid.

(Plaintiff's bill annexed.)

Form of claim filed by a Brickmaker, against William Burns, owner, and Samuel Dean, contractor, for materials furnished for two or more buildings, where the amount claimed is unequally divided.

John Jones *vs.* William Burns & Samuel Dean.	In the Court of Common Pleas of Erie County, No. 36, November Term, 1844.

John Jones, brickmaker, of the County of Erie, files this his claim for the payment of the sum of four hundred dollars, against all those two certain brick houses, situate in the borough of Erie, in the county aforesaid, the one in Peach street, between Ninth and Tenth streets, the other in Tenth street, between State and Peach streets, and the lots or pieces of ground and curtilages appurtenant to the said buildings; being a debt contracted for materials, viz., bricks, &c., furnished by the said John Jones within six months last past, for and about the erection and construction of the said buildings, of which the said William Burns was and is the owner or reputed owner, and Samuel Dean the architect, builder and contractor for said materials, at whose instance and request they were furnished as aforesaid: And the said John Jones hereby designates the amount he claims to be due to him for the same, on each of the said buildings, as follows: viz., on the said house in Peach street, between Ninth and Tenth streets, which is a three story brick house, twenty-four feet in front on said Peach street, by thirty-six in depth, and the lot or piece of ground and curtilage appurtenant to said building, the sum of two hundred and fifty dollars; on the said house in Tenth street, between State and Peach streets, which is a two story brick house, twenty feet in front on said Tenth street, by thirty feet in depth, and the lot or piece of ground and curtilage appurtenant to said building, the sum of one hundred and fifty dollars; according to the Act of Assembly in such case made and provided, and claims to have a lien on the said buildings and appurtenances for the same, from the time of their commencement: And said claimant hereto annexes a bill of particulars of the amount of his said debt, showing the kind and amount of materials furnished, and the time when said materials were furnished, as aforesaid.

(Plaintiff's bill annexed.) JOHN JONES.

Form of claim filed by Lumber-merchants (partners) against one who is owner and contractor, for lumber furnished for two or more buildings, where the amount claimed is unequally divided.

A. B. & C. D., lumber-merchants, in co-partnership, trading under the firm of A. B. & Co. *vs.* E. F.	In the —— Court for the County of ——, —— Term 18—, No. ——.

A. B. & C. D., lumber-merchants, in co-partnership, trading under the firm of A. B. & Co., of the county of ——, file this their claim, for the payment of the sum of —— dollars and —— cents, against all those certain houses situate in the —— of ——, in the county aforesaid, in —— street, between —— and —— streets, Nos. —— and ——, and the lots or pieces of ground and curtilages appurtenant to said buildings; being a debt contracted for materials, to wit: lumber furnished by the said A. B. & C. D., within —— months last past, for and about the erection and construction of the said buildings, of which the said E. F. was and is the owner or reputed owner, and at his instance and request, he being the architect, contractor and builder thereof: and the said A. B. & C. D. hereby designate the amount they claim to be due to them for the same, on each of the said buildings, as follows, viz., on the northernmost of the said buildings, which is a three story (or as the case may be) brick house, —— feet in front on said —— street, by —— feet in depth, and the lot or piece of ground and curtilage appurtenant to said building, the sum of —— dollars and —— cents: on the southernmost of said buildings, which is a two story (or as the case may be) brick, —— feet in front on said —— street, by —— feet in depth, and the lot or piece of ground and curtilage appurtenant to said building, the sum of —— dollars and —— cents, according to the Act of Assembly in such case made and provided; and claim to have a lien on said buildings and appurtenances thereto for the sum aforesaid, from the time of their commencement: and said claimants hereto annex a bill of particulars of the amount of their said debt, showing the kind and amount of materials furnished, and the time when said materials were furnished, as aforesaid.

(Plaintiffs' bill annexed.)

MORTGAGE.

Remarks.

Mortgages are of several kinds: As they concern the kind of property mortgaged, they are mortgages of lands, tenements and hereditaments; or of goods and chattels. As they effect the title of the thing mortgaged, they are legal and equitable. A legal mortgage of lands may be described to be a conveyance of lands by a debtor to his creditor as a pledge and security for the repayment of a sum of money borrowed, or performance of a covenant, with a proviso, that such conveyance shall be void on payment of the money and interest on a certain day, or the performance of such covenant by the time appointed, by which the conveyance of the land becomes absolute at law, yet the mortgagor has an equity of redemption, that is, right in equity on the performance of the agreement within a reasonable time, to call for a re-conveyance of the land. Cruise, Dig. t. 15, c. 1, s 11; 1 Pow. on Mort. 4.

As to the form, such a mortgage must be in writing when it is intended to convey the legal title. 1 Penn. R. 240. It is either in one single deed which contains the whole contract, and which is the usual form, or it is two separate instruments, the one containing an absolute conveyance, and the other a defeasance. 2 Johns. Ch. R. 189; 15 Johns. R. 555; 2 Greenl. R. 152; 12 Mass. 456.

As the money borrowed on mortgage is seldom paid on the day appointed, mortgages are now become entirely subject to our courts, where it is an established rule that the mortgagee holds the estate merely as a pledge or security for the re-payment of his money; therefore a mortgage is considered in equity as personal estate. The mortgagor is held to be the real owner of the land, the debt being considered the principal, and the land the accessory. Whenever the debt is discharged, the interest of the mortgagee in the lands determines of course. The Act of Assembly of 28th March, 1820, 7 Smith, p. 303, declares that all mortgages shall have priority according to the date of recording the same, without regard to the time of making or executing the same. And no mortgage or defeasible deed in the nature of a mortgage, shall be a lien, until such mortgage or defeasible deed shall have been recorded, or left for record. There is also another act of 28th May, 1715, 1 Smith, p. 94, which requires all deeds and mortgages to be recorded within six months after the date thereof. The following are some of the decisions of the Supreme Court of Pennsylvania on these Acts of Assembly. The recording of a mortgage amounts to a constructive notice to all men, and supersedes the necessity of express personal notice. 1 D. 435; 1 Y. 172. A mortgage not recorded within six months, according to the provisions of the acts of 1715 and 1775, is good against the mortgagor. 1 D. 430.

A mortgage, though not recorded according to the Act of Assembly, is good against a purchaser, who knew of the existence of the mortgage at the time of his purchase. 4 D. 153.

A mortgage not recorded within six months, gave no lien under the acts of 1715 and 1775, against a subsequent judgment creditor. 7 S. & R. 286. But it seems such mortgage would have been a lien if recorded before the entry of a judgment, although after the six months. Same 292–3.

If a second purchaser from the original grantor have notice of the existence of the first deed and defeasance, he is in equity bound to the same extent as the grantor, 7 W. 261. But the law is otherwise as respects a judgment creditor and the purchaser under an execution on such judgment; since a judgment has priority over an unrecorded mortgage, 7 W. 261. When a mortgage is payable by instalments, every payment made upon it should be receipted upon the record of the mortgage in the office, as they are severally made.

An equitable mortgage of lands is one where the mortgagor does not convey regularly the land, but does some act by which he manifests his determination to bind the same for the security of a debt he owes. An agreement in writing to transfer an estate as a security for the repayment of a sum of money borrowed, or even a deposit of title deeds, and a verbal agreement will have the same effect of creating an equitable mortgage. 1 Rawle, R. 328; 5 Wheat. R. 284; 1 Cox's R. 211.

A mortgage of goods is distinguishable from a mere pawn. By a grant or conveyance of goods in a gage or mortgage, the whole legal title passes conditionally to the mortgagee, and if not redeemed at the time stipulated, the title becomes absolute at law, though equity will interfere to compel a redemption. But in a pledge, a special property only passes to the pledgee, the general property remaining in the pledger. There have been some cases of mortgages of chattels, which have been held valid without any actual possession in the mortgagee; but they stand upon very peculiar grounds, and may be deemed exceptions to the general rule. 2 Pick. R. 607; 5 Pick. R. 59; 5 Johns. R. 261. See 12 Mass. R. 300; 4 Mass. R. 352; 6 Mass. R. 422; 15 Mass. R. 477; and Powell on Mortgages.

The remedies on a legal mortgage in Pennsylvania are various. 1st, by ejectment; 2d, by *scire facias;* 3d, by debt on the bond accompanying the mortgage, and on some by covenant. But nothing more than debt, interest and cost can be recovered by *scire facias,* or action of debt.

A Mortgage of Indemnity to Bail.

This indenture, made the tenth day of May, A. D. one thousand eight hundred and forty-four, between A. B., of ——, in the county of —— and State of Pennsylvania, of the one part, and C. D. and E. F., of, &c., of the other part: Whereas the real estate of C. B., late of, &c., deceased, father of the aforesaid A. B., has lately been valued, under a writ of partition or valuation, issued out of the Orphans' Court of Berks county, aforesaid, at the sum of twelve hundred dollars, and has been adjudged to the aforesaid A. B., eldest son of the said C. B., deceased: And whereas, the said C. D. and E. F. were approved of by the court aforesaid, as sureties of the said A. B., and have this day become bound with him in four bonds or writings obligatory, bearing even date herewith, to wit: in one bond to G. H., intermarried with M. [late M. B.] in the sum of four hundred dollars, lawful money of the United States, conditioned for the payment of two hundred dollars in like money, on or before the first day of January next ensuing the date thereof: and the further sum of one hundred dollars, at and immediately after the decease of N., widow of the said C. B., deceased, the said sums being the said M.'s share of the valuation money aforesaid; in one other bond to D. B., a son of the said C. B., deceased, in the same sum aforesaid, and conditioned for the payment thereof, in like manner and at the time aforesaid, being his share, &c., [here mention the two other bonds in a similar manner,] the whole sum for which the said C. D. and E. F. have become bound as aforesaid, with the said A. B., being twelve hundred dollars, and being also for the proper debt or debts of the said A. B.

Now this indenture witnesseth, that the said A. B., for and in consideration of the sum of one dollar, to him in hand paid by the said C. D. and E. F., and for the purpose of securing and indemnifying the said C. D. and E. F., and each of their heirs, executors and administrators, for or on account of the suretiship aforesaid, hath granted, bargained, sold, released and confirmed, and by these presents doth grant, bargain, sell, release and confirm, unto the said C. D. and E. F., and to their heirs and assigns, all that messuage, &c. [Here describe the premises.] Together with all and singular the buildings, improvements, ways, woods, waters, water-courses, rights, liberties, privileges, hereditaments and appurtenances whatsoever, thereunto belonging, or in anywise appertaining, and the reversions and remainders, rents, issues and profits thereof: To have and to hold the said messuage, &c., hereditaments and premises hereby granted, or mentioned or intended so to be, with the appurtenances, unto the said C. D., his heirs and assigns, to the only proper use and behoof of the said C. D., his heirs and assigns forever. Provided always nevertheless, that if the said A. B., his heirs, executors, administrators, or any of them, shall and do well and truly pay, or cause to be paid, unto the said

G. H., D. B., &c., the said sums mentioned in the said bonds, [or notes, as the case may be,] or by other lawful means, save, keep harmless and indemnified, the said C. D., and E. F., their heirs, executors and administrators, from the payment of the said bonds, and all costs, damages or charges, as sureties aforesaid, [or as endorsers of the said note, as the case may be] then and from thenceforth, as well this present indenture, and the estate hereby granted, as the said recited obligation, shall cease and determine, and become absolutely null and void, any thing herein contained to the contrary notwithstanding. In witness whereof, &c.

Common form of Mortgage for securing the payment of Money due on a Bond.

This indenture made the twentieth day of April, in the year of our Lord one thousand eight hundred and forty-four, between Allen Sisty, of Middletown, in the county of ——, yeoman, of the one part, and John Black, of the city of Hartford, merchant, of the other part: Whereas, the said Allen Sisty, in and by a certain obligation, or writing obligatory, under his hand and seal, bearing even date herewith, stands bound unto the said John Black, in the sum of one thousand dollars, conditioned for the payment of five hundred dollars, on the twentieth day of July, next ensuing the date hereof, with lawful interest for the same, as in and by the said recited obligation and condition thereof, relation being thereunto had, more fully and at large appears. Now this indenture witnesseth, that the said Allen Sisty, as well for and in consideration of the aforesaid debt or sum of five hundred dollars, and for the better securing the payment thereof, with its interest unto the said John Black, his executors, administrators and assigns, in discharge of the said recited obligation, as of the further sum of one dollar, to him in hand paid, by the said John Black, at and before the sealing and delivery hereof, the receipt whereof is hereby acknowledged, hath granted, bargained, sold, released and confirmed, and by these presents doth grant, bargain, sell, release and confirm, unto the said John Black, his heirs and assigns, all that messuage, &c., together with all and singular the buildings, improvements, ways, woods, waters, water-courses, rights, liberties, privileges, hereditaments, and appurtenances whatsover, thereunto belonging, or in anywise appertaining; and the reversions and remainders, rents, issues, and profits thereof. To have and to hold the said messuage, &c., hereditaments and premises hereby granted, or mentioned or intended so to be, with the appurtenances, unto the said John Black, his heirs and assigns, to the only proper use and behoof of the said John Black, his heirs and assigns forever. Provided always, nevertheless, that if the said Allen Sisty, his heirs, executors or administrators, shall and do well and truly pay, or cause to be paid unto the said John

Black, his executors, administrators or assigns, the aforesaid debt or sum of five hundred dollars, on the day and time hereinbefore mentioned and appointed for payment thereof, with lawful interest for the same, according to the condition of the said recited obligation, without fraud or further delay, and without any deduction, defalcation, or abatement to be made of any thing for, or in respect of, any taxes, charges or assessments whatsoever, then and from thenceforth, as well this present indenture, and the estate hereby granted, as the said recited obligation, shall cease, determine, and become absolutely null and void, to all intents and purposes, any thing hereinbefore contained to the contrary in anywise notwithstanding. In witness whereof, &c.

For continuing a Mortgage by Indorsement.

Whereas the within-named Philip Green hath advanced and lent unto the within-named Isaac Wallace the further sum of five hundred dollars, the receipt whereof the said Isaac Wallace doth hereby acknowledge, and thereupon the said Isaac Wallace hath entered into one bond or writing obligatory, under his hand and seal, bearing even date with these presents, to the said Philip Green, in the penal sum of one thousand dollars, in lawful money of the United States, with condition thereunder written, for making the same void, upon payment unto the said Philip Green, his executors, administrators or assigns, of the sum of five hundred dollars, of like lawful money, with interest for the same, after the rate of ——, on the —— day of ——, as in and by the said bond or writing obligatory, and the condition thereof, relation being thereunto had may more fully appear. Now know ye, that as well for the better securing and more sure payment unto the said Philip Green, his executors, administrators and assigns, of the said further sum of five hundred dollars, and interest on the said —— day of —— next ensuing, according to the true intent and meaning of the said recited bond or obligation, he, the said Isaac Wallace, doth hereby for himself, his heirs, executors, administrators and assigns, covenant, promise and agree, to and with the said Philip Green, his executors, administrators and assigns, the messuages, &c., and all and singular other the premises, with the appurtenances, by the within written indenture of demise or mortgage, mentioned to be granted, bargained, sold, and demised, and every part and parcel thereof, shall stand chargeable, remain, continue, and be a security unto him, the said Philip Green, his executors, administrators and assigns, as well for the payment of the sum of five hundred dollars within mentioned, and the interest thereof, as also for the payment of the said further sum of five hundred dollars, now lent, and advanced as aforesaid, and the interest thereof; and that the said premises, or any part thereof, shall not be redeemed or redeemable, either in law or in equity, until not only the said sum of five hundred dollars, before lent, and the interest thereof, but also the said sum of five hundred dollars, now lent, and the interest thereof shall be paid and satisfied, unto the said Philip Green, his executors, administrators and assigns, according to the true intent and meaning of these presents.

In witness whereof, I have hereunto set my hand and affixed my seal, this —— day of ——.

Mortgage to secure endorsers in Bank.

This indenture, made, &c., [here insert the parties.] Whereas the said C. D. and E. F. have endorsed for the said A. B., a certain promissory note for the sum of five hundred dollars, dated the —— day of —— last past, and payable —— months after date, which is now discounted at the Bank of ——, in the city of ——, and which said note it is contemplated to renew from time to time; and the said A. B., being desirous to secure and save the said C. D. and E. F., against all responsibility as endorsers of the note aforesaid, thereof, this indenture witnesseth, that the said A. B., as well for and in consideration of securing the said endorsers from the payment of the note aforesaid, as the sum of one dollar to him in hand paid, by the said C. D. and E. F., at and before the sealing and delivery hereof, the receipt whereof is hereby acknowledged, hath granted, bargained, sold, released, and confirmed, and by these presents doth grant, bargain, release and confirm, unto the said C. D. and E. F., their heirs and assigns, all that certain messuage, &c., [here describe the premises and recite the title.] Together with all and singular the buildings, improvements, ways, woods, waters, water-courses, rights, liberties, privileges, hereditaments and appurtenances whatsoever, thereunto belonging, or in anywise appertaining; and the reversions and remainders, rents, issues, and profits thereof. To have and to hold the said messuage, &c., hereditaments and premises hereby granted, or mentioned, or intended so to be, with the appurtenances, unto the said C. D., his heirs and assigns, to the only proper use and behoof of the said C. D., his heirs and assigns, forever. Provided always, nevertheless, that if the said A. B., his heirs, executors or administrators, shall and do well and truly pay, or cause to be paid, unto the said bank, the aforesaid promissory note for —— dollars, on the day and time hereinbefore mentioned, and appointed for payment thereof, or by other lawful means, save, keep harmless, and indemnified, the said C. D. and E. F., their heirs, executors and administrators, from the payment of the said note, and all costs, damages or charges, as sureties aforesaid, then and from thenceforth, as well this present indenture and the estate hereby granted, as the said recited obligation shall cease, determine, and become absolutely null and void, any thing herein contained to the contrary notwithstanding.

In witness whereof, &c.

A short Mortgage of Goods.

Know all men by these presents, that I, A. B., of ——, gentleman, in consideration of the sum of —— dollars, to me paid, by C. D., of ——, Esq., the receipt, &c., have granted, bargained and sold, and by these presents do grant, &c., unto the said C. D., all the goods and chattels, wares, effects and merchandise, mentioned and specified in the schedule hereunder written: To have and to hold all and singular the said, &c., unto the said C. D., his executors, administrators and assigns, forever. (*Add a covenant to warrant, &c.*)

Provided, nevertheless, that if I, the said A. B., my executors, administrators or assigns, or any of them, do and shall, well and truly pay, or cause to be paid, unto the said C. D., his executors, &c., the sum of ——, then these presents and every clause, article and thing herein contained, shall cease and be void. Otherwise, &c.

In testimony, &c.

Where Deeds and Evidences are delivered to Mortgagee upon the execution of the Mortgage the following acknowledgment should be signed.

I do hereby acknowledge, that the several deeds and evidences comprised in the above-written schedule, were delivered to me upon the execution of a mortgage to me for —— dollars and interest, of which the within written —— is a counterpart. And I do hereby promise and undertake that the same shall be delivered, uncanceled and unaltered, to the within-named W. W., his heirs, executors, administrators or assigns, or as he or they shall direct, upon his or their paying to me, my executors, administrators or assigns, all principal and interest due on the said mortgage, unless I, my executors, administrators or assigns, shall be prevented or hindered by fire or other inevitable accident. As witness my hand the day and year first within written.

NOTICES.

A notice, is the information given of some act done, or the interpellation by which some act is required to be done. Notices should always be in writing; they should state, in precise terms, their object, and be signed by the proper person, or his authorized agent, to be dated, and addressed to the person to be effected by them. The notice should be served by leaving a copy with the party to whom it is addressed. With respect to the necessity for giving notice, says Mr. Chitty, 1 Pr. 496, the rules of law are most evidently founded on good sense, and so as to accord with the intention of the parties.

Notice to Respondent of the taking of Depositions in application for Divorce.

A. B., by her next friend, C. D., *vs.* E. F.	In the Common Pleas of ——, County of ——, Term 18—. No. ——.

Sur Libel for Divorce.

[Here insert the interrogatories.]

Sir:—You will please take notice that the above interrogatories, to be addressed to the witnesses, to be produced in this case, on the part of the ——, have been filed, and that the said witnesses will be produced, sworn or affirmed, and examined before G. H., Esq., examiner appointed by the said court for that purpose, on the —— day of —— next, at —— o'clock, P. M., of that day, when and where you may attend, or file cross interrogatories, as you may think proper.

Notice of the Execution of a Writ of Inquiry.

John Jones *vs.* William Burns.	In the Common Pleas of Lancaster County of May Term, 1844. No. 200.

Sir:—Take notice, that a writ of inquiry of damages will be executed in this cause on ——, the —— day of —— next, at —— o'clock, P. M., at the house of ——, in the borough of ——.

Notice of the filing of Accounts in Court.

Public notice is hereby given, that A. B., —— of C. D., have filed in the —— office in and for the county of ——, at ——, his final account, as —— of the said ——, and that the same will be presented to the —— court of said county, for confirmation and allowance on ——, the —— day of —— next, at the court house at ——, in the county aforesaid.

Notice to Constable of a desire to vote for an increase of the number of Justices in a District.

Sir:—You are hereby notified, that it is our wish at the next constable election, to be holden in and for the township of ——, to vote for an increase of the number of justices of the peace in said township. You will please govern yourself accordingly.

Note.—This must be signed by fifty electors in the township or ward, and addressed to ——, constable of the —— of ——.

Notice of an Election to change the place of holding Township Elections.

To William Graham, Constable of the Township of North East, in the County of Erie, and State of Pennsylvania.

Sir:—The undersigned, qualified electors of the township of North East, in the county and state aforesaid, desirous of changing the place of holding the township election in said township, do hereby require you to give notice thereof to the electors of said township, in pursuance of the requirements of the first division of the fifty-sixth section of the Act relating to elections, passed July 2d, A. D. 1839.

[Signed by the requisite number of voters.]

Notice, by Constable, of the time and place of holding such Election.

Notice is hereby given, that a meeting of the qualified electors residing within the bounds of the township of North East, will be held at ——, in the said township, on ——, the —— day of ——, A. D. 1844, at —— o'clock, A. M., for the purpose of determining upon the expediency of changing the place of holding the township elections in said township.

WILLIAM GRAHAM,
Constable of North East Township.

Notice of an Appeal by Overseers of the Poor, from an Order of Removal.

Crawford County, *ss.*

To the overseers of the poor of the township of ——, in said county.

Take notice, that we, the overseers of the poor of the township of ——, in said county, do intend, at the next General Court of Quarter Sessions of the Peace, to be holden in and for the said county at Meadville, to commence and prosecute an appeal from the order of A. B. and C. D., two of the justices of the peace of the county aforesaid, for the removal of J. C., a pauper, from the township of —— to the township of —— aforesaid.

Notice of Captain of Militia to non-commissioned officers and privates on a requisition from the Governor or President.

To A. B.

SIR:—Take notice, that you are hereby required personally, or by a sufficient substitute, to appear properly armed and equipped for service at ——, on the —— day of ——, to march when required.

Given under my hand, &c.

Notice to Officers of their Election.

Take notice, that at an election held at the house of ——, A. B., in the —— of ——, county of ——, on ——, the —— day of —— instant, you were duly elected to the office of —— for said —— for the ensuing year.

Given under my hand at —— aforesaid, this —— day of ——, A. D. ——.

Notice of a Rule to take Depositions.

[Here insert a full copy of the rule.]

Take notice, that in pursuance of the above rule, the deposition of ——, of the —— of —— in the county of ——, will be taken before J. B., Esq., one of the justices of the peace in and for the county aforesaid, at his office in the borough of ——, on ——, the —— day of —— next, between the hours of —— and —— o'clock in the ——noon, at which time and place you are required to attend if you think proper.

Notice of proceedings to remove Pauper.

Lancaster County, *ss.*

To the overseers of the poor of the township of —— in the county of ——.

You are hereby notified and required to appear before ——, and such other of the justices of the peace of the said county as shall be at the house of —— in the —— of ——, and county aforesaid, on ——, the —— day of ——, at —— o'clock in the ——noon, to show cause, [if any you have,] why A. B., a pauper, should not be removed from the said township of —— to the township aforesaid.

Given under my hand and seal this —— day of ——, in the year of our Lord ——.

Notice of a motion upon a Justice's Judgment.

John Jones *vs.* William Burns. } Before J. B., Esq. Judgment for John Jones, for —— dollars.

To John Jones, plaintiff in the above cause.

At the instance of William Burns, the defendant, I hereby notify you to appear before me at my office in ——, on ——, the —— day of ——, at —— o'clock in the —— noon, to show cause, (if any you have,) why the above judgment should not be opened and another hearing given.

Witness my hand and seal at ——, this —— day of ——, in the year of our Lord one thousand eight hundred and ——.

Notice of Lumber taken up in Rivers.

Public notice is hereby given, that a lot of lumber was taken up while floating in the ——, on the —— day of ——, consisting of ——, a list and description of which are lodged in my office at —— for the inspection of all concerned. The owner or owners thereof are required to prove property, pay all legal charges, and take it away within three months from the date hereof, otherwise it will be forfeited.

Notice of sale in Attachment.

Public notice is hereby given, that by virtue of an order from A. B., one of the justices of the peace in and for the —— of ——, will be exposed to public sale on the —— day of —— instant, at —— o'clock in the ——, at the house of ——, in the —— of —— in the said county, the following articles, viz: (——.) Attached as the property of ——, late of the said ——. Attendance will be given and the terms of sale made known by ——.

Notice of Landlord to Sheriff or Constable to pay Rent out of proceeds of Sale.

To A. B., Sheriff of —— County.

SIR:—You are hereby required to pay over to the undersigned, the sum of —— dollars out of the proceeds of the sale of the property of ——, that being the amount of rent in arrear, and due by him to me for the premises now in his occupancy.

Notice to Justice of intention to bring suit unless he tender amends.

To A. B., Esq., Justice of the peace of ——.

SIR:—Take notice, that if you do not tender sufficient amends within thirty days from the date hereof, I will bring my action against you in the Court of Common Pleas of the county of ——, in the following case, to wit: that you maliciously, illegally, oppressively, and without probable cause, &c., [here state the grievance at length, omitting no material part of it.]

By reason of all which illegal, malicious and oppressive conduct of yours, I have sustained material injury and damage.

P. S.—L. M., Esq., is my attorney; his place of abode is ——.

See 2 S. & H. Pr., p. 472; 6 Binn. 84; 17 S. & R. 75, for other forms of these notices.

Notice by Commissioners of the time and place of taking Depositions.

Whereas the undersigned have received a commission issuing out of the Common Pleas of the county of ——, in the state of ——, to us and others [*or to me*] directed for the examination of witnesses in a certain cause, depending between A. B., plaintiff, and C. D., defendant.

These are to give you notice, that we will execute the said commission on behalf of the ——, at the house of —— in —— street, in the borough of ——, on —— the —— day of —— next, at the hour of —— o'clock in the ——noon of the same day, when and where you may attend with your witnesses and commissioners if you think proper.

Witness our hands this —— day of ——, A. D. ——.

Notice of time and place of taking Depositions on rule of Court.

A. B. *vs.* C. D. } In the Common Pleas of ——, County of ——, Term A. D. ——. No. ——.

[Here copy the rule as certified by the Prothonotary.]

To A. B., the plaintiff above named, or E. F., his attorney.

Take notice, that in pursuance of the above rule, the deposition of witness to be read in evidence on the trial of the above cause, on the part of the defendant, will be taken at the house of ——, in the —— of ——, between the hours of —— and —— o'clock of the same day, before L. M., Esq., a justice of the peace in and for said county, or before some other justice of the peace or judge, when and where you may attend if you think proper.

Notice of Special Matter.

A. B. *vs.* C. D. } In the Common Pleas of ——, County of ——, Term A. D. ——. No. ——.

Take notice that the defendant has added the pleas of *non-assumpsit infra sex annos, payment,* &c., to the pleas already pleaded in this cause.

And that under the plea of payment, he intends to give in evidence on the trial of the cause, the following matters, to wit: [*here insert the special matter.*]

Notice of Justification.

A. B. *vs.* C. D. } In the Common Pleas of ——, County of ——, Term A. D. ——. No. ——.

Please take notice, that on the trial of this cause the defendant will give evidence in justification of, &c., [*here insert the matter relied on.*]

Notice to produce Papers.

A. B. *vs.* C. D. } In the Common Pleas of ——, County of ——, Term A. D. ——. No. ——.

Take notice, that you are hereby required to produce to the [*court and jury*], on the trial of this cause, a certain deed, &c., [*describing the papers particularly,*] and all other letters, books, papers and writings whatsoever, in anywise relating to the matter in question in this cause.

Notice to Constable before bringing suit against him for acts done under the authority of a Warrant.

To A. B., constable of the —— of —— in the county of ——.

Whereas on or about the —— day of ——, A. D., you [*here recite the act done*], under colour of a warrant of ——, or some other justice of the peace, authorizing you to do so.

Now, I do hereby, as attorney of the said ——, and on his behalf, demand of you the perusal and a copy of all and every warrant, warrants, execution and executions, under and by virtue of which you —— as before mentioned.

Notice by purchaser at Sheriff's Sale, to Tenant in possession.

John Jones
vs.
William Burns.

To Mr. William Burns, the defendant above named.

Sir :—Take notice, that by virtue of a writ of *venditioni exponas*, which issued out of the Court of Common Pleas of the county of ——, returnable to the —— day of ——, A. D., ——, against you at the suit of John Jones, the sheriff of the said county, Richard Roe, Esq., did on the —— day of ——, last past, expose to sale a certain ——, then and now in your possession, situate in ——, and containing one hundred acres, and that at the said sale, I became the purchaser thereof. Whereupon you are hereby notified and required to surrender up the said one hundred acres of land, with the appurtenances, to me, the purchaser thereof as aforesaid, within three months after the date of this notice, as you shall answer your default herein at your peril.

Notice to Overseers of the Poor who neglect or refuse to comply with the orders of relief.

To A. B. and C. D., Overseers of the Poor of the —— of ——.

You are hereby notified that unless you make the weekly payments directed by the order of E. F. and G. H., Esqrs., two of the Justices of the Peace in and for the county of ——, for the relief of J. J., dated the —— day of May, A. D. 1844, you will be prosecuted for your default and contempt herein.

Notice of Bail.

John Jones *vs.* William Burns. } In the Common Pleas of Montgomery County, No. [illegible] of May Term, 1844.

Take notice, that bail was this day put in for the defendant in this cause, before ——, and that the names and additions of such bail are A. B., yeoman, and C. C., carpenter, of ——.

Notice of exception to Bail.

John Jones *vs.* William Burns. } In the Common Pleas of Lancaster County, No. —— of May Term, 1844.

Take notice, that I have excepted against the bail put in for the defendant in this cause.

Notice of Justification of Bail.

John Jones *vs.* William Burns.	In the Common Pleas of Lancaster County, May Term, 1844. No. 12.

Take notice, that J. R. and L. P., the bail already put in by the defendant, and of whom you have had notice, will, on the —— day of —— next, justify themselves before ——, as good and sufficient bail for the defendant in this cause.

N. B. (Where bail is added and justified, say) That Q. S., of ——, will, on the —— day of —— next, add himself to the bail already put in, &c.

PAPER BOOK.

A paper book is a book or paper containing an abstract of all the facts and pleadings necessary to a full understanding of a case. Courts of error and other courts, on arguments, require that each of the judges shall be furnished with such a book before the arguments are made.

It should first contain the evidence on the side of the plaintiff, then of the defendant, and the bills of exception.

The following will answer for a form in making up a paper book for the Judges of the Supreme Court of Pennsylvania.

A. B., plaintiff in error, *vs.* C. D., defendant in error.	Error to the Common Pleas of —— county. *Sci. fa.* on a mortgage.

The plaintiff gave the following evidence:

1. Mortgage given by —— to ——, dated ——, for —— dollars.

2. Bond from same to same, dated ——, for —— dollars.

3. Assignment of said bond and mortgage by said —— to ——, on the —— day of ——, in the following words, &c. &c.

Thereupon the plaintiff closed.

The defendant to maintain the issue on his part, called E. F., who being sworn, testified as follows: [*Here add the testimony as received.*] The defendant then offered to ask the witness, &c. To the admission of which evidence, the plaintiff objected. The court sustained the objection and admitted the evidence, to which decision the plaintiff excepted and prayed the court to seal this his bill of exceptions, which is done accordingly.

Add thus the whole of the material testimony with all the

bills of exceptions as they were sealed, and close with the charge of the court to the jury, which must be signed and sealed by the president judge.

PATENTS.

Information to persons having business at the Patent Office at Washington, under the Act of Congress, August 29, 1842.

Art. 1. This act authorizes the Treasurer of the United States to repay any money which has been paid into the Treasury by actual mistake, as for patent fees, thus precluding the necessity of special application to Congress for relief.

Art. 2. The privilege of renewal of lost patents is now extended to those *granted* before the fire of December, 1836. Heretofore it has been limited to those actually *lost* before the fire, and thus excluding many lost subsequently, and before they were recorded anew in this office, leaving the inventor without remedy.

Art. 3. Protection is by this act extended to a *new* class of objects, viz:

To new and original *Designs:*

—for a manufacture of metal and other materials:

—for the printing of woolen, silk, cotton, or other fabrics:

—for busts, statues, or bas reliefs, or composition in alto or basso relievo:

—for any impression or ornament, or to be placed on any article of manufacture in marble or other material:

—for any new and useful pattern, print, or picture, to be in any manner attached to or fixed on any article of manufacture:

—for any new or original shape of configuration of any article of manufacture: all such designs not being previously known or used by others.

Art. 4. American ministers, consuls, &c., residing abroad, may administer the oath required for applicants not resident in the United States. Heretofore such functionaries were not authorized to perform this act, thus subjecting applicants, in foreign countries, to much inconvenience.

Art. 5. The stamping or affixing the name of any patentee on any article without authority so to do, or the affixing the word *patent* or *letters patent*, or the stamp, mark, or device of any patentee on any unpatented article, for the purpose of deceiving the public, is forbidden under a penalty not less than one hundred dollars.

Art. 6. Patentees or their assigns are now required to affix the date of the patent on each article vended or offered for sale, under a like penalty—thus affording to the public notice of the duration of the patent—when the article is of such a nature that the date cannot be printed thereon, it should be affixed to the case or package containing it.

It will be observed that this act does not repeal or change the law under which patents have heretofore been granted, but is merely additional thereto—all patents, except for *designs*, being granted for fourteen years, and the fee, as hitherto, being thirty dollars.

Before the grant of any patent under this act the application must be made by petition to the Commissioner of Patents, signed by the inventor.

He is also required to furnish a written description or specification of his invention or production, in which the same shall be fully and clearly described—such specification to be signed, witnessed by two witnesses, and verified by his oath or affirmation.

In all cases which admit of representation by drawings, the application must be accompanied by duplicate drawings and a specimen—and in other cases by duplicate specimens.

The provisions of the 6th section do not apply to patents granted prior to the passage of this act.

Fees payable at the Patent Office.

Sec. 40. All fees must be paid in advance; the amount fixed by law, except in the case of drawings, the expense of which will be communicated on application for the same.

Sec. 41. Every applicant must pay into the Treasury of the United States, or into the Patent Office, or into any of the deposit banks, a deposit to the credit of the Treasurer, on presenting his petition or application, as follows:

Sec. 42. If a citizen of the United States, as a patent fee - - - - - - -	$30 00
Sec. 43. If a foreigner, who has resided in the United States one year next preceding the application for a patent, and shall have made oath of his intention to become a citizen - - - - -	30 00
Sec. 44. If a subject of the Sovereign of Great Britain - - - - - -	500 00
Sec. 45. All other foreigners - -	300 00
Sec. 46. On entering a caveat - - -	20 00
Sec. 47. On entering an application for an appeal from the decision of the Commissioner - -	25 00
Sec. 48. On extending a patent beyond the fourteen years - - - - - - -	40 00
Sec. 49. For adding to a patent the specification of a subsequent improvement - - - - -	15 00

In case of re-issues, for every additional patent - 30 00

Sec. 50. On surrender of an old patent, to be re-issued, to correct a mistake of the patentee - 15 00

Sec. 51. For a disclaimer - - - - 10 00

Sec. 52. For copies of patents, or any other paper on file, for each 100 words - - - - 10

Sec. 53. For copies of drawings, a reasonable sum, in proportion to the time occupied in making the same.

Sec. 54. Communications to and from the Patent Office, are free of postage.

Sec. 55. All fees under five dollars, if sent to the Commissioner of Patents, should be transmitted in specie.

Sec. 56. It is recommended to make a deposit in a specie-paying deposit bank, of the fee for a patent or other application, and to remit the certificate. Where this cannot be done without much inconvenience, gold may be remitted by mail free of postage.

Sec. 57. In case of deposits made in the deposit banks, a duplicate receipt should be taken, stating by whom the payment is made, and for what object. The particular invention should be referred to, to enable the applicant to recover back the twenty dollars, in case of the withdrawal of the petition. The certificate of deposit may be in the following form:

Sec. 58. *Bank of*

The Treasurer of the United States has credit at this office for dollars in specie, deposited by of the town of in the county of , and state of , the same being for a patent [*or whatever the object may be*] for a steam-boiler.

Sec. 59. N. B. The Patent Office does not make original drawings to accompany applications for patents, and furnishes copies of the same only after the patent is completed. Draughtsmen in the city of Washington are always ready to make drawings, at the expense of the patentees.

FORMS WHICH MAY BE USED IN MAKING APPLICATIONS AT THE PATENT OFFICE.

Form of Petition.

To the Commissioner of Patents:

The petition of Sebastian Cabot, of Cabotville, in the County of Hampden, and State of Massachusetts,

Respectfully represents:

That your petitioner has invented a new [and improved mode of preventing steam-boilers from bursting], which he verily believes has not been known or used prior to the invention thereof by your petitioner. He therefore prays that letters patent of the United States may be granted to him therefor, vesting in him and his legal representatives the exclusive right to the same, upon the terms and conditions expressed in the Act of Congress in that case made and provided; he having paid thirty dollars into the treasury, and complied with other provisions of the said act.

SEBASTIAN CABOT.

Form of Specification.

To all whom it may concern:

Be it known that I, Sebastian Cabot, of Cabotville, in the County of Hampden, and State of Massachusetts, have invented a new and improved mode of preventing steam-boilers from bursting, and I do hereby declare that the following is a full and exact description:

The nature of my invention consists in providing the upper part of a steam-boiler with an aperture in addition to that for the safety-valve, which aperture is to be closed by a plug, or disk, of alloy, which will fuse at any given degree of heat, and permit the steam to escape, should the safety-valve fail to perform its functions.

To enable others skilled in the art to make and use my invention, I will proceed to describe its construction and operation: I construct my steam-boiler in any of the known forms, and apply thereto gauge-cocks, a safety-valve, and the other appendages of such boilers; but, in order to obviate the danger arising from the adhesion of the safety-valve, and from other causes, I make a second opening in the top of the boiler, similar to that made for the safety-valve, as shown at A, in the accompanying drawing; and in this opening I insert a plug or disk of fusible alloy, securing it in its place by a metal ring and screws, or otherwise. This fusible metal, I, in general, compose of a mixture of lead, tin and bismuth, in such proportions as will insure its melting at a given temperature, which must be that to which it is intended to limit the steam, and will of course vary with the pressure the boiler is intended to sustain. I surround the opening containing the fusible alloy by a tube, B, intended to conduct off any steam which may be discharged therefrom. When the temperature of the steam, in such a boiler, rises to its assigned limit, the fusible alloy will melt, and allow the steam to escape freely, thereby securing it from all danger of explosion.

What I claim as my invention, and desire to secure by letters patent, is the application to steam-boilers of a fusible alloy, which will melt at a given temperature, and allow the steam to escape, as herein described; using for that purpose any metallic compound which will produce the intended effect.

Witness: { John Doe, Richard Roe. } SEBASTIAN CABOT.

When the application is for a machine, the specification should commence thus:

Be it known that I, Sebastian Cabot, of Cabotville, in the county of Hampden and State of Massachusetts, have invented a new and useful machine for—[stating the use and title of the machine; and if the application is for an improvement, it should read thus: a new and useful improvement on a, or on the, machine, &c.]—and I do hereby declare that the following is a full, clear and exact description of the construction and operation of the same, reference being had to the annexed drawings, making a part of this specification, in which figure 1 is a perspective view, figure 2 a longitudinal elevation, figure 3 a transverse section, &c. [thus describing all the sections of the drawings, and then referring to the parts by letters.] Then follows the description of the construction and operation of the machine, and ending with the claim, which should express the nature and character of the invention, and identify the part or parts claimed separately or in combination. If the application is for an improvement, the original invention should be disclaimed, and then the claim confined to the improvement.

Form of Oath.

County of Hampden, State of Massachusetts, *ss.*

On this tenth day of January, 1845, before the subscriber, a justice of the peace in and for the said county, personally appeared the within-named Sebastian Cabot, and made solemn oath [or affirmation] that he verily believes himself to be the original and first inventor of the mode herein described for preventing steam-boilers from bursting, and that he does not know or believe that the same was ever before known or used; and that he is a citizen of the United States.

Signed, A. B.

Form of Withdrawal.

To the Commissioner of Patents:

Sir:—I hereby withdraw my application for a patent for improvements in the steam-boiler, now in your office, and request that twenty dollars may be returned to me, agreeably to the provision of the Act of Congress authorizing such withdrawal.

SEBASTIAN CABOT.

Cabotville, Mass., March 1, 1845.

Form of surrender of a Patent for Re-issue.

To the Commissioner of Patents:
The petition of Sebastian Cabot, of Cabotville, in the County of Hampden, and State of Massachusetts,

RESPECTFULLY REPRESENTS:

That he did obtain letters patent of the United States for an improvement in the boilers of steam-engines, which letters patent are dated on the first day of March, 1835. That he now believes that the same is inoperative and invalid, by reason of a defective specification, which defect has arisen from inadvertence and mistake. He therefore prays that he may be allowed to surrender, and he hereby does surrender the same, and request that new letters patent may issue to him for the same invention, for the residue of the period for which the original patent was granted, under the amended specification herewith presented; he having paid fifteen dollars into the Treasury of the United States, agreeably to the requirements of the Act of Congress in that case made and provided.

SEBASTIAN CABOT.

Form of Assignment of a right in a Patent.

Whereas I, Sebastian Cabot, of Cabotville, in the county of Hampden, and State of Massachusetts, did obtain letters patent of the United States, for certain improvements in steam-engines, which letters patent bear date the first day of March, 1835; and whereas John Doe, of Cabotville aforesaid, is desirous of acquiring an interest therein: Now this indenture witnesseth, that for and in consideration of the sum of two thousand dollars, to me in hand paid, the receipt of which is hereby acknowledged, I have assigned, sold, and set over, and do hereby assign, sell, and set over, all the right, title and interest, which I have in the said invention, as secured to me by said letters patent, for, to, and in, the several states of New York, New Jersey and Pennsylvania, and in no other place or places. The same to be held and enjoyed by the said John Doe for his own use and behoof, and for the use and behoof of his legal representatives, to the full end of the term for which said letters patent are or may be granted, as fully and entirely as the same would have been held and enjoyed by me, had this assignment and sale not have been made.

In testimony whereof, I have hereunto set my hand, and affixed my seal, this first day of March, 1845.

Witness: { A. B., C. D.

SEBASTIAN CABOT. [L. S.]

Form of Disclaimer.

To the Commissioner of Patents:

The petition of Sebastian Cabot, of Cabotville, in the county of Hampden, and State of Massachusetts,

RESPECTFULLY REPRESENTS:

That he has, by assignment duly recorded in the Patent Office, become the owner of a right, for the several states of Massachusetts, Connecticut and Rhode Island, to certain improvements in the steam engine, for which letters patent of the United States were granted to John Doe, of Boston, in the State of Massachusetts, dated on the first day of March, 1835. That he has reason to believe that, through inadvertence and mistake, the claim made in the specification of said letters patent is too broad, including that of which the said patentee was not the first inventor. Your petitioner, therefore, hereby enters his disclaimer to that part of the claim in the aforenamed specification, which is in the following words, to wit: "I also claim the particular manner in which the piston of the above-described engine is constructed, so as to insure the close fitting of the packing thereof to the cylinder, as set forth;" which disclaimer is to operate to the extent of the interest in said letters patent vested in your petitioner, who has paid ten dollars into the treasury of the United States, agreeably to the requirements of the Act of Congress in that case made and provided. SEBASTIAN CABOT.

When the disclaimer is made by the original patentee, it must, of course, be worded so as to express that fact.

Form of Caveat.

To the Commissioner of Patents:

The petition of Sebastian Cabot, of Cabotville, in the County of Hampden, and State of Massachusetts,

RESPECTFULLY REPRESENTS:

That he has made certain improvements in the mode of constructing the boilers of steam-engines; and that he is now engaged in making experiments for the purpose of perfecting the same, preparatory to his applying for letters patent therefor. He therefore prays that the subjoined description of his invention may be filed as a *caveat*, in the confidential archives of the Patent Office, agreeably to the provisions of the Act of Congress, in that case made and provided; he having paid twenty dollars into the treasury of the United States, and otherwise complied with the requirements of the said act.

Cabotville, March 1, 1845. SEBASTIAN CABOT.

Here should follow a description of the general principles of the invention, so far as it has been completed.

Form for Addition of new Improvements.

To the Commissioner of Patents:

The petition of Sebastian Cabot, of Cabotville, in the County of Hampden, and State of Massachusetts,

RESPECTFULLY REPRESENTS:

That your petitioner did obtain letters patent of the United States for an improvement in the boilers of steam-engines, which letters patent are dated on the first day of March, 1835; that he has, since that date, made certain improvements on his said invention; and that he is desirous of adding the subjoined description of his said improvements to his original letters patent, agreeably to the provisions of the Act of Congress in that case made and provided; he having paid fifteen dollars into the treasury of the United States, and otherwise complied with the requirements of the said act. SEBASTIAN CABOT.

Form of Assignment before obtaining Letters Patent, and to be recorded preparatory thereto.

Whereas I, Sebastian Cabot, of Cabotville, in the county of Hampden and State of Massachusetts, have invented certain new and useful improvements in the boilers of steam-engines, for which I am about to make application for letters patent of the United States; and whereas John Doe, of Cabotville aforesaid, has agreed to purchase from me all the right, title and interest which I have, or may have, in and to the said invention, in consequence of the grant of letters patent therefor, and has paid to me, the said Cabot, the sum of five thousand dollars, the receipt of which is hereby acknowledged. Now, this indenture witnesseth, that for and in consideration of the said sum to me paid, I have assigned and transferred, and do hereby assign and transfer, to the said John Doe, the full and exclusive right to all the improvements made by me, as fully set forth and described in the specification which I have prepared and executed preparatory to the obtaining of letters patent therefor. And I do hereby authorize and request the Commissioner of Patents to issue the said letters patent to the said John Doe, as the assignee of my whole right and title thereto, for the sole use and behoof of the said John Doe and his legal representatives.

In testimony whereof, I have hereunto set my hand and affixed my seal, this first day of March, 1838.

Witness: { A. B.,
C. D.

SEBASTIAN CABOT.

Form of Application for Patents on Designs under the Act of August 29, 1842.

To the Commissioner of Patents:

The petition of Sebastian Cabot, of Cabotsville, in the County of Hampden, and State of Massachusetts,

RESPECTFULLY REPRESENTS:

That your petitioner has invented or produced [a new design or figure to be stamped or printed on fabrics, which, when thus printed, are termed calicoes], which he verily believes has not been known prior to the production thereof by your petitioner. He therefore prays that letters patent of the United States may be granted to him therefor, vesting in him and his legal representatives the exclusive right to the same, upon the terms and conditions expressed in the Act of Congress in that case made and provided; he having paid fifteen dollars into the treasury, and complied with other provisions of the said act. SEBASTIAN CABOT.

Specification.

To all whom it may concern:

Be it known that I, Sebastian Cabot, of Cabotsville, in the County of Hampden, and State of Massachusetts, have invented or produced a new [design or figure to be printed on fabrics, which, when thus printed, are termed calicoes], and I do hereby declare that the following is a full and exact description of the same. [Here follows a description of the design or figure with reference to the specimen, or to a drawing of it in all cases which admit of representation by drawings.]

The specification to conclude with declaring what the inventor or producer claims to be expressed in terms which will give the character of the design, &c.

Form of Oath.

County of Hampden, State of Massachusetts, *ss.*

On this tenth day of January, 1845, before the subscriber, a justice of the peace in and for said county, personally appeared the within-named Sebastian Cabot, and made solemn oath [or affirmation as the case may be], that he verily believes himself to be the original and first inventor or producer of the design for figures to be printed on fabrics which, when thus printed, are termed calicoes, and that he does not know or believe that the same was ever before known or used, and that he is a citizen of the United States. Signed, A. B.

Letters Patent for a new Invention.

Whereas J. S., of the —— of ——, in the county of ——, has alleged that he has invented a new and useful machine, which he states has not been known or used before his application; has made oath that he is a citizen of the United States—that he verily believes that he is the original and first inventor of the said machine, (discoverer of the improvement,) and that the same hath not, to the best of his knowledge and belief, been previously known or used; has paid into the treasury of the United States the sum of thirty dollars, and presented a petition to the Commissioner of Patents, signifying his desire of obtaining an exclusive property in the said improvement, and praying that a patent may be granted for that purpose.

These are, therefore, to grant, according to law, to the said J. S., his heirs, executors, administrators and assigns, for the full term of fourteen years from the —— day of ——, A. D. ——, the full and exclusive right and liberty of making, using and vending to others to be used, the said machine, a description whereof is given in the words of the said J. S., in the schedule hereto annexed, and is made part of these presents.

In testimony whereof, I have caused these letters to be made patent, and the seal of the Patent Office has been hereto affixed.

Given under my hand, at the city of Washington, this —— day of ——, A. D. ——, and of the Independence of the United States of America the ——.

PETITIONS.

Remarks.

A petition is an instrument containing a prayer from the person or persons who signed it, to the body or person to whom it is presented, for the redress of some wrong, or the grant of some favour, which the latter has the right to give. By the constitution of the United States, the right "to petition the government for a redress of grievances," is secured to the people. Amendment to Constitution, Art. 1. Petitions are frequently presented to the courts in order to bring some matters before them. It is a general rule in such cases, that an affidavit should be made that the facts therein contained are true, as far as known to the petitioner, and that those facts which he states as knowing from others, he believes to be true.

To the Governor of a State.

To his Excellency, J. R., Governor of the Commonwealth of Pennsylvania: The petition of the subscribers, citizens of the borough of Reading, in the County of Berks, respectfully showeth: [Here state the subject matter petitioned for.] And your petitioners, as in duty bound, will ever pray, &c.

To the Congress of the United States.

To the Honourable, the Senate and House of Representatives, of the United States of America, in Congress assembled: The petition of the subscribers, citizens of the city of Lancaster, in the State of Pennsylvania, respectfully showeth: [here state the subject matter petitioned for.] And your petitioners will ever pray, &c.

To the Legislature of Pennsylvania.

To the Honourable, the Senate and House of Representatives of the Commonwealth of Pennsylvania, in General Assembly met: The petition, &c., [as above.]

Petition for laying out a Road.

To the Honourable, the Judges of the Court of Quarter Sessions of the Peace in and for the County of ——.

The petition of divers inhabitants of the township of —— in the said county, respectfully showeth, that your petitioners labour under great inconveniences for want of a road or highway, to lead from —— to ——. Your petitioners, therefore, humbly pray the court to appoint proper persons to view and lay out the same, according to law. And they will pray, &c.

(There must be no intermediate points made in the road prayed for.)

Appointment of Viewers.

—— County, *ss.*

[*Seal.*] At a Court of Quarter Sessions of the Peace of the County of ——, held at —— in and for the said County, on —— the —— day, &c., before A. B., C. D. and E. F., Judges of the same court.

Upon the petition of divers inhabitants of the township of ——, in the said county, setting forth that they labour under great inconveniences for want of a road or highway, to lead from —— to —— and, therefore, praying the court to appoint, &c., [as in petition to "law."] The court, upon due consideration had of the premises, do order and appoint G. H., I. K., L. M., N. O., P. Q. and R. S., to view the ground proposed for the said road, and if they, or any five of them, view the same, and any four of the actual viewers agree that there is occasion for such a road, they shall proceed to lay out the same, as agreeable to the desire of the petitioners as may be, having respect to the best ground for a road, and the shortest distance, and in such a manner as to do the least injury to private property, and that they make report of their proceedings to the next Court of Quarter Sessions to be held for the said county, stating particularly whether they judge the same necessary for a public or private road, together with a plot or draft thereof, and the courses and distances, and references to the improvements through which it may pass.

By the Court, J. B., *Clerk.*

Return of Viewers in favour of the Road.

To the Honourable, the Judges within named.

We, the persons appointed by the within order of court, to view and lay out the road therein mentioned, do report, that in pursuance of the said order, we have viewed and laid out, and do return for public [or private] use, the following road, to wit: Beginning, &c., [here describe the courses and distances in letters (*not figures*) with references to the improvements through which it passes] a plot or draft whereof is hereunto annexed. Witness our hands the —— day of ——.

☞ At least five of the viewers must view the ground, and any four of the actual viewers may lay out the road, and whenever practicable, the viewers shall lay out the said roads at an elevation not exceeding five degrees, except at the crossing of drains and streams, where by moderate filling and bridging, the declination of the road may be preserved within that limit.

Return of Viewers against the Road.

To the Honourable, the Judges within named.

We, the subscribers, do report, that in pursuance of the within order of court, we have viewed the place where the road within mentioned is requested, and are of opinion that there is no occasion to lay out the same. Witness our hands, the —— day of ——.

Order of Confirmation.

At a Court of Quarter Sessions of the Peace, &c., G. H., I. K., L. M., N. O., P. Q., and R. S., the persons appointed by an order of this court of —— sessions last past, to view and lay out a road from —— to ——, do report, that in pursuance of the said order, they have viewed and laid out, and do return for public use, the following road, to wit: Beginning, &c., a plot or draft, whereof is to the said report annexed, which report being read the first time at —— sessions last, and the second time on the —— day of —— instant, the court approve of and confirm the said road for public use, and order and direct that it be entered of record, and opened and cleared of the breadth of —— feet, agreeably to the courses and distances aforesaid, of which the supervisors of the highways of the townships through which the said road runs, are to take notice. The breadth of any such road shall not in any case exceed fifty feet; the breadth of roads from the habitations of individuals, to the public highway, or other place of public resort, shall not exceed twenty-five feet, and the same shall be opened and kept in repair at the expense of the persons for whom it was laid out, and of such as have occasion to use it.

Petition for a Review.

To the Honourable, the Judges of the Court of Quarter Sessions of the Peace in and for the County of ——.

The petition of divers inhabitants of the township of, &c.: Respectfully showeth, that a road hath been lately laid out by order of court from —— to ——, which road, (if confirmed by the court,) will be very injurious to your petitioners, and burthensome to the inhabitants of the township through which the same will pass.

Your petitioners, therefore, pray your honours to appoint proper persons to review the said road, and parts adjacent, and make report to the court according to law. And they will ever pray, &c.

Appointment of Reviewers.

At a Court of Quarter Sessions of the Peace, &c.

Upon the petition of, &c., [as in petition] setting forth, &c., and therefore praying, &c. The court, upon due consideration, do order and appoint A. B., &c., [six discreet and reputable freeholders of the neighbourhood of the road prayed for,] to review the said road and parts adjacent, and if any five of them review the same, and any four of the actual reviewers agree that there is occasion for such a road, &c., [as in the order, *ante.*]

Report of Reviewers in favour of the Road.

To the Honourable, &c.

We, the persons appointed to review the road within mentioned, and parts adjacent, do report, that in pursuance of the said order, we did review the same, and have laid out for public use the following road, to wit: Beginning, &c. Witness our hands, the —— day of ——.

Against the Road.

To the Honourable, &c.

We, the persons appointed to review the road within mentioned, and parts adjacent, do report, that in pursuance of the said order, we did review the same, and in our opinion there is no occasion for such a road. Witness our hands, the —— day of ——.

Petition to vacate a Road.

To the Honourable, &c.

The petition of, &c., respectfully showeth, that a road has been long since laid out from, &c., which road [or part of which road, beginning, &c.,] your petitioners humbly conceive is now become useless, inconvenient and burthensome to the inhabitants thereabouts. Your petitioners, therefore, humbly pray your honours, that the said road may be vacated, agreeably to the act of the General Assembly in such case made and provided. And they will pray, &c.

☞ The petition must set forth, in a clear and intelligible manner, the length, breadth, situation and other circumstances of the road (or of the parts of the road) to be vacated.

Appointment of Viewers.

At a court, &c., upon the petition, &c., stating, &c., and therefore praying, &c., which petition being openly and audibly read in open sessions, the court do order and appoint A. B., &c., to view the road in the said petition prayed to be vacated, and to consider and judge whether it is become useless, inconvenient and burthensome, and if they, or any five of them, view the said road, and any four of the actual viewers agree that the same is become useless, inconvenient and burthensome, as aforesaid, then to make report accordingly to the next court.

Report of Viewers in favour of Vacation.

To the Honourable, &c.

We, the subscribers, appointed by the within order of court to view the road therein mentioned, do report, that in pursuance of the said order, we have viewed the said road, and that the same is, in our opinion, useless, inconvenient and burthensome. Witness, &c.

Report of Viewers against the Vacation.

To the Honourable, &c.

We, the subscribers, appointed by the within order of court to view the road therein mentioned, do report, that in pursuance of the said order, we have viewed the said road, and that, in our opinion, there is no cause for vacating the same. Witness, &c.

Confirmation by the Court.

A. B., &c., [five of] the persons appointed by the order of this Court of —— Sessions, A. D., &c., to view a road leading from —— to ——, and to consider and judge whether the same is become useless, inconvenient and burthensome, do report, that they have viewed the said road, and are of opinion that it is become useless, inconvenient and burthensome to the inhabitants thereabouts, which report being openly and audibly read, the court do approve of and confirm the said report, and order that the said road be vacated.

Petition to value Lands, in case of a Public Road.

To the Honourable, &c.

The petition of, &c., respectfully showeth, that a public road or highway was lately laid out, and opened, by order of this court from —— to ——, which road is laid out and opened through the land of your petitioners. Your petitioners, therefore, humbly pray your honours to appoint proper persons to view and adjudge the value of so much of their lands respectively as is or may be taken up for the use of the said road: And they will pray, &c.

Petition to value Lands in case of a Private Road.

To the Honourable, &c.

The petition of, &c., respectfully showeth, that a private road has been lately laid out and opened, by order of this court, on the petition of A. B., &c., extending over the lands of your petitioners. Your petitioners, therefore, humbly pray your honours to appoint proper persons to value their lands, so as aforesaid, taken up for the use of the said road, and to settle and ascertain the proportions to be paid to them by the several persons for whose use the same is laid out. And they will pray, &c.

☞ No application for compensation, in case of a public road, can be received after one year.

Appointment of Viewers.

At a court, &c., upon the petition, &c., stating, &c., and therefore praying, &c. The court, upon due consideration, do order and appoint A. B., &c., [six disinterested men,] to view and adjudge the amount of the damage, (if any,) sustained by the petitioners, by reason of the said road; who and every of whom, before they proceed to assess the damages, shall take the oath or affirmation prescribed by the Act of Assembly: And the court do further order that the said petitioners give notice of the time of holding such view, to one or more of the commissioners of —— county, and that the viewers aforesaid do make report of their proceedings herein to the next court according to law.

Oath of Viewers.

"You and every of you do swear [or 'solemnly and sincerely and truly declare and affirm,'] that you will justly and truly value the damages (if any) which the petitioners in this order mentioned have sustained by reason of the road which has been laid out through their lands, and that you will also consider the advantage as well as the disadvantage of the said road. So help you God."

This oath or affirmation is to be taken before some magistrate of the county, or may be administered by one of the viewers.

Report of Viewers.

To the Honourable, &c.

We, the subscribers, appointed by the within order of court, to view and adjudge the value of so much of the lands of A. B., as are taken up by the road therein mentioned, and do value and adjudge the loss thereby occasioned to the within-named A. B., at the sum of ——, and the loss thereby occasioned to C. D., at the sum of ——, respectively. Witness, &c.

Another.

We, the subscribers, within appointed to view and assess the damages sustained by the petitioner, A. B., by reason of the premises in the within order mentioned, do report, that having been previously sworn and affirmed according to law, we did view the lot through which the within-mentioned road passes, and that upon due consideration, as well of the advantages as disadvantages arising to the petitioner, we are of opinion that he has received damage to the amount of ——, and we do accordingly assess the same. Witness, &c.

Confirmation, as before, making the necessary alterations—concluding, "which report being read, the court, on due consideration, do approve of and confirm the same, and direct that the said sum of —— shall be paid to the petitioner, by the treasurer of the county of ——, out of the county stock."

☞ In case of a private road, the damage must be paid by the person at whose request it was laid out.

Petition for a Gate.

To the Honourable, &c.

The petition of, &c., respectfully showeth, that your petitioners labour under great inconveniences for want of the privilege of hanging a swinging gate or gates on a private road, leading from, &c. They, therefore, humbly pray the court to appoint proper persons to view and judge of the utility of granting them the privilege aforesaid. And they will pray, &c.

Appointment of Viewers.

(*As before.*) The court, upon due consideration had of the premises, do order and appoint A. B., &c., to view the said road, and inquire and judge whether such gate or gates may, without much inconveniency to the persons for whose use the said road was granted, be hung on the same, and do direct that they or any four of them, do make report accordingly to the next court of Quarter Sessions.

Report of Viewers.

To the Honourable, &c.

We, the persons appointed by the within order to view and judge of the propriety of hanging a gate or gates on the road therein mentioned, do report, that we have viewed the premises, and are of opinion that a gate may be hung upon the said road, at, &c., and another gate at, &c., according to the prayer of the petitioners, without inconveniency to the persons using the said road. Witness, &c.

Confirmation by the Court.

[*As before*, making the necessary alterations, and conclude thus:—"Which report being read, the court, on due consideration, do approve of, and confirm the same, and do order that the said gates may be hung on the said road accordingly, and that the same shall be made and kept in repair, by the owner of the said land, and made easy for the passage of persons using the said road."

Petition for a Bridge.

To the Honourable, &c.

The petition of, &c., respectfully showeth, that a bridge is much wanted over —— creek, at the place where the public highway to ——, crosses the said creek, in the township aforesaid, the ford there being frequently rendered impassable by reason of ice and high waters; and that the expense thereof would be too heavy and burthensome upon the inhabitants of said township. Your petitioners, therefore, pray your honours to take such order in the premises, as in your wisdom shall seem meet and consistent with the Act of the General Assembly in such case made and provided. And they will pray, &c.

☞ The court may take it up, either on the representation of the supervisors, or on petition as above.

Appointment of Viewers.

Upon the petition of, &c., setting forth, &c., and therefore praying the court, &c. The court, upon due consideration had of the premises, do order and appoint A. B., &c., to view the place proposed for the said bridge, and if they, or any five of them, view the same, and any four of the actual viewers agree that there is occasion for such a bridge, and that the erecting of such a bridge would require more expense than it would be reasonable the said township should bear, they are to make report thereof to the next Court of Quarter Sessions to be held for the said county.

Report of Viewers.

We, the persons appointed by the court to view the place proposed for the bridge in the within order mentioned, do report, that in our opinion, a bridge over —— creek, at the place where the public highway to —— crosses, the said creek is indispensably necessary, and that the expense of erecting such a bridge would be attended with more cost than the said township of —— could bear, [or, that "in our opinion, there is no occasion for the same."] Witness, &c.

Petition of Commissioners.

To the Honourable, &c.

The petition of A. B., C. D., and E. F., commissioners of the county of ——: Respectfully showeth, that it appearing to your honourable court, to the grand jury of the said county, and to your petitioners, that a bridge over —— creek, at the place where the public highway to —— crosses the said creek, in the township of ——, in the said county, was necessary, and that it would be too expensive for the said township to erect; the same was entered of record, and your petitioners did procure an estimate as nearly as might be of the money which would be necessary to erect such bridge, amounting to the sum of ——, which sum they have provided out of the county taxes, and did proceed to have such bridge erected, by entering into a contract with G. H., of, &c., for the building of the same—that the said bridge is now completed, and the said G. H. hath, in every respect, fulfilled the contract so as aforesaid made. Your petitioners, therefore, pray the court to appoint fit persons to inspect the said bridge and the workmanship thereof, and make report accordingly to the next court.

Order.

Upon the petition of, &c., stating, &c., and therefore praying the court, &c. The court do appoint A. B., &c., [six fit persons,] to inspect said bridge and the workmanship thereof, and make report accordingly to the next court.

Report of Viewers.

We, the persons appointed by the court to inspect a certain bridge in the within order mentioned, do report, that we have viewed and carefully examined the same, and are unanimously of opinion that it is completed in a substantial and workmanlike manner, and according to contract, and in a style much to the credit of the undertaker. Witness, &c.

Confirmation by Court.

A. B., &c., the persons appointed by an order of last sessions, to view the bridge lately erected, &c., do report, that, &c., [as in report] which report being read and considered, is approved of and confirmed by the court.

Petition where Deed is lost, or has become defaced.

To the Honourable, &c.

The petition of J. A., of, &c. Humbly showeth:

That, &c., [setting forth the case and the circumstances of it,] whereby your petitioner's title to the premises hath become defective and imperfect; and your petitioner being desirous to have the said losses, defects and imperfections in the said title supplied, therefore humbly prays your honours will be pleased to issue a subpœna for such person or persons as may appear to be interested in the matters above set forth, requiring them to appear before your honours, to make their answer upon oath or affirmation to the facts above alleged: And as some of the parties and their witnesses are very ancient and infirm, and cannot attend your honours, your petitioner, therefore, prays your honours will be pleased to authorize and appoint some person or persons to take their depositions respecting the facts above alleged, and make such order and decree in the premises as to justice and equity shall appertain, &c.

Affidavit:—J. A., the petitioner, on his solemn oath doth declare and say, that the material facts set forth in the above petition are true, to the best of his knowledge and belief.

Sworn in open court, &c.

Petition for Guardian for Minor under the age of fourteen years.

To the Honourable, the Judges of the Orphans' Court of the County of Erie.

The petition of James Jones, a minor child of John Jones, deceased, late of the county of Erie, by his mother Mary Jones, respectfully represents: That the petitioner is under the age of fourteen years, and has no person legally authorized to take charge of his person and estate. He, therefore, prays the court to appoint some suitable person his guardian for that purpose. And he will, &c.

MARY JONES for
JAMES JONES.

Petition for Guardian by Minor over the age of fourteen years.

To the Honourable Judges of the Orphans' Court of the County of Allegheny.

The petition of James Jones respectfully represents: That the petitioner is a minor child above the age of fourteen years, of John Jones, deceased, late of the county of Allegheny; that he has no person legally authorized to take care of his person and estate, and he prays the court, that he may be permitted to make choice of a suitable guardian for that purpose. And he will, &c.

JAMES JONES.

Petition for Sale of Land by Administratrix.

To the Honourable, the Judges of the Orphans' Court of the County of Erie.

The petition of A. B. and C., his wife, late C. F., widow and administratrix of all and singular the goods and chattels, lands and tenements which were of D. F., late of the township of Amity in said county, yeoman, deceased, at the time of his death, who died intestate, humbly showeth: That the said intestate left issue four children, to wit: A., (now the wife of G. H.,) B., C. and D., the last two named of whom are yet in their minority. That the personal estate of said intestate is insufficient for the payment of his debts, as by the account herewith produced, appears: And that the said intestate died seised in his demesne as of fee, of, and in a certain messuage, &c. [Here describe the premises,] situated in the township of Amity and county aforesaid. Your petitioners, therefore, pray your honours, to grant them an order to make sale of the said messuage, &c., with the appurtenances, for the payment of the debts, and the maintenance and education of the minor children of the said intestate.

A. B.
C. B.

☞ A petition for the sale of lands by an administrator, must be accompanied by the following statements, or such as the case may be.

1. A true and perfect inventory and conscionable appraisement of all the personal estate whatsoever of the decedent.

1 horse - - - - - -	$50 00
15 sheep - - - - - -	15 00
2 cows - - - - - -	20 00
1 wagon - - - - - -	30 00
1 clock - - - - - -	10 00
1 promissory note against R. S. - - -	25 00
Total	150 00

2. A full and correct statement of all the real estate of the decedent, wherever situated.

A certain messuage and piece of land situate in Amity township, Erie County, containing one hundred acres.

One other certain piece of land situate, &c.

3. A just and true account upon oath or affirmation of all the debts of the decedent, which have come to the knowledge of your petitioners.

One note payable to S. P. & Co. - - -	$95 00
One " " " John Jones - - -	31 00
An account " J. M. - - -	43 00
do do " " S. P. &. Co. -	67 00
do do " " N. T. - - -	21 50
Total	$257 50

A. B.
C. B.

Affidavit.

Erie County, *ss.*

A. B. and C. B., the above-named petitioners, being duly sworn [or affirmed, as the case may be], according to law, doth depose and say that the facts set forth in the foregoing petition are just and true, and that the inventory and appraisement of the personal estate of the said decedent, and the statement of said decedent's real estate, and the account of his debts which have come to the knowledge of said petitioners, which are thereunto annexed, are just and true, to the best of their knowledge and belief.

A. B.
C. B.

Sworn and subscribed before me this }
—— day of ——, A. D. 1844. }

THOMAS BROWN, J. P.

Petition of same for further Time.

To the Honourable, the Judges of the Orphans' Court of the County of Erie.

The petition of A. B. and C., his wife, late C. F., widow and administratrix of all and singular the goods, &c., which were of D. F., late of the township of Amity, in the said county, yeoman, deceased, at the time of his death, who died intestate, humbly showeth: That, in pursuance of an order of the said court, made the first day of January, last past, for the sale of a certain messuage, &c., [as in the order], late the estate of the said intestate, your petitioners did, on Monday, the twentieth day of January, instant, expose the premises aforesaid for sale, by public vendue or outcry, but no person offering a sufficient price, the same remains still unsold. Your petitioners, therefore, pray your honours to grant them such further time, for sale of the premises aforesaid, as to your honours may seem meet. And they will pray, &c.

A. B.
C. B.

Return upon Order of Sale.

To the Honourable Judges of the Orphans' Court of the County of Erie.

A. B. and C., his wife, late C. F., widow, and administratrix of all and singular the goods and chattels, lands and tenements, which were of D. F., late of the township of Amity, in said county, deceased, reports: That pursuant to the within order of court, they did, at the time and place therein mentioned, having given due public and timely notice thereof, in one newspaper published in said county, and also by handbills affixed in three or more of the most public places in the vicinity of said estate, twenty days or more before the day appointed therefor, expose the premises therein described, to sale by public vendue or outcry, and sold the same to G. H., of the county of Erie, for the sum of two hundred and fifty dollars, he being the highest and best bidder, and that the highest price bidden for the same. And they respectfully pray that the sale so made may be confirmed by the court.

A. B.
C. B.

Affidavit.

Erie County, *ss.*

A. B. and C. B., the persons named in the above return being duly sworn [or affirmed] according to law, do depose and say, that the facts set forth in the above return are just and true, to the best of their knowledge and belief.

A. B.
C. B.

Sworn and subscribed before me this
——day of ——, A. D. 184–.

THOMAS BROWN, J. P.

N. B. Notice of sale of land by administrators or guardian, must be advertised in at least one weekly newspaper published in the county, if one be published in the county; if not, then in an adjoining county, at least twenty days before the time appointed for the sale; and also by handbills set up in at least three of the most public places in the vicinity, for the same time, as required by Act of Assembly of Pennsylvania.

Petition by Guardian for sale of Land.

To the Honourable, the Judges of the Orphans' Court of the County of Cumberland.

The petition of John Jones duly sets forth, that on the —— day of ——, A. D. 1844, he was by your honourable court duly appointed guardian of the person and estate of Mary Burns, a minor under the age of fourteen years. That the personal estate of said minor is wholly insufficient for her maintenance and education, [or, "that the estate of said minor is in such a state of dilapidation and decay, or so unproductive and expensive that it will be to the interest and benefit of the said minor that the said estate be sold."] That your petitioner herewith exhibits attached to this his prayer, a true and perfect inventory and conscionable appraisement of all the personal estate of the said minor, together with a full and correct statement and description of all the real estate of said minor, wheresoever situated, which has come to the knowledge of your petitioner.

JOHN JONES,
Guardian of Mary Burns.

N. B. To this petition must be attached an inventory, and appraisement of all the personal estate, and a full and correct statement of all the real estate of the minor, with an affidavit of the truth of all the facts set forth, for forms of which, see proceedings under title of "*Petition for sale of land by administratrix;*" making the necessary alterations. Advertisement of sale, report of sale and affidavit are the same as required of administrators.

Petition where Master compels Apprentice to work at another business, beats him, &c.

To the Honourable, &c.

The petition of A. B., a minor, respectfully showeth: That your petitioner on the —— day of ——, at ——, with the assent of his father, bound himself by indenture, an apprentice to C. D., of the —— of ——, in and for the purpose of learning the art, trade, and mystery of a ——. That your petitioner has always conducted and demeaned himself as a good and faithful apprentice ought to do: that the said C. D. covenanted in the said indenture, to use the utmost of his endeavours to teach or cause to be taught and instructed, the said A. B., in the said art, trade, or mystery of a ——, during the term of —— years, —— months and —— days, from the said —— day of ——. Nevertheless, the said C. D., not regarding his said covenant, has not used his best endeavours to teach or cause to be taught or instructed, the said apprentice in the said art, trade or mystery, but has compelled him to labour in other business, to wit, in the business of a ——, and has cruelly and without any sufficient cause, beaten, wounded, and otherwise ill treated your petitioner in such a manner as to make his life miserable. Your petitioner, therefore, humbly prays your honours to discharge him from his said indenture, &c.

Petition where Apprentice has been disobedient, idle, &c.

To the Honourable ——, &c.

The petition of the subscriber, A. B., humbly showeth: That at ——, on the —— day of ——, C. D., a minor, with the assent of his father, E. F., was bound by indenture to petitioner for the term of —— years —— months and —— days, to learn the art, trade and mystery of ——. That your petitioner has complied in all things with the covenants covenanted to be kept and performed in said indenture on his part. But that the said C. D. has on several occasions, viz., on the —— day of ——, and on various other days and times during his apprenticeship, without the leave of petitioner, absconded and absented himself from the habitation and business of petitioner, and has, by disobedience, idleness and other misbehaviour, altogether failed and neglected to discharge his duty as an apprentice to petitioner according to his covenants. Your petitioner, therefore, prays your honourable court to impose such punishment on his said apprentice as your honours in your discretion shall think his offence deserves, &c.

Petition where Apprentice has committed larceny, &c.

To the Honourable ——, &c.

The petition of A. B., of the county of ——, humbly showeth: That on the —— day of ——, C. D. was, &c., bound to your petitioner to serve for the term of —— years to learn the art, trade and mystery of a ——, as by his indenture will appear: that the said C. D., hath lately and frequently been guilty of wasting your petitioner's effects, as also hath committed several acts of larceny, of which he now stands indicted before this court. Your petitioner, therefore, prays the court, that he may have a hearing respecting the conduct of the said apprentice, and that the court will give him relief against the indenture before mentioned agreeably to the Act of Assembly in such case made, &c.

Petition for Inquest to make Partition.

To the Honourable, the Judges of the Orphans' Court of the County of Bucks.

The petition of John Jones respectfully showeth: That William Burns, late of the borough of Doylestown, printer, died on the —— day of ——, A. D. 1842, leaving him surviving three children, to wit, I., B., &c. The said William Burns, some time prior to his decease, to wit, on the —— day of ——, &c., made, published and declared his last will and testament, duly proven and registered at ——, wherein and whereby he gave, devised and bequeathed, after the payment of certain debts and specific legacies, (as will appear on reference to the said will, a true copy whereof is hereto annexed,) all the rest, residue and remainder of his estate, real and personal, whatsoever and wheresoever, unto the said I., B., &c., to hold to them, their heirs, executors, administrators and assigns, in equal parts, share and share alike. The said William Burns died, seised in his demesne as of fee, of and in the following described real estate, to wit, &c. &c, [describing the real estate fully and accurately.] Your petitioner, therefore, prays that your honours award an inquest, to make partition of the premises aforesaid, to and among the said parties interested therein, in such manner and in such proportions, as by the said will and the laws of this commonwealth is directed, if such partition can be made without prejudice to, or spoiling the whole, but if such partition cannot be made thereof, then to value and appraise the same, and make return of their proceeding according to law. And as in duty bound, &c.

JOHN JONES.

(Add the usual affidavit.)

For Review of Account under the Act of 13th October, 1840.

To the Honourable, the Judges of the Orphans' Court of the County of ——.

In the matter of the estate of A. B., deceased.

The prayer of your petitioner, C. D., respectfully sets forth that the said A. B., of the county of ——, died intestate, on the —— day of ——, A. D. 18—, owning and possessing at the time of his decease personal property of great value. Letters of administration were afterwards, to wit, on the —— day of ——, 18—, issued in favour of and granted to G. H., in due form of law, and by virtue thereof, the said G. H. took possession of the said property, and realized the same, and expended certain sums of money, as will more fully and specifically appear, reference being had to the original (and supplementary) account of such administrator. Your petitioner respectfully represents that there are great and material errors in the said account which ought to be revised and corrected, and which errors he sets forth and assigns as follows, to wit: —— first ——, &c., &c. [*Specify them in detail.*]

Your petitioner is interested in said account and estate being ——, and is by such errors greatly injured. In consequence of —— (*the petitioner should explain the occasion of his delay in excepting to the account*) and, therefore, it is that until the present time your petitioner was not aware of the existence of the said errors, and did not except thereto. The said account (*such errors not having been excepted to*) was on the —— day of ——, 18—, referred to X. Y. and Z., &c., auditors, to audit, settle and adjust the same, and report distribution of the funds in hands of the administrator aforesaid; the said auditors, through inadvertence, did not correct the said errors, their attention not having been called to the same, and filed their report on the —— day of ——, 18—, which report was afterwards, on the —— day of ——, 18—, to wit: within five years last past, confirmed by decree of your honourable court, as will more fully appear on reference to the records of your said court: and your petitioner is credibly informed, and verily believes that the balance found due from G. H., the administrator as aforesaid, has not been actually paid or discharged by said administrator, but still remains in his hands.

For all which errors and imperfections in the said account and the said decree of confirmation, your petitioner has brought this his bill or petition of review, and humbly conceives that he should be relieved therein; to the end, therefore, that the petitioner may have the privilege of a re-hearing of so much of the said account as is hereinbefore alleged to be in error, and may have such relief as equity and justice may require, may it please your honours to grant to this petitioner a citation upon the said G. H., and all other persons interested, commanding them upon a day certain to be therein specified, to appear before your honourable court, and show cause, if any they have, why so much of the said account as is hereinafter alleged to be in error, should not be referred back to the said auditors, to be by them reviewed, reversed and corrected.

And as in duty bound, &c.

A. B., being duly sworn, doth depose and say, that all and singular the statements contained in the above petition and assignment of errors are just and true, to the best of his knowledge and belief. Sworn, &c.

Petition for the appointment of seven men to make Partition.

To the Honourable, the Judges of the Orphans' Court of the County of Erie.

The petition of John Jones respectfully showeth, that William Burns, late of Waterford, tanner, died on the, &c., [proceed to set forth the death, probate of will, devise, and description of the real estate, as in the foregoing petition, then continue as follows:]

No partition or valuation of said premises has been made, and your petitioner respectfully represents, that C. D., &c., [naming "seven or more disinterested persons,"] have been chosen, on behalf, and with the consent of all parties concerned, to make partition of the real estate of the said decedent, to wit: the premises afore-described, or in case the same cannot be divided among the said parties without prejudice to or spoiling the whole, to make, and as by law required, to return, a just appraisement thereof to your said court. Whereupon your petitioner prays that the said C. D., &c. &c., may be appointed for the purpose aforesaid, and as in duty bound, &c. JOHN JONES.

(The usual affidavit.)

We, the undersigned, heirs and devisees of William Burns, deceased, do consent and agree that the Orphans' Court for the County of Erie, appoint C. D., &c. &c., to make partition, &c., [as in the petition.]

Petition for Citation to Widow to accept or refuse a Device or Bequest.

To the Honourable, &c.

The petition of J. M., &c., respectfully represents: That he is one of the legatees under the will of S. M., deceased: that by said will, certain personal estate was bequeathed (or real estate devised) to J. M., the now widow and relict of said decedent; that said decedent has been dead longer than twelve months, and the said J. M. has not made her election to take or refuse the said bequest, which, if accepted, leaves her right of dower, as by the act in such case made and provided is directed.

The petitioner, therefore, prays the court to award a citation, directed to the said J. M., commanding her to be and appear at an Orphans' Court, to be holden on the —— day of ——, then and there to make her election, either to accept such [devise] [or bequest] in lieu of dower, or waive such devise or bequest, and to take her dower, pursuant to the directions of the Act of Assembly in such case made and provided. And he will, &c.

Petition for a Rule on the heirs to come in and accept or refuse to take the Real Estate of Decedent at the valuation.

To the Honourable, the Judges of the Orphans' Court of the County of Erie.

The petition of John Jones, one of the heirs of William Burns, deceased, who died intestate, respectfully represents: That the inquest appointed by this court on the —— day of ——, to make partition or valuation of the real estate of said decedent, have returned that the said premises cannot be divided, so as to accommodate all the heirs, but that the same may accommodate one of the heirs of said decedent, and they have reported the same accordingly: the petitioner, therefore, prays the court to grant a rule upon the heirs and representatives of said decedent, requiring them to be and appear at the Orphans' Court to be holden the —— day of —— next, then and there to accept or refuse the said estate at the valuation thereof, agreeably to the Acts of Assembly in such case made and provided: and in case all the heirs and representatives refuse to take same as aforesaid, then to show cause, if any they have, why the said premises should not be sold, according to the Act of Assembly in such case made and provided. And he will, &c. JOHN JONES.

(Add the usual affidavit.)

Petition for a citation to Executors to give security for the execution of their trust.

To the Honourable, the Judges of the Orphans' Court of the County of Erie.

The petition of John Jones, husband of Mary, daughter of William Burns, late of the borough of Erie, deceased, respectfully showeth: That William Burns, late of the borough of Erie, merchant, died on the —— day of ——, leaving him surviving three children, to wit, Mary, wife of your petitioner, Samuel and Thomas. The said William Burns, some time prior to his decease, to wit, on the —— day of ——, &c., made and published his last will and testament, duly proven and registered at Erie, wherein and whereby he gave, devised and bequeathed, after the payment of his debts, (as will appear on reference to the said will, a true copy whereof is hereto annexed,) all the rest, residue and remainder of his estate, real and personal, whatsoever and wheresoever, unto the said Mary, &c , subject to the right of dower of Anna Burns, widow of the said William Burns. That the said Anna was by said last will and testament appointed executrix thereof, and directed to sell and dispose of the said real and personal estate, and divide the proceeds equally among the children of the said decedent without delay. That the said William Burns died seised in his demesne as of fee, of and in the following described real estate, to wit, &c., [describe the real estate.]

That although more than —— years have elapsed since the said Anna took upon herself to execute said will and administer upon the estate of said decedent, yet she hath not distributed unto said Mary the share she is entitled to in said estate by said will. But on the contrary has sold and disposed of a large portion of said real estate, for a large sum of money, to wit, three thousand dollars and upwards, and has, as this petitioner verily believes, appropriated the same to her own use. That she, &c., [here insert any other facts that may be required in the particular case.] That she is wasting and mismanaging the property intrusted to her by the said last will and testament, so as the legatees of the said will will be left without remedy, unless prevented by order of this court. Your petitioner, therefore, prays your honourable court to issue a citation to the said Anna Burns, executrix as aforesaid, requiring her to appear on a day certain before the Orphans' Court, to show cause, if any she has, why she shall not be required to give security, conditioned for the performance of her respective trusts as executrix aforesaid. And your petitioner will, &c. JOHN JONES.

(Add the usual affidavit.)

Petition for Habeas Corpus, where Petitioner is under arrest on Civil Process.

To the Honourable J. B., Esq., Associate Judge of the Court of Quarter Sessions of the County of Erie.

The petition of John Jones respectfully showeth: That your petitioner is unjustly held and detained in custody by Daniel Martin, one of the constables [or A. B., keeper of the debtor's department, &c., or C. D., the sheriff], of Erie County, who refuses to discharge him and set him at liberty, and that your petitioner is not detained or confined by virtue of any commitment for any criminal or supposed criminal matter.

Your petitioner, therefore, prays, that your honour will direct to be issued, a writ of habeas corpus, returnable forthwith, agreeably to the Act of Assembly in such case made and provided, against the said Daniel Martin or such other person in whose custody your petitioner may be found, that cause may be shown, if any exist, why he should not be discharged and set free. And he will, &c.
JOHN JONES.

Personally appeared the above-named John Jones, before me, the subscriber, one of the —— of the —— of ——, and made solemn oath, in due form of law, that the facts set forth in the above petition are true to the best of his knowledge and belief.
JOHN JONES.

Sworn and subscribed before me
the —— day of ——, A. D. 1844.
THOMAS BROWN, *J. P.*

Petition for Habeas Corpus, where the Petitioner is in the Criminal Department.

To the Honourable, &c.

The petition of John Jones respectfully showeth: That your petitioner is confined unjustly (as he apprehends), in the jail of the county aforesaid, for some criminal or supposed criminal matter, as appears by a copy of the warrant of the commitment hereto annexed. To be relieved from which imprisonment, your petitioner now applies, praying that a writ of habeas corpus may be issued according to the Act of Assembly in such case made and provided, so that your petitioner may be brought before your honour, to do, submit to and receive what the laws may require.
(Add the affidavit.) JOHN JONES.

Petition for Habeas Corpus, where Petitioner is deprived of liberty by master or any other person.

To the Honourable, &c.

The petition of John Jones respectfully showeth: That he is now restrained of his liberty by Daniel Stone, illegally and wrongfully, for no criminal or supposed criminal matter. He therefore prays your honour to grant a writ of habeas corpus, directed to the said Daniel Stone, commanding him to bring before your honour, his the petitioner's body, to do as and abide such order as your honour may direct. And he will, &c.
(Add the affidavit.) JOHN JONES.

Petition for Habeas Corpus by a Parent for a Child.

To the Honourable, &c.

The petition of John Jones respectfully showeth: That your petitioner's daughter, Mary Jones, aged —— years, is restrained of her liberty by Daniel Stone, of the township of ——, that she is not detained for any criminal or supposed criminal matter. The petitioner therefore prays your honour to grant a writ of habeas corpus, agreeably to the Act of Assembly in such case made and provided, to bring up the body of the said Mary Jones. And he will ever pray, &c. JOHN JONES.

(Add the affidavit.)

Petition for Habeas Corpus ad testificandum.

To the Honourable, &c.

The petition of John Jones, of the —— of ——, respectfully showeth: That your petitioner is the party in a cause now pending before arbitrators appointed out of your honourable court, [or before your honourable court,] in a certain cause therein pending, in which a certain Daniel Stone is the defendant, that the said arbitrators are appointed to meet for the purpose of considering the said cause, [or the said cause will come on for trial,] on the —— day of ——, A. D. 1845, at ——, that Samuel Dean, a prisoner under custody of Thomas Brown, keeper of the prison, is a material witness for your petitioner. The petitioner therefore prays the court to award a writ of habeas corpus, directed to the said Thomas Brown, requiring him to produce the body of the said Samuel Dean, before the said arbitrators, [or the honourable court,] to testify on behalf of your petitioner. JOHN JONES,

by his att'y, ROBERT MARTIN.

John Jones [or Robert Martin,] being duly sworn, says, that the facts set forth in the above petition are true as he believes.

JOHN JONES,

[or ROBERT MARTIN.]

Petition to enter an Appeal from an Order of removal of Pauper.

To the Honourable, &c.

The petition of the undersigned overseers of the poor of the township of ——, in the said county, respectfully showeth: That they feel themselves aggrieved by an order made by A. B. and C. D., two of the justices of the peace for the said county for the removal of M. H., a poor person from the township of —— to the township of —— in said county, which order of removal is dated the —— day of ——, A. D. ——, a copy whereof is hereto annexed. That notice has been given by your petitioners to the overseers of the poor of the said township of ——, of their intention to appeal from said order of removal to your honour, a copy of which notice is also hereto annexed.

Your petitioners, therefore, pray your honours to permit them to enter an appeal from the said order of removal. And they will pray, &c.

Petition for Mandamus.

To the Honourable, &c.

The petition of A. B., of ——, humbly showeth: That, &c., (*here state all the facts and matters complained of as they occurred.*)

Your petitioner, therefore, prays that a mandamus may be issued to the said ——, commanding them to ——, or to grant a rule on the said —— to show cause why a mandamus should not be issued for the purposes aforesaid. And he will pray, &c.

Add affidavit.

Petition for the appointment of persons to appraise Assigned Property.

To the Honourable, &c.

The petition of C. D., of the —— of ——, in the county of ——, respectfully represents: That on the —— day of ——, A. D. ——, E. F., of ——, and G., his wife, executed a deed of assignment of all their property, real, personal and mixed, to your petitioners in trust for the benefit of the creditors of the said E. F., as in the said deed is more particularly set forth.

Your petitioner, therefore, prays your honour to appoint two or more disinterested and competent persons to appraise the estate and effects so as aforesaid assigned to him as is required by the Act of Assembly in such case made and provided. And he will pray, &c.

Petition for a Pedlar's License.

To the Honourable, &c.

The petition of E. F., of ——, respectfully showeth: That he is a citizen of the United States of America, and by reason of bodily infirmity is incapable of procuring a livelihood by labour,—that being desirous of traveling as a hawker and pedlar with —— horses and wagon or other vehicle, he has this day paid into the hands of ——, Esq., treasurer of said county, the sum of —— dollars.

He therefore prays your honours to grant him a license to travel as a hawker and pedlar for one year, with —— horses and wagon. And he will ever pray, &c.

Petition for the appointment of Auditors on the accounts of Guardian.

To the Honourable, &c.

The petition of J. F., respectfully represents: That S. J., his late guardian, has filed the account of his guardianship, which he prays may be referred to auditors appointed by the court to audit and adjust the same, and make report thereon. And he will, &c.

Petition where Trustee of a fund is Insolvent, mismanaging, &c.

To the Honourable, the Judges of the Court of Common Pleas of the County of ——.

The petition of A. B. respectfully showeth: That a certain C. D., in and by his last will and testament, dated the —— day of ——, A. D. ——, and proved before the Register of Wills of the —— of ——, on the —— day of ——, A. D. ——, among other things made the following bequest: [insert bequest,] (or as by a certain deed or indenture ——, bearing date the —— day of ——, A. D. ——, between ——, of the first part, ——, of the second part, and —— of the third part.) That since the decease of the said testator, [or since the execution of the said deed] one of the said trustees died, and the trust reposed thereby became exclusively vested in the said E. F. his executors, administrators and assigns. That the said E. F. has not, as your petitioners are informed and verily believe, placed the said sum of —— dollars at interest, as directed by said last will and testament, (or indenture of trust,) nor has the interest of the said sum of —— dollars, or any part thereof, been used and applied for the purpose specified in the said last will and testament, (or deed of trust,) or accounted for by the said E. F., although the said E. F. has been often requested so to do. Your petitioners, therefore, allege that the said E. F. has neglected and abused the uses and trusts reposed in him as aforesaid, and that the said trust has not been duly executed by the said E. F. They, therefore, pray the said court to grant them a rule upon the said E. F., to appear before the said court on a day to be named by the said court, to answer the complaint of your petitioners agreeably to the directions of the Act of the General Assembly, to account before this court, or before auditors, as the court shall direct, of and for the execution of the said trust, and also to show cause why he should not be removed from the said trust, and another person appointed in his place and stead.

Petition where Trustee under Marriage Settlement is Insolvent, &c.

To the Honourable the Judges of the Court of Common Pleas for the County of ——.

The petition of A. B. of the —— of ——, and C., his wife, respectfully showeth: That by indenture tripartite, bearing date the —— day of ——, in the year of our Lord one thousand eight hundred and ——, between the said C., then C. D., with the approbation of her guardian, E F., of the first part, your petitioner, A. B., of the second part, and G. H., of the third part, in contemplation of the marriage then about to be solemnized between your petitioners, a large —— estate, to the amount of upwards of —— dollars, belonging to your petitioner, C. B., then a minor, and in the hands and possession of the said C. F., as her guardian, was assigned, transferred and set over unto the said G. H., to have and to hold, unto him, his executors and administrators, upon the trusts and for the uses and purposes in the said indenture mentioned, and which by reference to the same, will more fully appear. That the said G. H. took upon himself the duties of trustee, and the —— estate above-mentioned, went into his hands, or remained there, upon the trusts and for the uses and purposes in the said indenture mentioned. That the said G. H. has mismanaged the said estate committed, as aforesaid, to his care, and has neglected to perform the duties of the trust thus confided to him. That the said G. H. is in insolvent circumstances, and has lately made an assignment for the benefit of his creditors. Your petitioners, therefore, pray that a citation may be issued to the said G. H., to show cause why he should not be dismissed from the said trust, according to the directions of the Act of Assembly in such case made and provided. And they will pray, &c.

Petition after Trustee is dismissed, for Appointment of a new one.

To the Honourable the Judges of the Court of Common Pleas for the County of ——.

The petition of A. B., of the —— of ——, and C., his wife, respectfully showeth: That whereas under and by virtue of an Act of Assembly of the Commonwealth of Pennsylvania, entitled "A supplement to the Act" entitled "An Act to compel assignees to settle their accounts, and for other purposes," passed the twenty-ninth day of March, Anno Domini one thousand eight hundred and twenty-three, your petitioners lately presented a petition to the said court, praying that a citation might be issued to D. E., the trustee named in a certain indenture tripartite, mentioned in the said petition, bearing date the —— day of ——, Anno Domini one thousand eight hundred and ——, to show cause why he should not be dismissed from the trust in the said indenture specified.

And whereas, the said citation was duly granted by the said court, and issued, directed to the said D. E. And upon the hearing thereupon had by the said court, they did actually dismiss the said D. E. from the said trust, pursuant to the said Act of Assembly. And whereas it is agreeable to your petitioners, the cestui que trust in the said indenture named, that F. G. of the —— of —— should be appointed a new trustee in lieu and in the place of the said D. E., so as aforesaid dismissed from the said trust. They, therefore, pray that the said F. G. may now be appointed by the said court, such new trustee as aforesaid, under, by virtue, and in pursuance of the said Act of Assembly. And your petitioners will ever pray, &c.

Petition for leave to prove Contract of decedent to convey.

To the Honourable the Judges of the —— Court for the County of ——.

The petition of A. B., of the —— of ——, respectfully showeth: That C. D., late of the —— of ——, died on the —— day of ——, at ——, intestate, (*or* having first duly made and published his last will and testament, wherein and whereby O. P. and Q. R., both of the said county, were nominated the executors thereof, which said will has been duly proved according to law, and letters testamentary thereon issued to the said O. P. and Q. R., of whose executorship accounts your honourable court have jurisdiction,) and letters of administration have been issued, in due course of law, to O. P. and Q. R., administrators of all and singular the goods, chattels and estate of said C. D. The said C. D., in his life-time, to wit: on the —— day of ——, in the year of our Lord one thousand eight hundred and ——, was seised in fee of and in ——, to wit: All that, &c. (*Here describe the property.*)

That being so seised, the said C. D. did, (or by E. F. and G. H., his lawful attorneys, duly constituted by power in writing, with the full knowledge, consent and approbation of the said C. D., did,) by a bargain or contract in writing, bind himself to sell and convey the said real estate with the appurtenances, unto your petitioner, A. B., in fee simple, in consideration of —— dollars, to be paid to the said C. D. That your petitioner paid unto the said C. D., in the life-time of the said C. D., the sum of —— dollars, a part of the purchase-money, and by direction of the said C. D., (or the said E. F. and G. H.,) a deed was prepared, but its execution was prevented by the death of the said C. D., (or enter into a parol contract for the conveyance of the said real estate to your petitioner.) That your petitioner is ready and willing to pay the said consideration money, but that no sufficient provision for the performance of the said bargain or contract appears to have been made by the said deceased in his life-time, though he was well satisfied, and intended that the same should be consummated.

Your petitioner, therefore, prays that this honourable court will be pleased to designate some day certain at which notice may be given to the executors (or administrators) and heirs, of the said deceased C. D., (or the devisees of the afore-mentioned real estate, if such there be,) to appear in your said court and answer this bill or petition: and furthermore, that this honourable court will be pleased to decree the specific performance of the said contract according to the true intent and meaning thereof, in order to the completing of her title according to the Act of Assembly, in such case made and provided.

A. B., the petitioner, being duly ——, declares, that the facts stated in the foregoing petition are true to the best of his knowledge and belief.

Sworn, &c.

Petition for Commission de Inebritate Inquirendo.

To the Honourable, &c.

The petition of A. B., of the —— of ——, and State of Pennsylvania, respectfully showeth, that —— is a citizen of this commonwealth, and is a relation by blood or marriage (or is interested in the estate) of C. D., of the —— of ——, being (brothers) to the said C. D., and that ——, the said C. D. has become an habitual drunkard, by reason of habitual drunkenness become incapable of managing his estate, and is wasting and destroying the same; that he, the said C. D., is seised of considerable real estate, and possessed of some personal property, and has a —— and —— children. Your petitioner, therefore, prays this honourable court to appoint a commissioner, (or commissioners,) and issue their precepts to the same, directing them to proceed in the same manner as has heretofore been used in cases of persons *non compos mentis*, and to inquire whether the said C. D. has or has not, by reason of habitual drunkenness, become incapable of managing his estate, and also to do such further things as the Act of Assembly, in such case made and provided, may require. And he will ever pray, &c.

Petition of Defendant, alleging reformation, and praying the Court to revoke the original order.

To the Honourable, &c.

The petition of C. D. respectfully showeth: That your petitioner was found by inquisition, under a commission issued by your honours, to have been an habitual drunkard, and your honours in consequence thereof, in —— term, 18—, appointed —— a committee of your petitioner; he now represents to your honours, that —— has become reformed and habitually sober, and that the said committee as well as your petitioner's family, are convinced of ——'s said reformation and sobriety, and are now willing and desirous that the stigma upon your petitioner and —— family, as well as ——'s incapacity to transact business for —— and their support, should be removed by this honourable court as far as in them lies. Your petitioner, therefore, prays your honours, to take proof of the said facts, and upon full proof being made of the truth of the foregoing allegations, to make an order that the said commission and the inquisition taken thereon, and the appointment of a committee, and all proceedings relating thereto, be altogether superseded, and determined, and he will, &c.

(The usual affidavit.)

Petition for a Tavern License.

To the Honourable, the Judges of the Court of Quarter Sessions of the Peace for the County of Erie.

The petition of John Jones respectfully showeth: That your petitioner occupies a commodious house, situate in the township of Amity, on the road leading from —— to ——, which is well calculated for a public house of entertainment, and from its neighbourhood and situation, is suitable as well as necessary for the accommodation of the public, and the entertainment of strangers and travelers.

That he is well provided with stabling for horses, and all conveniences necessary for the entertainment of strangers and travelers: he, therefore, respectfully prays the court to grant him a license to keep an inn, or public house of entertainment there. And your petitioner will pray, &c. JOHN JONES.

AMITY, January 10, 1845.

We, the undersigned, citizens of the township of Amity aforesaid, being personally acquainted with John Jones, the above-named petitioner, and also having a knowledge of the house for which the license is prayed, do hereby certify that such house is necessary to accommodate the public, and entertain strangers or travelers, that he is a person of good repute for honesty and temperance, and that he is well provided with house room and conveniences for the lodging and accommodation of strangers and travelers. We, therefore, beg leave to recommend him for a license, agreeably to his petition.

☞ The above certificate must be signed by at least *twelve* respectable citizens of the borough, ward or township, in which the tavern is proposed to be kept. Petitions for tavern licenses must be presented at the *first* or *second* term of the court of Quarter Sessions in each year, and notice given of the intended application in accordance with the first section of the Act of Assembly of Pennsylvania, of the 29th March, 1841, which is as follows.

Be it enacted, &c. That every person intending to apply for a tavern license in any city or county of this commonwealth, from and after the first day of April next, shall give public notice of the same, by at least three publications in two newspapers, where the application is made in any of the cities, and in one, where the application is made in any of the counties of this commonwealth, (if so many there be in said city or county, or if there be no newspaper published, then by printed hand-bills, to be posted throughout the township in six of the most public places, of which fact an affidavit, together with a copy of the printed notices, shall be attached to the application,) which publication shall be made nearest the place where such tavern is intended to be kept, and shall embrace the certificate required by the fourth section of the act passed on the eleventh of March, one thousand eight hundred and thirty-four, entitled, "An act relating to inns and taverns, and so forth," the last of which publications shall be at least ten days before the first day of the term of the court, to which the application shall be made.

Petition to the Legislature for a Turnpike Road.

To the Honourable, the Senate and House of Representatives of the Commonwealth of Pennsylvania, in General Assembly met:

We, the undersigned citizens, inhabitants of ——, respectfully represent, That, whereas many parts of this commonwealth, as well as parts of the adjoining states, derive peculiar advantages from the turnpike roads which are interspersed through various sections of them, while other sections, presumed to be equally entitled to such advantages, labour under great inconveniences for want of advantages of a similar kind, particularly that part of this state which lies between the —— end of —— and ——, the great thoroughfare in that direction, of teams, carriages and other vehicles of transportation, all which justifies the call for a good and commodious road, to facilitate the transportation of country produce and other commodities to an eligible and ready market.

We, therefore, pray your honourable body to enact a law, authorizing the governor to incorporate a company to survey, lay out, construct and make a turnpike road ——, in the county of ——, by the nearest and best route to ——, and from thence to ——, aforesaid.

We also pray your honourable body, to authorize the governor to subscribe, on behalf of the commonwealth, for —— shares, to be paid in such manner as they in their wisdom may deem meet and proper, for the furtherance of the object of your petitioners, and they will pray, &c.

Petition to the Legislature for a State Road.

To the Honourable, [as above.]

Your petitioners, inhabitants of the county of ——, aware that the Legislature of Pennsylvania is at all times favourably disposed towards all useful internal improvements, which tend to benefit and add comfort to her fellow citizens, most respectfully represent: That in consequence of the bridge at ——, over the ——, being completed for the passage of teams, carriages, horses and travelers of every description, and the outlet west of said river, being inconvenient in many directions, especially for the greater part of the inhabitants of said county, lying in the direction of ——, on the ——, &c. It is, therefore, the opinion of your petitioners, that if a road was laid out and opened from the west end of said bridge, the nearest and best route to ——, aforesaid, on the ——, it would not only be convenient and useful to the inhabitants in the north and north-west end of said county, but open a direct communication with the neighbouring counties, upon and adjacent to the ——, and thereby afford easy and safe access to a good market, as well as to the seat of government, where many people in the northern and western counties beyond ——, have frequent and necessary business, during almost every season of the year, but particularly when your honourable body is in session. Your petitioners, therefore, pray that a law may be passed, authorizing the appointment of commissioners, to view and lay out a road, in such direction, as the end of your petitioners' prayer may be accomplished: And they will pray, &c.

Petition for erecting a Bridge on County Line.

To the Honourable, the Judges, &c.

The petition of the subscribers, inhabitants of the counties of Green and Fayette, respectfully represent: That a bridge is much wanted over the Monongahela river, being the line of the said counties, at the place where the public highway to Union crosses the said river, in the township of —— in Greene County, and in the township of —— in Fayette County, and that the erection of such bridge will require more expense than it is reasonabe the said townships should bear. Your petitioners, therefore, pray the court to appoint proper persons to view the premises, and to take such order on the subject as is required and directed by the Acts of Assembly in such cases made and provided. And they will, &c.

Petition to authorize the Recorder to enter satisfaction upon a Mortgage.

To the Honourable J. B., President Judge of the Court of Common Pleas of Berks County.

The petition of A. B. respectfully showeth: That on the tenth day of February, A. D. 1837, C. D., of the township of Maiden Creek, executed to E. F., of the township of Windsor, a certain indenture of mortgage, in due form of law, which is recorded in Mortgage Book A., page 365, for securing the payment of the sum of eleven hundred dollars, lawful money of the United States, relation being thereunto had will more fully and at large appear. That the said E. F. being the legal holder of the said mortgage, has died, without entering satisfaction upon the record of the same; and that payment has been made of all the money or amount due thereon, and has so continued for more than two years; and that your petitioner is the owner of the premises mortgaged as aforesaid. Wherefore, he respectfully prays your honourable court, to direct the sheriff to serve a notice, stating the facts in this petition set forth, on G. H. and I. K., the legal representatives of the said E. F., who are to be found in the said county, requiring them to appear at the next term, and answer the petition as aforesaid. And your petitioner further prays, that upon due proof being made, that the full amount for which the said mortgage was given, has been paid, that your honourable court will decree and direct, that satisfaction shall be entered upon the record of the said mortgage, by the recorder of deeds, on payment of the costs due, relative to the entry of the said mortgage, or any proceedings thereon, and that said satisfaction so entered, shall forever discharge, defeat and release the same mortgage, according to Act of Assembly in such case made and provided. And he will pray, &c. A. B.

Petition to compel a Deed for property sold by former Sheriff.

To the Honourable the Judges of the Court of Common Pleas of the County of Berks.

The petition of A. B., of the township of Rockland, respectfully showeth: That, by virtue of a writ of *venditioni exponas*, issued out of this honourable court, C. D., Esquire, then sheriff of the county, sold to your petitioner, all that [here describe the premises,] for the sum of fifteen hundred dollars; that before a deed was executed, the said C. D. died, and E. F., Esquire, hath since been duly elected sheriff: That your petitioner, having complied with the conditions of sale, is desirous of having his title to the premises perfected. He, therefore, prays your honours to order and direct the said E. F., the present sheriff, to perfect the title, by executing to him a deed for the premises so by him purchased, according to Act of Assembly in such case made and provided. And he will, &c. A. B.

Where former Sheriff has gone out of Office.

To the Honourable, &c., [as above.]

That C. D., then sheriff of the county of Erie, by virtue of a writ of *venditioni exponas*, to him directed, issuing out of this honourable court, returnable to August Term, A. D. 1844, and numbered 49 of that term, in a suit wherein E. F. was plaintiff and G. H. defendant, did expose to sale a certain piece or parcel of land therein described, and sold the same to him, the said petitioner, as in and by the said sheriff's return, indorsed on said writ appears. But the said sheriff executed no deed to your petitioner, nor have any further proceedings been since had in the matter; and the said sheriff has since gone out of office by the limitation of his term. Your petitioner, therefore, prays this honourable court to order and direct the present sheriff to make and execute a sufficient deed to him for the property aforesaid, he paying the purchase-money. And he will, &c. A. B.

Petition for Subpœna in Divorce, for desertion.

To the Honourable the Judges of the Court of Common Pleas of the County of Erie.

The petition of John Jones, of Erie, carpenter, in all humble manner, showeth: That your petitioner was on the —— day of ——, &c., lawfully joined in marriage, with Mary Burns, his present wife, and from that time lived and cohabited with her, and hath in all respects demeaned himself as a kind and loving husband; and although by the laws of God, as well as by the mutual vows plighted to each other, they were bound to that constancy and uniform regard and chastity which ought to be inseparable from the marriage state,[*] yet the said Mary, in violation of her marriage vow, hath wilfully and maliciously deserted and absented herself from the habitation of your petitioner, without reasonable or probable cause, for the space of two years and upwards next preceding the date hereof. Wherefore, your petitioner further showing that he is a citizen of this state, and hath resided therein for upwards of one whole year previous to the filing of this his petition, prays your honours that a subpœna may issue in due form of law, directed to the said Mary, commanding her to appear at the next Court of Common Pleas to be held at Erie, to answer the petitioner's libel, and to show cause, if any she hath, why the petitioner should not be divorced from the bond of matrimony. And he will pray, &c.

JOHN JONES.

The above-named John Jones being duly sworn according to law, doth depose and say, that the facts contained in the above petition or libel, are true, to the best of his knowledge and belief: and that the said complaint is not made out of levity, or by collusion between him and the said Mary his wife, and for the mere purpose of being freed and separated from each other, but in sincerity and truth, for the causes mentioned in the said petition or libel.

JOHN JONES.

Sworn and subscribed before me this —— day of —— A. D. ——.

THOMAS BROWN, J. P.

Petition for Subpœna in Divorce, for intolerable treatment.

To the Honourable, &c.

The petition of Mary Jones, by her next friend Samuel Dean, &c., [as in the foregoing petition to the asterisk, with the necessary change of parties,] yet so it is that the parties being at the time domiciled within the commonwealth of Pennsylvania, the said John Jones has offered such indignities to the person of your petitioner, as to render her condition intolerable, and her life burthensome, and thereby forced her to withdraw from his house and family. Wherefore, your petitioner further showing that she is a citizen of the State of Pennsylvania, and has resided therein for upwards of one whole year previous to filing this her libel, prays &c., [as in the preceding form.]

Petition for Subpœna in Divorce.

On the ground of Adultery.

To the Honourable, &c.

The petition, &c., [as in the first petition to the asterisk,] yet so it is, that the said —— in violation of his [or her] marriage vow, hath for a considerable time past, being at such time domiciled within the commonwealth of Pennsylvania, given himself [or herself] up to adulterous practices, and been guilty of adultery with a certain M. S., and divers other persons, to your petitioner unknown. Wherefore, your libellant further showing that, &c., [as in the first petition for divorce.]

Petition for divorce from bed and board, and for Alimony.

For Abandonment of Family.

To the Honourable, the Judges of the Court of Common Pleas, for the County of Erie.

The petition of Mary Jones, by her next friend, Samuel Dean, respectfully showeth: That your petitioner on the —— day of —— in the year, &c., [as in the first petition to the asterisk, making the necessary alterations as to parties,] yet so it is, that the said John Jones from the —— day of ——, in the year, &c., hath, the said parties being at that time domiciled within the commonwealth of Pennsylvania, wilfully and maliciously absented himself from the habitation of this libellant, and abandoned his family without just or reasonable cause, and has from the said date persisted in such desertion. Wherefore, your petitioner further showing, that she is a citizen of this state, and hath resided therein for upwards of one whole year previous to the filing of this petition, prays your honours that a subpœna may issue from the said court directed to said John Jones, commanding him to appear at the next term of the said court to answer this petition; and also that a decree of this court may be given, granting this libellant a divorce from bed and board, and also allowing her such alimony as the said John Jones' circumstances will admit of, so as the same do not exceed the third part of the annual profit or income of his estate, or of his occupation and labour. And she will pray, &c.

(Affidavit as to the first petition.)

Petition for divorce from bed and board, and for Alimony, on the ground of intolerable treatment.

To the Honourable, &c.

The petition of Mary Jones, by her next friend, Samuel Dean, respectfully showeth: That your petitioner on the —— day of

—— in the year, &c., [as in the first petition to the asterisk, making the necessary change as to parties,] yet so it is, that the said John Jones did, on the —— day of ——, the said parties being at that time domiciled within the commonwealth of Pennsylvania, and at other various days and times, turn this libellant (his wife), out of doors, or offer such indignities to her person as to render her condition intolerable, or life burthensome, and thereby force her to withdraw from his house and family, (or by cruel and barbarous treatment endanger her life;) Wherefore, your libellant further showing, &c., [as in the last preceding form.]

Petition of a Husband, respondent, that the decree of Divorce, a mensa et thoro, be annulled.

A. B., by her next friend, C. D., *vs.* E. F.	In the —— Court of the —— of ——, of —— Term, 18—. No. ——.

The petition of E. F., the respondent above-named, respectfully showeth: That he is informed and understands, that on —— the —— day of ——, in the year of our Lord one thousand eight hundred and ——, this honourable court made a sentence or decree, conformably to the prayer of the libellant above-named, that your petitioner and the said libellant should be, and they accordingly were, divorced from bed and board.

Your petitioner does not deem it proper for him at this stage of the proceeding, to deny the allegations contained in the bill of the above libellant, nor to dispute the justice of the sentence pronounced by this honourable court, grounded upon the ex-parte evidence produced to them: he is informed and advised that the said sentence is absolute, and precludes contradiction on matters of fact. But your petitioner is well convinced that he and the libellant can live happily together hereafter, and that their doing so will be essential to the comfort, education and morals of their young children, and he anxiously avails himself of an indulgent provision of the law, and now offers to this honourable court, to receive and cohabit with the said libellant again, and to use her as a good husband ought to do: he, therefore, prays that this honourable court suspend the aforesaid decree, and that in case the said libellant refuse to return and cohabit with your petitioner under the protection of this court, your honours may discharge and annul the aforesaid sentence or decree. And for the faithful performance of this offer and engagement on his part, your petitioner will, if necessary, give to this honourable court, such security as in their discretion they may consider the case to require.

*Petition to the Legislature of Pennsylvania for Divorce.

To the Honourable, the Senate and House of Representatives of the Commonwealth of Pennsylvania, in General Assembly met.

The petition of John Jones of the County of Erie, in the said commonwealth, humbly showeth: That your petitioner, on the —— day of ——, in the year of our Lord one thousand eight hundred and thirty-nine, was bound in matrimony, and married to a certain Anna Burns, of said county, and from that time continued to live and cohabit with her until about the —— day of ——, one thousand eight hundred and forty-one, at which time your petitioner and his said wife were at ——, in the State of Indiana, to which place your petitioner and his said wife, had, a short time previously journeyed, for the purpose of visiting the said Anna's father, who then resided in the said State of Indiana; that on the said —— day of ——, one thousand eight hundred and forty-one, the said Anna, without any just or reasonable cause, left your petitioner, and refused to return with him to the County of Erie aforesaid; that your petitioner returned to his place of residence in the County of Erie, where he resided and has ever since continued to reside; that the said Anna hath persisted in such desertion, and still doth continue to absent herself from your petitioner. And your petitioner would further represent that he and his said wife are yet young, he being twenty-nine, and she not yet twenty-six years old.

Your petitioner, therefore, humbly prays your honourable bodies will be pleased to pass an act dissolving the marriage contract between him and the said Anna, so that they may be freed and separated from each other in all time to come. And as in duty bound he will ever pray, &c. JOHN JONES.

(Add the same affidavit as to the first petition.)

To the Honourable Judges of the Court of Common Pleas of the County of Erie.

The petition of divers inhabitants of the township of North East, in the County of Erie, and Commonwealth of Pennsylvania,

* By the constitution of Pennsylvania, the Legislature has no power to enact laws annulling the contract of marriage in any case where by law the courts of the commonwealth are empowered to decree a divorce.

A petition to the Legislature for a divorce, should be accompanied by the depositions of witnesses. It should also appear that the opposite party had due notice of the intended application, and of the time and place of taking depositions; unless the place of residence of the opposite party should be unknown. In that case, the want of such notice might be excusable, but such unknown residence should be proved. The depositions proving the facts set forth in the petition, &c., should accompany it.

respectfully showeth: That whereas the members of the Methodist Episcopal Church in the township of North East aforesaid, wish to be incorporated according to the articles hereunto attached, would respectfully recommend to your honourable court to incorporate said church accordingly. And your petitioners, as in duty bound, will ever pray, &c.

[Here will follow the names of the signers of the petition, and to the said petition will be annexed the articles as proposed for incorporation.]

Be it decreed by the Court of Common Pleas of Erie County, by virtue of the power vested in said court by the laws of the Commonwealth of Pennsylvania: That the members of the Methodist Episcopal Church of the township of North East, in the county and commonwealth aforesaid be, and they are hereby made and constituted into a body corporate and politic, in deed and in law, by the name, style and title of the "first Methodist Episcopal Church in North East," and by the same name, shall have perpetual succession, and be able to sue, and be sued, implead and be impleaded in all courts of law and elsewhere, and shall be able and capable in law and equity, to take, hold and enjoy for the use of said church, such lands and tenements, goods and chattels, as now are, or shall hereafter become the property of the said congregation, or to be held for their use by gift, grant, devise, bequest or otherwise, from any person or persons whomsoever, capable of making the same, and the same to grant, bargain, sell, or otherwise dispose of for the use of the said congregation.

Sec. 2d. A. B., C. D., E. F., G. H. and J. K. shall be trustees of the said church until others are appointed their successors in office, according to the form of discipline by which said church is governed. The said trustees or their successors in office to be appointed according to the form of discipline of the Methodist Episcopal Church aforesaid, shall have the care and management of the property, real, personal or mixed, belonging to said corporation; shall be members thereof and shall be accountable thereto for their official conduct, and shall in all respects conform to its instructions; provided, that the same are not inconsistent with the Constitution or laws of the United States, or of this Commonwealth, or with the form of discipline by which said corporation is governed as a church.

Sec. 3d. Every male member in full communion in the said church, of the age of twenty-one years and upwards, being a citizen of Pennsylvania, and having resided in the said township of North East and county aforesaid, for the space of six months, shall be considered a member of said corporation, and be as such entitled to the privilege of speaking and voting at its meetings.

Sec. 4th. The said corporation shall have full power to make and use one common seal, with such device or inscription thereon, as they may deem proper, and the same at pleasure to break, alter or renew, and also to enact and enforce such by-laws and ordinances from time to time, as they may judge expedient for the prosperity and good government of the said corporation; provided, the same shall not be inconsistent with the constitution and laws of the United States, or of this Commonwealth, or with the form of discipline by which said church is governed.*

PRECIPES.

A precipe is the name of the written instructions given by a plaintiff or an attorney, to the clerk or prothonotary of a court, whose duty it is to make out the writ for the making of the same. It is the authority which the prothonotary has for what he does, and it is the instrument by which any subsequent error may be amended.

Precipe for an Original Writ in the Common Pleas.

John Jones *vs.* William Burns. } In the Common Pleas of Erie County, issue summons in debt (or as the case may be) returnable to the next term.

R. S., Att'y for plaintiff,
January 1st, 1845.

W. K. Esquire, Prothonotary.

A Precipe in Foreign Attachment.

John Jones *vs.* William Burns. } In the Common Pleas of Crawford County, issue writ of Foreign Attachment, (in debt or case) returnable to next term. Bail in $— required.

Attach goods and chattels, moneys, rights and credits, lands and tenements of the defendant in the hands, possession, or custody of Eli Brooks, and summon him as garnishee.

R. S., Attorney for plaintiff,
January 1st, 1845

A. B., Esquire, Prothonotary.

* This form can be varied to suit a church corporation for any denomination associated for religious purposes, or associations for literary or charitable purposes, or for the formation of fire-engine or hose companies or beneficial societies. The Supreme Court and also the Court of Common Pleas of Pennsylvania have power to incorporate for the aforesaid purposes. See Act of 13th of October, 1840; Pamph. L. p. 5 of 1841. The Act is entitled "an Act relating to Orphans' Courts, and for other purposes. As to powers of the Supreme Court, see Act of 6th April, 1791; 3 Smith, p. 20.

John Jones
vs.
William Burns. } In the Common Pleas of Mercer County, May Term, A. D. 1844.

Issue writ of inquiry of damages returnable to next term.

R. S., Attorney for plaintiff,
January 1st, 1845.

A. B. Esquire, Prothonotary.

Precipe in Foreign Attachment.

Issue writ of inquiry of damages returnable to next term.

Precipe for Scire Facias to Garnishee.

John Jones
vs.
William Burns, garnishee of Ira Wilson. } In the Court of Common Pleas of —— County. Original action of foreign attachment to —— Term, A. D. ——. No. —.

Issue writ of scire facias returnable to next term.

Precipe in Domestic Attachment.

John Jones
vs.
William Burns. } Issue writ of domestic attachment per affidavit filed. Stipulations in $ ——.

Precipe in Attachment against Vessels.

John Jones
vs.
The schooner called the Betsy, William Burns owner. } Issue attachment and mention stipulations in the sum of $——.

Precipe for fi. fa. for residue of Judgment.

John Jones
vs.
William Burns. } In the Common Pleas of ——, County of ——, Term A. D. ——. No. ——.

Issue fi. fa. for residue of debt and costs not produced by former execution, returnable to next term.

Precipe for Certiorari to Justice of the Peace.

John Jones *vs.* William Burns.	Issue certiorari to L. M., Esq., returnable to next term.

Precipe for Summons in Covenant.

John Jones *vs.* William Burns.	Issue summons to answer plaintiff of a plea, that he keeps with him the covenants between them made, according to the force, form and effect of certain articles of agreement heretofore made between them.

Precipe for Execution on Judgment affirmed on Certiorari.

John Jones *vs.* William Burns.	In the Common Pleas of ——, County of ——, Term A. D. ——. No. ——.

Issue fi. fa. against defendant for *damages*, as per judgment of the justice affirmed by the court, and for all costs as well of the proceedings before the justice, as of the proceedings on certiorari in this court. Returnable to next term.

Precipe for Writ of Replevin.

John Jones *vs.* William Burns.	Issue replevin for two oxen, three cows, and one —— of the value of $——. Returnable to next term.

Precipe for sci. fa. on Writ of Inquiry.

John Jones *vs.* William Burns.	In the Common Pleas of ——, County of ——, Term A. D. ——.

Issue sci. fa., to show cause why a writ of inquiry should not issue to inquire of the damages in the above suit. Returnable to next term.

Let the sheriff return a nihil or this writ.

Precipe for fi. fa. against Plaintiff for Costs.

John Jones *vs.* William Burns.	Issue fi. fa. against the plaintiff for costs. Re turnable to next term.

Precipe for sci. fa. to revive Judgment.

John Jones *vs.* William Burns.	Issue sci. fa. to revive judgment. No. ——, to —— Term, A. D. ——. Entered, A. D. ——. Returnable to next term.

Precipe for a sci. fa. on Mortgage.

John Jones
vs. } In the District Court of Lancaster County.
William Burns.

Issue sci. fa. sur mortgage, recorded in Mortgage Book B., page 56, returnable to May Term, 1845.

Precipe for Certiorari on proceedings to deliver possession to Sheriff's Vendee.

In the case of John Jones, &c.

Issue certiorari to John Doe and Richard Roe, Esquires, two of the justices, &c., to remove all proceedings, judgments and executions, before them had and depending between William Burns, complainant, and the said John Jones, under the Act of Assembly, to enable purchasers at sheriff's or coroner's sales to obtain possession, returnable to May Term, 1845.

Precipe for a Writ in Trespass.

John Jones
vs. } In the District Court of Allegheny County.
William Burns.

Issue summons against defendant to answer plaintiff of a plea, wherefore, &c., [setting forth briefly the witness,] returnable to May Term, 1845.

PROCLAMATION.

A proclamation is the declaration made by the crier by authority of the court, that something is about to be done. It usually commences with the French word Oyez, do you hear, in order to attract attention. It is particularly used on the meeting or opening of the court, and at its adjournment. It is also frequently employed to discharge persons who have been accused of crimes or misdemeanors.

Proclamation of a Court Crier on opening Court.

Oyez, Oyez, Oyez. All manner of persons who have any thing to do before the Honourable, the Judges of the Court of Common Pleas, (Orphans' Court, Oyer and Terminer and General Jail Delivery, and Court of Quarter Sessions,) here holden this day, let them come forward, and they shall be heard.

Proclamation for Grand Jurors.

——. All you who have been summoned to serve as Grand Jurors, please answer to your names.

Proclamation for Returns of Constables.

——. All you who have been *elected* to serve as constables of the borough and several townships in the county of ——, come forward when called and render your returns.

Proclamation for Discharge of Insolvent Debtors.

——. If any person have aught to say why A. B., an insolvent debtor, should not be discharged, according to an Act of Assembly in such case made and provided, let them now come forward with their objection, or he will be discharged.

Proclamation for forfeiting Recognizance.

——. A. B., the principal, (*thrice*) come forth and appear as you have undertaken to do, or you will forfeit your recognizance.

——. C. D., (the surety,) bring forth the body of A. B., as you have undertaken to do, or you will forfeit your recognizance.

Proclamation for Acknowledgment of Sheriff's Deed.

——. The sheriff of —— county is about to acknowledge a deed to —— for a ——, situate in the —— of ——, taken in execution and sold as the property of ——.

Proclamation of Sheriff for holding Court.

Whereas, the honourable N. E., President of the Court of Common Pleas in the —— judicial district, consisting of the counties of ——, and the honourable J. B. and W. D., Esqs., Associate Judges in —— county, having issued their precept, bearing date the —— day of ——, 18—, to me directed, for holding a Court of Oyer and Terminer and General Jail Delivery, at ——, for the county of ——, and to commence on the —— Monday of —— next, being the —— day, 18—, and to continue —— weeks.

Notice is therefore hereby given, to the coroner, justices of the peace, and constables of the said county of ——, that they be then and there in their proper persons, at —— o'clock in the —— noon of said day, with their records, inquisitions, examinations and their other remembrancers, to do those things which to their offices appertain to be done; and those who are bound in recognizances to prosecute against the prisoners that are or shall be in the jail of —— county, be then and there to prosecute against them as shall be just.

Given under my hand at Erie, the first day of January, in the year of our Lord one thousand eight hundred and forty-five, and in the sixty-ninth year of the independence of the United States.

PUBLIC SCHOOLS.

Form of Bond of District Treasurer.

—— County, *ss.*

Know all men by these presents, that we ——— and ———, are held and firmly bound to ——— president of the board of school directors of —— district, in the county aforesaid, and to his successors in office, for the use of the district aforesaid, in the sum of ——, (here insert double the amount of the sum which will probably come into the hands of the treasurer in one year for school purposes,) lawful money, to be paid to the said ——— or his successors, to the which payment, well and truly to be made, we bind ourselves, jointly and severally, our heirs, executors and administrators, and every of them, by these presents. Sealed with our seals, dated the —— day of ——, in the year of our Lord, 18—. Whereas the said ——— has been duly appointed treasurer of the said school district, for and during the term of one year from the date hereof. Now the condition of this obligation is such, that if the said ——— shall, and do well and truly, execute and perform the duties of said office according to law, and shall, at the end of the term aforesaid, faithfully account for the school money he shall have received during the term aforesaid, and shall pay over into the hands of his successor in office, such balance as may then remain in his possession, this obligation to be void, or else to remain in full force and virtue.

Sealed and delivered in presence of us, }

Form of Bond of District Collector.

Know all men by these presents, that we, ——— and ——— are held and firmly bound to ———, president of the board of school directors of —— district, in the county aforesaid, and to his successors in office, for the use of the district aforesaid, in the sum of ——, (here insert double the amount of the duplicate,) lawful money, to be paid to the said ——— or his successors; to the which payment, well and truly to be made, we bind ourselves, jointly and severally, our heirs, executors and administrators, and every of them, by these presents. Sealed with our seals, dated the —— day of ——, in the year of our Lord, 18—. Whereas the said ———, has been duly appointed collector for the school year, which will terminate on the first Monday of June, 18—, of the school tax of —— district aforesaid. Now the condition of this obligation is such, that if the said ———, shall, and do well and truly, execute and perform the duties of said office, according to law, and shall faithfully account for, and pay into the hands of the proper treasurer of said district, the money which shall come into his hands as collector aforesaid, and shall settle up his duplicate on or before the —— day of —— next, according to law, then this obligation to be void, or else to be and remain in full force and virtue.

Sealed and delivered in the presence of us, }

Form of Warrant to Collector of School Tax.

—— County, —— District, *ss.*

To ———, of ———, in said county. These are to authorize and require you to demand and receive of, and from every person in the annexed duplicate named, the sum wherewith such persons stand charged, and you are to collect and pay over all such moneys as you may have received, to ———, treasurer of the said school district, and his successor in office, on or before the —— day of —— next; at which time abatement or allowance for mistakes or indigent persons will be made, and within —— months from the date hereof, you shall pay into the hands of the said treasurer, the whole amount of the taxes charged and assessed in the annexed duplicate, without further delay, except such sum as the directors may, in their discretion, exonerate you from.

And if any person shall neglect, or refuse to make payment within thirty days from the time of such demand, it shall and may be lawful to and for you, and you are hereby commanded, to levy the said tax by distress and sale of the goods and chattels of such delinquent, giving ten days' public notice of such sale, by written or printed advertisements, and rendering the overplus, (if any there be, after such sale,) to the owner. Hereof fail not.

Given under my hand and seal, at —— the —— day of —— A. D.

President of the Board of Directors of —— district.

Form of Certificate of Assessment of School Tax.

[Here insert the amount of tax assessed, in figures.]

[Date.]

To the Superintendent of Common Schools:

SIR:—I do hereby certify, that a school tax, amounting to —— dollars, —— has been regularly levied and assesssed for the school year, —— ending on the first Monday of June,* A. D. —— upon —— district —— county; that a warrant for the collection thereof has been delivered to the district collector, according to law; and that the aforesaid sum, is, at least, equal to the amount of this district's share of annual state appropriation.

I do further testify that —— (of —— Post Office, county of ——,) is lawfully appointed treasurer of this school district.

Attest: (Signed,) *President.*
Secretary, *Post Office.*

* See Act of 1836, Sect. 21, and Remarks on "School Year," page 32.

Form of Order on District Treasurer.

$, [Date.]

To the Treasurer of —— }
District, —— county: }

Sir:—Pay to —— or order, —— dollars, ——, (being one quarter's salary due him as teacher, up to —— or on account of salary, or for fuel furnished to —— school house, or for rent of school house, &c., as the case may be,) for which this will be your sufficient voucher, on settlement of your accounts.

By order of the Board.

Attest: (Signed,) *President.*

Secretary.

Form of Certificate of non-payment of tax on unseated land.

To the Commissioners of the County of ——

Gentlemen:—I do hereby certify, that the following school tax on unseated land within the district of ——, was regularly assessed and set forth in the duplicate of school tax for the year ——, delivered to me for collection by the president of the board of directors thereof, and that the same has not been voluntarily paid to me: you are therefore required to cause the same to be collected and paid over, agreeably to the 7th section of the Act, entitled "An Act to consolidate and amend the several Acts relative to a general system of education by Common Schools," passed the 13th day of June, 1836.

	DOLLARS.	CENTS.
Viz: Upon land of A. B.	—	—
Upon land of C. D.	—	—
	——	——

(Signed,)

Collector of School Tax for the District of ——.

[Date.]

Form of Deed of Land to School Directors.

Know all men by these presents, that we, ——, of ——, for and in consideration of —— dollars, to us paid at the ensealing hereof, by ——, Directors of Common Schools, of —— township, district in the county of ——, the receipt of which is hereby acknowledged, do grant, bargain, sell, assure and convey, to the said directors aforesaid, their successors and assigns, a piece of ground, situate in said township of ——, described as follows, viz: Beginning ——, containing ——; being part of the premises conveyed by —— to the grantors, by deed dated, [here insert the necessary recitals,] together with all its rights, members and appurtenances; to have and to hold the said piece of ground and appurtenances, to the said ——, directors aforesaid, their successors and assigns forever, for the establishment and support of common schools in said district, according to law. And ——, the said ——, do —— covenant with the said directors, their successors and assigns, that they are lawfully seised, in fee of the afore-granted premises; that they are free of all incumbrances; that they have a good right to sell and convey the same to the said directors, and will warrant and defend the same premises to the said directors, their successors and assigns, for ever, against the lawful claims and demands of all persons. [This constitutes a *general warranty*. If a *special* warranty be desired, let the following words be added:] claiming, by, from or under them, or any of them. In witness, &c.

Sealed and delivered in our presence:

[Receipt for the purchase money, and acknowledgment before a justice, to be in the usual form.]

Form of Lease of School House and Lot to School Directors.

Know all men by these presents, that I, ——, of ——, agree to let and rent to ——, Directors of Common Schools, for —— district, in —— county, and their successors, [here insert the words "and assigns," if it is agreed to confer upon directors power to assign the lease,] a house or building in said township, with about —— of ground, adjoining lands of ——, for the establishment and support of Common Schools in said district, according to law, for the term of ——, from the —— day of ——, at the annual rent of ——; to be paid in —— payments. The premises to be surrendered at the expiration of said term, in good order—casualties excepted. In witness, &c.

Sealed and delivered in presence of us:

Form of Agreement between School Directors and Teacher.

It is agreed by and between ——, Teacher, and ——, President of the Board of Directors of Common Schools, of —— district, in —— county, that said —— shall, under the supervision and exclusive direction of the Board of Directors of said district, and their successors, teach in the school house, or building, at or near ——, for the term of ——, at and for the compensation of ——, to be paid ——; reserving the right for the Board of Directors, for the time being, to dismiss said —— at the end of any month [or quarter] of said term. The actual possession of the said school house and building, and premises before mentioned, to remain and be considered by all parties as remaining and being at all times in the said Board of Directors and their successors. In witness whereof, we have hereunto set our hands and seals, on the —— day of —— A. D. ——.

Witness,

* *Form of Certificate to a Teacher.*

We, the undersigned, members of the Board of School Directors of —— district, county of ——, do certify that having examined ——, who wishes to be employed as a teacher in said district, we have found him [or her] to be of good moral character, and qualified to teach the following branches: [here name the branches.]

Witness our hands, this —— day of —— A. D. ——.

(Signed,) } *School Directors.*

* This Certificate will be good for one year only.—[See Supplement of 1840.]

RECEIPTS.

Remarks.

A receipt is an acknowledgment in writing, that the party giving the same has received from the person therein named, the money or other thing therein specified. Although expressed to be in full of all demands, it is only *prima facie* evidence of what it purports to be, and upon satisfactory proof being made that it was obtained by fraud, or given either under a mistake of facts or an ignorance of law, it may be inquired into and corrected, in a court of law as well as in equity. 1 Pet. C. C. R. 182; 3 S. & R. 355; 7 S. & R. 309; 3 S. & R. 564, 589; 12 S. & R. 131; 1 Sid. 44; 1 Lev. 43; 1 Saund. 285; 2 Lutw. 1173; Co. Lit. 373; 2 Stark. C. 382; 1 W. C. C. R. 328; 2 Mason's R. 541; 11 Mass. 27; 1 Johns. Cas. 145; 9 Johns. R. 310; 8 Johns. R. 389; 5 Johns. R. 68; 4 Har. & McH. 219; 3 do. 433; 2 Johns. R. 378; 2 Johns. R. 319. A receipt in full, given with a full knowledge of all the circumstances, and in the absence of fraud, seems to be conclusive. 1 Esp. C. 172; Benson *vs.* Bennet, 1 Camp. 394. A receipt on the back of a bill of exchange is *prima facie* evidence of payment by the acceptor. Peake's C. 25. The giving of a receipt does not exclude parol evidence of payment. 4 Esp. N. P. C. 214.

In Pennsylvania it has been held that a receipt, not under seal, to one of several joint debtors, for his proportion of the debt, discharges the rest. 1 Rawle, 391.

General form of Receipt.

Pittsburgh, May 10, 1844.

Received from Daniel Stone, the sum of ninety-one dollars, in full for a horse sold and delivered to him. JOHN JONES.

$91

Receipt for Rent.

Washington, May 12, 1845.

Received from Adam Miller, the sum of thirty dollars, being the amount of one quarter's rent of the dwelling-house by me rented to him, due and ending the first of April last.

$30 DANIEL DICK.

Another.

Carlisle, April 1, 1845.

Received from John Jones, the sum of sixty dollars, being the amount of one quarter's rent of the dwelling-house rented by me to him, as per agreement, dated the first day of April, 1844, and in full of all demands. CHARLES SIMONS.

$60

Another, paid by a third person.

Philadelphia, June 10, 1844.

Received from William Gilmore, by the hand of George Gilmore, the sum of one hundred dollars, being the amount of one quarter's rent of a farm near Germantown, due and ending the first day of April last, and by me rented to William Gilmore.

$100 HENRY CHASE.

Receipt for Money received from a third person.

Chester, January 20, 1845.

Received from Silas Morton, by the hand of John Price, the sum of two hundred and twenty-five dollars, in full for sundry articles of merchandise, bought by the said Silas Morton from me.

$225 SAMUEL STEVENS.

Receipt for Money received for the use of another.

Beaver, January 10, 1845.

Received from Richard Rush, the sum of one hundred and sixty-two dollars and twenty-five cents, in full for work done by Asa Brown for the said Richard Rush. WILLIAM COOPER.

$162 25

Receipt for Money received in part of a Bond.

Doylestown, May 1, 1845.

Received from Thomas Brown, the sum of four hundred and fifty dollars, in part payment of a larger sum due me on bond, by the said Thomas Brown. JAMES MILES.

$450

Receipt for Interest due on Bond.

Erie, December 8, 1844.

Received from Byron Lewis, the sum of seventy-two dollars, in full for one year's interest of twelve hundred dollars, due to me on the first of December instant, on bond, by the said Byron Lewis. HORATIO ADAMS.

$72

Receipt to an Administrator.

Lancaster, May 1, 1844.

Received from David Hopkins, administrator of the estate of Thomas Nicholson, late of Lancaster, deceased, the sum of seventy-one dollars, in full for a debt due to me in his lifetime, for a horse sold and delivered to the said deceased. JOHN MORRIS.

$71

Receipt for a Promissory Note.

Erie, May 10, 1845.

Received from Richard Lee, his promissory note, payable to me, or order, six months after date, for two hundred and thirty-three dollars and thirty-three cents, for certain goods bought from me by the said Richard Lee, which when paid will be in full of all demands. JAMES OTIS.

$233 33

Receipt for an Order drawn upon a third Person.

Harrisburg, July 20, 1845.

Received from Oliver Prescott, an order drawn in my favour, upon William Jackson, for the sum of eighty-five dollars, upon sight, which, when paid, will be in full of all demands I have against the said Oliver Prescott. EDWARD BURNS.

$85

Receipt for Writings left in a person's hands.

Newcastle, May 10, 1844.

Received from George Clark, two several deeds or conveyances; one of them purporting to be a lease of, &c., and made between, &c., the other of them to be an assignment of the said lease, and made between, &c., for which several deeds of writing, I hereby engage to be accountable, and to re-deliver the same to the said George Clark on demand. Witness my hand the day and year aforesaid. WILLIS GREEN.

Receipt for Grain from a Miller.

Fairmount Mill, May 1, 1844.

Received from Hiram Newman, seventy-five bushels good wheat, fifteen bushels rye, and twenty bushels Indian corn, which I engage severally to deliver to his order, as he may want them.

WILLIAM MILLER.

Receipt for Cattle, or Horses put out to Winter.

Mercer, November 29, 1844.

Received from Daniel Warner, eight head of horned cattle, viz., four cows and four young oxen, [or horses, sheep, swine, as the case may be,] which I promise to keep through the winter, and feed them with good hay, &c., and return them on the first day of May next, casualties excepted, in good condition, he paying me five dollars each for the same. Witness my hand.

JACOB STONE.

Receipt for Lading.

Philadelphia, December 28, 1844.

Received from Edward Livingston, on my wagon, the following goods, marked, numbered, and weighing as follows, viz.:

E. L. No.	1. Tierce, weighing	400	pounds.
"	2. one hogshead	890	do.
"	3. one do.	845	do.
"	4. one bale	375	do.
"	5, 6 & 7. three kegs	58	do.
"	8. one barrel	180	do.
		2748	pounds.

All in good order and well conditioned, with which load I promise to proceed without delay, or unnecessary detention, to the city of Pittsburgh, and deliver them in the same good order and condition, unto the said Edward Livingston, or to his order, for which he is to pay me the sum of four dollars for each hundred pounds, the one fourth thereof he is to pay me before my departure from Philadelphia, and the other three-fourths on the delivery of said goods at Pittsburgh, as aforesaid. In witness whereof, I have signed two receipts of the same tenour and date, the one satisfied, the other to be void. JOSIAH WAGNER.

Receipt upon the above.

Received of Edward Livingston, the sum of twenty-seven dollars and forty-eight cents, being the one-fourth part of the freight within-mentioned. JOSIAH WAGNER.

$27 48

Receipt for a Legacy.

York, January 21, 1845.

Received of George Wolf, executor of the last will and testament of Robert Findlay, deceased, the sum of one thousand dollars in full, of a legacy bequeathed to me by the said deceased.

$1000 WILLIAM FINDLAY.

☞ A refunding bond sometimes accompanies a receipt for a legacy, for which see "Indemnifying Bond to Executor on payment of a legacy."

Receipt for Boarding.

Received of William Burns, guardian of John Andrews, one of the minor children and heirs of Enos Andrews, deceased, the sum of twenty dollars in full, for boarding the said John Andrews from the first day of May, until the first day of August, A. D. 1844. GEORGE SNYDER.

Easton, August 1, 1844.

Receipt for Money at coming of Age.

Easton, May 10, 1845.

Received of William Burns, my late guardian, the sum of one hundred dollars, being in part [or in full, as the case may be,] of my proportion of the estate of my late father, Enos Andrews.

JOHN ANDREWS.

$100

Receipt for a Legacy.

Easton, May 10, 1845.

Received of William Burns, my late guardian, the sum of two hundred dollars, being in full of a legacy bequeathed to me in the will of my late uncle, Thomas Andrews, deceased.

JOHN ANDREWS.

$200

RECITALS.

Remarks.

A recital is the repetition of some former writing, or the statement of something which has been done. Touchst. 76. Recitals are used to explain those matters of fact which are necessary to make the transaction intelligible. 2 Bl. Com. 298. In preparing deeds, it is frequently necessary to recite certain matters connected with the titles; for the purpose of explaining the object and extent of the conveyance.

Recital of Title by Patent.

Whereas the commonwealth (or the honourable John Penn, &c., late proprietaries) of Pennsylvania, by patent or grant under the great seal, bearing date the first day of January, Anno Domini one thousand seven hundred and sixty-eight, for the consideration therein mentioned, did grant and confirm unto A. B., and to his heirs and assigns, a certain tract of land, situate in the township of Moyamensing, in the county of Philadelphia aforesaid, by marks and bounds in the same marks particularly described, containing one hundred acres and the allowance of six per cent. for roads, &c., with the appurtenances: To hold the same to him, his heirs and assigns forever, as in and by the said recited patent, (recorded in the Land Office, in Patent Book B., vol. 4, page 119,) relation being thereunto had, more fully and at large appears.

Recital of Title by Grant.

And whereas the said A. B., by indenture, under his hand and seal, bearing date the tenth day of April, Anno Domini one thousand seven hundred and seventy-three, for the consideration therein-mentioned, did grant and confirm unto C. D., and to his heirs and assigns, all that tract or piece of land, (part of the said above-mentioned tract,) bounded and described as follows, to wit: Beginning, &c., containing two hundred acres, and allowance aforesaid, with the appurtenances: To hold the same to him, his heirs and assigns, forever, as in and by the said recited indenture (recorded at Harrisburg,) &c., relation being thereunto had, appears.

Recital of Title by Devise.

Whereas by force and virtue of which said recited indenture, or of some other good conveyances or assurances in the law duly had and executed, the said C. D. became in his lifetime lawfully seised in his demesne as of fee, of and in the said tract of fifty acres of land, with the appurtenances; and being so thereof seised made his last will and testament in writing, bearing date the tenth day of December, Anno Domini one thousand eight hundred and twenty-two, wherein and whereby (amongst other things) he did give and devise the said tract of land unto his son C. D., and his heirs, as in and by the said recited will, (since his decease duly proved, and remaining in the register's office at Reading,) recourse being thereunto had, appears.

Recital of Title by Descent.

By force and virtue of which said recited indenture, or of some other good couveyances or assurances in the law duly had and executed, the said A. B. became, in his lifetime, lawfully seised in his demesne, as of fee, of and in the said tract of land, with the appurtenances, and being so thereof seised, died intestate, leaving issue four children, to wit: John, James, Mary (the wife of I. S.,) and Thomas, to whom the same, by the laws of Pennsylvania relating to intestates, did descend and come.

Recital of Title by Sheriff.

And whereas I. S., High Sheriff of the County of Berks aforesaid, by deed poll, under his hand and seal, bearing date the first day of October, one thousand seven hundred and ninety-two, for the consideration therein mentioned, did, by virtue of a certain writ of *venditioni exponas,* therein recited, grant and confirm unto C. D., and to his heirs and assigns, all that the said messuage or tenement and tract of land, containing fifty acres, late the estate of the said A. B., with the appurtenances: To hold the same to the said C. D., his heirs and assigns, forever, according to the act of General Assembly in such case made and provided, as by the said recited deed poll, duly acknowledged, and entered among the records of the Court of Common Pleas of the said county, relation being thereunto had, appears.

Recital of Title by Attorney.

And whereas the said C. D. by his attorney, E. F., (by letter of attorney, under the hand and seal of the said C. D., bearing date the tenth day of December, one thousand eight hundred and thirty, lawfully constituted,) did, by indenture, bearing date the first day of May, Anno Domini one thousand eight hundred and thirty-one, for the consideration therein mentioned, grant and confirm unto G. H., and to his heirs and assigns, all that messuage or tenement, plantation and tract of sixty acres of land, with the appurtenances: To hold the same to him, his heirs and assigns, forever, as in and by the said last recited indenture, (recorded in the office for the recording of deeds at Reading aforesaid, in book A., volume 10, page 104, &c.,) relation being thereunto had, appears.

Recital of Title by Executors.

And whereas the said M. R. and E. R., executors of the testament and last will of the said I. R., deceased, by virtue of the power and authority to them given by the said will, and pursuant to the directions thereof, did, by indenture, under their hands and seals, bearing date the tenth day of November, one thousand eight hundred and twenty-two, for the consideration therein mentioned, grant and confirm unto E. F., and to his heirs and assigns, all that the said messuage or tenement and tract of one hundred acres of land, with the appurtenances: To hold the same to him, his heirs and assigns, forever, as in and by the said recited indenture (recorded at, &c.,) relation being thereunto had, appears.

Recital of Title by Administratrix.

And whereas C. B., administratrix of all and singular the goods and chattels, rights and credits, which were of the said A. B. at the time of his death, who died intestate, (by virtue and in pursuance of an order of the Orphans' Court of the said county of Berks, for the sale of the real estate of the said intestate,) by indenture, under her hand and seal, bearing date the first day of April, one thousand eight hundred and nineteen, for the cousideration therein mentioned, did grant and confirm unto F. G., and to his heirs and assigns, all that the said above-mentioned and described tract of fifty acres, and allowance, aforesaid, with the appurtenances: To hold the same to him, his heirs and assigns, forever, as in and by the said last-recited indenture, (recorded at Reading aforesaid, &c.,) relation being thereunto had, appears.

Recital of Title partition by Writ.

And whereas, by virtue of a certain writ *de partitione faciendi*, issuing out of the County Court of Common Pleas of the county of Berks aforesaid, bearing date the tenth day of January, one thousand eight hundred and forty, for partition of the said tract of land, with the appurtenances, there was duly allotted and assigned unto the said G. H., a certain piece or parcel of land [part of the said tract,] bounded and described as follows, viz: beginning at a post, &c., containing one hundred acres, and allowance aforesaid, with the appurtenances: To hold the same to him, the said G. H., his heirs and assigns, in severalty forever, as by the said writ *de partitione faciendi*, and return of the sheriff thereupon duly made, and remaining amongst the records and proceedings of the said court of the term of September, one thousand eight hundred and forty, recourse being thereunto had, appears.

Recital of Title partition by Deed.

And whereas, by indenture of partitions between the said A. B. of the one part, and the said G. H. of the other part, made, bearing date the second day of September, Anno Domini one thousand eight hundred and twenty-eight, partition of the said messuage, &c., with the appurtenances, was made between the said parties, wherein and whereby the piece or parcel thereof, bounded and limited as follows, to wit: Beginning, &c., containing five hundred acres and allowance aforesaid, was released and confirmed to the said G. H., his heirs and assigns: To hold to him, the said G. H., his heirs and assigns, in severalty for ever, as in and by the said indenture of partition, (recorded at Philadelphia, &c.,) relation being thereunto had, appears.

Recital of Sale by Order of Orphans' Court.

And whereas at an Orphans' Court held at Reading, in and for the county of Berks, the tenth day of November, one thousand eight hundred and twenty-five, upon the petition of C. B., administratrix of all and singular the goods and chattels, rights and credits, which were of the said A. B. at the time of his death, who died intestate, praying the court to grant her an order to make sale of the said messuage and tract of land, for the payment of the debts, and maintenance and education of the minor children of the said intestate, it was ordered by the said court, that the said petitioner should, on Monday, the first day of December then next, expose the premises aforesaid to sale, by public vendue or outcry, and sell the same for the purposes aforesaid, and that she should make report of her proceedings therein to the next Orphans' Court, to be held for the said county, after such sale. In pursuance of which order, the said C. B. (after due public and timely notice by her given of the time and place of sale) did, on the day and time therein mentioned, expose the premises aforesaid to sale, by public vendue or outcry, and sold the same to the said E. F. for the sum of one thousand dollars; he being the highest bidder, and that the highest and best price bidden for the same; which sale, on report thereof made to the justices of the said court, the tenth day of January last, was confirmed by the said Court; and it was considered and adjudged by the said court, that the same should be and remain firm and stable forever, as by the records and proceedings of the said court, relation being thereunto had, appears.

SHORT FORMS.

Recital of Title by Deed.

It being the same premises (or part of the same) which E. F. and M. his wife, by indenture bearing date the first day of April,

Anno Domini one thousand eight hundred and sixteen, for the consideration therein mentioned, did grant and confirm unto the said A. B , (party hereto,) and to his heirs and assigns forever, as in and by the said in part recited indenture, recorded in the office for recording of deeds at Reading, in and for the county of Berks, in Book A. vol. 15, page 224, &c., relation being thereunto had, more fully and at large appears.

Recital of Title by Will.

It being the same lot of ground which H. H., late of the township of Blockley and county aforesaid, farmer, deceased, in and by his last will and testament, in writing, bearing date the tenth day of July, Anno Domini one thousand eight hundred and sixteen, did give and devise unto the said A. B. (party hereto) in fee, as in and by the said recited will, since his decease duly proved, and remaining in the Register's office at Philadelphia, recourse being thereunto had, more fully and at large appears.

Recital of Title by Deed and Will.

It being the same premises which T. V. and M., his wife, by indenture bearing date the first day of June, Anno Domini one thousand eight hundred and sixteen, for the consideration therein mentioned, did grant and confirm unto C. B., and to his heirs and assigns, as in and by the said in part recited indenture, (recorded, &c.,) relation being thereunto had, appears. And the said C. B., being so thereof, in his lifetime, lawfully seised in his demesne, as of fee of and in the said premises, made his last will and testament in writing, bearing date the tenth day of July, Anno Domini one thousand eight hundred and sixteen, wherein and whereby (amongst other things) he did give and devise the same unto his son A. B (party hereto) in fee, as in and by the said recited will, (since his decease duly proved, and remaining in the register's office at Philadelphia,) recourse being thereunto had, appears.

Recital of Estate of an Intestate, conveyed by the Heirs.

It being the same tract of land which the Commonwealth of Pennsylvania, by patent, bearing date the seventh day of March, 1788, (enrolled in the Rolls Office for the state of Pennsylvania, in Patent Book No. 12, page 53, &c.,) for the consideration therein mentioned, did grant and confirm unto K. E. in fee, who being thereof lawfully seised, died intestate, leaving issue E. E. and N., intermarried with N. S., to whom the same, by the laws of Pennsylvania, did descend and come. And the said E. E. and N. S., and N. his wife, by their joint indenture, bearing date the twenty-fourth day of April, one thousand eight hundred and four, for the consideration therein mentioned, did grant and confirm the same unto the said A. B. (party hereto) in fee, as in and by the said indenture, (recorded, or intended to be recorded, &c.,) relation being thereunto had, appears.

Same, valued by Order of Court, and accepted by one of the Heirs.

It being the same premises of which A. B. died intestate, and upon which, on due application to the Orphans' Court of Berks county, an order was granted by the said court, whereupon the said premises were duly valued and appraised, and by the said court adjudged and confirmed unto the said L. K., son-in-law [or eldest son] of the said deceased. To hold the same to the said L. K. and to his heirs and assigns forever, as in and by an exemplification of the records of the said court, dated at Reading, the seventh day of April, Anno Domini one thousand eight hundred and thirty-two, relation being thereunto had, appears.

Recital of Title by Sheriff.

It being the same lot of ground, No. 250, which E F., High Sheriff of the county of Berks, by deed poll, under his hand and seal, bearing date the fifth day of November, Anno Domini one thousand eight hundred and thirty-one, for the consideration therein mentioned, did, (as late the estate of S. E.) grant and confirm unto the said K. L., party hereto, in fee, as in and by the said deed poll entered among the records of the Court of Common Pleas of Berks county, (and recorded in the Recording Office at Reading, &c.,) relation being thereunto had, appears.

RELEASE.

Remarks.

Releases are of two kinds. 1st. Such as give up, discharge, or abandon a right of action. 2d. Such as convey a man's interest or right to another, who has possession of it, or some estate in the same. Touch. 320; Litt. sec. 444. The words generally used in such conveyance, are, "remised, released, and forever quit claimed." Litt. sec., 445. Releases of land are also, in respect of their operation, divided into four sorts. 1st. Releases that inure by way of passing the estate. 2d. Releases that inure by way of passing the right. 3d. Releases that inure by enlargement of the estate: and 4th. Releases that inure by way of extinguishment.

Release to an Executor.

Know all men by these presents: That we, Henry Benson, of, &c., and Mary, his wife, late Mary Miles, one of the daughters and legatees named in the will of William Miles, late of, &c., deceased, do hereby acknowledge, that we have this day had and received of and from David Jones, executor of the last will and testament of the said William Miles, deceased, the sum of three thousand dollars, in full satisfaction and payment of all such sum or sums of money, legacies and bequests as are given and bequeathed to the said Mary, by the last will and testament aforesaid, and all interest accrued thereon.

And therefore, the said Henry Benson and Mary, his wife, do by these presents, release, acquit, and forever discharge the said David Jones, his heirs, executors and administrators, of and from the said legacy or legacies, and of and from all actions, suits, payments, accounts, reckonings, claims and demands whatsoever, for or by reason thereof, or of any other act, matter, cause or thing whatsoever, from the beginning of the world to the day of the date of these presents. In witness, &c.

Release to an Administrator.

Know all men by these presents: That I, Samuel Wells, of, &c., one of the sons of Henry Williams, late of the township of Blockley, in the county of Philadelphia and state of Pennsylvania, deceased, who died intestate, do hereby acknowledge, that I this day have had and received of and from Thomas Robinson, administrator of the estate of the said Henry Williams, deceased, the sum of two hundred dollars, in full satisfaction and payment of all such sum or sums of money, share or shares, purparts and dividends, which were due, owing, payable and belonging to me, by any means whatsoever, for or on account of my full share, part, or dividend of the real and personal [or personal, as the case may be] estate of my said father deceased. And therefore I, the said Samuel Wells, do by these presents, release, acquit, and forever discharge the said Thomas Robinson, his heirs, executors and administrators, of and from the said share or dividend of the estate aforesaid, and of and from all actions, suits, payments, accounts, reckonings, claims and demands whatsoever, for or by reason thereof, or of any other act, matter, cause or thing whatsoever, from the beginning of the world to the day of the date of these presents. In witness, &c.

Release to Guardian.

Know all men by these presents: That I, D. E, of, &c., spinster, having attained the age of twenty-one years, do hereby acknowledge, that I this day have had and received, of and from E. E., my guardian, duly appointed by the Orphans' Court of the said county of Philadelphia, the sum of five hundred dollars, together with the bond to him given by my brother, J. S, and his sureties, agreeably to the order of the said court, in full satisfaction and payment of my share of the estate, real and personal, of my late father, W. S., deceased, and therefore I do, by these presents, release, acquit and forever discharge the said E. E., his heirs, executors and administrators, of and from the said guardianship, and of and from the said legacy or legacies, and of and from all actions, suits, payments, accounts, reckonings, claims and demands whatsoever, for or by reason thereof, or of any other act, matter, cause or thing whatsoever, from the beginning of the world to the day of the date of these presents. In witness, &c.

Release to the Father of a Bastard.

Know all men by these presents: That whereas A. B., of, &c., spinster, has lately been delivered of a male bastard child, [or is now pregnant with child, as the case may be,] in said township, and has charged C. D., of the same place, with being the father thereof; and whereas the said A. B. has this day agreed with the said C. D. to take the sum of one hundred dollars, in full satisfaction, for the lying-in expenses, maintenance, educating and bringing up the said child: Therefore know ye, that the said A. B., for and in consideration of the said sum of one hundred dollars, lawful money of the United States, to her in hand paid by the said C, D., at and before the ensealing and delivering hereof, the receipt whereof is hereby acknowledged, hath remised, released, acquitted and forever discharged, and by these presents, doth remise, release, acquit and forever discharge, the said C. D., his heirs, executors and administrators, of and from all manner of criminal and civil action or actions, now brought, or hereafter to be brought, against him, and also, of and from all debts, payments, accounts, claims and demands whatsoever, the said A. B. ever had, now hath, or hereafter shall or may have, against the said C. D., his heirs, executors and administrators, for or on account of the birth, maintenance, educating and bringing up the said child; or for, or by reason of any matter, cause or thing whatsoever, touching or concerning the same. In witness, &c.

[If surety be given for the due observance of the covenants, in the above-mentioned release, then add the following:]

And further, for the true observance of the covenants aforesaid, the said A. B. and her friend E. F., do hereby bind themselves, their heirs, executors and administrators, and every of them, unto the said C. D., his executors, administrators or assigns, in the penal sum of three hundred dollars, lawful money as aforesaid: Upon condition, that the said A. B. shall and do, in all things, well and truly observe, fulfil and keep, the covenants aforesaid, which on her part and behalf are to be observed and kept, according to the true intent and meaning of the same, as mentioned in the above-written release, then this obligation to be void, or else to be and remain in full force and virtue. In witness, &c.

Release of all Demands.

Know all men by these presents, That I, A. B., of, &c., as well for and in consideration of the sum of one dollar, to me in hand paid by C. D., of, &c., at and before the sealing and delivering hereof, the receipt whereof I do hereby acknowledge, as for divers other good causes and valuable considerations, me thereto specially moving, have remised, released, quit-claimed, and forever discharged, and by these presents, for me, my heirs, executors and administrators, do remise, release, quit-claim and forever discharge the said C. D., his heirs, executors and administrators, and every of them, of and from all, and all manner of action and actions, cause and causes of action and actions, suits, debts, dues, duties, sum and sums of money, accounts, reckonings, bonds, bills, specialties, covenants, contracts, agreements, promises, variances, damages, judgments, extents, executions, claims and demands, whatsoever, in law or equity; or otherwise, howsoever, which against the said C. D. I ever had, now have, or which I, my heirs, executors or administrators hereafter can, shall or may have, for, upon or by reason of any matter, cause or thing whatsoever, from the beginning of the world, to the day of the date of these presents. In witness whereof, &c.

Release upon a Mortgage.

Whereas A. B., by indenture of mortgage, dated the first day of January, A. D. 1844, recorded at Reading, in Mortgage-book B., page 263, did grant in mortgage to me, C. D., of Amity township, Berks County, to secure the payment of the sum of one thousand nine hundred dollars, with interest, a certain messuage, tenement, &c. [Here describe the premises as set forth in the mortgage.] And the said A. B., being desirous of having his said messuage and lot relieved from the operation of said mortgage:

Now, I, the said C. D., in consideration of the premises, and of the sum of one dollar, to me in hand paid, by the said A. B., the receipt whereof I do hereby acknowledge, have, and hereby do, for myself, my executors, administrators and assigns, covenant, promise and agree with the said A. B., his heirs and assigns, that no execution, or other final process, or proceeding in law, shall be sued, levied, taken or executed by me, my heirs, executors, administrators or assigns, by virtue of the said mortgage, on, for or against the messuage and lot, conveyed by the said A. B., to me, the said C. D., as above recited; and, by these presents, do remise, release and for ever quit claim, unto the said A. B., his heirs, executors, administrators or assigns, the aforesaid described premises.

In testimony whereof, the said C. D. hath hereunto set his hand and seal, the —— day of ——, one thousand eight hundred and forty-four.

Signed, sealed and delivered in the presence of }

C. D.

The —— day of ——, A. D. 1844, before me, one of the justices of the peace in and for Berks county, came the above [or within] named C. D., and acknowledged the above [or within] instrument of writing, to be his act and deed, and desires that the same may be recorded as such, according to law. Witness my hand and seal.

C. D.

Release between Copartners or Traders on settling Accounts.

Whereas sundry accounts current, and otherwise, and divers dealings in trade, have been subsisting and depending, for many years last past, between A. B., of the borough of Reading, in the county of Berks, and State of Pennsylvania, and C. D, late of the borough aforesaid, but now of the city of Philadelphia, which said accounts and dealings they have balanced and adjusted; by which it appears that nothing remains due from one to the other: therefore, to prevent any further disputes, touching and concerning such accounts and dealings, and to ascertain and confirm such balance and adjustment, they, the said A. B. and C. D., have mutually agreed to give and execute reciprocal releases to each her.

Now know all men by these presents, that he, the said A. B., for the considerations aforesaid, and to prevent all future disputes, for himself, his heirs, executors and administrators, hath remised, released, and for ever quit claimed, and by these presents, doth remise, release, and for ever quit claim, unto the said C. D., his heirs, executors and administrators, all and all manner of actions, causes of action, suits, debts, dues, sums of money, accounts, reckonings, bonds, specialties, covenants, contracts, controversies, agreements, promises, variances, damages, judgments, extents, executions, claims and demands, whatsoever, both at law and in equity, which against the said C. D., his heirs, executors and administrators, he, the said A. B., now hath, or ever had, on account of their said mutual dealings: or for or by reason of any other cause, matter or thing whatsoever, from the beginning of the world to the day of the date of these presents.

In witness whereof, he, the said A. B., hath hereunto set his hand and seal, this tenth day of May, one thousand eight hundred and forty-four.

Sealed and delivered }
in presence of }

E. F.

A. B.

☞ To make the release mutual and reciprocal, the counterpart should be written by C. D. to A. B., reversing the names, each party of course retaining one..

Release of Dower, by Indorsement.

Know all men by these presents, that I, M. W., widow and relict of the within-named H. W., deceased, for divers good causes and considerations, and especially for and in consideration of the sum of one dollar, to me in hand paid, by the within-named C. D., at and before the ensealing and delivering hereof, the receipt whereof I do hereby acknowledge, have remised, released, and forever quit claimed, and by these presents, do remise, release, and forever quit claim, unto the said C. D., and to his heirs and

and other interest, right, or title whatsoever, which I, the said M. W., now have, may, might, should, or of right ought to have, or claim of, in, to, or out of, all that the within-mentioned messuage, &c., granted to the said C. D., and every part and parcel thereof, with the appurtenances: And also, all manner of action and actions, writ and writs of dower, or other actions, and right to making distress, whatsoever; so that neither I, the said M. W., nor any other person or persons whatsoever, for me, or in my name, right or stead, any manner of dower, or writs of dower, or actions, right or title of dower, or other interest, claim or demand whatsoever, of or in the said messuage, &c., hereditaments and premises within mentioned, or of or in any part or parcel thereof, at any time hereafter, shall or may have, claim or prosecute against the said C. D., his heirs or assigns. In witness, &c.

Sealed and delivered }
in presence of }
S. R.

M. W.

REPORT.

A report is a certificate to the court made by an officer or other person appointed by the court, of the facts or matters to be ascertained by him, or of something of which it is his duty to inform the court. If the parties in the case accede to the report, and no exceptions are filed, it is in due time confirmed; if exceptions are filed to the report, they will, agreeably to the rules of the court, be heard; and the report will either be confirmed, set aside, or referred back for the correction of some error. 2 Madd. Ch. 505; Blake's Ch. Pr. 230.

Report of Examiners of Attorney at Law.

We, the undersigned, examiners appointed by the Court of Common Pleas of —— county, do hereby certify that having examined Mr. C. D., on his application to be admitted to practice in the said court, we are unanimously of opinion that he is sufficiently qualified to practice as an attorney of the said court, and that we have received satisfactory evidence that he is a gentleman of good moral character.

Report of an Alien.

—— *County, ss.* Be it remembered, that at a Court of Common Pleas, held at ——, in and for the said county, (or) before me, the prothonotary of the court of, &c., personally came A. B., a native of ——, who upon his solemn —— did depose and say, that he is a native of ——, now residing in the —— of ——, aged —— years, or thereabouts, and that it is his *bona fide* intention to become a citizen of the United States, and to renounce forever all allegiance and fidelity to any foreign prince, state, potentate or sovereignty whatever, and particularly the emperor of ——, of whom before he was a subject.

In witness whereof, I have hereunto set my hand and the seal of the court this —— day of ——, A. D. ——.

Report of Auditors to Orphans' Court on application of Executor, Administrator or Guardian, to sell or mortgage Real Estate.

To the Honourable, the Judges of the Orphans' Court of the County of ——.

The undersigned, appointed by this honourable court, on the —— day of ——, A. D. ——, to ascertain the truth of the facts set forth in the petition of A. B., —— of ——, do respectfully report:

That upon investigating the accounts filed by the said ——, it appears that the personal estate of the said —— is inadequate to ——, and that in our opinion it is necessary to sell or mortgage the following described real estate of the said —— for that purpose.

Witness our hands this —— day of ——, A. D. ——.

Report of Auditors on settlement of an Account.

To the Honourable, &c.

The undersigned, auditors appointed by the court to audit and adjust the accounts of A. B., —— of ——, respectfully beg leave to report:

That having examined the said accounts, with the vouchers, papers and other evidences thereof, we have found the same to be just and true according to the preceding statement, by which it appears that there is a balance of —— remaining in the hands of the said accountant, [*if authorized to distribute, say*] for *pro rata* distribution among the —— of the said ——, and which we have divided among the said —— according to the amount of their respective claims, at the rate of —— per centum as per the annexed schedule.

Report of Commissioners appointed to lay out State Road.

To the Honourable, &c.

We, the commissioners appointed by an Act of Assembly of the Commonwealth of ——, passed the —— day of ——, A. D. ——, to view, lay out and mark a state road, beginning at ——, in the county of ——, thence by the nearest and best rout to ——, thence by the nearest and best to ——, &c. &c., do report: That in pursuance of said appointment we met at ——, on the —— day of ——, A. D. ——, and being first sworn, (or affirmed,) according to the direction of the said act, we proceeded to perform the duties therein, and have viewed, laid out, and clearly and distinctly marked on the ground the rout agreed upon, as in said act we were directed, and viewed and laid out said road, according to the requirement of the said act, a fair and accurate draft of which is hereto annexed, on which the courses and distances as they occurred, the improvements through which it passes, the crossing of county and township lines, roads and waters are accurately noted, together with such other matter as may serve for explanation, having begun at —— and ended at —— as directed.

All which is respectfully submitted.

RETURN BY SHERIFF.

Remarks.

The return of writs is a short account in writing, made by the sheriff, or other ministerial officer, of the manner in which he has executed a writ. Steph. on Pl. 24.

It is the duty of such officer to return all writs on the return day; on his neglecting to do so, a rule may be obtained on him to return the writ, and if he do not obey the rule, he may be attached for contempt. See 19 Vin. Abr. 171; Com. Dig. Return; 2 Lilly's Abr. 476.

On Attachment.

Attached prout Return.

To the Honourable, the Judges within named.

I do humbly certify, that by virtue of the within-named writ to me directed, I have attached all and singular the goods, chattels, moneys and effects of the within-named C. D., in my bailiwick, in the hands and possession of E. F., as by the within writ I am commanded, as by the schedule hereunto annexed appears. So answers A. B., sheriff.

Attached by Pledges.

The within-named C. D. is attached by his pledges I. S., and E. F.

Nihil, &c.

The within-named C. D. hath nothing in my bailiwick whereby he can be attached, nor is he found in the same.

On Capias ad Respondendum.

Cepi Corpus.

By virtue of this writ to me directed, I have taken the body of the within-named I. S., which I have ready before the judges within named, at the day and place within contained, as within I am commanded.

Languidus.

By virtue, &c., [as above], I have taken the body of the within-named I. S., who remains in my custody in prison, so sick, weak, and infirm, that without great danger of his death, I cannot have his body before, &c., [as above].

Non est Inventus.

The within-named A. B. is not found in my bailiwick. [If there be more than one defendant, say, "the within-named A. B., C. D. and E. F. are not found, nor is either of them found in my bailiwick."]

Rescue.

By virtue of this writ to me directed, I made my certain warrant, directed to T. P., my bailiff, to take and arrest the within C. S., which said bailiff, by virtue of the said warrant, did, on the —— day of ——, in the year, &c., at —— in the county of ——, take and arrest the body of the said C. S., and him in his custody then and there had. Whereupon a certain G. R., of, &c., yeoman, in and upon said bailiff, then and there made an assault, and the said C. S., then and there out of the custody of my said bailiff, with force and arms did rescue. And the said C. S., himself, then and there from the custody of my said bailiff, with force and arms, &c., did rescue, withdraw and escape. And afterwards the same C. S. was not found in my bailiwick.

☞ This may be returned as a rescue from the sheriff himself.

On Capias ad Satisfaciendum.

Cepi Corpus.

By virtue of this writ to me directed, I have taken the body of the within-named A. B., which I have ready before the judges within named, at the day and place within contained, to satisfy the within-named C. D., of the debt and damages within mentioned, as within I am commanded.

Non est Inventus.

The within-named A. B. is not found in my bailiwick [as before].

On Distringas.

Attached.

The within-named A. B. is attached by his pledges, C. D. and E. F.

Nihil.

The within-named A. B. hath nothing in my bailiwick whereby he may be distrained.

Dower.

Return of Writ of Seisin.

I, I. M., Esquire, high sheriff of the county of ——, to the judges in the writ to this schedule annexed named do certify, that by virtue of the said writ to me directed, on the —— day of ——, in the year, &c., I caused R. S., widow, in the writ aforesaid named, to have full seisin of one-third part of one messuage, &c., with the appurtenances, in the same writ specified, to wit, of the lower room in the front part of the said messuage, towards the west; of a back chamber of the said messuage, one story high towards the east, &c., in the tenure of R. H., also of one other messuage, &c., with free ingress and egress to and from the same respectively, to hold to the said R. S. in severalty, by metes and bounds, in the name of the whole dower of her, the said R. S., in the said writ specified, as by the same writ I am commanded.

On Writ of Error.

Return of Writ of Error.

The record and process within mentioned, with all things touching the same, before the judges within named, at the day and place within contained, in a certain record to this writ annexed, we do certify and send as within we are commanded.

Of Sci. Fa. to hear Errors.

By virtue, &c., I have made known to T. R. and E., his wife, within named, (by A. B. and C. D., &c.,) that they be and appear before the judges within named, at the day and place within contained, to hear the record within mentioned: and further to do and receive as in the said writ is required.

On Fieri Facias.

Fieri Feci.

By virtue of this writ to me directed, of the goods and chattels of the within-named T. E., I have caused to be levied the debt and damages specified, and these moneys I have ready before the judges within named, at the day and place within contained, as within I am commanded.

Nulla Bona.

The within-named R. B. hath no goods or chattels, (lands or tenements,) whereof I can cause the moneys within mentioned, or any part thereof, to be levied.

Goods not Sold.

By virtue, &c., of the goods, &c., I have caused to be levied to the value of the debt and damages within mentioned, which said goods remain in my hands, for want of buyers; therefore, I cannot have the moneys within mentioned, before the judges within named, at the day and place within contained, as within I am commanded.

Levied as to Part.

By virtue, &c., of the goods, &c., I have caused to be levied —— parcel of the debt and damages within mentioned, which moneys I have ready, &c., [as before,] and I do further certify that the aforesaid C. D. hath no other goods or chattels, lands or tenements, in my bailiwick, whereof I can cause to be levied the residue of the said debt.

Same on Fi. Fa. against Executors.

By virtue of a writ of *fieri facias,* to me directed, and to this schedule annexed, to the judges in the same writ named, at the day and place therein contained, I do certify, that of the goods and chattels, which were of T. H., at the time of his death, in the hands of S. D., in the same writ named to be administered, I have caused to be levied the sum of ——, parcel of the debt and damages in the said writ specified; which said sum of ——, I have ready before the judges aforesaid, to render to F. D., in the same writ named, in part of the said debt.

And I do also certify that the aforesaid S. D. hath no other goods and chattels in my bailiwick, which were of the said T. H., at the time of his death, in her hands to be administered. And I do further certify that the aforesaid S. D. hath no goods or chattels of her own in my bailiwick, whereof I can cause the damages in the said writ mentioned to be levied.

Devastavit.

To the judges, &c. I do certify that the within-named L. G., after the death of the within-named K. P., had divers goods and chattels in my bailiwick, which were of the aforesaid K. P., at the time of his death, in his hands to be administered, to the value of the debt within mentioned; but before the coming of this writ, the aforesaid L. G., the goods and chattels aforesaid, to the value of the debt aforesaid, had wasted and to his own proper use had converted, whereby the debt and damages aforesaid, or any part thereof, I cannot cause to be levied as within I am commanded.

Rescue.

To the judges, &c. I do certify that by virtue of this writ to me directed, I made my certain warrant, directed to a certain F. B., my bailiff, to the debt and damages within mentioned, of the goods and chattels of the within-named J. S., according to the command of the said writ which said F. B. afterwards and before the return of the said writ, to wit: the —— day of ——, in the year, &c., at ——, in the county aforesaid, by virtue of my said warrant, did seize and take into his hands, divers goods and chattels of him, the said J. S., to the value of the debt and damages aforesaid, and the same in his custody then and there had and detained, until J. S., Jr., and W. S., with many other persons unknown, afterwards, to wit, &c., at, &c., in and upon my said bailiff with force and arms, &c., an assault did make, and him, my said bailiff, did beat, wound and evilly treat. And the goods and chattels aforesaid, out of the custody of the said F. B. then and there with force and arms did rescue, against the will of my said bailiff, and against the peace, &c.

Or thus: By virtue of this writ to me directed, I seized and took into my hands divers goods, &c., and the same in my custody had, until a certain J. S., &c., afterwards, to wit, &c., in and upon me, the said sheriff, with force and arms, an assault did make, and me, the said sheriff, did beat, &c.

On Habeas Corpus.

On Habeas Corpus to the Common Pleas.

The execution of this writ appears in a certain schedule to this writ annexed.

On same to the Sheriff or Gaoler.

The body of the within-named G. R., by me before taken and detained before the judges within named, at the day and place within contained, I have ready as within I am commanded.

Cum Causa.

The body of the within-named A. B., in my custody, together with the day and cause of his being taken and detained, before, &c., I have ready, as within I am commanded.

Not detained in prison, &c.

To the judges, &c. I do certify that the within-named J. S. is not detained in prison in my custody, nor was he detained therein on the day of the receipt of this writ; nor is there any cause of detention of him, the said J. S., remaining before me.

Detained by Writ.

To the judges, &c. I do certify, that before the coming of this writ, the within-named W. B. was taken and committed to the prison of ——, in my custody, by virtue of a certain other writ to me before directed, a true transcript whereof I send annexed to this writ. Nevertheless, the body of the said W. B. I have ready, &c.

In Execution.

To the judges, &c. I do certify that the body of the within-named T. C. is in execution, at the suit of T. B., for the sum of ——, returnable before, &c., on the —— day of ——. Nevertheless, &c.

On Warrant.

To the judges, &c. I, T. B., Esq., High Sheriff of the county of ——, do certify, that before the coming of this writ to me directed, to wit, on the —— day of ——, last past, J. M., in the said writ named, was committed to my custody by virtue of a certain warrant [or mittimus] under the hands and seals of E. H. and T. C., Esqs., two of the justices of the peace of the county aforesaid, the tenor of which said warrant follows in these words: "To the keeper of the gaol," &c., [as in the warrant] and this is the cause of the taking and detaining of the aforesaid J. M. in my custody. Nevertheless, &c.

On Suspicion.

To the judges, &c. I do certify that before the coming of this writ, the within-named C. D. was committed to the prison of ——, on suspicion of counterfeiting the moneys of the United States, and for that cause and no other, in the same prison is detained.

Or thus: On suspicion of larceny, and because he could not find sufficient sureties to abide the laws of the state, &c., [as before.]

On Indictment.

—— That before the coming of this writ, to wit, at a court of, &c., held, &c., before, &c., the within-named A. B. was indicted for, &c., and by the same court was committed to the prison of ——, which said indictment remains before the said judges at, &c. Nevertheless, &c.

On other Causes.

And also the said E. G. is detained in the prison of the said county, by virtue of a certain writ of *latitat.* against him at the suit of J. A., of a plea of trespass. And also of the bill of the said J. A. against him, the said E. G., for two hundred dollars, returnable before the judges at ——, the —— day of ——, last past. And these are the causes of the taking and detaining of the aforesaid E. G. Nevertheless, &c.

On Habere Facias Possessionem.

Cum Fi. Fa.

By virtue of this writ to me directed, on the —— day of ——, in the year within mentioned, I caused the within-named H. H. to have possession of his term within specified, of the tenements within mentioned, with the appurtenances. And I have also caused to be levied of the goods and chattels of the within-named W. W., the damages within mentioned, which moneys I have ready before the judges within named, at the day and place within contained, to render to the said H. H. as within I am commanded.

On Replevin.

Replevied.

By virtue, &c., I have caused to be replevied unto the within-named R. S., the goods and chattels within mentioned, as within I am commanded.

Elongata.

Before the coming of this writ, the goods and chattels within mentioned were eloined by the within-named W. C., to places by me unknown. Therefore, I cannot replevy the same as within I am commanded.

The same as to part.

To the judges, &c. I do certify, that by virtue of this writ to me directed, I have caused to be returned to the within-named A. B., two colts, part of the cattle within mentioned, as within I am commanded, and that before the coming of this writ, the residue of the cattle aforesaid were eloined by the within-named C. D. to places to me unknown, &c.

No Pledges.

The within-named A. B. hath not found any pledges to prosecute this writ; therefore nothing hath been done towards the execution thereof.

Nullus venit, &c.

To the judges, &c. I do certify, that no one came on the part of the plaintiff to show the goods to me.

On Scire Facias.

Scire Feci.

By virtue of this writ to me directed by A. B. and C. D., honest and lawful men of my bailiwick, I have made known to the within-named J. S., that he be before the judges within named, at a day and place within contained, to show if any thing for himself he hath or knows to say, why, &c., [according to the writ,] as within I am commanded.

Or thus: "To show in manner and form as by this writ it is required." Or, "to do those things which by this writ are required."

Same as to Terre Tenants.

I, R. B., Esq., High Sheriff of the county of ——, to the judges in the writ hereunto annexed named, do certify, that by virtue of the said writ to me directed, and to this schedule annexed, by J. B. and L. M., honest and lawful men of my bailiwick, I have made known to J. B., tenant of one messuage, &c., with the appurtenances, situate, lying and being in ——, in the county aforesaid. And also to J. H., tenant of, &c., [naming the several tenants,] of which said lands and premises, the within-named R. B. was seised in his demesne, as of fee, on the —— day of ——, in the year, &c., (on which day judgment was rendered of the debt and damages within mentioned,) that they be before the judges aforesaid, at the day and place within contained, to show in manner and form as by this writ it is required. And I do also certify that there are no other tenants of any further or other lands or tenements, which were of the said R. B. at the time of the rendering of the judgment aforesaid, in my bailiwick, to whom I could make it known, as within I am commanded.

RETURNS BY CONSTABLE.

Constable's return to Court of Constable's Election.

To the Honourable the Judges of the Court of Quarter Sessions of the Peace of the County of Lancaster.

At an election held at the house of James Smith, of the township of ——, innkeeper, on Friday, the —— day of ——, instant, Simon Straub having one hundred and sixty-nine votes, and Samuel Steel having ninety votes, were duly elected to the office of constable of the said township for the ensuing year, certified by us at the township aforesaid, the —— day of ——, A. D. 1845.

J. M., *Constable of —— Township.*

R. C.,
S. W. } *Judges.*

Notice to Constables elected.

To Simon Straub and Samuel Steel, of the township of ——, in the County of Lancaster.

Take notice, that at an election held at the house of James Smith, of the township aforesaid, innkeeper, on Friday, the —— day of ——, instant, you were duly elected to the office of constable of the said township for the ensuing year. Given under my hand at —— township aforesaid, the —— day of ——, A. D. one thousand eight hundred and forty-five.

J. M., *Constable of —— Township.*

Constable's return to Court.

To the Honourable the Judges of the Court of Quarter Sessions of the Peace for the County of Lancaster.

J. M., constable of the township of ——, in the said county, makes his return to the said court, of a list of all the wholesale and retail dealers described in the Act of 7th April, 1830, dealing within the district and township aforesaid, as far as he can ascertain the same.

John Stark,
Elias Brown.

Lancaster County, *ss.*

J. M., constable as aforesaid, on his oath, says that the above return and list is just and true to the best of his knowledge and belief. J. M.

Sworn and subscribed before me this —— day of ——, 1845.
O. N. Justice.

Return of Constable on Domestic Attachment.

June 10, 1845, attached one colt, one cow, one bureau, two barrels of cider, &c. &c. Attached the same in the hands of A. B., of —— township, carpenter. So answers

J. M., *Constable of —— Township.*

☞ If the constable cannot find property of the defendant, he may return, "the defendant has no goods and chattels within the county whereby he can be attached." So answers, &c.

Return of Constable on Warrant.

The within-named Charles Dean is not found in my bailiwick. So answers J. M., *Constable of —— Township.*

Return of Constable on Warrant.

I have taken the within-named John Shaw, whose body I have ready, as within I am commanded. So answers

J. M., *Constable of —— Township.*

Return of Constable on a Warrant.

By virtue of this warrant to me directed, on the tenth day of June, instant, I took and arrested the within-named A. B., and safely kept him in my custody, until S. B., of —— township, and divers other persons, to me unknown, on the eleventh day of June, instant, at the township aforesaid, assaulted and ill treated me, and the said A. B. out of my custody then and there rescued. And afterwards the said A. B. is not found in my bailiwick. So answers J. M., *Constable of —— Township.*

Return of Constable on Warrant for Affray.

I have taken the within-named A. B., whose body I have ready, as within I am commanded; but the within-named C. D. is not found in my bailiwick. So answers

J. M., *Constable of —— Township.*

SUBPŒNA.

Remarks.

A subpœna is a process to cause a witness to appear and give testimony, commanding him to lay aside all pretences and excuses, and appear before a court or magistrate therein named, at a time therein mentioned, to testify for the party named, under a penalty therein mentioned. On proof of service of a subpœna upon the witness, and that he is material, an attachment may be issued against the witness for a contempt, if he neglects or refuses to attend as commanded.

Subpœna with clause of Duces Tecum.

Erie County, *ss.*

The Commonwealth of Pennsylvania to A. B., greeting: We command you, that setting aside all manner of business and excuses whatsoever, you be and appear in your proper person, before our judges at Erie, at our Court of Common Pleas for the County of Erie, there to be held the —— day of ——, 1845, at 10 o'clock in the forenoon of that day, to testify all and singular, those things which you shall know in a certain action now depending and undetermined, between C. D., plaintiff, and E. F., defendant, on the part of the plaintiff, and that you bring with you all and singular, the day books, ledgers, letter books, and all papers and documents whatever of the said C. D. And this you are not to omit under the penalty of one hundred pounds. Witness the honourable G. H., President of our said court at Erie, the —— day of ——, in the year of our Lord one thousand eight hundred and forty-five. W. K., *Prothonotary.*

Common Form, before Arbitrators.

Erie County, *ss.*

The Commonwealth of Pennsylvania to ——, greeting: We command you and each of you, that you be and appear in your proper persons, before A. B., C. D. and E. F., arbitrators, appointed to hear and decide all matters in variance, between the parties, in a certain action wherein G. H. is plaintiff and J. K. defendant, at the house of R. M., in the township of ——, on Thursday, the —— day of —— next, then and there to give evidence on the part of the plaintiff [or defendant, as the case may be]. Hereof fail not, under the penalty which may ensue. Witness my hand the —— day of ——, A. D. 1845.

C. D., *one of the Arbitrators.*

WILL.

Remarks.

A will or testament, is the legal declaration of a man's intentions of what he wills to be performed after his death. Co. Litt. 111; Shep. Touch. 399. The terms will and testament are generally used as synonymous. There are five essential requisites to make a good will. 1. The testator must be legally capable of making a will. 2. The testator, at the time of making his will, must have a serious intention to make such will, and not jestingly or boastingly. 3. The mind of the testator, in making his will, must be free, and not moved by fear, fraud or flattery. 4. There must be a person to take, capable of taking. 5. The will must be put in proper form. Wills are either written or nuncupative. A will in writing must be, 1st, written on paper or parchment, and it may be in any language. It is very important that the design of the testator be clearly expressed. 2d. It must be signed by the testator or some person authorized by him, but a sealing has been held to be a sufficient signature. 2 Str. 764. And it ought to be signed by the attesting witnesses. In some states three witnesses are required, who should sign the will as such, at the request and in the presence of the testator and of each other. This formality should generally be pursued, as the testator may have lands in such states, which would not pass without it. 3d.

It must be published, that is, the testator must do some act from which it can be concluded that he intended the instrument to operate as his will. 4th. To make a good will of goods and chattels, there must be an executor named in it; otherwise, it will be a codicil only, and the party is said to die intestate; in such a case, administration must be granted. Bac. Abr. Wills, D. 2. It is a rule that the last will revokes all former wills. A nuncupative will or testament, is a verbal declaration by a testator of his will before a competent number of witnesses. The Act of Assembly of Pennsylvania, 8th April, 1833, Pamph. L. p. 249, requires that every will shall be in writing, and signed by the testator, unless he be prevented by the extremity of his last sickness. There is a proviso, however, in favour of sailors, soldiers, &c. Much care should be taken in drafting wills, so that the wishes of the testator may be clearly expressed in proper terms. The want of that care causes most of the difficulties concerning them.

A form for a Will.

In the name of God, Amen. I, John Hook, of the city of Lancaster, in the Commonwealth of Pennsylvania, merchant, being in health of body [or weak in body, as the case may be,] and of sound mind, memory and understanding, praised be God for the same, do make this, my last will and testament in manner and form following:

I give, devise and bequeath, unto my beloved wife, Mary Hook, her heirs and assigns forever, all my property, real, personal and mixed, of what nature or kind soever, and wheresoever the same shall be at the time of my death.

And I do nominate, constitute and appoint my said wife sole executrix of this, my last will and testament, hereby revoking and making void all and every other will or wills at any time heretofore by me made, and do declare this to be my last will and testament.

In witness whereof, I, the said John Hook, have hereunto set my hand and seal this tenth day of January, in the year of our Lord one thousand eight hundred and forty-five.

Signed, sealed, declared and published by the above-named John Hook, as and for his last will and testament, in the presence of us, who, at his request, and in his presence, have subscribed our names as witnesses thereto.

JOHN EVANS,
WILLIAM SMITH.

JOHN HOOK.

Another form of a Will.

I, William Smith, of the city of Pittsburgh, in the County of Allegheny and Commonwealth of Pennsylvania, hatter, do make and publish this, my last will and testament, hereby revoking and making void all former wills by me at any time heretofore made. And first, I direct that my body be decently interred in the burying ground of the Episcopal Church of St. Paul's, in the said city, according to the rites and ceremonies of the said church, and that my funeral be conducted in a manner corresponding with my estate and situation in life. And as to such worldly estate as it hath pleased God to entrust me with, I dispose of the same as follows: First, I direct that all my debts and funeral expenses be paid as soon after my decease as possible, out of the first moneys that shall come into the hands of my executors, from any portion of my estate, real or personal: Also, I direct that a fair valuation or appraisement be made by three judicious neighbours, of all my said estate, including my household furniture, and after being signed with their names, that a copy of the same shall be given by them to each of my executors: Also, I direct that all my stock in trade be sold by public auction, for good current money, but not upon credit; and that all the real estate of which I shall die seised or possessed, shall be sold by my executors for its reasonable value, for like current money, or on such credit, and the amount thereof secured in such manner as is usual in like cases to insure the full and punctual payment thereof: And to effectuate this my intention, I do hereby vest in my executors full power and authority to dispose of my real estate, in fee simple, or for a term of years, or otherwise in as full and large a manner, in every respect, as I could myself do, if living: Also, I do direct that the whole of my household furniture [excepting such articles hereafter bequeathed to my several children, as the case may be] shall be and remain the absolute property of my beloved wife, if she shall be living at the time of my decease; but if she shall not survive me, then that the same shall be given absolutely to such of my daughters, then unmarried, as shall be then living, share and share alike, and to be apportioned by three impartial neighbours, mutually chosen by my said daughters for that purpose: Also, I do direct that the nett produce of my personal estate, heretofore ordered by me to be disposed of, be divided equally, as soon as it can be done, share and share alike, amongst my said wife, and my several children who shall survive me; and that the produce of the real estate, if sold on credit, shall be divided in like manner, as soon as it shall come into the hands of my executors; the heirs or representatives of any of my children, who shall have died between the time of my decease and the time of such division or distribution, to be entitled to such share or shares as their respective ancestors would have been entitled to receive, if then living; and the share of my real and personal estate, thus bequeathed to my wife, to be in lieu of her dower at common law, if she shall so elect. And I do hereby make and ordain my esteemed neighbours, Daniel Stone and Charles Dean, executors of this my last will and testament.

In witness whereof, I, Jonathan Francis Smith, the testator, have to this my will written on one sheet of paper, set my hand and seal, this first day of January, in the year of our Lord one thousand eight hundred and forty-five.

Signed, sealed, published and declared by the above-named Jonathan Francis Smith, as and for his last will and testament, in the presence of us, who have hereunto subscribed our names as witnesses thereto in the presence of the said testator, and at his request.

A. B.
C. D.

JONATHAN FRANCIS SMITH.

Another form of a Will.

In the name of God, Amen. I, A. B., of the county of Philadelphia, in the state of Pennsylvania, farmer, being weak in body, [or in perfect health of body, as the case may be,] and of sound mind, memory and understanding: but considering the uncertainty of this transitory life, do make and publish this, my last will and testament, in manner and form following, to wit:

First: It is my will, and I do order, that all my just debts and funeral expenses be duly paid and satisfied, as soon as conveniently can be after my decease.

Item: I give and bequeath unto my dear wife, D., one bed, one cow, &c., together with such of my household furniture, and kitchen utensils, as she may choose to keep for her own use.

Item: I give and bequeath unto my said wife, the use and occupation of my plantation, &c., until my son A. shall attain the age of 21 years, (she maintaining and educating my minor children thereout,) and from and after his arrival at such age, then I give and devise the said plantation, &c., unto my son A., his heirs and assigns forever; he or they paying thereout, unto my other children hereinafter named, the several sums of money, to them respectively bequeathed; and also paying unto my said wife, the sum of one hundred and fifty dollars (which sum I hereby bequeath to her) yearly, and every year, during her natural life, for her maintenance and support; all which legacies to my said wife I do hereby declare to be in lieu and stead of her dower, at common law. And, in case of the death of my said son A. before his arrival at the age aforesaid, then I do order and direct, that my executors, hereinafter named, or the survivor of them, shall, as soon as conveniently may be, after his decease, sell and dispose of my said plantation, &c., to such person or persons, and for such price or prices, as may be reasonably gotten for the same; and for that purpose, I do hereby authorize and empower my said executors, or the survivor of them, to sign, seal, execute and acknowledge, all such deed or deeds of conveyance, as may be requisite and necessary, for the granting and assuring the same to the purchaser or purchasers thereof, in fee simple: And the moneys arising from such sale, to put and place out to interest, on good security, for the payment of the said annuity hereby bequeathed to my said wife; the residue of the interest to be applied to the maintenance and education of such child, or children, as shall then be under age.

Item: I give and bequeath unto my son C. the sum of one hundred dollars, to be paid to him six months after my decease.

Item: I give and bequeath unto my daughter E the sum of one hundred dollars, to be paid to her on her arrival at the age of 21 years, or the day of her marriage, whichever shall first happen.

And, as touching all the rest, residue and remainder of my estate, real and personal, of what kind or nature, whatsoever the same may be, in the county of Philadelphia aforesaid, or elsewhere, I give and devise the same, unto my said wife, D., during her natural life; and from, and immediately after her decease, I give and devise the same unto my three children, A., C., and E., and to their heirs and assigns forever, to be equally divided among them.

And, lastly, I nominate, constitute and appoint my said wife, and my son A., to be the executors of this my will, hereby revoking all other wills, legacies and bequests, by me heretofore made, and declaring this, and no other, to be my last will and testament.

In witness whereof, I have hereunto set my hand and seal, the fourth day of July, one thousand eight hundred and forty-four.

Signed, sealed, declared and published, by the above-named A. B. as and for his last will and testament, in presence of us, who at his request and in his presence, have subscribed our names as witnesses thereto.

W. R.
J. D.

A. B.

Another form of a Will.

I, A. B., of the township of Amity, in the county of Berks, and state of Pennsylvania, do make and publish this my last will and testament, in manner and form following, that is to say:—

First: It is my will that my funeral shall be conducted without pomp, unnecessary parade or ostentation, and that the expenses thereof, together with all my just debts, be fully paid.

Second: I give, devise and bequeath to my beloved wife, M. B., in lieu of her dower, if she should so elect, the plantation on which we now reside, situate in the township aforesaid, and containing two hundred and ten acres, or thereabouts, during her natural life: And all the live-stock, horses, cattle, sheep, swine, &c., by me now owned and kept thereon: Also, all the household furniture and other items, not particularly named and otherwise disposed of, in this my will, during her said life; she, however, first disposing of a sufficiency thereof to pay my just debts, as aforesaid. And, that at the death of my said wife, all the property hereby devised or bequeathed to her, as aforesaid, or so much thereof, as may then remain unexpended, I give unto my three sons, F., W., and I., and to their heirs and assigns for ever.

Third: I give and devise to my eldest son, F. the farm on which he now resides, situate, &c., and containing one hundred and fifty acres, or thereabouts, and to his heirs and assigns for ever.

Fourth: I give and devise to my second son, W., the farm now in the occupancy of G. H., situate, &c., and containing one hundred and ten acres, to him, the said W., his heirs and assigns, in fee simple.

Fifth: I give and devise to my third son, I., the house and lot, in the borough of Reading, in the county and state aforesaid, now in the occupancy of I. K., known and designated in the plan of said borough, by No. 47, to him, the said I., his heirs and assigns for ever.

And last: I hereby constitute and appoint my said wife, M., and my said son F., to be the executrix and executor of this my last will and testament, hereby revoking and annulling all former wills by me made, and ratifying and confirming this, and no other, to be my last will and testament.

In testimony whereof I have hereunto set my hand and seal the tenth day of May, one thousand eight hundred and forty four.

Signed, published and declared by the above-named A. B., as and for his last will and testament, in presence of us, who, at his request, have signed as witnesses to the same.

M. S.
R. T.

A. B.

Codicil, or Supplement to a Will.

I, A. B., the within-named testator, do hereby make and publish this codicil, to be added to my last will and testament in manner following, to wit: I give and bequeath, &c.

And, whereas, in my said will, I have given and bequeathed unto my son C. (who is since deceased), the sum of one hundred dollars, to be paid to him six months after my decease, I do hereby declare that my will is, that the same be paid unto my daughter E. immediately after my decease. And lastly, it is my will and desire, that this, my present codicil, be annexed to and made a part of my last will and testament aforesaid. In witness whereof I have hereunto set my hand and seal, this tenth day of May, one thousand eight hundred and forty-five.

Signed, sealed, published and declared by the said A. B. as and for a codicil to his last will and testament, in the presence of us, who in his presence, and in the presence of each other, have, at his request, subscribed our names as witnesses thereto.
Q. R.
S. T.

A. B.

Another form of Codicil or Supplement to a Will.

This is a codicil, to be added to and taken as part of the last will and testament of me, A. B., which bears date the fourth day of July, 1837, whereby I do revoke the devise in my said will contained, to my son F., of all that farm, situate, &c., and containing one hundred and fifty acres, and do give and devise the same to my daughter C., her heirs and assigns for ever. I give and bequeath to my said son F., in lieu of the said farm the sum of four thousand dollars; and do hereby ratify and confirm my said will in all other respects. In witness whereof, I have hereunto set my hand and seal, this tenth day of September, 1845.

Signed, sealed, &c., as above.

A. B.

Clauses to be inserted in a Will.

Clause, forgiving Debts due from Relations.

And whereas there are considerable sums of money due and owing to me, upon bonds, bills and otherwise, from my relations hereinbefore named, it is my will and true meaning, and I do hereby direct, that the same bonds, bills, &c., immediately after my death, shall be canceled and destroyed by my said executors. And I do hereby discharge my aforesaid relations, and every of them, their and every of their heirs, executors and administrators, from the payment of every debt and debts due and owing to me or my estate, upon any account whatsoever, without any abatement or deduction from or out of their legacies, before by me given or devised to them respectively, in and by this my last will and testament.

Proviso, in case a Wife should sue for Dower and Thirds.

Provided further, and my will expressly is, that in case my said wife D. shall not accept of the provisions and legacies hereinbefore by me made and given her as aforesaid, and shall, at any time or times hereafter, prosecute any action or suit for dower, thirds, or any other part of my estates, real or personal, other than what I have so hereinbefore devised and given her, then and in that case, the several annuities of ——, and amounting together to ——, and each of them, and all other legacies and bequests, hereby by me before given, or intended her, shall cease and be void, to all intents and purposes, any thing to the contrary notwithstanding.

To make void Limitations where persons dispute the Validity of a Will.

Provided always, and I do hereby declare my will to be, that if any person or persons, to whom any estate or interest is given or limited, by this my will, shall, in any court of law or equity, or otherwise, controvert the same, or dispute or call in question the validity thereof, or of any of the estates, limitations, powers, provisos, or dispositions, hereby limited, or given, or made, or herein contained, then, and in such case the estates, interests, limitations, &c., so hereby limited, &c., to or in favour of such person or persons, so controverting my said will, shall cease, determine, and be absolutely void, to all intents and purposes whatsoever, as if such person or persons was or were naturally dead: And then, and from thenceforth, such estates, interests, limitations, powers, provisos, and dispositions, shall go, and belong to, and be vested in the person or persons, who, by virtue of this my will, shall be next in remainder, after the person or persons so disputing as aforesaid. *Provided* he, she, or they shall not controvert or dispute the validity of this my will, or any of the devises, limitations, powers, provisos, or dispositions herein contained, or hereby made.

Clause concerning Disputes.

My express will and desire is, that if any difference or dispute, question or controversy, shall arise or happen concerning any gift, bequest, or other matter or thing in this my will, the same shall be referred wholly to the award, order and determination of my esteemed neighbours, R. S. and T. V., with power for them to choose an umpire; but if they or either of them should not be able or willing to act in the premises, then I do direct that my eldest son and eldest daughter shall each appoint an arbitrator or arbitrators, with the same power of choosing an umpire; and what they or a majority of them shall order, direct or determine therein, shall be binding and conclusive, to and on all and every person and persons therein concerned.

Clause as to Guardianship of Children.

And in case I shall leave any child or children living at the time of my decease, my will is, and I do appoint, that my said dear wife shall have the guardianship and tuition of them during their minority so long as she shall continue to be sole; and, in case of her death or marriage, during the minority of such my children, then I will and appoint that my much esteemed and loving friend John Williamson shall have the tuition and guardianship of them during such their minority; and in case of his refusal, renunciation, or decease, I will that my other executor, James Richards, shall exercise the said guardianship; and I earnestly entreat their utmost care, respectively, in and about the morals and education of my children, if any such shall happen to be, and to survive me; and desire that they may be brought up and instructed in the doctrines and religion of the ——— church.

Conclusion and Attestation of a Will written on several sheets.

I do hereby make, ordain, constitute and appoint A. B. and C. D. executors of this my last will and testament, hereby revoking all former wills, by me at any time heretofore made, and do declare this to be my last will and testament. In witness whereof, I, the said J. S., have to this my last will and testament, contained in this and the four preceding sheets (or skins of parchment), set my hand and seal, to wit, my hand to the bottom of each of the said four sheets (or skins) and my hand and seal to this last sheet (or skin) and my seal at the top of the said sheets (or skins) where all the said sheets (or skins) are fixed together, this —— day of ——, one thousand eight hundred and forty-four.

The writing contained in this and the four preceding sheets (or skins) was signed and sealed by the above-named J. S., and by him published and declared as and for his last will and testament, in the presence of us, who have hereunto subscribed our names in his presence, and in the presence of each other.

N. S.
T. B.
G. H.

Renunciation of Executorship.

Know all men by these presents, that I, D. B., of, &c., widow, executrix named in the last will and testament of A. B., late of the same place, yeoman, have renounced, released and quit claimed, and by these presents do renounce, release and quit claim, all my right and title to the said executorship, and to the administration of the goods and chattels, rights and credits whatsoever, which were of the said deceased; and desire that the same may be committed to my son, H. B., or to such person or persons as may be entitled thereto. In witness, &c.

Release of right to Administration, by Widow.

To I. A., Esquire, Register for the Probate of Wills and granting Letters of Administration, in and for the county of Berks.

Whereas my late husband, A. B., died intestate, whereby the right of the administration of the estate of the said deceased did devolve upon me, D. B., widow and relict of the said deceased: Now know ye, that for divers good causes and considerations me thereunto moving, I have released, and hereby do release, all my right and title to the administration of the said estate. Witness my hand and seal the first day of March, Anno Domini, one thousand eight hundred and thirty-seven.

M. B. [L.S.]

Appointment of a Guardian by a Father for his Son.

Know all men by these presents, that I, Andrew Brown, of the city of Norfolk, and state of Virginia, tanner, have committed and disposed, and by these presents do commit and dispose, unto Paul Davidson, of the said city, the custody, tuition, and education of my son Robert Brown, from and immediately after my decease, until my said son shall attain the age of twenty-one years; and if it shall happen that the said Paul Davidson dies before me, or before my said son attains the age of twenty-one years, then and in such case I do commit and dispose unto Isaac Donaldson, of ——, such custody, tuition, and education after my decease, and the decease of the said Paul Davidson, until my said son attains the age of twenty-one years, and desire the said Isaac Donaldson to take upon him the trouble for the good of my said son.

☞ Till the age of twenty-one years, the empire of the father continues even after his death; for he may, by deed or will, appoint a guardian to any of the children unmarried, until such child attain the age of twenty-one, or for any less time.—*Black. Com.* 462.

Nuncupative Wills.

The will of A. B., of ——, made and declared by him on the —— day of ——, &c., at the house of ——, No. — in —— street, in the city of Philadelphia, being then and until and after his decease, his habitation or dwelling, where he had resided for the space of —— days, &c., next before the making of his said will in the presence of us, who have hereunto subscribed our names, as witnesses hereto. "My will is," &c., [recite the very words.] These words or the like effect, the said deceased declared in the presence of the witnesses whose names are hereunto subscribed, with an intention that the same should stand for and be his last will and testament, and he, the said A. B., bid the witnesses or some of them, to bear witness that such was his last will.

C. D.
E. F.

Proviso,—that if the estate prove insufficient to pay all legacies, the legatees to sustain loss equally.

And my further will is that in case the said several legacies or sums of two hundred dollars each hereinbefore given and made payable to my said three children in manner aforesaid, shall by reason or on account of any debt or debts due and owing, or which may hereafter grow due and owing to my personal estate, or by any other losses, misfortunes or means whatsoever, my said estate shall prove or become insufficient to answer and pay to my said three children, or any of them, their respective full legacies of

before directed and appointed for the payment thereof, then and in such case I do hereby order, will, direct and appoint, that all such losses or deficiencies so happening to my said estate, shall be borne and sustained by all and every my said three children, who shall then be entitled to the said legacies of two hundred dollars each, and that in equal proportions, share and share alike, any thing in this my will contained to the contrary thereof in any wise notwithstanding.

WRIT OF ERROR.

Precedents to obtain Writ of Error to the Supreme Court of Pennsylvania.

Precipe.

A. B., plaintiff in error and plaintiff below [or defendant below, as the case may be]
vs.
C. D., defendant in error and defendant below [or plaintiff below, as the case may be].

Issue writ of error to the Court of Common Pleas of Erie County, returnable to September and October Term, 1845.

E. F.,
Att'y for Plaintiff in Error.

December 10, 1844.

A. L. Pentland, Esq., Proth'y., Western Dis. Supreme Court, Pa.

Affidavit.

Erie County, *ss.*

A. B., the above-named plaintiff in error, being duly sworn according to law, deposeth and saith that the writ of error in this case is not intended for delay.

Sworn and subscribed the —— day of ——, A. D., 1844, before me.

☞ The oath may be made by the agent or attorney, by Act of Assembly of the 11th June, 1832.

Recognizance.

Erie County, *ss.*

A. B., G. H. and J. K., each acknowledges himself to owe and stand indebted to C. D. in the sum of —— dollars, to be levied of their goods and chattels, lands and tenements respectively, upon this condition, that the above-named A. B., plaintiff in error, prosecute his writ of error with effect, or in default thereof will pay the costs and condemnation money, together with the costs of this writ of error.

Taken and acknowledged the 10th day of December, 1844, before me.

☞ In order to operate as a supersedeas to an execution, it is necessary there should be two sureties in the recognizance.

A GLOSSARY

OF

TECHNICAL LAW TERMS.

A

Ab initio.—From the beginning.

Actor.—A Plaintiff.

Ad finem litis.—To the conclusion of the suit.

Ad hominem.—"To the person." This is used as meaning an argument touching the prejudice or qualities of the person addressed.

Ad idem.—"To the same." To the like intent.

Ad infinitum.—"To eternity." To the utmost.

Ad inquirendum.—To make inquiry.

Ad libitum.—At pleasure: at will.

Ad litem.—To (or in) the suit or (controversy).

Ad matrimonium colendum.—To contract matrimony.

Ad medium filum aquæ.—To the middle line of the water.

Administrator de son tort.—Administrator in his own wrong.

Ad pios usus.—For pious purposes.

Ad sectam.—At the suit of.

Affidare.—To plight one's faith, or give, or swear fealty, i. e., fidelity.

Affrayer.—To terrify.

A fortiori.—By so much the stronger; by a more powerful reason.

Agalma.—The impression, or image on a seal.

A gratia.—From (or by) favour.

Alias ca. sa.—Another writ to take (the person) to make satisfaction.

Alias scire facias.—"That you again cause to be informed." A second writ of *scire facias.*

Alibi.—"In another place."

Alibi natus.—Born in another place.

A mensa et thoro.—"From bed and board." A divorce between husband and wife, which does not make the marriage void, *ab initio,* or from the beginning.

Ancient demesne.—An ancient inheritance.

Animalia feræ naturæ.—Animals of a wild nature.

Annates.—First fruits.

Apprendre.—To learn—whence the word "apprentice."

A prendre.—To take—to seize.

A priori.—From the former.

Arbiter.—An arbitrator.

Arrester.—To stay: to arrest.

Assumpsit.—He undertook (or promised).

Assumpsit pro rata.—He undertook agreeably to the proportion.

Autre droit.—Another's right.

A vinculo matrimonii.—From the bond of marriage.

B

Banco.—"In bench." As "*dies in banco,*" or days in which the court sits.

Bancus ruptus.—"A broken bank." From which the word "Bankrupt."

Barat.—"A quarrel," a dispute. From which the word "Barratry."

Baron et feme.—The husband and wife.

Basileus.—A king: a governor.

Billa vera.—A true bill.

Bona.—Goods: personal estate. Lord Coke says this word includes all chattels, as well real as personal. Co. Lit. 118, 6. It is, however, generally used to designate movable property.

Bona fide.—In good faith.

Bona fidei.—Of good faith, or credit.

Bonus.—A consideration given for what is received: a premium paid to a grantor or vendor.

Botes.—Wood cut off a farm by the tenant for the purposes of repairing dwelling-houses, barns, fencing, &c., which the common law allows him, without any prior agreement made for that purpose.

C

Camera stellata.—"The star chamber." An odious court once held in England, but many years since abolished.

Capias.—"You may take." A writ authorizing the defendant's arrest.

Capias ad computandum.—That you take (defendant) to make account.

Capias ad respondendum.—That you take (defendant) to make answer.

Capias ad satisfaciendum.—That you take (defendant) to make satisfaction.

Capias ad valentiam.—That you take to the value.

Capias in withernam.—That you take a reprisal.

Capas pro fine.—That you take for a fine.

Causa causans.—The moving cause.

Causa impotentiæ.—On account of impotence.

Causa mortis.—On account of death: in prospect of death.

Caveat.—That he beware: a warning.

Cepi corpus.—I have taken the body.

Certiorari.—"To be certified of: to be informed of." A writ directing the proceedings, or record of a cause, to be brought before a superior court.

Cestui que trusts.—Persons for whose use another is seised of lands, &c.

Cestui que use.—A person for whose use land, &c., be given or granted.

Cestui que vies.—Persons for whose lives a gift or grant is made.

Chose in action.—A thing in action.

Clausum fregit.—He broke the close, or field.

Cognovit actionem.—"He has acknowleged the action." After suit brought, the defendant frequently confesses the action; judgment is then entered on the record without trial: or the defendant signs an instrument called a *cognovit.*

Committitur.—He, or she is committed.

Compensatio criminis.—A compensation for crime.

Compos mentis.—"Of sound mind." A man in such a state of mind as to be qualified legally to sign a will, or deed, &c.

Connubium.—Matrimony between citizens.

Consanguinei.—Relations.

Contra bonos mores.—Against good morals.

Corpora cepi.—I have taken the bodies.

Covert.—Married.

Crim. con.—Illicit connection (adultery).

D

Damage feasant.—Doing damage.

Data—"Things granted." We must proceed on certain "*data,*" that is, on matters previously admitted to be correct.

Datum.—A thing granted: a point fixed upon: a first principle.

De bene esse.—Conditionally.

Debet et detinet.—He owes and detains.

De bonis non.—Of goods not (administered).

De bonis non administrandis.—Of goods unadministered.

Decemviri.—"Ten men." They were appointed to compose the twelve tables of the laws for the *Roman* people.

De clauso facto.—Of a close made.

De clauso fracto.—Of a close broken.

De corpore suo.—Of his own body.

De die in diem.—From day to day.

De facto.—Of the deed: in fact.

Defeasance.—A conditional undertaking to annul the effect of a bond, &c.

De gratia.—As a matter of grace or favour.

De jure—de facto.—"From the law: from the fact." Sometimes an offender is guilty the moment the wrong is committed—then he may be said to be guilty "*de facto.*" In other cases he is not guilty until he be convicted *by law,* then he is guilty "*de jure.*"

Delictum.—A fault, offence or crime.

De novo.—Anew: afresh.

De præsenti.—Of the present time.

Dernier resort.—The last resort.

Desiderata.—Requisites.

De son don.—Of his gift.

De son tort.—"Of his own wrong." This was part of a plea very similar to *son assault demesne.*

Detinet.—He keeps: he detains.

Detinuit.—He has detained.

De ultra mari.—Of (the matter) beyond sea.

Devastavit.—He wasted.

Devastavit, nolens volens.—He wantonly (or wickedly) committed waste.

De vasto facto.—Of waste committed.

Dicta.—Sayings: remarks: observations.

Dies amoris.—The days of grace: the Essoin days.

Dies communis in banco.—The common (or usual) day in bank.

Dies in banco.—"Days in bank." Days on which the courts sit to hear motions in arrest of judgment; for new trials, &c.

Domesday—or *Domesday Book*—A book, showing the tenures, &c., of most of the lands in England, in the time of William the Conqueror.

Domitæ naturæ.—Of a tame nature.

Donatio.—A gift: a donation.

Droit des gens.—The law of nations.

Duces tecum.—"That you bring with you."

[A subpœna so called when the person is commanded to produce books, papers, &c., to the court and jury.]

Dum fuit non compos mentis.—Whilst he (or she) was of unsound mind.

E

Eat sine die.—Let him go without day (or be discharged).

E converso.—On the other hand: on the contrary.

Elegit.—"He has chosen." A judicial writ directed to the sheriff, empowering him to seize one moiety of the defendant's lands for damages recovered.

Ensient per A.—Pregnant by A.

En ventre sa mere.—In the womb.

Error coram nobis.—Error (lying) before us.

Eruditus in lege.—"Learned in the law." A counsel.

Escrow.—A deed or writing left with another, to be delivered on the performance of something specified.

Essoiner.—To excuse.

Estoppel.—"A stop:" a preventive plea.

Estovers.—Wood cut from a farm by the tenant, which by the common law he

Et non alibi.—And in no other place.
Excerpta.—Extracts.
Ex contractu.—By way of agreement.
Ex curia.—Out of court.
Ex delicto.—By (or from) a fault or offence.
Executor de son tort.—"An executor of his own wrong:" one who acts illegally in the office.
Ex facto.—From (or by) the deed.
Ex justa causa.—For a good reason (or cause).
Ex lex.—An outlaw.
Ex officio.—Officially: by virtue of the office.
Exoneretur nunc pro tunc.—Let him (or it) be now discharged, instead of at some past time.
Ex parte materna.—On the part of the mother.
Ex parte paterna.—On the part of the father.
Ex parte quærentis.—On the part of the plaintiff.
Ex post facto.—From (or by) an after act.
Ex relatione.—"By, or from, relation." Sometimes the words mean "*by the information.*"
Ex tempore.—Out of hand (without delay, or premeditation).
Ex visitatione Dei.—From the visitation of God.

F

Facias.—That you do (or cause to be done).
Fac simile.—Do the like: a close imitation.
Falsare curiam.—To deceive the court.
Felo de se.—A suicide: a self-murderer.
Feme covert.—A married woman.
Feme sole.—An unmarried woman.
Feme sole sub modo.—A single woman, to a certain extent.
Feoffare.—To enfeoff: or grant in fee.
Feræ naturæ.—Of a wild nature.
Feudum.—A fee: land held in fee simple.
Fiat.—Let it be done.
Fief.—"A fee." What we call a fee, is in other countries, the contrary to *chattels.* In Germany, certain districts or territories are called "*Fiefs,*" where there are *Fiefs* of the Empire.
Fieri.—To be made, or done.
Fieri Facias.—That you cause to be made, or done; or levied. A writ of execution so called.
Filum aquæ.—The middle of the water (or stream).
Flotsam.—Goods floating on the sea.
Forma legalis.—A legal form.
Forum.—A court, or place of justice.
Franchise.—A privilege, or exemption.
Frank-almoign.—A free gift.

G

Gavelkind.—A peculiar tenure of land.
Generosus.—A gentleman.
Gleaning.—*Leasing*, or *Lesing*, from "*glainer,*" i. e., gathering loose corn in the fields after reaping.
Guardian ad litem.—A guardian in the suit.

H

Habeas corpora.—That you have the bodies.
Habeas corpus.—"That you have the body." The great writ of the people's liberty.

Habeas corpus ad respondendum.—That you have the body to answer.

Habeas corpus ad satisfaciendum.—That you have the body to make satisfaction.

Habeas corpus ad testificandum.—That you have the body to give evidence.

arrested).

Habendum et tenendum.—To have and to hold.

Hiatus.—An opening: a chasm.

Hospitia curiæ.—Inns of court.

Hospitium.—An Inn.

I

Idem dies.—The same day: a like day.

Idem per idem.—Like by like.

Ignoramus.—"We are ignorant." A word written on a bill of indictment when the evidence is insufficient to put the accused on his trial.

Imparlance.—A time granted by the court for the defendant to plead.

Imperium in imperio.—"One government within another:" which has been wittily expressed "a power behind the throne." Some power acting irresponsibly within the government, but not always discernible.

Impetere.—To impeach—to sue—to attach.

In abstracto.—In the abstract.

In articulo mortis.—At the point of death.

In autre droit.—In right of another.

In banco Regis.—In the King's Bench.

In capite.—In chief. Lands held "*in capite*" are those held of the chief lord of the fee.

Incipitur.—It is begun.

In colloquio.—In a discourse.

In delicto.—In an offence: or in default.

In dominio suo.—In his demesne; or lordship.

In dorso—On the back.

In dubiis.—In doubtful cases.

In esse.—In being.

In eventu.—In the end, or event.

In extenso.—At large: to the extent.

In extremis.—In the last moments; near death.

Infeudare.—To enfeoff: grant in fee.

In infinitum.—To infinity—time without end.

In loco hæredis.—In the place of the heir.

In loco parentum.—In the place of the parents.

In mortua manu.—In mortmain: in a dead hand or possession.

In omnibus.—In all things.

In pais.—In the country.

In pari delicto.—In a like offence (or crime).

In personam.—To or against the person.

In pios usus.—For pious purposes.

In pleno comitatu.—In full assembly of the county: in full county court.

In potestate parentis.—In the power of the parent.

In præsenti.—At the present time.

In proprio jure.—In (his) proper (or peculiar) right.

In propria persona.—In his own person: in personal attendance.

In puris naturalibus.—In a state of nature.

In rem.—To, or against the property. To the point.

In rerum naturâ.—In the nature (or order) or things.

Inscriptum.—An indorsement.

Instar dentium.—"Like teeth"— similar to the top of an ancient indenture, that word being, as supposed, derived from "*instar dentium.*"

In stirpes.—To the stock or lineage.

Insultus.—An assault.

In suo jure.—In his own right.

2 D

Insurrectio populi.—An insurrection of the people.
Inter mœnia.—Within the walls: within the domicile.
Inter nos.—Between ourselves: that is (*inter nos*) to keep a secret.
Interregnum.—A space between two reigns.
Interregnum quare clausum fregit?—In the mean time why did he break the close?
In terrorem.—By way of terror (or warning).
In toto.—In the whole: altogether: entirely.
In transitu.—"In the passage." Merchandize is said to be "*in transitu*," while on its way to the consignee.
In vadio.—In pledge.
In ventre sa mere.—In its mother's womb.
Ipso facto.—By the fact itself: positively.
Ipso jure.—By the law itself—or by that right.
Ita lex scripta.—So the law is written.

J

Jetsam.—Goods thrown into the sea.
Jura in re.—Rights in the matter, or thing.
Jura personarum.—The rights of persons.
Jura rerum.—The rights of things.
Jure divino.—By right divine.
Jure gentium.—By the law of nations.
Jure humano.—By human law (or right).
Jure mariti.—In right of the husband.
Jure naturæ.—By the law of nature.
Jure uxoris.—In right of the wife.
Jus ad rem.—A right to the property.
Jus civile.—The civil (or municipal law).
Jus in re.—The right in the property.
Jus suum.—His own right.

L

Laches.—Neglect: supineness.
Lacta.—"A defect in the weight of money:" whence probably comes the word "Lack."
Levari facias.—That you cause to be levied.
Levari facias de bonis.—That you cause to be levied of the goods.
Lex.—"The Law." This word among the ancient Romans, was often taken in the same general sense as *Jus* (Right). When we find *Lex* put *absolutely*, the law of the Twelve Tables is meant.
Lex fori.—The law of the court.
Lex non scripta.—The unwritten, or common law: that which has been received from time immemorial by tradition.
Lex scripta.—The written or statute law.
Lex talionis.—The law of requital in kind: "An eye for an eye," &c., as in the Mosaic law.
Libelli famosi.—Libels: infamous writings.
Libellus sine scriptis.—An unwritten libel.
Liber homo.—A free man.
Loco parentis.—In the place of the parent.

M.

Magna Charta.—The Great Charter: the bulwark of English liberty.
Mala fide.—In bad fai
Mala in se.—Things bad, or wicked, in themselves.
Mala prohibita.—Wrongs forbidden (by common law).
Malfeasance.—Doing wrong: a bad act.
Malo animo.—With a bad intent.

Malum in se.—Bad in itself: wrong in its own nature.
Malum prohibitum.—A prohibited offence.
Mandamus.—"We command." A peremptory writ, issued for many purposes.
Manu forti.—With a strong hand: by violence.
Mesne.—"Middle: intervening." The middle between two extremes, and that either in time, or dignity.
Meum et tuum.—Mine and thine.
Misfeasance.—A misdeed.
Modo et forma.—In manner and form.
Moot.—Doubtful: a term anciently used in the Inns of Court.
Mortis causa.—The occasion of death.
Mortmain—Manus mortua.—A dead hand, or an unchangeable possession.
Mulier.—"A woman." Generally applied to married women.
Mutatus mutandis.—The necessary changes.

N

Narratio.—Often abbreviated *Narr'.* A declaration: a count.
Naufrage.—Shipwreck.
Nihil debet.—He is not indebted.
Nihil dicit.—He says nothing.
Nil debet.—"He owes nothing." The usual plea in an action of debt.
Nil debet in assumpsit.—He is not indebted in (the action of) assumpsit.
Nil dicit.—He says nothing.
Nisi Prius.—"Unless before." These words generally designate the proceedings before a judge and jury in a suit at law, either at, or after the sittings of a term, or upon the circuit.
Nolens volens.—Willing or unwilling.
Nolle prosequi.—"To be unwilling to proceed." Generally used in criminal cases, when further proceedings are discontinued.
Non cepit.—He did not take.
Non compos mentis.—Not of sound mind: in a delirium of lunacy.
Non damnificatus.—Not damnified: not injured.
Non debet.—He does not owe.
Non est inventus.—"He is not found." The return made by a sheriff when the defendant is not found in his county.
Nonfeasance.—Non-performance.
Non pros'.—He will not prosecute.
Non prosequitur.—He does not proceed: he is nonsuited.
Non sum informatus.—I am not informed: I am ignorant.
Non tenuit.—He did not occupy (or hold).
Nudum pactum.—A bare (or naked) contract: one not binding in law.
Nul assets ultra.—No further effects.
Nulla bona.—No effects.
Nul tiel corporation.—No such corporation.
Nul tiel record.—"No such record." This is part of the plaintiff's rejoinder, that there is no such record; where the defendant alleges matter of record in bar of the plaintiff's action.
Nul tort.—"No wrong." A plea in a real action, that *no wrong* was done, and is a species of the general issue.
Nunc pro tunc.—"Now for that time." These words are frequently used in legal or equitable proceedings, where something is permitted to be done "*eo instanti,*" which should have been performed some time before.

O

On dit.—A loose report.
Ouster.—A dispossession.
Overt.—Open: public.
Oyer et terminer.—To hear and determine.

P

Parole.—Verbally.

Per annum: per diem.—By the year: by the day.

Per autre vie.—For the life of another.

Per capita.—"By the heads or polls:" a division share and share alike.

Per duellum.—By single combat.

Per se.—By himself, herself, or itself.

Per stirpes.—By stock: by lineage.

Per totam curiam.—By the whole court.

Per verba de futuro.—By words of future acceptation.

Per verba de præsenti.—By words of the present time.

Per viam ellemosynæ.—By way of charity, or alms.

Pie poudre.—The pie powder court. This is a court held at some of the great fairs, in England, where justice is administered *instantly*, even whilst the *dust is fresh upon the feet* of the suitors.

Plagium.—Man stealing; or enticing away men and children.

Plena fides.—Full credit.

Pluries.—"Very often." Also the name of a third writ, after two have issued against a defendant.

Pone.—"Put." The name of a writ or process in replevin.

Posse comitatus.—"The power of the county," which the sheriff is authorized to call out, whenever an opposition is made to his writ, or to the execution of justice.

Post diem.—After the day.

Postea.—"Afterwards." The name given to the endorsement of the verdict made on the record.

Post-mortem.—After the death.

Post nati.—After-born.

Post obit.—After the death.

Post terminum.—After the term.

Præcipe.—Command.

Præcipe in capite.—A writ of right so called.

Prætor.—A Magistrate: a Consul: a Judge among the ancient Romans.

Prætor fidei commissarius.—The Judge among the ancient Romans, who compelled the performance of trusts: and who appears to have had, in this respect, a similar office to our Chancellors.

Prendre.—To take.

Prima facie.—On the first view or appearance of the business.

Prochein ami.—The nearest friend.

Proprio jure.—In its proper right.

Proprio vigore.—In full force (or effect).

Pro rata.—According to the rate, proportion or allowance.

Pro tanto.—For so much.

Pur autre vie.—For the life of another.

Q

Quantum maximum.—Far the greatest.

Quantum valebat.—As much as it was worth.

Quare clausum fregit?—Wherefore (or why) did he break the close?

Quasi ex contractu.—In nature of a contract.

Quasi ex delicto.—As of an offence (or crime).

Quid pro quo.—A mutual consideration.

Quoad hoc.—With respect to this.

Quo animo?—With what intent?

Quod detinuit.—Which he (or she) detains.

Quo warranto.—"By what authority." The name of a writ against a person who has usurped a franchise, or an office.

Recordare.—To remember (to record).
Rectus in curia.—"Untainted in court." With clean hands.
Reddendum.—To pay: to yield: to render: the reservation of rent, &c., in a deed.
Registrum.—A registry: a place for depositing wills, deeds, &c.
Remitter.—To restore (or send back).
Replegiari facias.—That you cause to be replevied.
Rescous.—A rescue.
Residuum. "The remainder." Frequently applied to that part of the testator's estate not specially disposed of.
Res integra.—An entire (new, or untouched) matter.
Respondentia.—Bottomry.
Respondere non debet.—He ought not to answer.
Responsa prudentum.—The opinions of learned men.
Retorna brevium. The return of writs.
Reversetur.—Let it be reversed.

S

Sacrare.—To outlaw.
Sacrilegium.—Sacrilege. Also any detestable or odious crime.
Sans issue.—Without children.
Scandalum magnatum.—The scandal against the peerage.
Scienter.—Knowingly: wilfully.
Scintilla.—A tittle: a spark.
Scire facias.—That you make known. This is the name of a writ for many purposes, commanding the defendant to show cause why a certain specific thing should not be done, as why execution should not issue on an old judgment, &c.
Scire fieri.—To be informed.
Secta.—A suit: litigation: also the pledges produced that the plaintiff should prosecute his claim.
Secundis ventis.—With favourable winds.
Sed per curiam.—But by the court.
Semble.—It seems.
Sequestrari facias.—That you cause to be sequestered.
Sine die.—"Without day"—as the court adjourned "*sine die*"—no day being mentioned for sitting again.
Sine qua non.—An indispensable condition.
Soccagium.—"Socage." This was a tenure by which considerable estates were held under the feudal system. The tenants performed husbandry, &c., for the superior lord of the fee.
Son assault.—His own assault.
Sparsim.—Scattered about: in several places.
Sponsalia.—Marriage contracts.
Sponsio judicialis.—A judicial agreement.
Sponsiones ludicræ.—Ridiculous answers.
Stirps.—The stock: lineage: race.
Stricti juris.—Of strict right (or law).
Suaviter in modo fortiter in re.—Gentle in the manner, but vigorous in the execution.
Sub finem.—Under a penalty.
Sub modo.—Under a condition: within bounds.
Subpœna.—"Under a penalty." A writ so called to procure the attendance of witnesses.
Subpœna ad testificandum.—A subpœna to give evidence.
Subpœna duces tecum.—"Bring with you under a penalty." The name of a writ, by which a witness is commanded to produce something in his possession, to be given in evidence.
Sub potestate parentis.—Under the authority of the parent.

Sub potestate viri.—Under the control of the husband.
Subsidium justitiæ.—An aid to justice.
Sub spe reconciliationis.—In the hope of reconciliation.
Suggestio falsi.—A suggestion (or incitement) to falsehood, or wrong.
Sui generis.—"Of its own kind." Not to be classed under any ordinary description.
Sui juris.—Of his own right.
Supersedeas.—"You may remove or set aside." A writ so called to stay proceedings.
Supra protest.—An acceptance of a bill after protest.
Sur la pie.—At the foot.
Sur rebut.—Upon rebutter.
Sur rejoin.—Upon rejoinder.
Sursum redditio.—A surrender: a yielding back.
Sur trover, et conversion.—Upon trover, and conversion.

T

Tenendum.—"To hold." That clause in a deed wherein the tenure of the land is created, and limited.
Terminus.—The end, limit or boundary: sometimes it means the stock or root, to which, by reference, the future succession is to be regulated.
Terre tenant.—The tenant who occupies the land: he who has the actual possession.
Tertia.—The third part: the ancient term for dower.
Testari.—To be witnessed.
Testatum.—It is testified.
Testatum capias.—That you take the person testified (or to have been proceeded against elsewhere).
Testatum fieri facias.—That you cause the testified writ to be executed.
Testatum pluries.—A testified process issued more than twice.
Teste.—The date: the supposed issuing of process.
Tort.—A wrong: an injury.
Tort-feasor.—A wrong doer: a trespasser.
Tout ensemble.—The whole together.
Tresor trouvé.—"Treasure trove, or found." Money or property found, of which no person makes a claim within a year and a day; it
the lord of the manor.
Trespass, quare clausum fregit.—Trespass, wherefore he broke the close.
Trespass vi et armis, de uxore rapta et abducta.—Trespass with force and arms, concerning a wife taken and carried away.
Triens.—A third part: an ancient term for dower.
Trina admonitio.—The third summons.

U

Ubi supra.—"Where above mentioned." A reference to the preceding subject.
Ultimum supplicium.—The last atonement: death.
Ultra mare.—Beyond sea.
Usance.—Usury: interest.

V

Vacatur.—It is set aside: vacated.
Venditioni exponas.—That you expose to sale.
Venditor.—A seller.
Venire.—To come.
Venire ad respondendum.—To come to make answer.
Venire de novo.—To come anew.
Venue.—The place from which the jury come.

Vouchee.—The person vouched in a writ of right, &c.

Voucher.—A word of art when the tenant in a writ of right, calls another into the court, who is bound to him to *warranty;* and is either to defend the right against the demandant, or yield him other lands to the value.

APPENDIX.

PRECEDENTS FOR PROCEEDINGS IN ADMIRALTY COURTS.

Remarks.

Admiralty is the name of a jurisdiction which takes cognizance of transactions and proceedi
upon the sea.

The Constitution of the United States has conferred upon the Courts of the National Government, cognizance "of all cases of Admiralty and Maritime jurisdiction." The Act of Congress of September 24th, 1789, has given the District Courts of the United States "cognizance of all civil causes of Admiralty and Maritime jurisdiction," including all seizures under laws of imposts, navigation or trade of the United States, where the seizures are made on waters navigable from the sea, by vessels of ten or more tons burthen, within their respective districts, as well as upon the high seas. For further information see Dunlap's Admiralty Practice; Bett's Adm. Practice; Hall's Adm. Pr.; 1 Kent's Com. 353 to 380; 2 Gall. R. 398 to 476; 2 Chit. Pr. 508; Bac. Ab. Courts of Adm.; Story's L. U. S., vol. 1st, 56, 60; 2 do. 905; 3 do. 1564, 1696; 4 Sharswood Con. of Story's L. U.S., 2262; 1 U. S., Dig. tit. Admiralty Courts, and other works on that subject.

Libel for Mariners' Wages, with a Claim and Answer.

UNITED STATES OF AMERICA, EASTERN DISTRICT OF PENNSYLVANIA, *ss.*

——— Term, 18—.

To the Honourable ARCHIBALD RANDALL, *Judge of the District Court of the United States, in and for the Eastern District of Pennsylvania.*

The libel and complaint of A. B., of ———, late mariner of the ship ———, whereof C. D. now is or late was master, *against the said ship, her tackle, apparel and furniture, and against all persons lawfully intervening for their interest therein,* in a cause of subtraction of wages, civil and maritime.* And thereupon the said A. B. alleges and articulately propounds as follows:

* If the libel be *in personam,* it should commence as follows:

"The libel and complaint of A. B., of ——, late mariner of the ship ——, whereof C. D., of ——, now is or lately was master [or owner, as the case may be], *against the said C. D.,* in a cause of substraction of wages, civil and maritime," &c.

If the libel be *in personam* and *in rem,* it should commence as follows:

"The libel and complaint of A. B., of ——, late mariner of the ship ——, whereof C. D., of ——, now is or lately was master [or owner, as the case may be], *against the said ship, her tackle, apparel and furniture, and also against the said C. D.,* in a cause of subtraction of wages, civil and maritime," &c.

A corresponding variation should take place in the conclusion of the libel.

First. That in the month of ——, in the year of our Lord eighteen hundred and ——, the said ship ——, whereof the said C. D. was master, being at the port of ——, and destined on a voyage from thence to ——, he, the said C. D., by himself or his agent, on the high seas and within the ebb and flow of the tide, and within the Admiralty and Maritime jurisdiction of the United States and of this honourable court, did ship and hire the libellant to serve as a mariner on board the said ship, for and during said voyage, at the rate of wages of —— per month, as schedulate; and that for the due performance of the said voyage, the libellant signed and duly executed certain articles of agreement commonly called the shipping or mariners' articles, which now are in the possession of the said C. D., master [or owner] of the said ship, and which he prays may be produced for farther certainty in the premises and for the benefit of the libellant.* That in pursuance thereof, on or about the —— day of ——, he, the libellant, went on board and entered into the service of the said ship as such mariner, as aforesaid.

Second. That the said ship, having taken on board a cargo of divers goods and merchandise for the voyage, proceeded therewith, and with the libellant on board for the port of ——, and there safely arrived on or about ——, and delivered her cargo and made freight, and that the libellant continued on board and in the service of the said ship until the —— day of ——, when the said voyage, for which he had so engaged, was duly ended, and he was discharged from such service by the said C. D., the master.

Third. That during the whole time he was in the service of the said ship, to wit, from the time when he went on board thereof, to the time of his discharge therefrom, as aforesaid, he well and truly performed his duty as a mariner on board the said ship, according to his best ability, and was obedient to all the lawful commands of the said master and the other officers of the said ship, and well and truly deserved and is entitled to the wages in the schedule hereunto annexed, amounting to the sum of ——.

Fourth. That all and singular the premises are true, and within the Admiralty and Maritime jurisdiction of this honourable Court, in verification whereof, if denied, the libellant craves leave to refer to the depositions and other proofs to be by him exhibited in this cause.

WHEREFORE the libellant prays that process, in due form of law, according to the course of Courts of Admiralty, and of this Honourable Court in causes of Admiralty and Maritime jurisdiction, may issue *against the said ship, her tackle, apparel and furniture, wheresoever the same shall be found, and that all persons having or pretending to have any right, title or interest therein, may be cited to appear and* to answer upon oath† all and singular the matters so articulately propounded, and that this honourable court would be pleased to pronounce for the wages aforesaid, and for such other relief to the libellant as shall to law and justice appertain, and *also to condemn the said ship, her tackle, apparel and furniture, and the party intervening therefor in costs.*‡

(Signed) A. B., *Libellant.*

E. F., *Proctor.*

EASTERN DISTRICT OF PENNSYLVANIA, *ss.* ——, 18—.

§Sworn to by the libellant before me.

G. H., *Clerk.*

* See Act of Congress, cap. 56 [29], § 6, by which the master is obliged to produce the contract and log-book, if required.

† In regard to requiring the answer to be on oath, see Dunlap's Admiralty Practice, p. 122.

‡ If the libel be *in personam*, it should conclude as follows:

"WHEREFORE the libellant prays that process, in due form of law, according to the course of courts of admiralty and of this honourable court, in causes of admiralty and maritime jurisdiction, may issue *against the said C. D*, and that he may be required to answer upon oath all and singular the matters so articulately propounded, and that this honourable court would be pleased to pronounce for the wages aforesaid and for such other relief to the libellant as shall to law and justice appertain, and *also to condemn the said C. D. in costs.*"

§ The libel must be sworn to before the Judge or Clerk of the Court, or a U. S. Commissioner. If sworn to before an Alderman or Justice of the Peace, it will not be received. This applies to all libels in Admiralty.

Schedule Annexed.

Wages due to A. B., from —— to ——, being —— months —— days, at the rate of —— per month, $——
Out of which he has received, including hospital dues, $——

Sum due $——

Claim and Answer.

UNITED STATES OF AMERICA, EASTERN DISTRICT OF PENNSYLVANIA, *ss.*

—— Term, 18—.

To the Honourable ARCHIBALD RANDALL, *Judge of the District Court of the United States, in and for the Eastern District of Pennsylvania.*

And now C. D., of ——, *intervening for his interest in the ship* ——, appears before this honourable court, and for answer to the libel and complaint of A. B., of ——, *against the said ship, and against all persons lawfully intervening for their interest therein,* alleges and articulately propounds as follows:*

First. That the respondent now is the owner of the said ship ——, and also was the owner of the same during the time the said A. B. belonged thereto, and that the said A. B. was duly hired to serve on board the said ship for the voyage, as in the first article in the said libel is propounded; the articles of agreement for which voyage, signed by the said A. B., the respondent doth herewith produce in court according to the prayer in the said first article.

Second. That the said ship ——, having taken on board a cargo of divers goods and merchandise for the voyage, proceeded therewith for the port of ——, and there safely arrived and delivered her cargo and made freight, as in the second article in the said libel is propounded.

Third. That whilst the said —— was at the port of ——, the said A. B., &c., [here state the bad conduct of the libellant, amounting to mutiny or desertion, or other ground of forfeiture of wages, and such other matter showing that the shipping articles were substantially broken, and also any other matters calculated to support and establish the defence.]

Fourth. That all and singular the premises are true and within the admiralty and maritime jurisdiction of this honourable court, in verification whereof, if denied, the respondent craves leave to refer to the depositions and other proofs to be by him exhibited in this cause.

WHEREFORE the respondent prays, that this honourable court would be pleased to pronounce against the libel aforesaid and to condemn the libellant in costs, and otherwise right and justice to administer in the premises.

(Signed) C. D.

I. J., *Proctor.*

EASTERN DISTRICT OF PENNSYLVANIA, *ss.* ——, 18—.

†Sworn to by the respondent before me.

G. H., *Clerk.*

Libel in a Cause of Personal Damage, with an Answer.

UNITED STATES OF AMERICA, EASTERN DISTRICT OF PENNSYLVANIA, *ss.*

—— Term, 18—.

To the Honourable ARCHIBALD RANDALL, *Judge of the District Court of the United States, in and for the Eastern District of Pennsylvania.*

The libel and complaint of John Smith, of Philadelphia, in the district aforesaid,

* If the proceeding be *in personam*, the answer should commence thus:

"And now C D, of ——, *master [or owner, as the case may be] of the ship* ——, appears before this honourable court, and, for answer to the libel and complaint of A. B, of ——, *against him, the said C. D*, alleges and articulately propounds as follows:

"*First.* That the respondent was the master [or owner] of the said ship —— during the time the said A. B belonged thereto," &c.

† The answer must be sworn to in same manner as the libel. See note p. 346.

late a mariner on board the ship Venice, whereof James Brown, of the said Philadelphia, now is or late was master, against the said James Brown, in a cause of damage, civil and maritime. And thereupon the said John Smith alleges and articulately propounds as follows:

First. That in May, 1844, the ship Venice, whereof the said James Brown was then master, being in the port of Philadelphia, and bound on a voyage to China, the said James Brown did, on the high seas, and within the ebb and flow of the tide and within the admiralty and maritime jurisdiction of this honourable court, by himself or his agent, ship and hire the libellant to serve as seaman on board of the said ship, for and during the said voyage; and the said ship, having taken on board her complement of officers and crew, did, on or about the —— day of the said month of May, proceed thereon, with the libellant on board, and, having been to China, returned to the port of Philadelphia aforesaid, with a full ship in the month of April last.

Second. That during the whole time the libellant continued on board the said ship, he did well and truly perform his duty on board her, and was obedient to all the lawful commands of the said James Brown, the master, and others his superior officers on board the said ship.

Third. That during the time of the said voyage, and while the ship was lying off Whampoa, in China, (to wit) on the high seas, and within the ebb and flow of the tide and within the admiralty and maritime jurisdiction of this honourable court, on the 4th day of October, 1844, whilst the libellant was in the fore-hold handing up billet-wood, Jacob Johnson, the third officer on board the said ship or vessel, charged him with not working so well as he could, nor so fast as another seaman of the name of Thomas Robb. That the libellant replied, "that Thomas Robb worked too fast to last long," or he made use of words to that or the like effect; when the said Jacob Johnson immediately made complaint to Mr. Snowden, the chief officer, that the libellant had been very impertinent to him; whereupon, and for no other cause whatever, Mr. Snowden then ordered him to be taken from his duty and placed below in irons, where he continued until the 12th of October. That, upon the said James Brown coming on board the ship (from which he had been absent the whole of the before-mentioned period), he immediately, upon the complaint being made to him by the said Snowden, and without hearing the libellant in his defence, ordered him to the gangway and caused him to be flogged with three dozen lashes; and, although the libellant most humbly and repeatedly urged the said James Brown for some water to allay the thirst and fever that he then suffered from the punishment and previous imprisonment, he, the said James Brown, absolutely refused to let the steward give him any, nor would he permit the mate to give the libellant an ointment or lotion to apply to his back, but ordered him in his fainting and exhausted state to return to his duty. That the libellant, in consequence of the flogging aforesaid, suffered extreme pain and was greatly injured thereby.

Fourth. That the libellant, by reason of the said cruelty and violent assault which he suffered by the act of the said James Brown, as before pleaded, has sustained a damage to the amount of two thousand dollars.

Fifth. That all and singular the premises are true, and within the admiralty and maritime jurisdiction of this honourable court, in verification whereof, if denied, the libellant craves leave to refer to the depositions and other proofs to be by him exhibited in this cause.

WHEREFORE he prays that process, in due form of law, according to the course of courts of admiralty and of this honourable court in causes of admiralty and maritime jurisdiction, may issue against the said James Brown, and that he may be required to answer upon oath all and singular the matters so articulately propounded, and that this honourable court would be pleased to pronounce for the damages aforesaid and for such other relief to the libellant as shall to law and justice appertain, and also to condemn the said James Brown in costs.

(Signed) JOHN SMITH, *Libellant.*

A. B., *Proctor.*

EASTERN DISTRICT OF PENNSYLVANIA, *ss.* May 8, 1845.

Sworn to by the libellant before me.

FRANCIS HOPKINSON, *Clerk.*

Answer.

UNITED STATES OF AMERICA, EASTERN DISTRICT OF PENNSYLVANIA, *ss.*

—— Term, 18. —

To the Honourable ARCHIBALD RANDALL, *Judge of the District Court of the United States, in and for the Eastern District of Pennsylvania.*

And now James Brown, of Philadelphia, in the said district, late master of the ship Venice, appears before this honourable court, and for answer to the libel and complaint of John Smith, of the said Philadelphia, late mariner on board the said ship, against him, the said James Brown, alleges and articulately propounds as follows:

First. That the libellant was duly shipped and hired to serve as a seaman on board the said ship Venice, for and during a voyage to China and back again; and that the said ship, with the libellant on board, proceeded on the said voyage, and, having been to China, returned to the port of Philadelphia, as is alleged in the first article of the said libel.

Second. That the libellant did not, during the whole time he continued on board the Venice, that is to say, from May, 1844, until April, 1845, well and truly perform his duty on board the ship, nor was he obedient to all the lawful commands of the respondent, the master, and others, the officers on board the said ship, as in the second article of the libel is falsely alleged and pleaded. On the contrary, that the libellant frequently neglected to perform his duty, particularly during his watch; that he was disobedient and refused or neglected to obey the lawful commands of the master, and others the officers on board the ship, and treated them with great insolence and contempt, and was frequently reprimanded for such conduct; that on such occasions he made insolent and irritating replies, and said he was only on board "a bloody merchantman," and made use of many other expressions to that or the like effect.

Third. That on the 4th of October, 1844, the libellant, having heen ordered to assist in the handing some billet-wood from the fore-hold unto the deck of the ship, was idle and inattentive in the performance of such duty, and in receiving the wood from one person and handing it to another, and thereby greatly impeded and delayed the performance of the said duty; that Jacob Johnson, the third officer or mate of the ship, who was superintending the performance of the work, several times remonstrated with him on his conduct and desired him to be more diligent, but the libellant replied with great insolence and said, that he should take it easy,—there was plenty of time, that he should not hurry himself, or to that effect; that the man who handed wood to the libellant several times complained of his insolence, by which he was frequently kept with a billet in his hand, waiting until the libellant, who had delivered the preceding billet and was standing idle, chose to receive the billet from him; and, the said Jacob Johnson, observing such man standing with a large billet in his hands, and the libellant standing idle, he ordered the libellant to take the billet from such man, to which he insolently replied, that "he would be damned if he would," or words to that effect, and made use of other violent expressions, and treated the said Jacob Johnson with great insolence and contempt, whereupon the said Jacob Johnson made a faithful representation of such conduct to Robert Snowden, the chief officer, the respondent being then on shore at Canton, on the necessary concerns of the ship; that the said Robert Snowden ordered the libellant to be confined in irons, which was accordingly done, and he, by letter, informed the respondent of the aforesaid circumstances, who ordered a court of inquiry to be held, and on the next day the said Robert Snowden, and the second, third and fourth officers of the ship assembled, and in the presence of the libellant examined witnesses as to his conduct, and heard him in his defence; and, it clearly appearing from the testimony of the witnesses that the libellant had refused to obey the orders of the said Jacob Johnson, and had conducted himself in a mutinous manner, they were of opinion that he was deserving of punishment; and therefore he was continued in confinement until the respondent returned to the ship; and having returned on the 12th day of said month, and the conduct of the libellant, and the proceedings of the said court of inquiry, and the evidence given, having been represented to him, he directed that the libellant should receive thirty-six lashes as a punishment, and the same was accordingly inflicted on the same day; that after the libellant had received one or two lashes, he admitted that he had been very insolent to the said Jacob Johnson, and asked to be forgiven; that the libellant did not suffer any fever from his aforesaid confinement; nor did he at the time he was so punished as aforesaid, urge the respondent to let him have some water; nor did the respondent refuse to let the steward give him any, as in the third article of the said libel is falsely alleged and pleaded; that the punishment of the libellant was necessarily inflicted for the sake of example, and to preserve due discipline on board the ship; that the respondent did not refuse to permit the mate to give the libellant any ointment or lotion for his back; nor was the libellant in a fainting or exhausted state; nor did he suffer extreme pain; nor was he injured in consequence of the punishment he received, as in the said libel is falsely alleged and pleaded.

Fourth. That all and singular the premises are true, in verification whereof, if denied, the respondent craves leave to refer to the depositions and other proofs to be by him exhibited in this cause.

Wherefore the respondent prays, that this honourable court would be pleased to pronounce against the libel aforesaid, and to condemn the libellant in costs, and otherwise right and justice to administer in the premises.

(Signed) James Brown, (*the Respondent.*)

C. D., *Proctor.*

Eastern District of Pennsylvania, *ss.* May 11, 1845.

Sworn to by the respondent before me.

Francis Hopkinson, *Clerk.*

Another Libel in a Cause of Personal Damage.

United States of America, Eastern District of Pennsylvania, *ss.*

—— Term, 18—.

To the Honourable Archibald Randall, *Judge of the District Court of the United States, in and for the Eastern District of Pennsylvania.*

The libel and complaint of John Andrews, of Philadelphia, in the district aforesaid, late a mariner on board the ship Langdon Cheves, whereof William Green, of the said Philadelphia, now is or late was master, against the said William Green, in a cause of damage, civil and maritime. And thereupon the said John Andrews alleges and articulately propounds as follows:

First. That the said ship, called the Langdon Cheves, whereof the said William Green was master, being, in the month of ——, in the present year of our Lord, at Charleston, in South Carolina, and destined on a voyage from thence to the port of Philadelphia, he, the said William Green, upon the high seas and within the ebb and flow of the tide, and within the admiralty and maritime jurisdiction of this honourable court, did hire the libellant to serve as a mariner on board the said ship during her passage to Philadelphia aforesaid; and that the said ship, having taken in a cargo of goods and merchandises for the voyage aforesaid, did, on or about the —— day of ——, proceed from Charleston aforesaid with the libellant on board, for Philadelphia, where she safely arrived on or about the —— And that during the whole time of the said voyage, or run, the libellant did well and truly perform his duty as a mariner of the said ship (excepting only while he was rendered incapable of performing the same by the cruel usage of him, the said William Green, as hereinafter more particularly pleaded,) and was obedient to all the lawful commands of the said William Green, the master, and the other officers on board the said ship.

Second. That while the said ship Langdon Cheves was on her passage from Charleston to Philadelphia, as aforesaid, to wit, on or about the —— day of ——, the libellant being busy in setting the square sail of the said ship, the said William Green, without any provocation, did, upon the high seas and within the ebb and flow of the tide, and within the admiralty and maritime jurisdiction of this honourable court, with his fist clenched, strike the libellant a blow on the head, which knocked him down, and that then the said William Green did with his feet, with great force and violence, kick the libellant several times, whereby he was dangerously hurt and bruised.

Third. That while the said ship was on her aforesaid passage, to wit, on or about the —— day of ——, the libellant being at work on board the said ship, and having hold on the cable thereof, the said William Green, without any reasonable cause or provocation, did, upon the high seas and within the ebb and flow of the tide, and within the admiralty and maritime jurisdiction of this honourable court, with a large handspike, with great force and violence strike the libellant on his right arm, and thereby bruised his said arm very severely and put him in great pain and suffering.

Fourth. That while the said ship was off Cape Henry, on the passage aforesaid, he, the said William Green, did, upon the high seas and within the ebb and flow of the tide, and within the admiralty and maritime jurisdiction of this honourable court, with his fist clenched, without any just cause or provocation, strike the libellant on his left ear with great force and violence, and thereby knocked him down and caused blood to gush from his ears, nose and mouth; that the libellant was thereby deprived of his senses or power of motion for several minutes, and rendered incapable of performing any kind of service for many hours.

Fifth. That during the whole time of the aforesaid voyage, the said William Green behaved with great cruelty and inhumanity towards the libellant, and on the high seas and within the ebb and flow of the tide, and within the admiralty and maritime jurisdiction of this honourable court, frequently attempted to throw the libellant overboard, and threatened to cut his throat, and many times, to wit, on —— days of the month of ——, did, without any reasonable cause or provocation, violently beat, kick, and ill treat the libellant, whereby he was put in great fear and danger of his life.

Sixth. That by reason of the cruelty exercised by the said William Green on the person of the libellant, as pleaded and set forth in the *second, third, fourth* and *fifth* articles of this libel, the flesh of the libellant became almost totally discoloured, and he had therein many severe and dangerous bruises and contusions, and he became very weak, and his constitution was so much impaired and injured, that he has not yet recovered his former health and strength.

Seventh. That by the cruelty and repeated ill usage, which the libellant received from the said William Green, as herein before pleaded and set forth, the libellant was and is damnified in the sum of two thousand dollars.

Eighth. That all and singular the premises are true, and within the admiralty and maritime jurisdiction of this honourable court, in verification whereof, if denied, the libellant craves leave to refer to the depositions and other proofs to be by him exhibited in this cause.

[Conclusion the same as in the preceding libel, p. 348.]

Libel for Collision, with a Claim and Answer.

United States of America, Eastern District of Pennsylvania, *ss.*

—— Term, 18—.

To the Honourable Archibald Randall, *Judge of the District Court of the United States, in and for the Eastern District of Pennsylvania.*

The libel and complaint of Richard Jones, Anthony Simms and William Potter, of Philadelphia, in the district aforesaid, merchants and copartners, doing business under the name of Richard Jones and Company, owners of the ship Lehigh (whereof Augustus Kemper now is or lately was master), her tackle, apparel and furniture, *against the ship Saranak (whereof Andrew Stevenson now is or lately was master), her tackle, apparel and furniture, and against all persons lawfully intervening for their interest therein,** in a cause of collision, civil and

* The above form is proper if the proceeding be entirely *in rem.* If it be *in personam,* the form should be as follows: "*against A. B., of the said Philadelphia, merchant, owner of the ship Saranak,*" &c. If it be *in rem* and *in personam,* the form should be as follows: "*against the ship Saranak, her tackle, apparel and furniture, (whereof Andrew Stevenson now is or*

maritime. And thereupon the said Richard Jones, Anthony Simms and William Potter allege and articulately propound as follows:

First. That in the month of December, 1843, the said ship Lehigh, whereof Augustus Kemper now is and then was master, was at the port of Calcutta in the East Indies, and destined on a voyage from thence to the port of Philadelphia, with a lading of East India Goods to the amount of $100,000 in value, or thereabouts; and was at that time a tight, staunch and well-built vessel, of the burthen of four hundred tons or thereabouts; and was then completely rigged and sufficiently provided with tackle, apparel and furniture; and then had on board and in her service twenty-five mariners or thereabouts, which was a full complement of hands to navigate the said ship on the voyage above mentioned.

Second. That in the said month of December, 1843, the said ship, provided and manned as aforesaid, sailed from the port of Calcutta on her aforesaid voyage to the port of Philadelphia, and in the prosecution of her said voyage, arrived in the river Delaware, off the city of Philadelphia, on or about the 5th day of May, 1844, and was there safely moored; and that it being about ten o'clock in the evening of the 5th day of May, 1844, within the ebb and flow of the tide and within the admiralty and maritime jurisdiction of this honourable court, at her aforesaid moorings, John Thomas, the first mate of the said ship Lehigh, who then had the watch and was the commanding officer on deck, and that part of the crew, which composed the said watch, observed the said ship Saranak, whereof the said Andrew Stevenson was then master, of the burthen of six hundred tons or thereabouts, with all her sails set, sailing up the said river Delaware towards the said ship Lehigh; and that thereupon the said John Thomas and others of the crew aforesaid several times with loud and audible voices called to the crew of the said ship Saranak, and desired them to keep clear of the said ship Lehigh, and which they had time and tide enough to do, and might with great ease and safety have done, but which they refused, or at least neglected to do; and that notwithstanding the said ship Lehigh was then lying at her aforesaid moorings, and could not possibly get out of the way of the said ship Saranak, and notwithstanding there was room sufficient for the said ship Saranak to pass, the crew thereof kept on their course with the wind and tide, and ran their ship, with very great force and violence, foul of and on board the said ship Lehigh, and thereby broke and parted her small bower cable, carried away the bumkin and jib-boom, and damaged her yawl and her standing and running rigging, and otherwise greatly damaged the said ship; and that, had not the crew immediately and with the greatest expedition possible let go another anchor, the said ship Lehigh must unavoidably have been very soon on shore; and that the said ship Saranak so continued foul of and on board the said ship Lehigh for about two hours and until the ebb tide forced her off.

Third. That at the time the damage mentioned in the next preceding article happened, it was impossible for the said ship Lehigh to get out of the way of the said ship Saranak by reason that the former was properly moored; that there was room enough for the said ship Saranak to steer clear of and pass by the said ship Lehigh without doing any damage whatever; and that, if the said Andrew Stevenson and the rest of the crew of the said ship Saranak had not refused, or at least neglected, to endeavour to keep clear of the said ship Lehigh, as desired by the said John Thomas and others, as mentioned in the next preceding article, which it was their duty to do, and which they might with ease and safety have done, the aforesaid damage would not have happened.

Fourth. That the said ship Lehigh, before and at the time of receiving the damage from the said ship Saranak, as hereinbefore mentioned, was a tight, strong and staunch vessel, and that the libellants then were, and now are, the true and lawful owners of the same, and of her tackle, apparel and furniture.

Fifth. That immediately after the damages mentioned in the second article of this libel happened, several men were employed to bring the said ship Lehigh to her moorings and to take up her sheet anchor and bower anchor and part of a cable which had been broken and turned adrift from the said ship; and

lately was master), and against A. B., of the said Philadelphia, merchant, owner of the said ship, and also against all persons lawfully intervening for their interest in the said ship," &c.

that the several other damages mentioned in the second article of this libel were repaired by shipwrights and others with all possible despatch, all which cost the sum of three hundred and twenty-five dollars and upwards; and that by reason of the said ship Lehigh having been run foul of, or run down, as aforesaid, the libellants have sustained damages for the services and repairs aforesaid to the amount of three hundred and twenty-five dollars.

Sixth. That all and singular the premises are true and within the admiralty and maritime Jurisdiction of this honourable court, in verification whereof, if denied, the libellants crave leave to refer to the depositions and other proofs to be by them exhibited in this cause.

WHEREFORE the libellants pray, that process, in due form of law, according to the course of courts of admiralty and of this honourable court in causes of admiralty and maritime jurisdiction, may issue *against the said ship Saranak, her tackle, apparel and furniture, and that all persons having, or pretending to have, any right, title or interest therein may be cited to appear* and answer upon oath all and singular the matters so articulately propounded; and that this honourable court would be pleased to pronounce for the damages aforesaid, and to decree such other relief to the libellants, as shall to law and justice appertain, also to condemn the said ship, her tackle, apparel and furniture, *and all persons intervening for their interest therein* in costs.*

(Signed) RICHARD JONES,
ANTHONY SIMMS,
WILLIAM POTTER,
Libellants.

A. B., *Proctor.*

EASTERN DISTRICT OF PENNSYLVANIA, *ss.*

Sworn to by the said Richard Jones, Anthony Simms and William Potter, before me. FRANCIS HOPKINSON, *Clerk.*

Claim and Answer.

UNITED STATES OF AMERICA, EASTERN DISTRICT OF PENNSYLVANIA, *ss.*

—— Term, 18—.

To the Honourable ARCHIBALD RANDALL, *Judge of the District Court of the United States, in and for the Eastern District of Pennsylvania.*

And now Thomas C. Graham, of Philadelphia, in the district aforesaid, *intervening for his interest in the said ship Saranak*, appears before this honourable court, and for answer to the libel and complaint of Richard Jones, Anthony Simms and William Potter, all of the said Philadelphia, merchants and copartners, doing business under the name of Richard Jones & Company, *against the said ship Saranak, her tackle, apparel and furniture, and against all persons lawfully intervening for their interest therein,* alleges and articulately propounds as follows:

First. That the respondent is the true and lawful owner of the said ship Saranak, a vessel of six hundred tons or thereabouts, now lying in the port of Philadelphia aforesaid.

Second. And the respondent, admitting the several matters in the first, fourth and fifth articles of the said libel pleaded to be true as therein alleged, further alleges and propounds, that the matters in the second and third articles of the said libel are in great part falsely alleged, and that the truth is as is hereinafter particularly propounded.

Third. That the said ship Saranak, being in good order and well and sufficiently equipped and manned, sailed from the port of Liverpool, in England, in the month of April, 1844, bound for the port of Philadelphia aforesaid; and in the prosecution of her voyage, on or about the 5th day of May, 1844, at seven o'clock in the forenoon, came in sight of the Cape May light-house; that shortly thereafter, the said ship was boarded by John Smith, a pilot, accustomed to conduct and manage

* The latter part of this form should be varied according to the nature of the proceeding. See note, p. 346.

ships in the Delaware bay and river, and to his charge and guidance, as pilot, the said Andrew Stevenson, master, immediately committed the navigation and government of the said ship; that the said ship having proceeded up the river Delaware until off the town of Chester, which place was reached by six o'clock in the afternoon of the day aforesaid, the said pilot and master consulted together whether it were better to endeavour to get the said ship up to Philadelphia that night, notwithstanding the darkness, or to cast anchor and keep her safely moored till the next morning; that the said pilot strongly advised the endeavouring to get the said ship up to Philadelphia on the night aforesaid, and urged that it was customary with him and other pilots of the said port of Philadelphia, to conduct ships up the river in the night time, notwithstanding the darkness; that it was accordingly determined to endeavour to get the said ship up to Philadelphia on the night aforesaid; and that powerful lights were placed in different parts of the said ship, and every other possible precaution taken, in order to facilitate the management of the same, and to enable other ships in the river to discern the said ship, for a long time before it came near.

Fourth. That very soon after it became dark on the night aforesaid, the wind, which until then had been quite moderate and favourable to sailing up the river aforesaid, suddenly began to blow in successive gusts, very strong, stormy and contrary, so that the said ship Saranak was compelled by means of repeated tacks to beat up against the wind; and that at the same time the night grew so very dark, that it was impossible to discern, without the assistance of a light, objects even when very near.

Fifth. That while the said ship was beating up, as aforesaid, against the wind, notwithstanding the precautions against accident which had been taken, as aforesaid, and also the excellent and seamanlike management by the said pilot, assisted by the master and crew, the said ship Saranak ran foul of the ship, which the respondent understands to have been the said ship Lehigh, whereof the present libellants then were and now are the true and lawful owners, as is alleged in the fourth article of the libel aforesaid.

Sixth. That the said ship Lehigh, at the time of the accident aforesaid, was lying moored in the channel of the river aforesaid, and directly in the path of the said ship Saranak, and that there were no lights visible aboard of the said ship Lehigh, which could enable the pilot, or master, or any of the crew of the ship Saranak then on deck, to discern that the said ship Lehigh was so lying in the channel, although they kept a good "look-out" for this purpose; also that neither the pilot, nor the master, nor any of the crew of the said ship Saranak, then on deck, heard the said John Thomas or any of the crew of the said ship Lehigh call to them, as it is alleged they did call in the second article of the libel aforesaid.

Seventh. That the said pilot and the master and crew of the said ship Saranak used the greatest care and skill in the management of the same on the night aforesaid, and took every possible precaution to prevent the occurrence of any accident.

Eighth. That the accident aforesaid was occasioned by the great negligence and want of care of the officers and crew of the said ship Lehigh, in the mooring of the said ship in the place where they did, and also in not providing powerful lights on deck, so that the said ship could be discerned at a distance; and that it was not occasioned by any want of care or skill, or by any malice or evil design, on the part of the said pilot or master or any of the crew on board the said ship Saranak, as is falsely alleged in the third article of the libel aforesaid; and that the owner of the said ship Saranak is not, therefore, liable to pay the damages by the libellants sustained.

Ninth. That all and singular the premises are true, in verification whereof, if denied, the respondent craves leave to refer to the depositions and other proofs to be by him exhibited in this cause.

Wherefore the respondent prays that this honourable court would be pleased to pronounce against the libel aforesaid, and to condemn the libellant in costs, and otherwise right and justice to administer in the premises.

(Signed) Thomas C. Graham, *Respondent.*

Eastern District of Pennsylvania, *ss.* ——.
Sworn to by the respondent, before me,
Francis Hopkinson, *Clerk.*

Libel by a dissentient Part-owner (having a majority or a moiety of interest) of a Ship, in order to procure Possession; with an Answer.

UNITED STATES OF AMERICA, EASTERN DISTRICT OF PENNSYLVANIA, *ss.*

—— Term, 18—.

To the Honourable ARCHIBALD RANDALL, *Judge of the District Court of the United States, in and for the Eastern District of Pennsylvania.*

The libel and complaint of Charles L. Mount, of Philadelphia, in the district aforesaid, and owner of three-quarter parts of the barque Jane (whereof William Jones now is or lately was master), against the said barque Jane, her tackle, apparel and furniture, and against John Rogers, of Philadelphia aforesaid, merchant, and owner of one-quarter part of the said barque, and also all persons lawfully intervening for their interest in the said barque, in a cause of possession, civil and maritime. And thereupon the said Charles L. Mount alleges and articulately propounds as follows:

First. That the libellant is the true and lawful owner of three-quarter parts of the said barque Jane, of the burthen of about three hundred tons, and now lying in the port of Philadelphia aforesaid.

Second. That the libellant is now, and has been for a long time desirous of sending the said barque on a voyage to Rio Janeiro, in Brazil, and from Rio Janeiro back to Philadelphia; but that the said John Rogers, owner of the remaining quarter part of the said barque, has refused, though repeatedly applied to in this regard, to join in the voyage aforesaid, or to suffer the said barque to sail on the account of the libellant on the voyage aforesaid.

Third. That all and singular the premises are true, and within the admiralty and maritime jurisdiction of this honourable court; in verification whereof, if denied, the libellant craves leave to refer to the depositions and other proofs to be by him exhibited in this cause.

WHEREFORE the libellant prays, that process, in due form of law, according to the course of courts of admiralty and of this honourable court, may issue against the said barque Jane, her tackle, apparel and furniture, wheresoever the same shall be found, and that the said John Rogers, owner of the quarter part as aforesaid, and all persons having or pretending to have any right, title, or interest therein, may be cited to appear before this honourable court, and to show cause, why the possession of the said barque should not be delivered to the libellant, as having the majority of interest therein; and that this honourable court would be pleased to decree the possession of the said barque to be delivered to the libellant, and to administer such other relief as shall to law and justice appertain, and also to condemn the said John Rogers and all persons intervening for ther interest in the said barque in costs. (Signed) CHARLES L. MOUNT,

A. B., *Proctor.* *Libellant.*

EASTERN DISTRICT OF PENNSYLVANIA, *ss.* ——.

Sworn to by the libellant before me.

FRANCIS HOPKINSON, *Clerk.*

Answer.

UNITED STATES OF AMERICA, EASTERN DISTRICT OF PENNSYLVANIA, *ss.*

—— Term, 18—.

To the Honourable ARCHIBALD RANDALL, *Judge of the District Court of the United States, in and for the Eastern District of Pennsylvania.*

And now John Rogers, of Philadelphia, in the district aforesaid, merchant, appears before this honourable court, and for answer to the libel and complaint of Charles L. Mount, of Philadelphia aforesaid, against the barque Jane, and against him the said John Rogers, and also against all persons lawfully intervening for their interest in the said barque, alleges and articulately propounds as follows:

First. That the libellant is the true and lawful owner of three-quarter parts of the said barque Jane, as in the first article of the said libel is alleged.

Second. That the respondent was the owner of a quarter part of the said barque from some time in the month of April, 1842, until the 6th day of January, 1844, on which last day, by a deed of indenture, he assigned all his property, real and personal, of whatsoever name or nature and wheresoever situated, to George Rogers and William Jones, in trust for the benefit of his creditors; and that he is not now, nor was he, at the time of filing the said libel, the owner of a quarter part of the said barque; but that the said quarter part has belonged to the trustees aforesaid, and could not be employed without their consent, ever since the date of the said assignment, and long before the time of filing the said libel.

Third. That the respondent refused to join in the voyage from Philadelphia to Rio Janeiro and from Rio Janeiro back to Philadelphia, as is alleged in the second article of the said libel, for reasons alleged in the next preceding article.

Fourth. That all and singular the premises are true; in verification whereof, if denied, the respondent craves leave to refer to the depositions and other proofs to be by him exhibited in this cause.

Wherefore the respondent prays that this honourable court would be pleased to pronounce against the libel aforesaid, and to condemn the libellant in costs, and otherwise right and justice to administer in the premises.

(Signed) John Rogers, *Respondent.*

C. D., *Proctor.*

Eastern District of Pennsylvania, *ss.*

Sworn to by the respondent before me.

Francis Hopkinson, *Clerk.*

Libel by dissentient Part-owners (owning less than a moiety) of a Ship, in order to obtain Security; with a Stipulation thereupon.

United States of America, Eastern District of Pennsylvania, *ss.*

—— Term, 18—.

To the Honourable Archibald Randall, *Judge of the District Court of the United States, in and for the Eastern District of Pennsylvania.*

The libel and complaint of Henry Davis and Louis Rankin, of Philadelphia, in the district aforesaid, merchants, and owners of one moiety of the brig Fanny (whereof James Green, of Philadelphia aforesaid, now is or lately was master), against the brig Fanny, her tackle, apparel and furniture, and against the said James Green, and also against Joseph Gray, of Philadelphia aforesaid, merchant, and owner of one moiety of the said brig, and against all persons lawfully intervening for their interest in the said brig, in a cause of possession, civil and maritime. And thereupon the said Henry Davis and Louis Rankin allege and articulately propound as follows:

First. That the libellants are the true and lawful owners of one moiety of the said brig Fanny, of the burthen of two hundred and fifty tons or thereabouts, which is now lying at the port of Philadelphia, and that the said moiety is worth the sum of three thousand five hundred dollars.

Second. That the said Joseph Gray, owner of another moiety of the said brig, has caused to be laden on board the said brig a cargo of flour, to be carried therein to Callao, a foreign and distant port in Peru, and is about to cause the said brig to be cleared at the custom-house for the said port; that he has constituted the said James Green master of the said brig for the voyage aforesaid, and that the said James Green is now making great haste and preparation for the entering upon and performance of the said voyage and sailing from the port of Philadelphia aforesaid.

Third. That the said voyage was planned, and the said cargo taken on board the said brig, and the said James Green constituted master of the same for the voyage aforesaid, without consulting the libellants, and contrary to their express desires often communicated to the said Joseph Gray, part-owner, as aforesaid; and that the libellants now object to, and dissent from, the said employment of the said brig on and for the voyage aforesaid.

Fourth. That all and singular the premises are true, and within the admiralty and maritime jurisdiction of this honourable court; in verification whereof, if denied, the libellants crave leave to refer to the depositions and other proofs to be by them exhibited in this cause.

Wherefore the libellants pray, that process, in due form of law, according to the course of courts of admiralty and of this honourable court in causes of admiralty and maritime jurisdiction, may issue against the said brig Fanny, her tackle, apparel and furniture, wheresoever the same shall be found, and that the said James Green, master as aforesaid, and Joseph Gray, owner of one moiety as aforesaid, and all persons having or pretending to have any right, title or interest in the said brig, may be cited to appear before this honourable court, and to show cause, why the said James Green should not be restrained from proceeding to sea with the said brig, until good and sufficient security shall be given in this court, to the amount of the value of the moiety of the libellants therein, for the return of the said brig to the said port of Philadelphia, to which she belongs; and that this honourable court would be pleased to pronounce that such security shall be given or the possession of the said brig be delivered to the libellants, and to administer such other relief as shall to law and justice appertain, and also to condemn the said James Green and Joseph Gray and all persons intervening for their interest in the said brig, in costs.*

(Signed) Henry Davis,
Louis Rankin
Libellants.

A. B., *Proctor.*

Eastern District of Pennsylvania, *ss.* ——.
Sworn to by the libellants, before me.
Francis Hopkinson, *Clerk.*

Stipulation by a Part-owner and Master of a Ship, with Sureties, on sending the Ship to Sea.

United States of America, Eastern District of Pennsylvania, *ss.*

—— Term, 18—.

On this 10th day of May, 1844, James Green, of Philadelphia, in the district aforesaid, master of the brig Fanny, and Joseph Gray, of Philadelphia aforesaid, merchant, appear in court and produce for sureties Jacob Robertson and William Jenks, both of Philadelphia aforesaid, merchants; and the said James Green and Joseph Gray as principals, and the said Jacob Robertson and William Jenks as sureties, submitting themselves to the jurisdiction of this court, do bind themselves, their heirs, executors and administrators, in the sum of *seven thousand dollars*, being double the appraised value of one moiety of the said brig, unto Henry Davis and Louis Rankin, both of Philadelphia aforesaid, merchants, owners of the said moiety of the said brig, for the safe return of the said brig to the port of Philadelphia, being the port to which the same belongs, or to pay to them the amount of the said moiety of the said Henry Davis and Louis Rankin; and, unless they shall so do, they do hereby severally consent that execution shall issue forth against them, their heirs, executors and administrators, goods and chattels, wheresoever the same shall be found, to the value of the sum aforesaid.

Libel by a Painter, for painting and furnishing a ship, with an Answer.

United States of America, Eastern District of Pennsylvania, *ss.*

—— Term, 18—.

To the Honourable Archibald Randall, *Judge of the District Court of the United States, in and for the Eastern District of Pennsylvania.*

The libel and complaint of Matthew Brown, of the district aforesaid, ship-painter, *against the barque W. H. Harrison (whereof Thomas Mason now is or late was master), her tackle, apparel and furniture, and also against all persons lawfully intervening for their interest therein*† in a cause of contract, civil and maritime.

* If a sale of the ship be desired, a prayer to this effect must be inserted.

† The commencement of this form should be varied to suit different cases. See notes, pp. 345, 351.

And thereupon the said Matthew Brown alleges and articulately propounds as follows:

First. That the said barque W. H. Harrison, in the month of November, 1844, being in the port of Philadelphia, within the ebb and flow of the tide and within the admiralty and maritime jurisdiction of this honourable court, and standing in need of repairs, necessaries and painting, in order to render her seaworthy and competent for her voyage to New Orleans and elsewhere, the libellant did, at the request of the said master, contract and undertake properly to repair, supply and furnish the same by painting said barque, so that she should be competent for such voyages.

Second. That the libellant, during the said month of November, 1844, the said barque being within the ebb and flow of the tide and within the admiralty and maritime jurisdiction of this honourable court, repaired and painted the said barque, furnishing her with certain materials, to wit, paints, oil, putty, &c., and labouring to paint the said barque; the particulars of which supplies and repairs aforesaid will fully appear in the account hereto annexed, amounting in the whole to the sum of forty-five dollars and fifty cents, of which your libellant has received twenty-five dollars, leaving a balance due and unpaid, of twenty dollars and fifty cents.

Third. That the above supplies and work were necessary for the said barque, and that the said supplies were furnished and work done, on the credit of the said barque, as well as of the owners and master thereof.

Fourth. That all and singular the premises are true, and within the admiralty and maritime jurisdiction of this honourable court; in verification whereof, if denied, the libellant craves leave to refer to the depositions and other proofs to be by him exhibited in this cause.

Wherefore the libellant prays, that process, in due form of law, according to the course of courts of admiralty and of this honourable court in cases of admiralty and maritime jurisdiction, may issue *against the said barque, her tackle, apparel and furniture, wheresoever the same may be found; and that all persons having or pretending to have any right, title, or interest therein, may be cited to appear* and answer all and singular the matters so articulately propounded; and that this honourable court would be pleased to pronounce for the claim or damages aforesaid, and to decree such other relief to the libellant as shall to law and justice appertain, and also to condemn *the said barque W. H. Harrison, her tackle, apparel and furniture, and all persons intervening therefor,* in costs.*

(Signed) Matthew Brown, *Libellant.*

A. B., *Proctor.*

Eastern District of Pennsylvania, *ss.* ——.

Sworn to by the libellant before me.

Francis Hopkinson, *Clerk.*

Claim and Answer.

United States of America, Eastern District of Pennsylvania, *ss.*

—— Term, 18—.

To the Honourable Archibald Randall, *Judge of the District Court of the United States, in and for the Eastern District of Pennsylvania.*

And now Robert Moore, of the district aforesaid, merchant, *intervening for his interest in the barque W. H. Harrison,* appears before this honourable court, and for answer to the libel and complaint of Matthew Brown, of the district aforesaid, ship-painter, *against the said barque W. H. Harrison, her tackle, apparel and furniture, and also against all persons intervening for their interest in the said barque,*† alleges and articulately propounds as fol

First. That it is true that the said Matthew Brown did contract and undertake

* The conclusion of this form should be varied according to the nature of the proceeding. See note, p 346

† The commencement of this form should be varied to suit other cases. See note, p. 347.

properly to repair, supply and furnish the same by painting the said barque so that she should be competent for her voyage to New Orleans and elsewhere.

Second. That the libellant, in pursuance of his said contract, did pretend to repair and paint the said barque, and to furnish her with certain materials, to wit, paints, oil, putty, &c., and that he received for his services the sum of twenty-five dollars. But the said libellant totally violated his contract for the repair and painting of the said barque, and did his work so negligently, and in such an unworkmanlike manner, that the respondent was obliged to employ other workmen to do over again the same work which the said libellant undertook to do, for which the respondents were obliged to pay them, and by reason of which the said barque was prevented from sailing on her voyage on her appointed day, to the great damage and loss of the respondents.

Third. That all and singular the premises are true; in verification whereof, if denied, the respondent craves leave to refer to the depositions and other proofs to be by him exhibited in this cause.

Wherefore the respondent prays that this honourable court would be pleased to pronounce against the libel aforesaid, *and to decree a restoration of the said barque to the respondent*, and to condemn the libellant in costs, and otherwise right and justice to administer in the premises.

(Signed) Robert Moore, *Respondent.*

C. D., *Proctor.*

Eastern District of Pennsylvania, *ss.* ——.

Sworn to by the respondent before me.

Francis Hopkinson, *Clerk.*

Libel in a Cause of Salvage, with a Claim and Answer.

United States of America, Eastern District of Pennsylvania, *ss.*

—— Term, 18—.

To the Honourable Archibald Randall, *Judge of the District Court of the United States, in and for the Eastern District of Pennsylvania.*

The libel and complaint of Edward Dale, of Philadelphia, in the district aforesaid, master and owner of the sloop Red Rover, and of John Colton, of Wilmington, in the State of Delaware, the master and owner of the sloop Jenny Dean, and of the respective crews of the said sloops, *against the ship Octorara (whereof George Walters now is or lately was master), her tackle, apparel and furniture, and all and singular the goods, wares and merchandises now or late on board the said ship,** in a cause of salvage, civil and maritime. And thereupon the said Edward Dale, John Colton, and the respective crews of the sloops aforesaid, allege and articulately propound as follows:

First. That on Saturday, the 10th day of December last, the said sloop called the Red Rover, of the burthen of ninety tons, or thereabouts, (whereof the said Edward Dale was master and owner,) sailed from Philadelphia aforesaid, bound to Boston, and that the said sloop was manned with a crew of seven men, exclusive of the said Edward Dale, and fully and completely equipped and set forth for the said voyage. And that on Sunday, the 11th day of the said month of December, the said sloop called the Jenny Dean, of the burthen of one hundred tons, or thereabouts, (whereof the said John Colton was master and owner,) sailed from Wilmington aforesaid, bound to Portland; and that the said sloop last mentioned was likewise manned with a crew of seven men, exclusive of the said John Colton, and fully and completely equipped and set forth for such voyage.

Second. That between ten and eleven o'clock in the forenoon of the following Wednesday, to wit, the 14th day of December, (it blowing hard and the sea running high,) the said two sloops were in company together, in the prosecution of their aforesaid voyages, when the said Edward Dale and John Colton, and their respective mariners descried a ship in distress upon the —— sands; and that both the said sloops made for the said ship in distress, and in about an hour after-

* The commencement of this form should be varied to suit different cases. See notes, pp. 345, 351.

wards were brought up near to her, in order to render to her every possible assistance; for which purpose the boats of the said two sloops were thereupon hoisted out, and the said Edward Dale, with four of his crew, and the said John Colton, with four of his crew, immediately proceeded therein to, and got on board of, the said ship, and which they found to be the Octorara, of Philadelphia, in the district aforesaid, of the burthen of four hundred tons, or thereabouts, (whereof George Walters was master,) having on board a crew of about twenty men and two ladies passengers, and laden with a valuable cargo of hemp, iron, and other merchandise, bound from St. Petersburgh to Philadelphia aforesaid, being the very ship proceeded against in this cause.

Third. That the said ship, the Octorara, was then in a very dangerous situation, and in great hazard of being lost, and that the said George Walters, the master, begged or requested the aforesaid Edward Dale and John Colton, that they, with their sloops and crews, would assist and preserve the said ship and cargo, or to that effect; and that the said ship and cargo were thereupon put under the care of them, the said Edward Dale and John Colton, who, with their men, immediately set about using their best endeavours to preserve the same.

Fourth. That the said Edward Dale and John Colton, having caused the boats belonging to their respective sloops, and also two boats belonging to the Octorara, to be made fast to the said ship, and having cleared the decks and set the sails of the said ship, in order, if possible, to force her off the said sand, they waited until about seven o'clock in the evening of the said 14th day of December, when, with the help of the tide, they got the said ship off the said sand, and brought her up to anchor in a fair channel; but, there being a great deal of sea, the said ship's long-boat was thereby stove.

Fifth. That the said ship rode at anchor the whole ebb with the wind blowing hard, and varying from WNW. to WSW.; but that, the said ship making much water, the pumps on board thereof were obliged to be kept constantly going, in order to keep her from sinking; that the people belonging to the said sloops, as well as the crew of the said ship, being all thereby much fatigued, and the wind blowing fresh, and the said ship and cargo then still being in great danger of sinking, it was thought advisable to endeavour to get the same into the harbour of ——, that being the nearest port of safety; and that accordingly about six o'clock of the following morning, being Thursday, the 15th day of December, the said Edward Dale and John Colton hove in the said ship, and with much difficulty and danger, about seven o'clock in the evening of the same day, got her into the harbour aforesaid, and there brought her to an anchor, it being too dangerous to attempt getting her on shore that night, the weather being thick and blowing hard.

Sixth. That during the night of the 15th day of December aforesaid, it blew a violent gale of wind, which continuing until the morning of Saturday, the 17th day of December aforesaid, the said Edward Dale and John Colton were obliged to keep the pumps constantly going, in order to save the said ship from sinking; but that about eight o'clock in the morning of the said Saturday, the 17th day of December aforesaid, the wind being abated, and the tide answering to put the said ship on shore, they got up her anchor and laid her on shore, the said Edward Dale and John Colton with their men continuing, however, on board the said ship and further assisting until the night of the next day, being Sunday, the 18th day of December aforesaid, when they left her on shore in safety; having previously, to wit, in the morning of the day last mentioned, returned on board the said ship the goods, which it had been necessary to take out in order to lighten her as aforesaid.

Seventh. That from the time of the said sloops going to the assistance of the said ship Octorara on the said 14th day of December last, to the time of her being laid on shore at the port of —— in safety on the 17th day of the same month, as mentioned in the next preceding article, the said sloops were constantly attending the said ship, the leaky condition whereof made it absolutely necessary to keep her pumps constantly going, by reason of the scarf or box of her keel and stem being open an inch (and which the party proponent doth allege could not be stopped, until the ship was laid on shore at the port of ——); and that the masters and crews of the said sloops used their utmost endeavours in preserving the said ship and cargo, and the lives of the crew of the same; and that, in attending to the preservation of the said ship and cargo, the masters and crews of the said sloops ran great risk, not only of their own lives, but also of the loss of their respective sloops, for that, in case a storm had arisen before the said ship's arrival in the harbour of ——, neither of the said sloops had sufficient hands left on board to manage them (the prime hands belonging to the sloops being all employed on board the Octorara).

Eighth. That on the night of Thursday, the said 15th day of December last, both the sloops, then lying near the Octorara, and the whole of the crews of the said sloops being employed in pumping on board the Octorara, excepting three hands left on board each of the said sloops, the Red Rover, by the violence of the weather and the insufficiency of the people left on board to her preservation, was virtually driven on shore on —— beach; but did not thereby receive any essential injury, owing to the providential circumstance of its having happened in harbour, without which the said sloop would in all probability have been lost or destroyed.

Ninth. That without the assistance hereinbefore pleaded, the said ship Octorara could not have been saved, for that she had been on —— sand, from about eight o'clock in the evening of Tuesday, the said 13th day of December last; and that, previous to the sloops' arriving to her assistance, she had been on shore two ebbs and a flood, but that such flood had not lifted or floated the said ship; and that, if she had continued on the said sand until the night of Thursday, the said 15th day of December, in the violent gale, which drove the Red Rover on shore although in harbour, as before alleged, the total loss of both ship and cargo could not have been prevented.

Tenth. That whilst the said sloops, the Red Rover and the Jenny Dean, were sailing towards the said ship in distress on the —— sand, in the forenoon of the said 14th day of December last, as mentioned in the second article of this libel, a boat was observed from the said sloops to be making towards the said ship, which proved to be the Octorara libellate: and that such boat was afterwards found to be one of the boats belonging to the said ship Octorara, which had quitted and left the said ship, with the master, two ladies passengers, and four of the crew, for personal preservation, by endeavouring to make the shore; but which boat returned to the said ship in consequence of the persons therein perceiving the sloops making to their assistance. And several of the crew of the said ship Octorara, who remained on board after the master and others had quitted her as aforesaid, declared to the persons belonging to the sloops, that they should all have likewise left the said ship, if the said sloops had not come to their assistance, or to that effect.

Eleventh. That the said Edward Dale, the master and owner of the sloop called the Red Rover, and the said John Colton, the master and owner of the sloop called the Jenny Dean, and the respective crews of the said sloops, by reason of the risk and hazard they ran, and the service they performed in saving the said ship Octorara and her cargo, deserve, and are justly entitled to, meet and competent salvage for such service, and to so much as has been, and is actually allotted by this court to persons doing and performing the like service, together with all charges and expenses attending the same.

Twelfth. That all and singular the premises are true, and within the admiralty and maritime jurisdiction of this honourable court; in verification whereof, if denied, the libellants crave leave to refer to the depositions and other proofs to be by them exhibited in this cause.

Wherefore the libellants pray that process, in due form of law, according to the course of courts of admiralty and of this honourable court in cases of admiralty and maritime jurisdiction, may issue *against the ship Octorara, her tackle, apparel and furniture, and against the cargo laden therein, wheresover the same shall be found, and that all persons having or pretending to have any right, title or interest in the said ship and cargo may be cited to appear* and answer upon oath all and singular the matters so articulately propounded; and that this honourable court would be pleased to decree such a sum of money, or proportion of the value of the said *ship Octorara and her cargo,* to be due to the libellants, as a compensation for their said salvage services, as shall seem meet and reasonable, together with their expenses in this behalf sustained, and to condemn *the said ship, her tackle, apparel and furniture, and the cargo laden therein, and all persons intervening for*

*their interest in the said ship,** in costs, and otherwise right and justice to administer in the premises. (Signed) Edward Dale,
John Colton,
for themselves and the respective crews of the sloops the Red Rover and the Jenny Dean.

A. B., *Proctor.*

Eastern District of Pennsylvania, *ss.* ——.
Sworn to by the said Edward Dale and John Colton before me.
Francis Hopkinson, *Clerk.*

Claim and Answer by the Owner of the Cargo.†

United States of America, Eastern District of Pennsylvania, *ss.*
—— Term, 18—.

To the Honourable Archibald Randall, *Judge of the District Court of the United States, in and for the Eastern District of Pennsylvania.*

And now George Powell, of Philadelphia, in the district aforesaid, merchant, *intervening for his interest in the cargo on board the ship Octorara,* appears before this honourable court, and claims the said cargo as his property, and for answer to the libel and complaint of Edward Dale, of Philadelphia aforesaid, master and owner of the sloop called the Red Rover, and of John Colton, of Wilmington, in the state of Delaware, master and owner of the sloop called the Jenny Dean, and of the respective crews of the said sloops, *against the said ship Octorara, her tackle, apparel and furniture, and against all and singular the goods, wares and merchandises now or late on board the said ship,*‡ alleges and articulately propounds as follows:

First. That the respondent is the true and lawful owner of the cargo now on board the said ship Octorara, consisting of 300 tons of iron, 200 tons of hemp, 1000 bolts of canvas and 150 bales linen goods, and which he alleges to be the same goods, wares and merchandises proceeded against by the libellants in the present cause.

Second. That the respondent, admitting all and singular the matters alleged in the libel to be true, as therein alleged, nevertheless further alleges and propounds, that the libellants, all and singular, do not deserve and are not entitled to salvage, because on a day unknown to the respondent, but since the arrival of the said ship Octorara and her cargo in the port of Philadelphia aforesaid, they have tortiously converted to their own use and embezzled certain of the goods, wares and merchandise aforesaid, and which were by them salved, to wit, 150 bolts of canvas and 25 bales of linen goods, which, after the arrival of the said ship at Philadelphia as aforesaid, they caused to be taken from her secretly and covertly, and without the knowledge of any party in interest, and conveyed to a store or warehouse in Philadelphia aforesaid, there to be sold on their own account.

Third. That in consideration of the premises, each and all of the libellants have forfeited all claim and title to compensation out of the cargo aforesaid or from the owner thereof for the salvage services alleged in the libel aforesaid, and that accordingly this honourable court ought not to decree such compensation.

Fourth. That all and singular the premises are true; in verification whereof, if denied, the respondent craves leave to refer to the depositions and other proofs to be by him exhibited in this cause.

Wherefore the respondent prays, that this honourable court would be pleased to pronounce against the libel aforesaid, *and to decree a restitution of the said goods, wares and merchandises, to the respondent,* and to condemn the libellants in costs, and otherwise right and justice to administer in the premises.
(Signed) George Powell, *Respondent.*

C. D., *Proctor.*

Eastern District of Pennsylvania, *ss.* ——.
Sworn to by the said George Powell before me.
Francis Hopkinson, *Clerk.*

* The latter part of this libel should be varied according to the nature of the proceeding. See note, p 346.

† A claim and answer should also be put in by the owner of the ship.

‡ The commencement of this form should be varied to suit other cases. See note, p. 347.

viction of having performed a noble duty, a justly merited reward for the care and labour bestowed to make the work worthy of the subject, is the ardent wish of your friend and obedient servant, HENRY A. MUHLENBURG.

From the Hon. A. V. Parsons, Judge of the Court of Common Pleas, late Secretary of the Commonwealth and Superintendent of Common Schools.

MR. EDWARD C. BIDDLE, *Philadelphia, Sept.* 18, 1843.

Sir,—I have examined with attention a Geography of Pennsylvania, by Charles B. Trego, Esq., which you have published. It is, in my opinion, a book which ought to be in every family in Pennsylvania, for its usefulness as a reference, if to answer no other purpose; and I trust it will be introduced into all the schools throughout the state.

It is a work that was much needed in the commonwealth; and I think the author has very happily arranged the various subjects which ought to be known to every Pennsylvanian, and to the world, relative to the Geographical Features, Soil, Climate, Geology, Botany, Zoology, Population, Education, Government, Finances, Productions, Railroads and Canals of our State.

It is a lamentable truth, that *too little* has been known of the Geography and Resources of this State, which, at no distant period, is destined to hold the first rank in the Union. The large amount of valuable information, well condensed in this work, cannot fail to do great good by diffusing a proper knowledge of much that is interesting and valuable within our boundaries.

I sincerely hope this *excellent* Geography will be universally circulated and read. I am, with respect, yours, &c., A. V. PARSONS.

From Thaddeus Stevens, Esq., late Member of the House of Representatives of Pennsylvania.

Lancaster, Oct. 28, 1843.

Dear Sir,—I have carefully examined the Geography of Pennsylvania, by Charles B. Trego, Esq. It is full of accurate information on useful and interesting subjects. Mr. Trego is well qualified for the task which he has so ably performed, both by scientific knowledge, practical acquaintance with facts, and a sound, discriminating judgment.

The work cannot fail of being useful to all classes. It is an admirable school book; and, it is to be hoped, may be introduced into all our common schools; and that such school districts may embrace every inch of territory within the commonwealth. With great respect, your obd. servt.,

EDWARD C. BIDDLE, ESQ. THADDEUS STEVENS.

From Judge Richards, of Berks County.

EDWARD C. BIDDLE, ESQ., *Reading, Oct.* 20, 1843.

Dear Sir,—An examination of the Geography of Pennsylvania by Mr. Trego, which I received through your kindness, has given me much pleasure. The great amount of interesting and valuable knowledge brought to view, especially that in relation to the mineral and other great resources of our State, cannot but be gratifying to a Pennsylvanian.

From the method in the arrangement of the various subjects of which it treats, the work is peculiarly adapted to become useful, and ought to be in the hands of every one. It is every way worthy the patronage of a discerning public.

Accept assurances of respect, M. S. RICHARDS.

From the Harrisburg Argus.

We confess, when we cast our eye over the variety of subjects which the author proposed to discuss, we expected, notwithstanding his known ability, to meet with a series of remarks necessarily so general as to afford little either of pleasure or profit to any one. But, on a perusal of the work, we have been most agreeably disappointed, and find the very opposite of what we had anticipated. Every article exhibits traces of the abundant care and extensive research the author must have employed: and contains a mass of information of the most definite and satisfactory description: so much so, that we are at a loss which to admire most, the unbounded acquaintance the author evinces with the various branches of his subject, or his power of expressing his ideas in so conspicuous a manner within such narrow limits.

Spotted something that isn't quite right?

Let us know and we'll fix it for future reprints. And as a thank you for your diligence, we'll send you a free Sothis book of your choice.

publisher@sothis.press

This page intentionally left blank

Made in the USA
Monee, IL
08 November 2026

67812130R00215